PMP®
Project Management Professional Exam
Review Guide
Fourth Edition

Kim Heldman

Vanina Mangano

Brett Feddersen

SYBEX®
A Wiley Brand

Senior Acquisitions Editor: Kenyon Brown
Development Editor: Mary Ellen Schutz
Technical Editor: Brett Feddersen, Vanina Mangano, and Warren E. Wryostek
Production Manager: Kathleen Wisor
Copy Editor: Judy Flynn
Editorial Manager: Mary Beth Wakefield
Executive Editor: Jim Minatel
Proofreader: Amy Schneider
Indexer: Johnna VanHoose Dinse
Project Coordinator, Cover: Brent Savage
Cover Designer: Wiley
Cover Image: ©Getty Images, Inc./Jeremy Woodhouse

Copyright © 2018 by John Wiley & Sons, Inc., Indianapolis, Indiana

Published simultaneously in Canada

ISBN: 978-1-119- 42104-7
ISBN: 978-1-119-42112-2 (ebk.)
ISBN: 978-1-119-42108-5 (ebk.)

Manufactured in the United States of America

For general information on our other products and services or to obtain technical support, please contact our Customer Care Department within the U.S. at (877) 762-2974, outside the U.S. at (317) 572-3993 or fax (317) 572-4002.

Wiley publishes in a variety of print and electronic formats and by print-on-demand. Some material included with standard print versions of this book may not be included in e-books or in print-on-demand. If this book refers to media such as a CD or DVD that is not included in the version you purchased, you may download this material at http://booksupport.wiley.com. For more information about Wiley products, visit www.wiley.com.

Library of Congress Control Number: 2017962408

10 9 8 7 6 5 4 3 2 1

To BB, *my forever love.*
—Kim Heldman

To Roshoud, *who inspires me with his imagination, creativity, and tenaciousness.*
—Vanina Mangano

To April, Kayla, Marcus, and Adric, *the light and joy of my life.*
—Brett Feddersen

Acknowledgments

I'd like to thank Vanina and Brett for an outstanding job writing this book. They were both lifesavers and bore the brunt of the work. I enjoyed seeing how they gave the content a fresh face, and their illustrations are terrific. I appreciate the diligence and the new ideas that Vanina brings to these projects. Brett's insights were a great contribution to this edition as well. He is a true friend and an outstanding leader. As always, it was a great pleasure to work with Vanina and Brett.

I also echo Vanina's thanks to Kenyon Brown, senior acquisitions editor, for the opportunity to update this book.

I also want to thank Neil Edde, former vice president and publisher at Sybex, for taking that leap of faith on a crazy project management study guide idea way back when. Thanks, Neil.

Mary Ellen Schutz, development editor, is the best. She had some great suggestions that improved the content and kept us on track with deadlines just like a seasoned project manager.

A very big thanks goes to all of the instructors who use my books in their classrooms. I appreciate you choosing Sybex and my books to help your students master PMP® concepts. Thank you also to all of the readers who choose this book to help them study for the PMP® exam.

—Kim Heldman

To start, thank you to the team at Sybex who devoted a great deal of effort toward making this review guide come together successfully. It is incredible to see the amount of teamwork and effort that goes into the making and editing of a book. The process is certainly thorough, and there are many people not named here who were key to producing a solid product. Once again, thanks to all of you!

I'd like to thank Kim Heldman for the opportunity to work together once again on this book. Kim's warm, positive, and dynamic nature always makes her a pleasure to engage with. I'd also like to give a special, heartfelt thanks to Brett Feddersen. Brett worked tirelessly to produce a great product and always had the reader in mind. Not only was Brett's positive attitude and outlook contagious, but he made the process fun, collaborative, and memorable.

Thank you to Kenyon Brown, our senior acquisitions editor, who saw the value of updating this book and whose great and supportive personality always comes through on the phone and in email. I appreciate you welcoming me back to the Sybex family!

A tremendous thank-you to Mary Ellen Schutz, development editor. It was great to reunite on this project after working together on the first edition. With your guidance and feedback, we were able to work through life's many challenges and produce a book that I am proud of! You ensured that everything stayed on course, and your recommendations were valuable and instrumental in creating this finished product. It was absolutely wonderful having an opportunity to work with you once again.

A special thanks to the individuals who are such a big part of my life and who have always influenced me in a magnificent way. This includes my family, Nicolas Mangano, Marysil Mangano, Nicolas Mangano Jr., Carina Moncrief; and my beautiful nieces, Kaylee, Alyssa, Yasmin, and Rianna—you mean everything to me! Thank you to Al Smith Jr., who has supported and encouraged me through my many projects. And finally, thank you to Roshoud Brown, who always encouraged me to write and inspired me with his own words.

—Vanina Mangano

I could not have asked for two better contributors to work with on a book than Vanina Mangano and Kim Heldman, and I want to thank them for the opportunity to join their team in collaborating on this book. Vanina's talent, experience, and drive are extraordinary, and she willingly shared her passion and knowledge with me. Her sense of humor and attention to detail helped make the process fun and helped us deliver a superior product to the reader. Kim Heldman is a superior mentor who freely shares her enthusiasm, knowledge, humility, and leadership, and her contributions are what makes this book great. She has consistently pushed me to believe in myself, helping me to grow into the best professional I can be. It has been an honor to work with this team and help others prepare to take the PMP® exam.

I would like to thank Kenyon Brown for giving me another shot at contributing on a book. And I would also like to thank Mary Ellen Schutz and the editorial team for their push to make this product.

A commitment of this size normally requires a compromise in another part of one's life. Accordingly, I want to thank my three children, Kayla, Marcus, and Adric, for being willing to have Papa retreat to working on this book. They all kept their sense of humor, though, and they know that I will follow my wireless mouse anywhere. However, without my wonderful wife, April, I would not have the successes in my life like finishing this book. April is always there to hear my stories, talk me down after a bad day, laugh at my jokes, share a movie with me, and encourage me to be even better than I thought I could be. There is no greater cheerleader in all the world, and I am humbled that she cheers for me.

—Brett Feddersen

We would like to thank Judy Flynn, copyeditor, who made sure grammar and spelling were picture perfect; Amy Schneider, proofreader, for catching those last little "oopses" and Dassi Zeidel and Kathleen Wisor, production editors, who made sure everything flowed through the production process. Thanks also to our compositor, and the indexer, Johnna VanHoose Dinse. The book couldn't happen without them.

—The Authors

About the Authors

Kim Heldman, MBA, PMP®   Kim is the senior manager of IT/CIO for the Regional Transportation District in Denver, Colorado. Kim directs IT resource planning, budgeting, project prioritization, and strategic and tactical planning. She directs and oversees IT design and development, enterprise resource planning systems, IT infrastructure, application development, cybersecurity, the IT program management office, intelligent transportation systems, and data center operations.

Kim oversees the IT portfolio for a range of projects, from projects that are small in scope and budget to multimillion-dollar, multiyear projects. She has over 25 years of experience in information technology project management. Kim has served in a senior leadership role for over 18 years and is regarded as a strategic visionary with an innate ability to collaborate with diverse groups and organizations, instill hope, improve morale, and lead her teams in achieving goals they never thought possible.

Kim is the author of the *PMP®: Project Management Professional Study Guide, Ninth Edition*. She is also the author of *CompTIA Project+, Second Edition*; *Project Management JumpStart, Third Edition*; and *Project Manager's Spotlight on Risk Management*. Kim has also published several articles.

Kim continues to write on project management best practices and leadership topics, and she speaks frequently at conferences and events. You can contact Kim at Kim.Heldman@gmail.com. She personally answers all her email.

Vanina Mangano   Over the past decade, Vanina has specialized in working with and leading project, program, and portfolio management offices (PMOs) across various industries and companies, most recently at NBCUniversal and AMN Healthcare. Currently, Vanina leads a PMO at Microsoft Corporation.

As part of her contribution to the community, Vanina devotes time to furthering the project management profession through her volunteer work at the Project Management Institute®. Vanina recently served as the chair for *The Standard for Program Management, Fourth Edition*, and participates in activities that seek to harmonize the four foundational standards of the PMI®. She has also served as a core committee member for *A Guide to the Project Management Body of Knowledge (PMBOK® Guide), Fifth Edition*, and has served as a subject matter expert on multiple PMI® Standards and Practice Guides.

Vanina holds a dual bachelor's degree from the University of California, Riverside, and holds the following credentials: Project Management Professional (PMP)®, PMI Risk Management Professional (PMI-RMP)®, PMI Scheduling Professional (PMI-SP)®, CompTIA Project+, and ITIL Foundation v3.

You may reach Vanina through LinkedIn: https://www.linkedin.com/in/vaninam/.

Brett Feddersen MPS, PMP®   Brett is a career public servant with 25 years of experience in government, including the United States Marine Corps, the state of Colorado, the city of Boulder (Colorado), and the Regional Transportation District (RTD) in the Denver metro area. Brett has been a certified project manager since 2007 and has contributed to several books as a technical editor and technical proofreader. He is the author of the *CompTIA Project+ Practice Tests: Exam PK0-004*, and served as a coauthor for the *PMP Project Management Professional Exam Review Guide, Third Edition*. In addition to his commitment to the project management community, Brett is passionate about leadership and organizational excellence, and he has contributed to several cultural revolutions, helping government agencies become high-performing organizations.

Brett holds a bachelor's degree from Colorado Mesa University and a master's degree from the University of Denver. He holds the following credentials: Project Management Professional (PMP)®, Gamification, CompTIA Project+ , and ITIL Foundation v3.

You can reach Brett through LinkedIn: https://www.linkedin.com/in/brettfeddersen.

Contents

Introduction

Congratulations on your decision to pursue the Project Management Professional (PMP)® credential, one of the most widely recognized credentials within the project management industry. The PMP® credential is offered by the Project Management Institute (PMI®), a not-for-profit organization with thousands of members across the globe. PMI® has been a long-standing advocate and contributor to the project management industry and offers several credentials for those specializing in the field of project management.

This book is meant for anyone preparing to take the PMP® certification exam as well as individuals who are looking to gain a better understanding of *A Guide to the Project Management Body of Knowledge, Sixth Edition (PMBOK® Guide)*. If you are studying for the Certified Associate in Project Management (CAPM)® exam, you may also find this book useful because the CAPM® exam tests your knowledge of the *PMBOK® Guide* contents.

This review guide has been formatted to work hand in hand with *PMP®: Project Management Professional Exam Study Guide, Ninth Edition*, from Sybex. The study guide provides a more comprehensive review of the concepts included on the exam along with real-world examples. This review guide will reinforce these concepts and provide you with further explanation and a handy reference guide to the project management processes within the *PMBOK® Guide*. You'll find references to the study guide throughout this book, guiding you to where you may find additional information as needed. With all of these great resources at your fingertips, learning and understanding the *PMBOK® Guide*, along with other project management concepts, has certainly become easier!

Book Structure

This book has been structured in a way that carefully follows the concepts of the *PMBOK® Guide*, allowing you to understand how a project is managed from beginning to end. For this reason, we will review the processes in the order of the process groups:

- Initiating
- Planning
- Executing
- Monitoring and Controlling
- Closing

We start by covering the project management framework and the *PMI® Code of Ethics and Professional Conduct* and then move to a comprehensive review of the process groups. You'll find that each chapter offers a concise overview of each project management process and concept as well as the process inputs, tools and techniques, and outputs. This structure allows you to go back and reference terms, definitions, and descriptions at a glance.

Overview of PMI® Credentials

PMI® offers several credentials within the field of project management, so whether you are an experienced professional or looking to enter the project management field for the first time, you'll find something to meet your needs. You may hold one or multiple credentials concurrently.

Over the years, PMI® has contributed to the project management body of knowledge by developing global standards used by thousands of project management professionals and organizations. In total, there are four foundational standards, 7 practice standards, and four practice guides, all grouped within the following categories:

- Projects
- Programs
- Profession
- Organizations
- People

Several credentials offered by PMI® are based on the *PMBOK® Guide*, which is part of the Projects category. As of the publication date of this book, PMI® offers eight credentials. Let's briefly go through them:

Project Management Professional (PMP)®   You are most likely familiar with the PMP® credential—after all, you purchased this book! But did you know that the PMP® certification is the most widely and globally recognized project management certification? The PMP®, along with several other credentials, validates your experience and knowledge of project management. This makes obtaining a PMP® in itself a great achievement. The following requirements are necessary to apply for the PMP® exam:

Work Experience   The following work experience must have been accrued over the past eight consecutive years:

- If you have a bachelor's degree or the global equivalent: three years (36 months) of nonoverlapping project management experience, totaling at least 4,500 hours
- If you have a high school diploma, associate's degree, or global equivalent: five years (60 months) of nonoverlapping project management experience, totaling at least 7,500 hours

Contact Hours   *Contact hours* refers to the number of qualified formal educational hours obtained that relate to project management. A total of 35 contact hours is required and must be completed before you submit your application.

Certified Associate in Project Management (CAPM)®   The CAPM® credential is ideal for someone looking to enter the project management industry. You may meet the requirements through work experience *or* through formal project management education. If you do not currently have project management experience, you may apply if you have accumulated the requisite number of formal contact hours:

Work Experience   1,500 hours of formal project management experience

Contact Hours   23 contact hours of formal project management education

Program Management Professional (PgMP)®   The PgMP® credential is ideal for those who specialize in the area of program management or would like to highlight their experience of program management. A PMP® is not required to obtain this or any other credential. You must meet the following requirements to apply for the PgMP® exam:

Work Experience   The following work experience must have been accrued over the past 15 consecutive years:

- If you have a bachelor's degree or global equivalent: four years of nonoverlapping project management experience, totaling at least 6,000 hours, *and* four years of nonoverlapping program management experience, totaling 6,000 hours
- If you have a high school diploma, associate's degree, or global equivalent: four years of nonoverlapping project management experience, totaling at least 6,000 hours, *and* seven years of nonoverlapping program management experience, totaling 10,500 hours

Portfolio Management Professional (PfMP)®   The PfMP® is meant for those specializing in the area of portfolio management. It reflects several years of hands-on portfolio management experience, geared toward achieving strategic objectives. You must meet the following requirements to apply for the PfMP® exam:

Work Experience   The following work experience must have been accrued over the past 15 consecutive years:

- If you have a bachelor's degree or global equivalent: 6,000 hours of portfolio management experience plus eight years (96 months) of professional business experience
- If you have a high school diploma, associate's degree, or global equivalent: 10,500 hours of portfolio management experience plus eight years (96 months) of professional business experience

PMI Risk Management Professional (PMI-RMP)®   The PMI-RMP® credential is ideal for those who specialize in the area of risk management or would like to highlight their risk management experience. The following are the requirements to apply for the PMI-RMP® exam:

Work Experience   The following work experience must have been accrued over the past five consecutive years:

- If you have a bachelor's degree or global equivalent: 3,000 hours of professional project risk management experience
- If you have a high school diploma, associate's degree, or global equivalent: 4,500 hours of professional project risk management experience

Contact Hours

- If you have a bachelor's degree or global equivalent: 30 contact hours in the area of risk management
- If you have a high school diploma, associate's degree, or global equivalent: 40 contact hours in the area of risk management

PMI Scheduling Professional (PMI-SP)®   The PMI-SP® credential is ideal for those who specialize in the area of project scheduling, or who would like to highlight their project scheduling experience. You must meet the following requirements to apply for the PMI-SP® exam:

Work Experience   The following work experience must have been accrued over the past five consecutive years:

- If you have a bachelor's degree or global equivalent: 3,500 hours of professional project scheduling experience
- If you have a high school diploma, associate's degree, or global equivalent: 5,000 hours of professional project scheduling experience

Contact Hours

- If you have a bachelor's degree or global equivalent: 30 contact hours in the area of project scheduling
- If you have a high school diploma, associate's degree, or global equivalent: 40 contact hours in the area of project scheduling

PMI Agile Certified Professional (PMI-ACP)®   The PMI-ACP® credential is ideal for those who work with Agile teams or practices. The PMI-ACP® covers approaches such as Scrum, Kanban, Lean, Extreme Programming (XP), and Test-Driven Development (TDD). You must meet the following requirements to apply for the PMI-ACP® exam:

Work Experience   The following work experience must have been accrued:

- 2,000 hours (12 months) working on project teams—accrued in the last five years
- 1,500 hours (8 months) working on project teams using Agile methodologies—achieved in the last three years

Contact Hours

- 21 hours of formal Agile training

PMI Professional in Business Analysis (PMI-PBA)®   The PMI-PBA® credential is meant for those specializing in business analysis. This credential is ideal for those managing requirements or product development. You must meet the following requirements to apply for the PMI-PBA® exam:

Work Experience   The following work experience must have been accrued over the past eight consecutive years:

- If you have a bachelor's degree or global equivalent: 4,500 hours of professional business analysis experience and 2,000 hours of general project experience
- If you have a high school diploma, associate's degree, or global equivalent: 7,500 hours of business analysis experience and 2,000 hours of general project experience

Contact Hours

- 35 hours of formal training in the area of business analysis practices

For the latest information regarding the PMI® credentials and other exam information, you can visit PMI®'s website at www.PMI.org.

How to Use This Book

We've included several learning tools in the book. These tools will help you retain vital exam content as well as prepare to sit for the actual exams.

Exam Essentials   Each chapter includes a number of exam essentials. These are the key topics that you should take from the chapter in terms of areas on which you should focus when preparing for the exam.

Chapter Review Questions   To test your knowledge as you progress through the book, there are review questions at the end of each chapter. As you finish each chapter, answer the review questions and then check your answers—the correct answers appear in the appendix, "Answers to Review Questions." You can go back to reread the section that deals with each question you got wrong to ensure that you answer correctly the next time you're tested on the material.

Interactive Online Learning Environment and Test Bank

The interactive online learning environment that accompanies *PMP® Project Management Professional Exam Review Guide, Fourth Edition,* provides a test bank with study tools to help you prepare for the certification exam—and increase your chances of passing it the first time! The test bank includes the following:

Sample Tests   All the questions in this book are provided, including the chapter tests that include the review questions at the end of each chapter. In addition, there are two practice exams. Use these questions to test your knowledge of the study guide material. The online test bank runs on multiple devices.

Flashcards   One set of questions is provided in digital flashcard format (a question followed by a single correct answer). You can use the flashcards to reinforce your learning and provide last-minute test prep before the exam.

Other Study Tools   A glossary of key terms from this book and their definitions is available as a fully searchable PDF.

> **NOTE**   Go to http://www.wiley.com/go/sybextestprep to register and gain access to this interactive online learning environment and test bank with study tools.

Day of the Exam

After you gain the necessary prerequisites to sit for the exam, the PMP® exam itself serves as the final measure to earning your certification. You are already well ahead of the game in preparing for the exam when you purchase this book. The preparation you put forth will help you show up on the day of the exam in a calm and confident state. Throughout the course of this book, you will find sections that offer tips on what to do on the day of the exam. While you are not allowed to take anything into the exam room, you are given scratch paper to work with during your exam. Before you begin the exam, you can use the tips in this book to help you jot down notes that will free your mind to focus fully on the questions. In the days leading up to the exam, we recommend that you practice creating your reference sheet by memorizing the mnemonics, formulas, and other information that you will need.

Clearly, standard test taking advice is relevant here, such as getting a good night's sleep, eating a good breakfast, and going through relaxation exercises before you are called into the exam room. In addition, consider the following items during the exam:

- Take the time to read through each question slowly and completely. Fully understanding what is being asked in the question can contribute greatly to getting the right answer.

- You will be given the ability to mark a question if you are unsure of your answer or are unable to come up with the answer. Take advantage of this feature so you can move on to the next question. At the end of the exam, you can come back and review your answers and take more time to answer questions that escaped your answer earlier in the process.

- You have four hours to complete an examination of 200 questions. Tell yourself that it is *more important to pass than it is to go home early*. If it will help, write that statement at the top of your reference scratch paper so you can remind yourself of this ideal. In a four-hour examination, it is possible to get fatigued and just want to be done with it. Make sure you keep your focus and energy on success.

It's a good idea to use scratch paper given to you for use during your exam to jot down formulas and other information you memorized but may forget if you become mentally exhausted midway through the exam. Keep in mind that you cannot use your scratch paper until the exam time officially starts. Some test takers practice getting their thoughts down on their scratch paper quickly when the test begins so they can relax and focus on the test questions.

For more information from PMI® on preparing for the exam, be sure you check out pmi.org and search for "PMP Exam Guidance" for more valuable resources.

PMP® Exam Objectives

The PMP® exam tests your knowledge of the competencies highlighted in the exam objectives. The following are the official PMP® exam objectives, as specified by PMI®.

Initiating the Project

The following objectives make up the Initiating the Project performance domain and are covered in Chapter 2 of this book:

- Perform project assessment based upon available information, lessons learned from previous projects, and meetings with relevant stakeholders in order to support the evaluation of the feasibility of new products or services within the given assumptions and/or constraints.

- Identify key deliverables based on the business requirements in order to manage customer expectations and direct the achievement of project goals.

- Participate in the development of the project charter by compiling and analyzing gathered information in order to ensure that project stakeholders are in agreement on its elements.

- Identify high-level risks, assumptions, and constraints based on the current environment, organizational factors, historical data, and/or expert judgment, in order to propose an implementation strategy.

- Obtain project charter approval from the sponsor in order to formalize the authority assigned to the project manager and gain commitment and acceptance for the project.

- Perform stakeholder analysis using appropriate tools and techniques in order to align expectations and gain support for the project.

- Conduct benefit analysis with relevant stakeholders to validate project alignment with organizational strategy and expected business value.

- Inform stakeholders of the approved project charter to ensure common understanding of the key deliverables, milestones, and their roles and responsibilities.

Planning Project Scope and Schedule Management

The following objectives make up a part of the Planning the Project performance domain and are covered in Chapter 3 of this book:

- Review and assess detailed project requirements, constraints, and assumptions with stakeholders based on the project charter, lessons learned, and by using gathering techniques in order to establish detailed project deliverables.

- Develop a scope management plan based on the approved project scope and using scope management techniques, in order to define, maintain, and manage the scope of the project.

- Develop the project schedule based on the approved project deliverables and milestones, scope, and resource management plans in order to manage timely completion of the project.

Planning Project Cost and Quality Management

The following objectives make up a part of the Planning the Project performance domain covered in Chapter 4 of this book:

- Develop the cost management plan based upon the project scope, schedule, resources, approved project charter, and other information, using estimating techniques, in order to manage project costs.

- Develop the quality management plan and define the quality standards for the project and its products, based on the project scope, risks, and requirements in order to prevent the occurrence of defects and reduce the cost of quality.

Planning Project Resource, Communication, Procurement, Change and Risk Management

The following objectives make up a part of the Planning the Project performance domain covered in Chapter 5 of this book:

- Develop the human resource management plan by defining the roles and responsibilities of the project team members in order to create a project organizational structure and provide guidance regarding how resources will be assigned and managed.

- Develop the communications management plan based on the project organizational structure and stakeholder requirements in order to define and manage the flow of project information.

- Develop the procurement management plan based on the project scope, budget, and schedule in order to ensure that the required project resources will be available.

- Develop the change management plan by defining how changes will be addressed and controlled in order to track and manage change.

- Plan for risk management by developing a risk management plan; identifying, analyzing, and prioritizing project risk; creating the risk register; and defining risk response strategies in order to manage uncertainty and opportunity throughout the project life cycle.

Planning Stakeholder Engagement and Obtaining Project Plan Approval

The following objectives make up a part of the Planning performance domain covered in Chapter 6 of this book:

- Present the project management plan to the relevant stakeholders according to applicable policies and procedures in order to obtain approval to proceed with project execution.

- Conduct kick-off meeting, communicating the start of the project, key milestones, and other relevant information in order to inform and engage stakeholders and gain commitment.

- Develop the stakeholder engagement plan by analyzing needs, interests, and potential impact in order to effectively manage stakeholders' expectations and engage them in project decisions.

Executing the Project

The following objectives make up the Executing the Project performance domain and are covered in Chapter 7 of this book:

- Acquire and manage project resources by following the human resource and procurement management plans in order to meet project requirements.

- Manage task execution based on the project management plan by leading and developing the project team in order to achieve project deliverables.

- Implement the quality management plan using the appropriate tools and techniques in order to ensure that work is being performed in accordance with required quality standards.

- Implement approved changes according to the change management plan in order to meet project requirements.

- Implement approved actions and follow the risk management plan in order to minimize the impact of the risks and take advantage of opportunities on the project.

- Manage the flow of information by following the communications plan in order to keep stakeholders engaged and informed.

- Maintain stakeholder relationships by following the stakeholder management plan in order to receive continued support and manage expectations.

Monitoring and Controlling the Project

The following objectives make up the Monitoring and Controlling the Project performance domain and are covered in Chapter 8 of this book:

- Measure project performance using appropriate tools and techniques in order to identify and quantify any variances and corrective actions.

- Manage changes to the project by following the changed management plan in order to ensure that project goals remain aligned with business needs.

- Verify that project deliverables conform to the quality standards established in the quality management plan by using appropriate tools and techniques to meet project requirements and business needs.

- Monitor and assess risk by determining whether exposure has changed and evaluating the effectiveness of response strategies in order to manage the impact of risks and opportunities on the project.

- Review the issue log, update if necessary, and determine corrective actions by using appropriate tools and techniques in order to minimize the impact on the project.

- Capture, analyze, and manage lessons learned, using lessons learned management techniques in order to enable continuous improvement.
- Monitor procurement activities according to the procurement plan in order to verify compliance with project objectives.

Closing the Project

The following objectives make up the Closing the Project performance domain and are covered in Chapter 9 of this book:

- Obtain final acceptance of the project deliverables from relevant stakeholders in order to confirm that project scope and deliverables were achieved.
- Transfer the ownership of deliverables to the assigned stakeholders in accordance with the project plan in order to facilitate project closure.
- Obtain financial, legal, and administrative closure using generally accepted practices and policies in order to communicate formal project closure and ensure transfer of liability.
- Prepare and share the final project report according to the communications management plan in order to document and convey project performance and assist in project evaluation.
- Collate lessons learned that were documented throughout the project and conduct a comprehensive project review in order to update the organization's knowledge base.
- Archive project documents and materials using generally accepted practices in order to comply with statutory requirements and for potential use in future projects and audits.
- Obtain feedback from relevant stakeholders using appropriate tools and techniques and based on the stakeholder management plan in order to evaluate their satisfaction.

Project Foundation

THE PMP® EXAM CONTENT FROM THE INITIATING THE PROJECT PERFORMANCE DOMAIN COVERED IN THIS CHAPTER INCLUDES THE FOLLOWING:

✓ **Be able to describe the difference between projects and operations.**

✓ **Be able to differentiate between project management, program management, portfolio management, and a project management office.**

✓ **Be able to list some of the skills every good project manager should possess.**

✓ **Be familiar with the components of the PMI Talent Triangle.**

✓ **Be able to define the role of the project manager.**

✓ **Be able to differentiate between the organizational structures and the project manager's authority in each.**

✓ **Be able to name the five project management process groups.**

Much of the focus and content of this book revolves heavily around the information contained in *A Guide to the Project Management Body of Knowledge, Sixth Edition (PMBOK® Guide)*, published by the Project Management Institute (PMI®). Because many exam questions will relate to the content of the *PMBOK® Guide*, it will be referenced throughout this book, and we'll elaborate further on those areas that appear on the test.

This chapter lays the foundation for building and managing a project. Understanding project management from a broad and high-level perspective is important and will prepare you to digest the rest of the information in this book. One of the concepts you will learn is that of progressive elaboration, which PMI® defines as an iterative process of increasing the level of detail in a project management plan as information and accurate estimates become available. In this context, we want to start with an overview of the general framework in which projects operate, and then we will get progressively more elaborate with defining what those steps entail.

Day of the Exam

This book provides targeted content to help you review and prepare to take the Project Management Professional (PMP)® certification exam (PMP® exam). Through the course of this book, we will be giving you tips on things you should do the day of the exam to help you achieve the greatest opportunity to pass and then join the worldwide network of certified project managers. Look for these tips throughout the book.

Defining a Project

Pop quiz: How do you tell the difference between a project and ongoing operations? Before delving into the aspects of project management, it's important to determine whether what you are dealing with is, in fact, a project. Projects are often confused with ongoing operations, and it's therefore important to understand how to define a project and know its characteristics.

Once you have determined that you are dealing with a project, all stakeholders will need to be identified. To be considered successful, a project must achieve its objectives and meet or exceed the expectations of the stakeholders.

For more detailed information on projects and stakeholders, see
Chapter 1, "What Is a Project?" in *PMP®: Project Management Professional
Exam Study Guide, Ninth Edition* (Sybex, 2017).

Project Characteristics

According to the *PMBOK® Guide*, the characteristics of projects, as shown in Figure 1.1,
are as follows:

- They are temporary in nature and have a definite start and finish.
- They produce a unique product, service, or result that didn't exist before.
- They often drive change within organizations.
- They typically enable the creation of business value.

FIGURE 1.1   Project

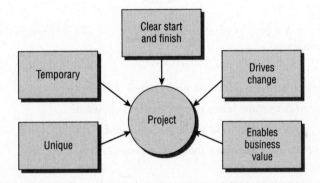

The unique deliverables from a project might include tangible products (a road or a
building); well-defined and specific services, such as consulting or project management; and
business functions that support the organization. Projects might also produce a result or an
outcome, such as a document that details the findings of a research study. The purpose of
a project is to achieve its goals and to conclude. Therefore, a project is considered complete
when one of the following occurs:

- The goals and objectives are accomplished to the satisfaction of the stakeholders.
- It has been determined that the goals and objectives cannot be accomplished or are no
  longer needed.
- The project is canceled due to lack of resources (i.e., funding, people, or physical
  resources) or for legal reasons.

After its completion, a project's product, service, or result may become part of an
ongoing operation.

Operations

Operations are ongoing, are repetitive, and involve work that is continuous without an end date. Often, operations involve repeating the same processes and producing the same results. Figure 1.2 shows the characteristics of operations. The purpose of operations is to keep the organization functioning.

FIGURE 1.2   Operations

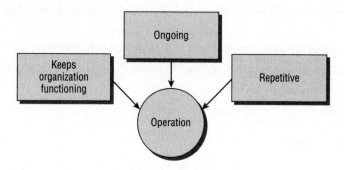

Unsure whether it is a project or an ongoing operation? Put it through the following test to make a determination:

- Is it unique?
- Does the work effort have a limited time frame?
- Is there a way to determine when the project is completed?
- Is there a way to determine stakeholder satisfaction?

If you answered yes to each question, then it is a project.

Remember that the temporary nature of a project does not necessarily mean the duration of the project is short.

Progressive Elaboration

Progressive elaboration means the characteristics of the product, service, or result of the project are determined incrementally and are continually refined and worked out in detail as the project progresses. Product characteristics are typically broad-based at the beginning of the project and are iterated into more and more detail over time until they are complete and finalized.

Stakeholders

A stakeholder is any person or group, including formal organizations, who are impacted by the project, who believe themselves to be impacted, or who can directly impact the project. The following are characteristics of various stakeholders:

- They are individuals, groups, or organizations with a vested interest in the project.
- They are actively involved with the work of the project.
- They have something to either gain or lose as a result of the project.

Identifying who these stakeholders are is not a onetime process, and it's important to identify stakeholders at the onset of the project. Here are some examples of project stakeholders, as shown in Figure 1.3:

- Customer
- Sponsor
- Contractors
- Suppliers
- Project manager
- Project team members
- Department managers
- Project management office (PMO)

FIGURE 1.3   Stakeholders

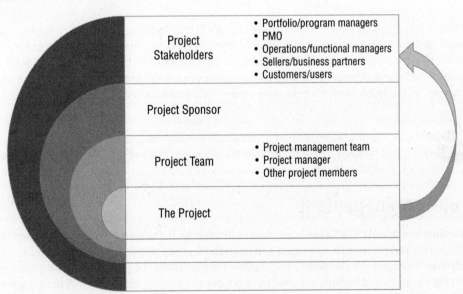

It's also important to note that stakeholders might have conflicting interests and that it is the project manager's responsibility to manage stakeholder expectations. When in doubt, stakeholder conflicts should always be resolved in favor of the customer.

The project sponsor, who is also a stakeholder, is generally an executive in the organization with the authority to assign resources and enforce decisions regarding the project. The project sponsor typically serves as the tiebreaker decision maker and is one of the people on the project's escalation path.

Stakeholders are identified early on within the life of the project and may change as the project evolves. Failure to identify stakeholders can result in failure of the project itself because unidentified stakeholders might not have their expectations satisfied if you do not give them a voice. Understanding the level of influence of each stakeholder is also critical to the success of the project.

Exam Essentials

Be able to describe the difference between projects and operations.   A project is temporary in nature with a definite beginning and ending date. Projects produce unique products, services, or results. Operations are ongoing and use repetitive processes that typically produce the same result over and over.

Defining Project Management

A project management framework provides the tools and techniques necessary for the successful initiation, planning, and execution of a project. Project management is the application of that framework to consistently deliver products and services to a stakeholder's satisfaction. Project management may involve more than a single project. In the bigger picture, a project may be part of a program, a portfolio, and/or a PMO.

 For more detailed information on project management basics, see Chapter 1 of *PMP®: Project Management Professional Exam Study Guide, Ninth Edition.*

Project Management

According to the *PMBOK® Guide*, project management is "the application of knowledge, skills, tools, and techniques to project activities to meet the project requirements."

Project managers are the people responsible for managing the project processes and applying the tools and techniques used to carry out the project activities. It is the responsibility of the project manager to ensure that project management techniques are applied and followed. In addition to this, project management is a process that includes initiating a new project, planning, putting the project plan into action, and measuring and reporting on performance. It involves identifying the project requirements, establishing project objectives, balancing constraints, and taking the needs and expectations of the key stakeholders into consideration.

Project management itself can exist beyond the management of a single project. In some organizations, programs and portfolios are also managed. Figure 1.4 shows the characteristics of a project, program, and portfolio as well as a PMO.

FIGURE 1.4   Project management overview

Project Management			
Project	**Program**	**Portfolio**	**PMO**
• Produces a unique product, service, or result	• Groups of related projects • Managed using similar techniques	• Collections of programs and projects • Supports specific business goals	• Centralized organizational unit • Oversees projects and programs

Programs

According to the *PMBOK® Guide*, programs are groups of related projects, subsidiary programs, and program activities that are managed in a coordinated way to obtain benefits not available from managing them individually.

In many cases, projects within a program have their own project manager(s), who report to a program manager. All the projects are related and are managed together so that collective benefits are realized and controls are implemented and managed in a coordinated fashion. The management of this collection of projects—determining their interdependencies, managing their constraints, and resolving issues among them—is called program management.

In addition to its project management certification, PMI® offers a certification for *program* management called the Program Management Professional (PgMP)®. For more detailed information on program management skills, see *The Standard for Program Management, Fourth Edition* (PMI®, 2017).

Portfolios

Portfolios are collections of projects, programs, subsidiary portfolios, and operations managed as a group to achieve strategic objectives. Programs and projects included as part of a portfolio may not necessarily relate to one another in a direct way.

Portfolio management encompasses managing the collection of programs, projects, other work, and sometimes other portfolios. It also concerns monitoring active projects for adherence to objectives, balancing the portfolio among the other investments of the organization, and ensuring the efficient use of resources.

 PMI® also offers a credential for *portfolio* management called the Portfolio Management Professional (PfMP)®. For more detailed information on portfolio management skills, see *The Standard for Portfolio Management, Fourth Edition* (PMI®, 2017).

Project Management Office

The project management office (PMO) is a centralized organizational unit that oversees or guides the management of projects and programs throughout the organization.

While there are different types of PMOs, a PMO is generally responsible for the following:

- Standardizing project-related governance processes

- Standardizing project management processes, tools, and techniques

- Managing the objectives of a collective set of projects

- Managing shared resources across the projects

- Managing the interdependencies of all the projects within its authority

- Maintaining and archiving project documentation for future reference

- Measuring project performance of active projects and suggesting corrective actions

- Evaluating completed projects for their adherence to the project plan

- Suggesting corrective actions pertaining to projects and programs as needed

The most common reason a company starts a project management office is to establish and maintain procedures and standards for project management methodologies and to manage resources assigned to the projects in the PMO. Project managers and team members may report directly to the PMO, or the PMO may provide support functions for projects and project management training or simply have experts available to provide assistance.

According to the *PMBOK® Guide*, there are several types of PMOs:

- Supportive, which provide resources and guidance on following project management best practices

- Controlling, which ensure adherence to policy and published framework or methodologies

- Directive, where project managers report directly into the PMO organization

Figure 1.5 shows the three common types of PMOs.

FIGURE 1.5   Common types of PMOs

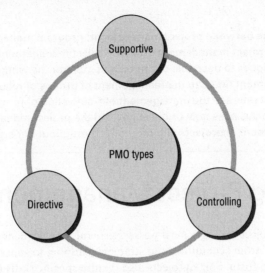

The overall purpose of a project manager and PMO differ to a certain extent. A project manager is focused on the project at hand, whereas the PMO takes more of an organizational approach to project management. The project manager is concerned with the project's objectives; the PMO is concerned with the organizational objectives. Table 1.1 outlines the differences between the overall objectives and perspectives of a project manager and PMO.

TABLE 1.1   Project manager vs. PMO

	Project manager	**PMO**
Overall goal	Achieve the project requirements	Achieve goals from an enterprise-wide perspective
Objective	Deliver project objectives	Deliver organizational objectives
Resources	Manage project resources	Optimize shared resources
Reporting	Project reporting	Consolidated reporting

PMOs can exist in any type of organizational structure. A major benefit for project managers working in an organization that has an existing PMO is the room for advancement that a PMO provides.

Although PMOs are common in organizations today, they are not required in order to apply good project management practices.

Identifying Project Management Skills

To be successful, a project manager must possess general management skills that span every area of management—from accounting and strategic planning to supervision, personnel administration, and so forth. Some projects also require specific skills in certain application areas, such as within an industry group, within a department, or by technical specialty. These skills prepare the project manager to communicate, solve problems, lead, and negotiate throughout a project.

For more detailed information on project management skills, see Chapter 1 of *PMP®: Project Management Professional Exam Study Guide, Ninth Edition.*

As shown in Figure 1.6, seven general management skills make up the foundation of good project management practices.

FIGURE 1.6   General management skills

General Management Skills
- Communications
- Organization and planning
- Budgeting
- Conflict management
- Negotiation and influencing
- Leadership
- Team building and motivating

Communication Skills   Many forms of communication exist within a project and are critical to its success. It is the job of the project manager to ensure that the information is explicit, clear, and complete. Once the information has been distributed, it is the responsibility of the recipient to confirm that the information has been understood. *Good project managers spend up to 90 percent of their time communicating.* This makes communication skills a critical asset for a project manager.

Organization and Planning Skills   Organization and planning skills are closely related and an important skill set that a project manager should possess. Project managers must track and locate many documents, meetings, contracts, and schedules. Doing so requires time management skills, which is why this skill set is tied closely to organization skills. Because there isn't any aspect of project management that doesn't first involve planning, it will be an area discussed extensively throughout this book.

Budgeting Skills   Project managers establish and manage budgets and are therefore expected to have some knowledge of finance and accounting principles. Cost estimates are an example of when budgeting skills are put to use. Other examples include project spending, reading and understanding vendor quotes, preparing or overseeing purchase orders, and reconciling invoices.

Conflict Management Skills   Conflict management involves problem solving, first by defining the causes of the problem and then by making a decision to solve it. After examining and analyzing the problem, the situation causing it, and the available alternatives, determine the best course of action. The timing of the decision is also important.

Negotiation and Influencing Skills   Both negotiation and influencing skills are necessary in effective problem solving and are used in all areas of project management. The following terms are related to this skill set:

Negotiation   Whether one on one or with teams of people, negotiation involves working with others to come to an agreement and is necessary in almost every area of the project.

Influencing   Influencing requires an understanding of the organization's structure and involves convincing the other party to consider the choice you think is the better one even if it is not what they want.

Power   Power is a technique used to influence people and is the ability to get people to do things they wouldn't otherwise do.

Politics   Politics involves getting groups of people with different interests to cooperate creatively even in the midst of conflict and disorder.

Leadership Skills   Leadership involves exhibiting characteristics of both a leader and a manager and knowing when to switch from one to the other throughout the project. A leader imparts vision, gains consensus for strategic goals, establishes direction, and inspires and motivates others. Managers focus on results and are concerned with getting the job done according to requirements.

Team Building and Motivating Skills The project manager sets the tone for the project team and walks the team members through various stages of team development to become fully functional. This can involve team-building groundwork and motivating the team even when team members are not direct reports.

PMI® publishes what is referred to as the PMI Talent Triangle™, which breaks out the skills a project manager needs in order to be effective. As demonstrated in Figure 1.7, the Talent Triangle consists of three key sets of skills:

- Technical project management, which refers to the skills needed in order to apply project management knowledge effectively to produce the desired results for a project. Examples are producing project management artifacts; tailoring project management methodologies, tools, and techniques; and managing against scope, budget, and schedule constraints.

- Leadership, which refers to the ability to direct, guide, and motivate others, as described previously in this section.

- Strategic and business management, which refer to skills needed to see the big picture of what an organization is aiming to accomplish and implement decisions that support strategic initiatives. Examples are understanding business benefits of a project, communicating effectively with the project sponsor and team, and maximizing the business value of the project.

FIGURE 1.7   PMI Talent Triangle™

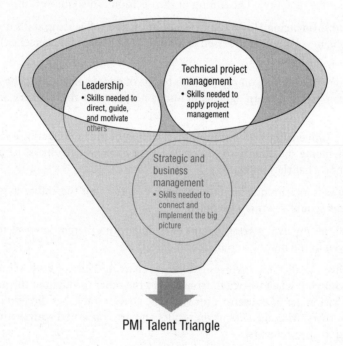

PMI Talent Triangle

Understanding the Role of the Project Manager

The role of the project manager is essential to the successful outcome of a project. As noted throughout this chapter, the project manager plays a different role than that of a functional manager or operations manager, although they often interact closely with these other key roles connected to the project. The role of project manager is defined by the *PMBOK® Guide* as "the person assigned by the performing organization to lead the team that is responsible for achieving the project objectives."

Project managers are tasked with achieving the objectives of a project and meeting the expectations of stakeholders. This requires that the project manager balance several competing constraints and effectively communicate with various stakeholders within and outside of their project. As noted earlier, communication is a key skill that every effective project manager excels in.

According to the *PMBOK® Guide*, good project managers work toward achieving the following within their organization:

- Increasing project management competency and capability

- Demonstrating the value of project management

- Increasing the acceptance of project management

- Advancing the effectiveness of the PMO, if one exists

Exam Essentials

Be able to list some of the skills every good project manager should possess. Communication, budgeting, organization, problem solving, negotiation and influencing, leading, and team building are skills a project manager should possess.

Be familiar with the components of the PMI Talent Triangle. The components are technical project management, leadership, and strategic and business management.

Be able to define the role of the project manager. The project manager is the individual assigned to lead the team that is responsible for achieving the project objectives.

Understanding Organizational Structures

Like projects, organizations are unique, each with its own style and culture—both have an influence on how projects are performed. Organizations in general can be structured in several different ways, including hybrids of the various types. For example, in some organizational types, the role of the project manager is not formal, and project management responsibilities are absorbed into other functional roles. In others, the role of the project manager is formal, and they may hold a high level of authority. In the past, three organizational structures were highlighted:

- Functional

- Matrix

- Projectized

According to the *PMBOK® Guide,* variations and combinations of these organizational structures exist, including multidivisional organizations, virtual, hybrid, and PMO. Figure 1.8 provides a simplified view of the primary three structures and where they fall in relation to one another, including the variations (weak, balanced, and strong) that exist in matrix organizations. Knowing the type of structure that an organization operates within is important and impacts how a project manager may proceed. One of the biggest determining factors of an organization's structure is the authority that a project manager holds.

FIGURE 1.8   Simplified spectrum of organizational types

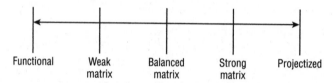

| Functional | Weak
matrix | Balanced
matrix | Strong
matrix | Projectized |

Since functional and projectized are the two extreme types of organizational structures, we'll cover them first.

> For more detailed information on functional, projectized, and matrix organizations, including sample charts, see Chapter 1 of *PMP®: Project Management Professional Exam Study Guide, Ninth Edition.*

Organizational Structure Types

Of the various organizational structures noted, there are two that reflect opposite ends of the spectrum: functional organizations and projectized organizations, also referred to as project-oriented organizations.

Functional Organizations   Functional organizations are the oldest style of organization; the functional style is known as the traditional approach to organizing businesses. These types of organizations have the following characteristics:

- They center on specialties.

- They are grouped by function.

- They are displayed as a hierarchy.

Importantly, workers within a functional organization specialize in an area of expertise, which allows them to become very good in a particular specialty (such as accounting, human resources, or engineering).

Within this hierarchical structure, a chain of command exists in which employees report to one manager and one person is ultimately in charge at the top. Each department or group is managed independently and has a limited span of control, therefore requiring that the chain of command be followed when input from another department on a project is needed. The mind-set behind this type of structure is that people with similar skills and experiences are easier to manage as a group, allowing for work assignments to be distributed and managed easily, and supervisors are experienced in the area they supervise.

Table 1.2 highlights the advantages and disadvantages of a functional organization.

TABLE 1.2   Functional organizations

Advantages	Disadvantages
There is an enduring organizational structure.	Project managers have little to no formal authority.
There is a clear career path with separation of functions, allowing specialty skills to flourish.	Multiple projects compete for limited resources and priority.
Employees have one supervisor with a clear chain of command.	Project team members are loyal to the functional manager.

Projectized Organizations   Projectized organizations, also referred to as project-oriented organizations, are nearly the opposite of functional organizations, focusing on the project itself and therefore developing loyalties to the project and not to a functional manager.

Project managers have high to ultimate authority within this type of organization and typically report directly to the CEO. The project manager makes decisions regarding the project, including dealing with constraints. As a side note, project managers in all organizational structures must balance competing project constraints such as these:

- Scope
- Quality
- Schedule
- Budget
- Resources
- Risk

Within a projectized organization, teams are often co-located, meaning that team members physically work at the same location and report to the project manager. Once the project is completed, the team is often dissolved and members are either put on the bench or let go. Resource utilization can be inefficient if a highly specialized skill is needed only at given times throughout the project and sits idle during other times.

Table 1.3 highlights the advantages and disadvantages of a projectized organization.

TABLE 1.3   Projectized organizations

Advantages	Disadvantages
Project managers have high to ultimate authority.	Project team members may find themselves out of work after project completion.
Project team members are loyal to the project.	There can be inefficiency with resource utilization.

Matrix Organizations   Matrix organizations are a blend of functional and projectized organizations, taking advantage of the strengths of both and combining them into one. Employees report to a functional manager and to at least one project manager.

Functional managers assign employees to projects and handle administrative duties, whereas project managers execute the project and assign project activities to employees. Both share the responsibility of performance reviews.

Within matrix organizations exists a balance of power ranging from that of a functional organization to that of a projectized organization:

Strong Matrix   A strong matrix organization has characteristics of a projectized organization, where the project manager has a high level of authority and can dictate resources.

Weak Matrix   On the other end of the spectrum is the weak matrix, which holds a resemblance to a functional organization in that the functional managers have a greater level of power and tend to dictate work assignments.

Balanced Matrix   In between a strong matrix and weak matrix is the balanced matrix, where the power is balanced between the project managers and functional managers.

Table 1.4 shows the subtle differences between the three types of matrix organizations. The majority of organizations today are a composite of functional, projectized, and matrix structures.

TABLE 1.4   Comparing matrix structures

	Weak Matrix	**Balanced Matrix**	**Strong Matrix**
Project manager's title	Project coordinator, project leader, or project expeditor	Project manager	Project manager
Project manager's focus	Split focus between project and functional responsibilities	Projects and project work	Projects and project work
Project manager's power	Minimal authority and power	Balance of authority and power	Significant authority and power
Project manager's time	Part-time on projects	Full-time on projects	Full-time on projects
Organization style	Most like functional organization	Blend of both weak and strong matrix	Most like a projectized organization
Project manager reports to	Functional manager	Functional manager, but shares authority and power	Manager of project managers

Exam Essentials

Be able to differentiate between the organizational structures and the project manager's authority in each.   Organizations are usually structured in some combination of the following: functional, projectized, and matrix (including weak matrix, balanced matrix, and strong matrix). Other types of organizational structures exist, such as multidivisional, virtual, hybrid, and PMO. Project managers have the most authority in a projectized organization and the least authority in a functional organization.

Understanding the Project Environment

The project environment is made up of internal and external factors that influence a project. When managing a project, the project manager must consider more than just the project itself. Proactively managing a project involves understanding the environment in which the project must function.

The following are some examples of the elements that make up the project environment:

Organizational Structure   The organizational structure itself plays a large role in how a project is managed and is a major influential factor within the project environment. This is intermingled with the company culture.

Physical Environment   The physical environment includes considerations such as the following:

- Local ecology
- Physical geography
- Environmental restrictions, such as protected areas or protected wildlife
- Amount of dedicated office and conference room space

Cultural and Social Environment   When referencing the cultural environment, consider these various layers:

- Corporate culture, including external stakeholders and vendors. This is intermingled with organizational structures but can take on a life of its own.
- Ethnic culture.
- Religious culture.
- Organizational risk tolerance.

To communicate effectively with customers, stakeholders, and project team members, it becomes necessary to understand cultural and social factors and how they can impact a project. In particular, cultural differences pose a common communication obstacle within projects. As virtual and global projects become a more common scenario, understanding how to function within this type of environment becomes critical.

A project manager should also understand how the project impacts individuals and how individuals impact the project.

International and Political Environment   The international and political environment involves considering the following:

- International, national, regional, and local laws and regulations
- Norms and customs
- Political climate
- Time zone and local holidays

It is important for a project manager to know, from the onset of the project, whether any of the items listed affect their particular project. Something as minor as a time zone difference or as large as the political climate can have a huge impact on a project.

There are other influential factors far beyond those listed here, and the list can become quite extensive. On a basic level, these factors provide you with an overview of a project from a broader perspective.

Understanding Project Life Cycles and Project Management Processes

Most projects begin with an idea. After soliciting support and obtaining approval, a project progresses through the intermediate phases to the ending phase, where it is completed and closed out. As a project passes through this life cycle, it is carried out through a set of project management processes. According to the *PMBOK® Guide*, these processes are interrelated and dependent on one another; they are divided into five project management process groups:

- Initiating
- Planning
- Executing
- Monitoring and Controlling
- Closing

Each of these process groups displays characteristics that reflect the level of a project's costs, staffing, chances for successful completion, stakeholder influence, and probability of risk.

Figure 1.9 shows the project management process groups and represents the life cycle of a project or project phase.

FIGURE 1.9   Project management process groups

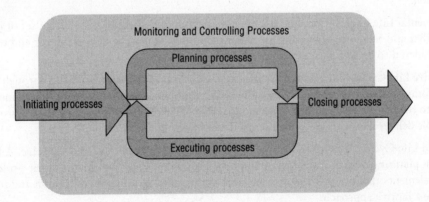

For more detailed information on the project management life cycle and processes, see Chapter 1 of *PMP®: Project Management Professional Exam Study Guide, Ninth Edition.*

Project Phases and Project Life Cycles

Most projects are divided into phases. Project phases consist of segments of work, and a project may have one or many phases, depending on the project complexity and industry. The phases that a project progresses through are collectively called the *project life cycle*. Project life cycles are similar for all projects, and the phases that occur within the project life cycle can vary, such as being sequential or overlapping.

All projects generally follow the same life-cycle structure:

- Starting the project, or initiating

- Organizing and preparing, or planning the work of the project

- Carrying out (or performing) the work of the project, or executing

- Closing out the project

A development life cycle often has one or more phases that are connected to the creation or output of the product, service, or result. According to the *PMBOK® Guide*, these life cycles can follow predictive, iterative, incremental, adaptive, or hybrid models.

Predictive Life Cycles   In a predictive life cycle, planning generally occurs at the front end of the project and changes to scope follow a change control process. These types of life cycles are also commonly referred to as plan driven.

Iterative Life Cycles   Iterative life cycles are similar to predictive in that planning occurs at the front end of the project. The difference is that estimates (such as time and cost) are refined as the project proceeds forward and the team gains a greater understanding of the project's end result. Incremental additions to functionality through repetitive cycles are common.

Incremental Life Cycles   Incremental life cycles produce deliverables through a set of iterations that add functionality within an established time frame. The deliverable, or end result, is considered to be complete after the final iteration occurs.

Adaptive Life Cycles   In an adaptive life cycle, deliverables are also produced through a set of iterations, similar to an incremental life cycle, although a detailed scope is determined prior to the start of an iteration. With an adaptive life cycle, the end of an iteration produces a usable deliverable. This life cycle is considered to be agile.

Hybrid Life Cycle   A hybrid life cycle is a combination of predictive and adaptive. A high level of planning occurs at the front end of the project for known elements of the project; other elements that are unknown at the start are planned in an iterative fashion and follow a more adaptive approach.

Figure 1.10 outlines the characteristics of each of the development life cycles.

FIGURE 1.10   Development life cycles

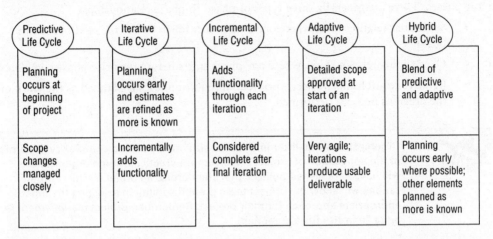

Predictive Life Cycle	Iterative Life Cycle	Incremental Life Cycle	Adaptive Life Cycle	Hybrid Life Cycle
Planning occurs at beginning of project	Planning occurs early and estimates are refined as more is known	Adds functionality through each iteration	Detailed scope approved at start of an iteration	Blend of predictive and adaptive
Scope changes managed closely	Incrementally adds functionality	Considered complete after final iteration	Very agile; iterations produce usable deliverable	Planning occurs early where possible; other elements planned as more is known

Exam Essentials

The *PMBOK® Guide* emphasizes that you should not confuse this generic life-cycle structure with the project management process groups because the processes in a process group will consist of activities that may be performed and recur within each phase of a project as well as for the project as a whole.

At the beginning of a phase, a feasibility study may be carried out. At the end of a phase, a phase gate or phase-end review of the accomplished deliverables may be performed before handoff to the next phase can occur. The following list expands further on several key terms used within this description of what occurs within a phase:

Handoffs   For the project to progress from one phase to the next, the phase deliverables should be reviewed for accuracy and approved. As each phase is completed, it's handed off to the next phase. Handoffs, or technical transfers, are phase sequences that signal the end of one phase and typically mark the beginning of the next.

Feasibility Studies   Some projects incorporate feasibility studies in the beginning phase. They are completed prior to the beginning of the next phase. A feasibility study determines whether the project is worth undertaking (or worth continuing if it is performed at a project checkpoint) and whether it will be profitable to the organization.

Deliverables   Each phase has at least one deliverable that marks the phase completion. A deliverable is a tangible output that can be measured and must be produced, reviewed, and approved to bring the phase or project to completion.

Phase-End Reviews   At the end of a phase, a phase-end review may take place so that those involved with the work can determine whether the project should continue on to the next phase. Phase-end reviews (also known as phase exits, phase gates, milestones, stage gates, decision gates, and kill points) give the project manager the ability to identify and address errors discovered during the phase.

Phase-to-Phase Relationships   As previously indicated, a project can consist of one or more phases. There are generally three types of phase-to-phase relationships:

- Sequential relationships, where one phase must finish before the next phase can begin

- Overlapping relationships, where one phase starts before the prior phase completes

- Iterative relationships, where work for subsequent phases is planned as the work of the previous phase is performed

> Organizations will differ in terms of size, maturity, and complexity. In terms of the application of project management practices, some organizations will have established policies that standardize all projects. Other organizations will allow the project team great flexibility in selecting the most appropriate approach for their project. Remember, project management is not a "one size fits all" model.

The act of overlapping phases to shorten or compress the project schedule is called fast-tracking. This means that a later phase is started prior to completing and approving the phase or phases that come before it.

Project Management Process Groups

Project management processes organize and describe the work of the project. As mentioned earlier, the following are the five process groups described in the *PMBOK® Guide*:

- Initiating process group
- Planning process group
- Executing process group
- Monitoring and Controlling process group
- Closing process group

These processes are performed by people; they are interrelated, are dependent on one another, and include individual processes that collectively make up the group. The five process groups are iterative and might be revisited and revised throughout the project's life as the project is refined.

The project manager and the project team are responsible for tailoring, which involves determining which processes within each process group are appropriate for the project. When the project is tailored, its size and complexity and various inputs and outputs are taken into consideration. The conclusion of each process group allows the project manager and stakeholders to reexamine the business needs of the project and determine whether the project is satisfying those needs.

Initiating Process Group   The processes within the Initiating process group occur at the beginning of the project and at the beginning of each project phase for large projects. This process group grants the approval to commit the organization's resources to working on the project or phase and authorizes the project manager to begin working on the project.

The Initiating process group contains the following actions:

- Developing the project charter, which formally authorizes the project
- Identifying project stakeholders

Planning Process Group   The Planning process group includes processes that formulate and revise project goals and objectives. It is also where the project management plan that will be used to achieve the goals the project was undertaken to address is created. Within this process group, project requirements are fleshed out and additional stakeholders are identified. Because projects are unique, planning must encompass all areas of project management.

The Planning process group contains the following actions:

- Developing the project management plan

    The project management plan itself contains several subsidiary plans and baselines. This collection of plans defines how the project will be planned, carried out, and closed.

- Collecting project requirements

    The project requirements define and document the needs of the stakeholders.

- Developing the project and product's scope
- Creating the work breakdown structure (WBS)

    The WBS contains a decomposition of the project work, from the major deliverables down to the work packages.

- Identifying the project activities necessary to carry out the project work
- Developing the order and duration of project activities
- Calculating the number of resources needed to carry out the project activities
- Creating the project schedule
- Identifying the cost of all of the activities needed for project success
- Developing the project's budget
- Estimating the cost of each project activity
- Identifying project risks

    This process also results in the creation of the risk register, where information about the identified risks will be documented.

- Assessing and prioritizing project risks that require further analysis or action, as well as the numerical analysis of risk on the overall project objectives
- Developing risk responses

Executing Process Group   The Executing process group involves putting the project management plan into action, keeping the project plan on track, and implementing approved changes.

The project manager coordinates and directs project resources, and costs are highest here since greater amounts of time and resources are utilized during the Executing processes.

The Executing process group contains the following actions:

- Performing the work defined in the project management plan
- Ensuring that the quality standards and operational definitions outlined in the Planning process group are followed according to the quality management plan
- Auditing the quality requirements
- Obtaining the human resources needed to complete the project work
- Enhancing the skills and interactions of the project team
- Enhancing the overall team environment
- Managing the project team and enhancing its performance
- Distributing the necessary information throughout the course of the project, as outlined within the communications management plan
- Selecting the external vendors used and awarding the necessary procurement contracts
- Managing the expectations of the stakeholders

Monitoring and Controlling Process Group   The Monitoring and Controlling process group is where project performance measurements are taken and analyzed to determine whether the project is aligned with the project plan. This process group tracks the progress of work being performed and identifies problems and variances within a process group and the project as a whole.

Processes from within the Monitoring and Controlling process group contain the following actions:

- Monitoring and controlling the work of the project, such as making sure the actual work performed is in line with the project management plan
- Using the integrated change control system to review, approve or deny, and manage all changes within the project
- Accepting the completed project deliverables
- Controlling the project and product scope

    This helps prevent scope creep and ensures that the project accomplishes what it set out to do.

- Controlling the project schedule to make sure the project is completed on time
- Controlling the project costs to make sure the project is completed within the allotted budget
- Monitoring the results of conducting quality activities

    This allows for an assessment of performance.

- Reporting the project performance through planned reports

    This also involves forecasting and measuring project performance.

- Implementing risk response plans
- Monitoring and controlling risks

    This includes monitoring the project for any new risks and evaluating the effectiveness of risk responses and risk management processes.

- Managing vendor relationships and vendor contracts
- Monitoring the relationships with project stakeholders and adjusting approaches as warranted

Closing Process Group   The Closing process group includes processes that bring a formal, orderly end to the activities of a project phase or to the project itself. Once the project objectives have been met, all the project information is gathered and stored for future reference. The closing process group contains finalizing the project work to formally complete the project or project phase.

The progression through the project management process groups exhibits the same characteristics as progression through the project phases. Table 1.5 shows the characteristics of the process groups.

TABLE 1.5   Characteristics of the project process groups

	Initiating	Planning	Executing	Monitoring and Controlling	Closing
Costs	Low	Low	Highest	Lower	Lowest
Staffing levels	Low	Lower	High	High	Low
Chance for successful completion	Lowest	Low	Medium	High	Highest
Stakeholder influence	Highest	High	Medium	Low	Lowest
Risk probability	Highest	High	Medium	Low	Lowest

Plan-Do-Check-Act Cycle

As the project progresses and more information becomes known, the project management processes might be revisited and revised to update the project management plan. Underlying the concept that process groups are iterative is a cycle called the Plan-Do-Check-Act cycle, which was originally defined by Walter Shewhart and later modified by Edward Deming. The idea behind this concept is that each element in the cycle is results oriented and becomes input into the next cycle. The cycle interactions can be mapped to work in conjunction with the five project management process groups.

Exam Essentials

Be able to name the five project management process groups.   The five project management process groups are Initiating, Planning, Executing, Monitoring and Controlling, and Closing.

Day of the Exam

You are not allowed to bring anything into the testing room when you take the exam. However, you will be given scratch paper as an aid. An excellent approach to take the test is to memorize formulas, acronyms, and mnemonics before you begin taking the test and then write these all out on the sheet of blank scratch paper provided during your exam time. This will allow you to focus exclusively on what is being asked on the test instead of taking brain power to try to remember these elements while answering a question.

The book *PMP®: Project Management Professional Exam Study Guide, Ninth Edition* mentions an acronym for the process groups that is helpful: it sounds like IPECC (Initiating, Planning, Executing, Monitoring and Controlling, and Closing), where you think of Monitoring and Controlling simply as "Controlling." Give it a try and see if it helps.

Recognizing Professional and Social Responsibility

A PMP® credential comes with several responsibilities that involve decisions and actions you make. By submitting your PMP® application, you agree to abide by the *PMI® Code of Ethics and Professional Conduct*. This oath touches on several elements within your personal and professional life and includes actions that are mandatory as well as actions and ideals to which we aspire.

Maintaining ethical and professional conduct applies to day-to-day activities and is therefore applicable to everything discussed earlier in this chapter and throughout the rest of the book. Meeting ethical and professional standards is an essential part of building a solid project management foundation. For the exam, you will be expected to be familiar with the code and answer questions based on its contents.

PMI® Core Values

The *PMI® Code of Ethics and Professional Conduct* addresses the following four elements: responsibility, respect, fairness, and honesty.

Responsibility

Responsibility is a major part of upholding integrity. It involves taking ownership for your actions, being proactive in doing the right thing, and doing what is necessary to resolve a situation that results from an initial lack of responsibility.

As shown in Figure 1.11, a variety of elements touch on the concept of responsibility:

- Ensuring a high level of integrity
- Accepting only those assignments for which you are qualified
- Following rules, regulations, laws, and policies
- Respecting confidential information
- Upholding the PMI® code of ethics and holding fellow project managers accountable

FIGURE 1.11   Elements of responsibility

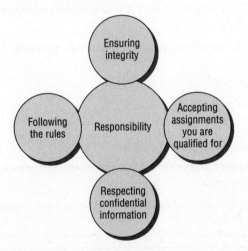

 Responsibility involves making decisions that are for the good of the organization rather than for yourself. It also involves admitting your mistakes and being accountable for the decisions you make and the consequences that result from those decisions and actions.

Ensuring Integrity   As a project manager, one of your professional responsibilities is to ensure integrity of the project management processes, the product, and your own personal conduct. This can entail the following:

- Applying the project management processes correctly to ensure integrity of the product
- Executing the process groups effectively to ensure the quality of the product
- Obtaining formal acceptance of the project and product

Accepting Assignments   Accepting appropriate assignments is tied to responsibility and honesty. This involves doing the following:

- Accurately and truthfully reporting your qualifications, experience, and past performance of services to potential employers, customers, PMI®, and others
- Declining assignments beyond your capabilities or experience
- Emphasizing your knowledge and how you've used it in your specific industry as opposed to making others believe that you have experience using certain processes and tools if, in reality, you don't
- Accurately representing yourself, your qualifications, and your estimates in your advertising and in person
- Completing the commitments that you undertake and ensuring that you do what you say you will do

Following the Rules   It is imperative that you follow all applicable laws, rules, and regulations, including these:

- Industry regulations
- Organization rules
- Project rules
- PMI® organizational rules and policies
- Intellectual property and other ethical standards and principles governing your industry
- Local, national, and international law governing your location, processes, and product

 Rules or regulations that apply in one country may or may not apply in other countries.

Respecting Confidential Information   Whether you are a direct employee, a consultant, or a contractor, it is likely that during the course of your project management career you will come across some form of sensitive information. You may collect or be exposed to sensitive information as part of a project. You may be required to provide such information to a contractor. You may have access to this type of information as part of your role. Whatever the situation, it is important that you comply with the *PMI® Code of Ethics and Professional Conduct*, which states that you agree not to disclose sensitive or confidential information or use it in any way for personal gain.

Handling company data, trade secrets, data from governmental agencies, and intellectual property are typical cases in which you will come across sensitive or confidential information. Don't forget to ask yourself the key questions shown in Figure 1.12 whenever you handle information. If you are unsure of the answer to any of the questions, find out before you share the information.

FIGURE 1.12   Handling information

Ask Yourself:		
Is this information private or protected?	Can this information be shared?	Does a nondisclosure agreement exist?

Trade Secrets   An organization's trade secrets or private information should not be used for personal gain. Understanding what information may be shared with vendors, other organizations, or even coworkers is important. In practice, there are often gray areas where the breach of information is not as obvious. Being conscious and sensitive about your organization's information can make a big difference. If ever in doubt, always ask.

Restricted Access   Working with the government is a great example of when data sharing can be sensitive. The fines and criminal penalties that can be incurred with breaches can be substantial when dealing with medical, financial, and other personally identifiable data. One governmental agency does not always have access to data from another, separate governmental agency. Depending on the data, others may have restricted access or no access at all. Restricted access isn't limited to governmental data; similar restrictions occur in the private sector as well. One department within an organization may not always have access to data from another department. Think of the sensitive nature of information housed within the human resources department. An employee's file may not always be accessible to department heads or others. It is a mistake to assume that others should have access to data because you believe it is logical that they do.

Nondisclosure Agreements   It is your responsibility to make sure vendors or organizations that will have access to sensitive data sign and understand the appropriate nondisclosure agreements before you release the data. Clearly, make sure there is key stakeholder support, including from the legal department, in the release of sensitive information.

Intellectual Property   You are likely at some point to come into contact with intellectual property. The business or person who created the protected material or item owns the intellectual property. Intellectual property typically includes the following items:

- Items developed by an organization that have commercial value but are not tangible
- Copyrighted or trademarked material, such as books, software, and artistic works
- Ideas, products, or processes that are patented
- An industrial process, a business process, or a manufacturing process developed by the organization for a specific purpose

You might have to pay royalties or request written permission to use the property. Intellectual property should be protected just like sensitive or confidential data.

Respect

Demonstrating respect involves how you conduct yourself, the way you treat others and the resources around you, and listening to the viewpoints of others. Respect is something that should be exhibited on a personal and professional level. Among other things, the level of respect you earn will be based on how well you do the following:

- Exhibit a professional demeanor
- Handle ethics violations
- Demonstrate a sense of cultural awareness
- Interpret experiences

Exhibiting Professional Demeanor

Exhibiting a professional demeanor is an important part of business. You are responsible for your own actions and reactions. Here are some examples of maintaining a professional demeanor and encouraging professional demeanor within others:

- Controlling your emotions and your reactions in questionable situations.
- Notifying the project team during the kickoff meeting where they can find a copy of organizational policies regarding conflict of interest, cultural diversity, standards and regulations, customer service, and standards of performance.
- Coaching and influencing team members who exhibit nonprofessional attitudes or behaviors to conform to the standards of conduct expected by you and your organization. As the project manager, it is your job to ensure that team members act professionally because they represent you and the project.

Reporting Ethics Violations

One of the responsibilities that falls to you as a project manager is the responsibility to report violations of the PMP® code of conduct. To maintain integrity of the profession, PMP® credential holders must adhere to the code of conduct that makes all of us accountable to one another. This includes notifying PMI® when you know a violation has occurred and you've verified the facts. The *PMI® Code of Ethics and Professional Conduct* includes the following violations:

- Conflicts of interest
- Untruthful advertising
- Falsely claiming PMP® experience and credentials
- Appearances of impropriety

Demonstrating Cultural Awareness

As project teams and organizations become increasingly more diverse, the need for a heightened awareness of cultural influences and customary practices becomes critical. Today, it's common for project teams to be spread out globally. It is rare *not* to come into contact with someone from another culture. For example, you may encounter some or all of the following:

- Virtual project teams with team members based in different physical locations
- Internal project stakeholders spread among offices globally
- Offshore vendors or suppliers
- Offshore partners
- Project team members who, while physically located in the same office, are from different cultures

It is important not to attempt to force your own culture or customs on others. When in a different country, you will need to respect the local customs. At the same time, it is not acceptable to do something that violates your ethics and the ethics of your company.

Do not forget that cultural awareness is an important component in your own country as well. Citizens of the same country can often have different cultural influences and customs, which should be recognized and respected.

As part of cultural awareness, you will need to be proactive in protecting yourself and your staff from experiencing culture shock. In order to do this, it becomes important to devote time to diversity training as needed and to always demonstrate respect for your neighbors, as follows:

Culture Shock   Working in a foreign country can bring about an experience called *culture shock*. Culture shock involves a separation from what you would normally expect. This can cause disorientation, frustration, breakdown of communication, and confusion. Here are some ways to prepare yourself and protect against culture shock (Figure 1.13):

- Read about the country you're going to work in before you go.
- Become familiar with customs and acceptable practices in foreign countries where you have dealings or will be visiting.
- When in doubt about a custom or situation, ask your hosts or a trusted contact from the company for guidance.

FIGURE 1.13   Avoiding culture shock

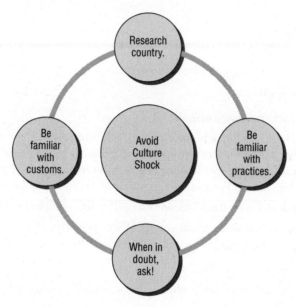

Diversity Training   Project team members may be from different countries or cultures. Providing your team members with training helps to prevent cultural or ethical differences from impacting the project.

Diversity training makes people aware of differences between cultures and ethnic groups and helps them gain respect and trust. Training involving the company culture should also be provided so that project team members understand how the organization functions.

Building Relationships   Some cultures require that a relationship be established before business can be conducted. Building that relationship may take days, depending on the culture.

Building relationships is valuable, regardless of whether a culture requires it. On the flip side, as you are building relationships, remember that you should not impose your beliefs on others because that is not the purpose of building relationships. Instead, building a relationship with others creates an atmosphere of mutual trust and cooperation. In this environment, all aspects of project planning and management, including negotiating and problem solving, become easier and smoother to navigate.

Interpreting Experiences

As part of exhibiting respect, it's important to be conscious of how experiences are interpreted and perceived. This is relevant on both ends of the communication spectrum. Others may interpret your actions in a way that you did not intend. Likewise, you may misinterpret the actions of others. Remember the following:

▪ Each member of your team brings a unique set of experiences to the project. Those experiences influence perception, behavior, and decisions.

- Your perception of a situation is influenced by your experiences and might be very different from the perceptions of others.

- Always give others the benefit of the doubt and ask for clarification if you think there is a problem.

- Avoid allowing feelings or emotions to get in the way of how you interpret a situation.

Fairness

According to the *PMI® Code of Ethics and Professional Conduct*, you have a responsibility to report to the stakeholders, customers, or others any actions or circumstances that could be construed as a conflict of interest. Avoiding conflicts of interest is a part of exhibiting fairness. Fairness includes the following:

- Treating everyone equally, without favoritism or discrimination

- Appropriately representing yourself and your organization to avoid conflict-of-interest situations, and quickly reporting any situation if conflict of interest occurs

- Maintaining impartiality in your decision-making process

A conflict of interest involves putting your personal interests above the interests of the project or using your influence to cause others to make decisions in your favor without regard for the project outcome. As Figure 1.14 illustrates, any of the following could be construed as conflicts of interest and compromise fairness:

- Not revealing your active associations and affiliations

- Accepting vendor gifts

- Using stakeholder influence for personal reasons

- Participating in discrimination

FIGURE 1.14   Elements to consider in exhibiting fairness

Associations and Affiliations   In maintaining associations and affiliations, it's important to consider whether any conflicts of interest exist as a result. For instance, sitting on the decision-making committee of a company that wins a bid for a contract relating to your project constitutes a conflict of interest. Even if you do not influence the decision in any way, others will assume that a conflict of interest occurred. This is also the case in personal associations—for instance, awarding a project to a relative, spouse, and so forth.

When these types of situations occur, do the following:

- Inform the project sponsor and the decision committee of the association or affiliation.
- Refrain from participating in the award decision committee.
- In cases of a contract with a personal association, appoint someone else in your organization to administer the contract and make the payments for the work performed.
- Document all of the decisions you make regarding the activities performed by the association and keep them with the project files.

Vendor Gifts   Vendor gifts are not uncommon. Vendors and suppliers often provide their customers and potential customers with lunches, gifts, ballgame tickets, and the like. However, some professionals are not allowed to accept gifts in excess of a certain dollar amount. This might be driven by company policy or the department manager's policy. Accepting vendor gifts may be construed as a conflict of interest—no matter how small the gift is. It is your responsibility to know the policy on accepting gifts and inform the vendor if they go beyond the acceptable limits. Likewise, do not give inappropriate gifts to others or attempt to influence a decision for personal gain.

 Don't accept gifts that might be construed as a conflict of interest. If your organization does not have a policy regarding vendor gifts, set limits for yourself.

Stakeholder Influence   Some stakeholders have a great deal of authority. As you engage with stakeholders who have a lot of power and influence, you should never use these engagements for your own personal benefit. The interests of the project or organization should be first and foremost when dealing with these powerful stakeholders. This is another potential area for conflict of interest. Keep in mind these guidelines:

- Weigh your decisions with the objectives of the project and the organization in mind—not your own personal gain.
- Do not use stakeholder influence for personal gain, such as receiving a promotion, bonus, or similar reward.

Discrimination   Maintaining a strong level of fairness is important on many levels, as you have seen so far. In practice, we sometimes fall prey to favoritism without realizing it. When issuing assignments, promotions, and the like, always use strong professional reasoning when making decisions. Choosing someone simply because you enjoy working with them is poor judgment and represents a conflict of interest.

It is also important to be conscious of discriminating against others. Whether based on age, disability, religion, sexual orientation, or personality, discrimination on any level is not acceptable. Remember that the *PMI® Code of Ethics and Professional Conduct* also requires you to report this type of behavior exhibited by someone else.

Honesty

You should be aware of several aspects of honesty that you must uphold (as shown in Figure 1.15):

- Report the truth regarding project status and circumstances.
- Avoid deception.
- Make only truthful statements.
- Be honest about your own experience.

FIGURE 1.15   Elements of honesty

Reporting Truthfully   Honesty involves information regarding your own background and experience as well as information about the project circumstances. Benefit to the project, and not your personal gain, should be the influencing factor when billing a customer or working on a project. Experiencing a personal gain as a result of your work is positive, but making a project decision simply to result in a personal gain is not.

As a project manager, you are responsible for truthfully reporting all information in your possession to stakeholders, customers, the project sponsor, and the public when required. This includes situations where personal gain is at stake. Always be truthful about the situation and up front regarding the project's progress. It is important.

Avoiding Deception   At times, being honest can feel difficult. In some cases, it may result in the end of a project, losing a job, missing out on a bonus, or other consequences that impact you and your team personally. Deceiving others and making false statements to prevent unfavorable consequences are not acceptable ways of handling situations. In terms of a project, telling the truth is a necessity.

Making Truthful Statements   Part of managing a good team involves leading by example. This includes making truthful statements, not just on your PMP® application but in the day-to-day management of a project. In some cases, delicate situations might present themselves; this is where your general management skills come into play. Being truthful doesn't mean being disrespectful, and a project manager must understand how to present the truth respectfully.

Representing Personal Experience

Being honest about your personal experience is just as important as not deceiving others. You may have heard that enhancing a résumé is a standard practice in business. While creating a résumé that greatly highlights your experiences and credentials is recommended, exaggerating experience or clearly embellishing credentials is unacceptable. This is equivalent to making false statements.

Correctly represent yourself on your PMP® application as well. Accurately stating your work experience, credentials, and background is an important part of maintaining high integrity.

The project management community has put together a variety of resources to communicate the values of the PMI® Code of Ethics, including video tutorials describing ethical conduct. Additionally, tools are available to help you work through a dilemma if you find yourself unsure of what to do in a certain situation. For more information, please visit the PMI® website at www.pmi.org/about/ethics.

Advancing the Industry

Promoting good project management and advancing the industry are part of your role as a project management professional. Professional knowledge involves knowledge of project management practices as well as specific industry or technical knowledge required to complete an assignment. As part of maintaining your credential, you have the following responsibilities:

- To apply project management knowledge to all your projects
- To educate others regarding project management practices by keeping them up-to-date on best practices, training your team members to use the correct techniques, informing stakeholders of correct processes, and then sticking to those processes throughout the course of the project
- To promote interaction among stakeholders

Becoming knowledgeable in project management best practices and staying abreast of the industry are important. Figure 1.16 touches on these responsibilities.

FIGURE 1.16 Elements of industry advancement

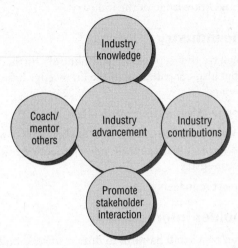

 While the PMP® exam is not expected to test your knowledge of this topic, the continuing credential requirements will become important to maintaining your credential.

Enhancing Your Industry Knowledge

Furthering knowledge in the field of project management (your own and others) is a part of your responsibility as a project manager. Project management is a growing field, which makes staying abreast of project management practices, theories, and techniques an ongoing process. For this reason, PMI® requires that once you achieve your PMP® certification, you maintain the credential by earning a given number of professional development units (PDUs) every three years. PDUs ensure that your knowledge of the industry and project management practices remains current. There are several ways to earn PDUs, such as taking project management classes, reading industry books and magazines, speaking on the subject of project management, and so forth. You can find additional details on the PMI® website (www.PMI.org).

Here are some ways that you can further and enhance your project management education:

- Join a local PMI® chapter.

- Read the PMI® monthly magazines.

- Take educational courses offered through PMI® chapters or other project management training companies.

Remember that as a project manager, you should be proactive in looking for ways to further enhance your skills and knowledge of the industry.

Contributing to the Industry

As a project manager you have the responsibility of not only furthering your own level of knowledge and skill set but also contributing to the knowledge base itself. This includes actions such as the following:

- Coaching and mentoring others within the field
- Contributing to the knowledge base itself, such as through volunteer efforts, writing articles relating to project management, and conducting research and studies that enhance or add to the industry
- Supporting other project managers

Promoting Stakeholder Interaction

Within a project, there can be a small handful to dozens of stakeholders. The greater the number of stakeholders, the more complex project communication and control become. Throughout this book, we review how stakeholders tend to have varying interests. Although everyone wants the project to succeed, the agendas may vary. Ways to promote interaction among stakeholders include the following:

- Working toward balancing their interests, requirements, and expectations
- Reducing the amount of conflict within the project
- Encouraging collaboration among the departments

Be sure to apply all of the stakeholder management techniques that we will cover later in this book from within the Project Communications Management Knowledge Area.

Review Questions

1. The following are characteristics of a project, *except*:
   A. It is temporary in nature.
   B. It is continuous.
   C. It is unique.
   D. It has a definitive end.

2. When is a project considered successful?
   A. All deliverables have been completed.
   B. The phase completion has been approved.
   C. Stakeholder expectations have been met.
   D. The customer has provided final payment.

3. You are currently managing multiple projects relating to a high-profile build-out of a major retail center. The project is extensive, with a two-year timeline. Bob is the project manager responsible for the east block of the build-out, and Sally is the project manager responsible for the north block of the build-out. Both Bob and Sally report to you. Your role can best be described as:
   A. Lead project manager
   B. Department manager
   C. Program manager
   D. Portfolio manager

4. Which of the following is the oldest organization type?
   A. Functional organization
   B. Projectized organization
   C. Matrix organization
   D. Balanced matrix organization

5. A project management office (PMO) is responsible for the following activities, *except*:
   A. Measuring project performance and suggesting corrective action
   B. Ensuring efficient use of resources toward a specific business goal
   C. Evaluating completed project for adherence to project plan
   D. Maintaining and archiving project documentation for future use

6. During a planning meeting, a discussion takes place to decide which resource will be assigned to perform an activity that will be fast-tracked. As the project manager, you unilaterally decide to assign Fred to the activity. What type of organizational structure is this?
   A. Functional organization
   B. Projectized organization
   C. Matrix organization
   D. Balanced matrix organization

7. All of the following are project management process groups, *except*:

    A. Integration

    B. Planning

    C. Executing

    D. Closing

8. During which process group are costs the highest?

    A. Planning

    B. Executing

    C. Monitoring and Controlling

    D. Closing

9. The concept that each element within a cycle is results oriented and becomes an input into the next cycle describes which of the following?

    A. Project management processes

    B. Phases

    C. Project life cycle

    D. Plan-Do-Check-Act cycle

10. All of the following statements are true, *except*:

    A. It is the job of the project manager to ensure that information is explicit, clear, and complete.

    B. A project manager must possess a strong knowledge of finance and accounting principles.

    C. Organizational and planning skills are an important skill set for a project manager to possess.

    D. Power is a technique that the project manager may use to influence people.

11. Which of the following *best* describes the level of authority that a project manager has within a functional organization?

    A. High to ultimate authority

    B. Authority to assign resources

    C. Minimal to no authority

    D. Authority to recommend resources

12. The *PMBOK® Guide* suggests that projects follow a series of project management phases that make up the project life cycle. Which answer represents the phases of the project life cycle?

    A. Planning, Acting, Doing, and Checking

    B. Initiating, Planning, Executing, Monitoring and Controlling, and Closing

    C. Discovery, Designing, Execution, and Finishing

    D. Initiating, Planning, Performing, and Closing Out

13. General management skills are a necessary foundation for the work of a project manager. Which of the following are not general management skills a project manager would need?

   A. Data management skills

   B. Communication skills

   C. Conflict management skills

   D. Budgeting skills

14. What two actions are performed as a part of the Initiating process group?

   A. Hold the project kickoff meeting and perform stakeholder identification

   B. Develop the project charter and project kickoff meeting

   C. Create the project plan and develop the project charter

   D. Develop the project charter and stakeholder identification

15. What actions are performed as a part of the Closing process group?

   A. Accepting project deliverables

   B. Managing stakeholder expectations

   C. Closing out all vendor contracts

   D. Finalizing project work

Initiating the Project

THE PMP® EXAM CONTENT FROM THE INITIATING THE PROJECT PERFORMANCE DOMAIN COVERED IN THIS CHAPTER INCLUDES THE FOLLOWING:

✓ Perform project assessment based upon available information, lessons learned from previous projects, and meetings with relevant stakeholders in order to support the evaluation of the feasibility of new products or services within the given assumptions and/or constraints.

✓ Identify key deliverables based on the business requirements in order to manage customer expectations and direct the achievement of project goals.

✓ Participate in the development of the project charter by compiling and analyzing gathered information in order to ensure project stakeholders are in agreement on its elements.

✓ Identify high-level risks, assumptions, and constraints based on the current environment, organizational factors, historical data, and expert judgment, in order to propose an implementation strategy.

✓ Obtain project charter approval from the sponsor, in order to formalize the authority assigned to the project manager and gain commitment and acceptance for the project.

✓ Perform stakeholder analysis using appropriate tools and techniques in order to align expectations and gain support for the project.

✓ Conduct benefit analysis with relevant stakeholders to validate project alignment with organizational strategy and expected business value.

✓ Inform stakeholders of the approved project charter to ensure common understanding of the key deliverables, milestones, and their roles and responsibilities.

Initiating is the first of the five project management process groups as defined by the Project Management Institute. Initiating acknowledges that a new project (or the next phase within a project) should begin. This process group culminates in the publication of a project charter and a stakeholder register.

Before diving into the Initiating process group, we'll provide a high-level review of the ten Project Management Knowledge Areas, which is another way of classifying the project management processes. This review offers a high-level look at the Knowledge Areas and insight as to how they are tied into the five process groups.

The Initiating process group accounts for 13 percent of the questions on the PMP® exam.

The process names, inputs, tools and techniques, outputs, and descriptions of the project management process groups and related materials and figures in this chapter are based on content from *A Guide to the Project Management Body of Knowledge (PMBOK® Guide), Sixth Edition* (PMI, 2017).

Understanding the Project Management Knowledge Areas

Throughout the project life cycle, a project utilizes a collection of processes that can be classified by the five process groups mentioned in Chapter 1, "Project Foundation." They are Initiating, Planning, Executing, Monitoring and Controlling, and Closing. Processes can also be classified into ten categories called the Project Management Knowledge Areas, which bring together processes that have characteristics in common. According to the *PMBOK® Guide*, the ten Knowledge Areas are as follows:

- Project Integration Management
- Project Scope Management
- Project Schedule Management
- Project Cost Management
- Project Quality Management
- Project Resource Management

- Project Communications Management
- Project Risk Management
- Project Procurement Management
- Project Stakeholder Management

Processes within the Knowledge Areas are grouped by commonalities, whereas processes within the project management process groups are grouped in more or less the order in which you perform them. Once again, these are two ways of classifying the same set of project management processes. Processes interact with other processes outside of their own Knowledge Area and, in many cases, are repeated multiple times as needed.

 For more detailed information on the Project Management Knowledge Areas, see Chapter 2, "Creating the Project Charter," of *PMP®: Project Management Professional Exam Study Guide, Ninth Edition* (Sybex, 2017).

Day of the Exam

For the ten Project Management Knowledge Areas, think of a phrase where each word begins with the first letter of each Knowledge Area. Here's an example:

I (Integration)

Saw (Scope)

Several (Schedule)

Cool (Cost)

Quails (Quality)

Readily (Resources)

Chuckling (Communications) **while**

Reciting (Risk) **and**

Perfecting (Procurement)

Songs (Stakeholder)

Using mnemonics is a great way of memorizing key information and makes preparing for the exam fun!

Project Integration Management

The Project Integration Management Knowledge Area consists of seven processes. Table 2.1 lists the processes and the process group for each. The Project Integration Management Knowledge Area involves identifying and defining the work of the project and combining, unifying, and integrating the appropriate processes. This is the only Knowledge Area that contains processes across all five of the project management process groups. The processes within Project Integration are tightly linked because they occur continually throughout the project, meaning that they are iterative in nature.

TABLE 2.1   Project Integration Management

Process Name	Project Management Process Group
Develop Project Charter	Initiating
Develop Project Management Plan	Planning
Direct and Manage Project Work	Executing
Manage Project Knowledge	Executing
Monitor and Control Project Work	Monitoring and Controlling
Perform Integrated Change Control	Monitoring and Controlling
Close Project or Phase	Closing

As a recap, remember that processes can be categorized by Knowledge Area and also by process group. The five project management process groups are Initiating, Planning, Executing, Monitoring and Controlling, and Closing.

The Project Integration Management Knowledge Area involves the following:

- Identifying and defining the work of the project
- Combining, unifying, and integrating the appropriate processes
- Managing customer and stakeholder expectations and meeting stakeholder requirements

The following tasks are typical of those performed during work covered by the Project Integration Management Knowledge Area:

- Making choices about where to concentrate resources
- Making choices about where to expend daily efforts
- Anticipating potential issues
- Dealing with issues before they become critical
- Coordinating the work for the overall good of the project
- Making trade-offs among competing objectives and alternatives

Figure 2.1 shows the highlights of the Knowledge Area's purpose.

FIGURE 2.1   Project Integration Management

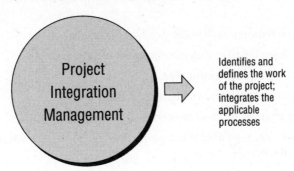

Project Integration Management

Identifies and defines the work of the project; integrates the applicable processes

Project Scope Management

The Project Scope Management Knowledge Area consists of six processes. Table 2.2 lists the processes and the process group for each. These processes are interactive and define and control what is strategically included versus intentionally excluded from the project scope.

TABLE 2.2   Project Scope Management

Process Name	Project Management Process Group
Plan Scope Management	Planning
Collect Requirements	Planning
Define Scope	Planning
Create WBS	Planning
Validate Scope	Monitoring and Controlling
Control Scope	Monitoring and Controlling

The Project Scope Management Knowledge Area encompasses the following:

Project Scope   According to the *PMBOK® Guide*, project scope identifies the work that needs to be accomplished to deliver a product, service, or result with the specified features and functionality. This is typically measured against the project management plan.

Product Scope   Product scope addresses the features and functionality that characterize the product, service, or result of the project. This is measured against the product
specifications to determine successful completion or fulfillment. Product scope entails the
following:

- Detailing the requirements of the product of the project
- Validating those details using measurement techniques
- Creating a scope management plan
- Creating a work breakdown structure (WBS)
- Controlling changes to these processes

The following tasks are typical of those performed during work covered by the Project
Scope Management Knowledge Area:

- Collecting the project requirements
- Defining the overall project scope
- Measuring the project against the project management plan, project scope statement,
  and WBS
- Measuring the completion of a product against the product requirements

Keep in mind that the Project Scope Management Knowledge Area is concerned with
making sure the project includes *all* the work required to complete the project—and *only*
the work required to complete the project successfully.

Figure 2.2 shows the highlights of the Knowledge Area's purpose.

FIGURE 2.2   Project Scope Management

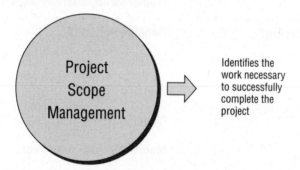

Project
Scope
Management

Identifies the
work necessary
to successfully
complete the
project

Project Schedule Management

The Project Schedule Management Knowledge Area consists of six processes. Table 2.3
lists the processes and the process group for each. On small projects, the Sequence
Activities, Estimate Activity Durations, and Develop Schedule processes are completed as
one activity.

TABLE 2.3   Project Schedule Management

Process Name	Project Management Process Group
Plan Schedule Management	Planning
Define Activities	Planning
Sequence Activities	Planning
Estimate Activity Durations	Planning
Develop Schedule	Planning
Control Schedule	Monitoring and Controlling

The Project Schedule Management Knowledge Area involves the following:

- Creating a detailed plan for how and when the project will produce the results defined by the project scope
- Keeping project activities on track and monitoring those activities against the project plan
- Ensuring that the project is completed on time

The flow of the Project Schedule Management Knowledge Area is very intuitive. First, the project activities are identified and put into the order in which they will occur. Next, duration of activities is estimated. Finally, the project schedule is developed and controlled as the project work moves forward.

Figure 2.3 shows the highlights of the Knowledge Area's purpose.

FIGURE 2.3   Project Schedule Management

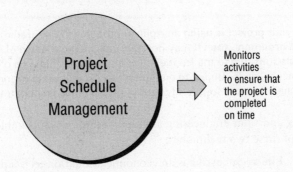

Project Schedule Management

Monitors activities to ensure that the project is completed on time

Project Cost Management

The Project Cost Management Knowledge Area consists of four processes. Table 2.4 lists the processes and the process group for each. For small projects, the Estimate Costs process and Determine Budget process may be combined into a single process. Remember that your ability to influence cost is greatest at the beginning of the project. Minimal resources have been used, in comparison with other stages. Therefore, changes made during these processes have a greater impact on cost reduction, and your opportunities to effect change decline as you move deeper into the project.

TABLE 2.4 Project Cost Management

Process Name	Project Management Process Group
Plan Cost Management	Planning
Estimate Costs	Planning
Determine Budget	Planning
Control Costs	Monitoring and Controlling

The Project Cost Management Knowledge Area involves the following:

- Establishing cost estimates for resources
- Establishing budgets
- Ensuring that the project is executed within the approved budget
- Improving the quality of deliverables through two techniques: life-cycle costing and value engineering

If your project is using an Agile approach, or is operating in an uncertain environment, then it may not gain value from the use of detailed cost calculations due to the frequency of changes. In this type of environment, if the project is subject to a strict budget, it will likely change the scope and schedule more frequently to stay within any cost constraints.

Life-cycle costing and value engineering are used to improve deliverables. The following is a brief overview of these two techniques:

Life-Cycle Costing   Life-cycle costing is an economic evaluation technique that determines the total cost of not only the project (temporary costs) but also owning, maintaining, and operating something from an operational standpoint after the project is completed and turned over.

Value Engineering   Value engineering is a technique that looks for alternative product ideas to make certain the team is applying the lowest cost for the same or better-quality results. So, for example, if the original engineer suggests a custom part for a step of the production process, a value engineering review might suggest an alternative that can use a readily available, lower-cost standard part that will produce the same output for a better value.

These are typical tasks performed during work covered by the Project Cost Management Knowledge Area:

- Developing the cost management plan
- Considering the effects of project decisions on cost
- Considering the information requirements of stakeholders

Figure 2.4 shows the highlights of the Knowledge Area's purpose.

FIGURE 2.4   Project Cost Management

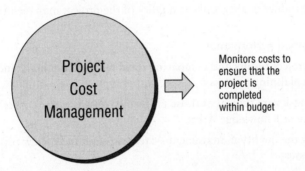

Project
Cost
Management

Monitors costs to
ensure that the
project is
completed
within budget

Day of the Exam

It is important to know what process group and Knowledge Area a process belongs to. In some instances, the name of a process can reveal this information. For example, the **Control Costs** process belongs to the Project **Cost** Management Knowledge Area and Monitoring and **Control**ling process group. Be on the lookout for similar clues to make memorization a cinch!

Project Quality Management

The Project Quality Management Knowledge Area consists of three processes. Table 2.5 lists the processes and the process group for each.

TABLE 2.5   Project Quality Management

Process Name	Project Management Process Group
Plan Quality Management	Planning
Manage Quality	Executing
Control Quality	Monitoring and Controlling

The Project Quality Management Knowledge Area involves the following:

- Ensuring that the project meets the requirements that it was undertaken to produce
- Converting stakeholder needs, wants, and expectations into requirements
- Focusing on product quality and the quality of the project management processes used
- Measuring overall performance
- Monitoring project results and comparing them with the quality standards established in the project planning process

The following tasks are typical of those performed during work covered by the Project Quality Management Knowledge Area:

- Implementing the quality management system through the policy, procedures, and quality processes
- Improving the processes
- Verifying that the project is compatible with applicable standards, such as ISO standards

Figure 2.5 shows the highlights of the Knowledge Area's purpose.

FIGURE 2.5   Project Quality Management

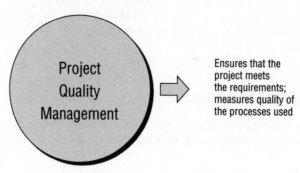

Project Quality Management

Ensures that the project meets the requirements; measures quality of the processes used

Project Resource Management

The Project Resource Management Knowledge Area consists of six processes. These processes identify, help acquire, and manage the resources needed for project success. Table 2.6 lists the processes and the process group for each. In addition to other resources, developing the project team is a key aspect of this Knowledge Area. Because the makeup of each team is different and the stakeholders involved in the various stages of the project might change, project managers use different techniques at different times throughout the project to manage these processes.

TABLE 2.6   Project Resource Management

Process Name	Project Management Process Group
Plan Resource Management	Planning
Estimate Activity Resources	Planning
Acquire Resources	Executing
Develop Team	Executing
Manage Team	Executing
Control Resources	Monitoring and Controlling

The Project Resource Management Knowledge Area involves the following:

- Addressing all aspects of people management and personnel interaction
- Ensuring that physical and human resources assigned to the project are used in the most effective way possible
- Practicing good project management by knowing when to enact certain skills and communication styles based on the situation

The Project Resource Management Knowledge Area also includes enhancing the skill and efficiency of the project team, which, in turn, improves project performance.

Keep in mind that the project management team and project team are different. The project management team is the group of individuals responsible for planning, controlling, and closing activities. They are considered to be the leadership team of the project. The project team is made up of all the individuals that have assigned roles and responsibilities for completing the project. They are also referred to as the project staff.

Physical resource management focuses on assigning and utilizing materials, equipment, and supplies that are needed for successful completion of the project. It is important for organizations to have data on demands, configuration, and supply of resources.

Figure 2.6 shows the highlights of the Knowledge Area's purpose.

FIGURE 2.6   Project Resource Management

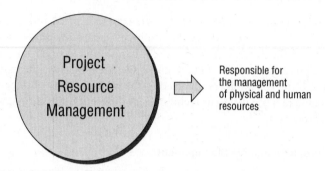

Project
Resource
Management

⇨ Responsible for
the management
of physical and human
resources

Project Communications Management

The Project Communications Management Knowledge Area consists of three processes. Together, these processes connect people and information for successful communication throughout the project. Table 2.7 lists the processes and the process group for each.

TABLE 2.7   Project Communications Management

Process Name	Project Management Process Group
Plan Communications Management	Planning
Manage Communications	Executing
Monitor Communications	Monitoring and Controlling

The Project Communications Management Knowledge Area involves the following:

- Ensuring that all project information is collected, documented, archived, and disposed of at the proper time.

- Distributing and sharing information with stakeholders, management, and project team members.

- Archiving information after project closure to be used as reference for future projects; this information is known as historical information.

As mentioned in Chapter 1 of this book, a good project manager spends up to 90 percent of their time communicating. Overall, much of the project manager's work involves managing project communication.

Figure 2.7 shows the highlights of the Knowledge Area's purpose.

FIGURE 2.7   Project Communications Management

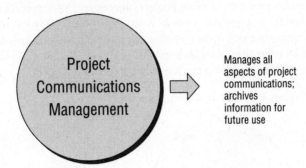

Project Risk Management

The Project Risk Management Knowledge Area consists of seven processes, some of which may be combined into one step. Table 2.8 lists the processes and the process group for each. Risks include both threats to and opportunities within the project.

TABLE 2.8   Project Risk Management

Process Name	Project Management Process Group
Plan Risk Management	Planning
Identify Risks	Planning
Perform Qualitative Risk Analysis	Planning
Perform Quantitative Risk Analysis	Planning
Plan Risk Responses	Planning
Implement Risk Responses	Executing
Monitor Risks	Monitoring and Controlling

The Project Risk Management Knowledge Area involves the following:

- Identifying, analyzing, and planning for potential risks, both positive and negative, that might impact the project
- Minimizing the probability and impact of negative risks, and increasing the probability and impact of positive risks
- Identifying the positive consequences of risk and exploiting them to improve project objectives or discover efficiencies that may improve project performance

According to the *PMBOK® Guide*, a risk is an uncertain event or condition that has a positive or negative effect on one or more project objectives. Every project has some level of uncertainty and, therefore, some level of risk. Keep in mind that a risk is different from an issue. A risk may or may not occur. But when a negative risk materializes and impacts the project, it becomes an issue that must be handled.

Figure 2.8 shows the highlights of the Knowledge Area's purpose.

FIGURE 2.8   Project Risk Management

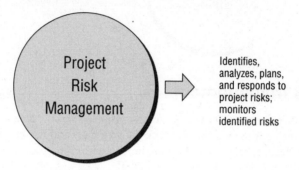

Project Risk Management

Identifies, analyzes, plans, and responds to project risks; monitors identified risks

In Chapter 5, "Planning Project Resource, Communication, Procurement, Change and Risk Management," we will talk more about the various types of risks, including positive versus negative risks.

Project Procurement Management

The Project Procurement Management Knowledge Area consists of three processes. Table 2.9 lists the processes and the process group for each. While reviewing the procurement processes, remember that you are viewing the process from the perspective of the buyer and that sellers are external to the project team. Together, these three processes allow you to manage the purchasing activities of the project and the life cycle of the procurement contracts.

TABLE 2.9   Project Procurement Management

Process Name	Project Management Process Group
Plan Procurement Management	Planning
Conduct Procurements	Executing
Control Procurements	Monitoring and Controlling

The Project Procurement Management Knowledge Area involves purchasing goods or services from vendors, contractors, suppliers, and others outside the project team.

Keep in mind that a contract can be simple or complex; contracts can be tailored to the needs of the project. The *PMBOK® Guide* defines a contract as an agreement that binds the seller to provide the specified products or services; it also obligates the buyer to compensate the seller as specified.

Figure 2.9 shows the highlights of the Knowledge Area's purpose.

FIGURE 2.9   Project Procurement Management

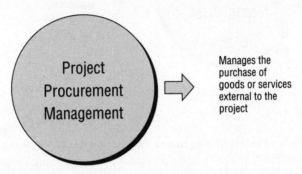

Project Procurement Management

Manages the purchase of goods or services external to the project

Project Stakeholder Management

The Project Stakeholder Management Knowledge Area consists of four processes. Table 2.10 lists the processes and the process group for each. This Knowledge Area is concerned with both internal and external stakeholders.

TABLE 2.10   Project Stakeholder Management

Process Name	Project Management Process Group
Identify Stakeholders	Initiating
Plan Stakeholder Engagement	Planning
Manage Stakeholder Engagement	Executing
Monitor Stakeholder Engagement	Monitoring and Controlling

The Project Stakeholder Management Knowledge Area is concerned with identifying all of the stakeholders of the project. These processes also assess stakeholder needs, expectations and involvement on the project.

According to the *PMBOK® Guide*, stakeholder engagement and satisfaction should be managed as a key project objective.

Figure 2.10 shows the highlights of the Knowledge Area's purpose.

FIGURE 2.10   Project Stakeholder Management

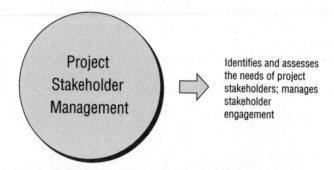

Project Stakeholder Management → Identifies and assesses the needs of project stakeholders; manages stakeholder engagement

---

Exam Essentials

Be able to name the ten Project Management Knowledge Areas.   The ten Project Management Knowledge Areas are Project Integration Management, Project Scope Management, Project Schedule Management, Project Cost Management, Project Quality Management, Project Resource Management, Project Communications Management, Project Risk Management, Project Procurement Management, and Project Stakeholder Management.

Performing a Project Assessment

Before an organization decides to embark on a project, several considerations must take place, such as an assessment of the various potential projects. As part of performing a project assessment, management will need to evaluate existing needs and demands, perform feasibility studies, and use project selection methods to help in making good decisions.

Project assessment should entail a careful evaluation of information carried out through meetings with the sponsor, customer, and other subject matter experts. This group of key individuals will then determine whether the new products or services are feasible under the existing assumptions and constraints.

Initiating a Project

Project initiation is the formal recognition that a new project, or the next phase in an existing project, should begin and resources may be committed to the project. A project may come about as a result of a need, demand, opportunity, or problem. Once those needs and demands are identified, the next logical step may include performing a feasibility study to determine the viability of the project.

For more detailed information on initiating a project, including a closer look at the project selection methods and a case study, see Chapter 2 of *PMP®: Project Management Professional Exam Study Guide, Ninth Edition.*

Identifying Needs and Demands

Needs and demands represent opportunities, business requirements, or problems that need to be solved. Management must decide how to respond to these needs and demands, which will, more often than not, initiate new projects. According to the *PMBOK® Guide*, projects come about as a result of one of the following 13 needs or demands:

Market Demand   The demands of the marketplace can drive the need for a project. Some companies must initiate projects in order to take advantage of temporary and long-term market changes.

Strategic Opportunity / Business Need   An organization may respond to an internal need that could eventually affect the bottom line. For example, this may include addressing company growth or even the need to downsize.

Customer Request   A new project may emerge as a result of internal or external customer requests.

Stakeholder Demands   Stakeholders may require that a new output be produced by an organization.

Technological Advance   New technology often requires companies to revamp their products as a way of taking advantage of the latest technology.

Business Process Improvement   The organization conducts a value streaming exercise in conjunction with a practice like Lean Six Sigma.

Competitive Forces   Industry pressures like price reductions on a product may lead to the need for an organization to reduce production costs to keep competitive.

Material Issues   A sinkhole in a highly used freeway might result in a project that corrects any problems and restores the road to safe operation.

Legal Requirement   Both private industry and government agencies generate new projects as a result of laws passed during a legislative season.

Environmental Consideration   Many organizations are undergoing greening efforts to reduce energy consumption, save fuel, reduce their carbon footprint, and so on.

Political Changes   A changing of the guard for elected officials brings new priorities and changes in funding.

Economic Changes   Positive or negative changes in the economy can result in the initiation of a project.

Social Need   Projects arise out of social needs, such as a developing country that offers medical supplies and vaccination in response to a fast-spreading disease.

Conducting a Feasibility Study

Some organizations require that a feasibility study take place prior to making a final decision about starting a project. Feasibility studies may be conducted as separate projects, as subprojects, or as the first phase of a project.

When evaluating the feasibility of new products or services, it's generally a good idea to meet with the sponsor, customer, and other subject matter experts. Here are some of the reasons that a feasibility study may be undertaken:

- To determine whether the project is viable

- To determine the probability of success

- To examine the viability of the product, service, or result of the project

- To evaluate technical issues related to the project

- To determine whether the technology proposed is feasible, reliable, and easily assimilated into the existing technology structure

Selecting a Project

As shown in Figure 2.11, there are a variety of selection methods an organization may choose to utilize. Selection methods help organizations decide among alternative projects and determine the tangible benefits to the company of choosing or not choosing a project. Project selection methods are also used to evaluate and choose between alternative ways to implement the project.

FIGURE 2.11   Project selection methods

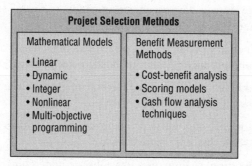

Project Selection Methods	
Mathematical Models	**Benefit Measurement Methods**
• Linear • Dynamic • Integer • Nonlinear • Multi-objective programming	• Cost-benefit analysis • Scoring models • Cash flow analysis techniques

Although project selection is considered to be out of the scope of a project manager's role, the project selection methods we'll talk about next are ones you should be familiar with for the exam.

Depending on the organization, a steering committee may be responsible for project review, selection, and prioritization. A *steering committee* is a group comprising senior managers and, sometimes, midlevel managers who represent each of the functional areas in the organization.

There are generally two categories of selection methods:

- Mathematical models (also known as constrained optimization methods)
- Benefit measurement methods (also known as decision models)

Mathematical Models

For the exam, simply know that mathematical models, also known as constrained optimization methods, use the following in the form of algorithms:

- Linear
- Dynamic
- Integer
- Nonlinear
- Multi-objective programming

Benefit Measurement Methods

Benefit measurement methods, also known as decision models, employ various forms of analysis and comparative approaches to make project decisions. These methods include comparative approaches, such as these:

- Cost-benefit analysis
- Scoring models
- Cash flow analysis techniques

 When applying project selection methods, you can use a benefit measurement method alone or in combination with others to come up with a selection decision.

Let's take a closer look at the benefit measurement methods.

Cost-Benefit Analysis

Cost-benefit analysis, also known as cost analysis or benefit analysis, compares the cost to produce the product, service, or result of the project with the benefit that the organization will receive as a result of executing the project.

Scoring Models

For weighted scoring models, the project selection committee decides on the criteria that will be used on the scoring model. Each of these criteria is then assigned a weight depending on its importance to the project committee. More-important criteria should carry a higher weight than less-important criteria. Each project is then rated on a numerical scale, with the higher number being the more desirable outcome to the company and the lower number having the opposite effect. This rating is then multiplied by the weight of the criteria factor and added to other weighted criteria scores for a total weighted score. The project with the highest overall weighted score is the best choice.

For example, if Project A contains a weighted score of 31, Project B contains a weighted score of 42, and Project C contains a weighted score of 40, which project would you choose? The correct answer is Project B, since it has the highest weighted score.

Cash Flow Analysis Techniques

The final benefit measurement methods involve a variety of cash flow analysis techniques:

- Payback period
- Discounted cash flows
- Net present value
- Internal rate of return

Figure 2.12 provides an overview of the cash flow analysis techniques.

FIGURE 2.12   Overview of cash flow analysis techniques

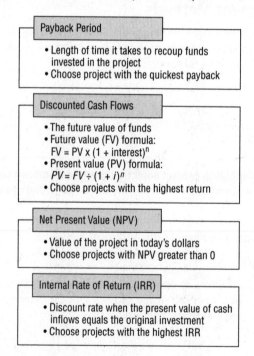

Let's take a closer look at these techniques.

PAYBACK PERIOD

The *payback period* is the length of time it takes the company to recoup the initial costs of producing the product, service, or result of the project. This method compares the initial investment to the cash inflows expected over the life of the product, service, or result.

Payback Period Example

The initial investment on a project is $200,000, with expected cash inflows of $25,000 per quarter every quarter for the first two years and $50,000 per quarter from then on. The payback period is two years and can be calculated as follows:

Initial investment = $200,000

Cash inflows = $25,000

Time frame = 4 quarters

Total cash inflows per year = $100,000 (4 quarters × cash inflows of $25,000)

Initial investment ($200,000) – year 1 inflows ($100,000) = $100,000 remaining balance

Year 1 inflows remaining balance – year 2 inflows = $0

Total cash flow year 1 and year 2 = $200,000

The payback is reached in two years.

The fact that inflows are $50,000 per quarter starting in year 3 makes no difference because payback is reached in two years.

The payback period is the least precise of all the cash flow calculations because it does not consider the time value of money.

DISCOUNTED CASH FLOWS

Money received in the future is worth less than money received today. Therefore, you can calculate what the value of funds will be in the future by using the following formula:

$$FV = PV (1 + i)^n$$

This formula says that the future value (FV) of the investment equals the present value (PV) times (1 plus the interest rate) raised to the value of the number of time periods (n) the interest is paid.

Future Value Example

What is the value of $2,000 three years from today, at 5 percent interest per year?

$FV = \$2,000(1.05)^3$

$FV = \$2,000(1.157625)$

$FV = \$2,315.25$

The discounted cash flow technique compares the value of the future cash flows of the project to today's dollars. It is literally the reverse of the FV formula. To calculate discounted cash flows, you need to know the value of the investment in today's terms, or the present value (PV). PV is calculated using the following formula:

$$PV = FV \div (1 + i)^n$$

 Real World Scenario

Present Value Example

If $2,315.25 is the value of the cash flow three years from now, what is the value today given a 5 percent interest rate?

$PV = \$2,315.25 \div (1 + 0.05)^3$

$PV = \$2,315.25 \div 1.157625$

$PV = \$2,000$

$2,315.25 three years from now is worth $2,000 today.

To calculate discounted cash flow for the projects you are comparing for selection purposes, apply the PV formula, and then compare the discounted cash flows of all the projects against each other to make a selection.

 Real World Scenario

Calculating Project Value Example

Project A is expected to make $100,000 in two years, and Project B is expected to make $120,000 in three years. If the cost of capital is 12 percent, which project should you choose?

Using the PV formula shown previously, calculate each project's worth:

PV of Project A = $79,719

PV of Project B = $85,414

Project B is the project that will return the highest investment to the company and should be chosen over Project A.

NET PRESENT VALUE

Net present value (NPV) allows you to calculate an accurate value for the project in today's dollars. NPV works like discounted cash flows in that you bring the value of future monies received into today's dollars. With NPV, you evaluate the cash inflows using the discounted cash flow technique applied to each period in which the inflows are expected instead of in one sum. The total present value of the cash flows is then deducted from your initial investment to determine NPV. NPV assumes that cash inflows are reinvested at the cost of capital.

Here are some important notes on NPV calculations:

- If the NPV calculation is greater than zero, accept the project.
- If the NPV calculation is less than zero, reject the project.
- Projects with high returns early in the project are better projects than projects with lower returns early in the project.

INTERNAL RATE OF RETURN

Internal rate of return (IRR) is the discount rate when the present value of the cash inflows equals the original investment. When choosing between projects or when choosing alternative methods of doing a project, projects with higher IRR values are generally considered better than projects with low IRR values.

Keep the following in mind:

- IRR is the discount rate when NPV equals zero.
- IRR assumes that cash inflows are reinvested at the IRR value.
- You should choose projects with the highest IRR value.

Exam Essentials

Be able to distinguish between the 13 needs or demands that bring about project creation. The 13 needs or demands that bring about project creation are market demand, stakeholder demand, business process improvement, competitive forces, material issues, organizational need, customer requests, technological advances, legal requirements, ecological impacts, political changes, economic changes, and social needs.

Be able to define decision models. Decision models are project selection methods that are used prior to the Develop Project Charter process to determine the viability of the project. Decision models include benefit measurement methods and mathematical models.

Be familiar with payback period. Payback period is the amount of time it will take the company to recoup its initial investment in the product of the project. It's calculated by adding up the expected cash inflows and comparing them to the initial investment to determine how many periods it takes for the cash inflows to equal the initial investment.

Understand the concept of NPV and IRR. Projects with an NPV greater than zero should be accepted, and those with an NPV less than zero should be rejected. Projects with high IRR values should be accepted over projects with lower IRR values. IRR is the discount rate when NPV is equal to zero and IRR assumes reinvestment at the IRR rate.

Defining the High-Level Project Scope

During the Initiating process group, the high-level project scope is defined and documented. As the project moves into the Planning process group, the high-level scope is further elaborated and defined. This is typically based on the business and compliance requirements and is documented to meet the customer's expectations. According to the *PMBOK® Guide*, the high-level project scope is contained within the project charter.

> For more information on the project charter, see the section titled "Developing the Project Charter" within this chapter.

Exam Essentials

Be able to identify where the high-level scope is documented and what it is based on. The high-level scope is defined and documented within the project charter and is based on the business and compliance requirements.

Identifying High-Level Risks, Assumptions, and Constraints

The Initiating process group focuses on documenting not only the high-level project scope, as mentioned previously, but also high-level risks, assumptions, and constraints. This information will be documented within the project charter and will be largely based on the existing environment, historical information, and expert judgment.

As you may have noticed, this process group is concerned with setting a foundation and common understanding of what the project is setting out to achieve. The Planning process group will later expand on this high-level information by working out the granular details.

> For more information on the project charter, see the section titled "Developing the Project Charter" within this chapter.

Exam Essentials

Be able to identify where the high-level risks, assumptions, and constraints are documented and what they are based on. The high-level risks, assumptions, and constraints are defined and documented within the project charter and are largely based on the existing environment, historical information, and expert judgment.

Developing the Project Charter

Creating the *project charter* is an important initial step to beginning any project because it formally initiates the project within an organization and gives authorization for resources to be committed to the project. The creation of this document involves gathering and analyzing stakeholder requirements, which will lead the way for properly identifying and documenting the project and product scope, milestones, and deliverables.

The project charter document is created out of the first process within the Project Integration Management Knowledge Area, called Develop Project Charter. This document attempts to not only formally recognize the project but also identify project limitations and propose an implementation approach. Until the project charter is created and formally approved, many organizations do not recognize the project.

The project charter documents the name of the project manager and gives that person the authority to assign organizational resources to the project. It also documents the business need, justification, and impact; describes the customer's requirements; sets stakeholder expectations; and ties the project to the ongoing work of the organization. The project is officially authorized when the project charter is signed.

Figure 2.13 shows the inputs, tools and techniques, and outputs of the Develop Project Charter process.

FIGURE 2.13   Develop Project Charter process

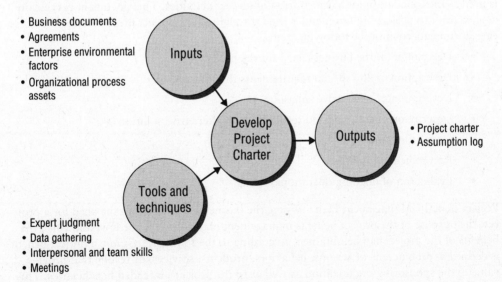

- Business documents
- Agreements
- Enterprise environmental factors
- Organizational process assets

Inputs

Develop Project Charter

Outputs

- Project charter
- Assumption log

Tools and techniques

- Expert judgment
- Data gathering
- Interpersonal and team skills
- Meetings

For more detailed information on the project charter, see Chapter 2 of *PMP®: Project Management Professional Exam Study Guide, Ninth Edition.*

Inputs of the Develop Project Charter Process

For the exam, you should know the following inputs of the Develop Project Charter process:

- Business documents
  - Business case
  - Benefits management plan
- Agreements
- Enterprise environmental factors
- Organizational process assets

Let's look at each of these inputs more closely.

Business Documents   Business documents describe the project's objectives and how the project will contribute to the business's goals and include documents such as the business case and the benefits management plan. The business case describes the product, service, or result the project was undertaken to complete from a business perspective. The project benefits management plan describes the positive aspects that the project will create and for whom.

Business Case   The purpose of a business case is to understand the business need for the project and determine whether the investment in the project is worthwhile. Performing an economic feasibility study is a great first step in establishing the validity of the benefits and is used as the foundation for authorization of project activities. This document is typically created prior to project initiation and is used throughout the project lifecycle. Most business case documents contain the following items:

- Description of the business need for the project
- Description of any special requirements that must be met
- Description of alternative solutions
- Description of the expected results of each alternative solution
- Cost-benefit analysis
- Recommended solution
- Evaluation of ongoing operational needs

Project Benefits Management Plan   Where the business case describes the need for a project, the purpose of the project benefits management plan is to describe how and when the benefits of the project can be obtained. According to the *PMBOK® Guide*, a project benefit is defined as an outcome of actions, behaviors, products, services, or results that provide value to the sponsoring organization as well as to the project's intended beneficiaries. This document is typically created early in the project life cycle. Most project benefits management plans contain the following items:

- Description of the target benefits
- Description of the project's strategic alignment with the organization

- A listing of the benefits' owners
- Time frames that define when benefits should be realized
- Metrics that will be used to measure the benefits
- Description of known assumptions and risks

Agreements   The agreements input is applicable only when the organization you are working for is performing a project for a customer external to the organization. The agreement is used as an input to this process because it typically documents the conditions under which the project will be executed, the time frame, and a description of the work.

Enterprise Environmental Factors   Enterprise environmental factors refer to the factors outside the project that may have significant influence on the success of the project. According to the *PMBOK® Guide*, the environmental factors, in relation to this process, include but are not limited to the following items:

- Governmental or industry standards, which include elements such as regulatory standards and regulations, quality standards, product standards, and workmanship standards
- Organizational culture and structure
- Marketplace conditions, referring to the supply-and-demand theory along with economic and financial factors

Organizational Process Assets   Organizational process assets are the organization's policies, guidelines, procedures, plans, approaches, or standards for conducting work, including project work.

These assets include a wide range of elements that might affect several aspects of the project. In relation to this process, organizational process assets refer to the following items:

- Processes, policies, templates, and procedures of the organization
- Corporate knowledge base, such as historical information and lessons learned

Tools and Techniques of the Develop Project Charter Process

The Develop Project Charter process has four tools and techniques that you should be familiar with:

- Expert judgment
- Data gathering
- Interpersonal and team skills
- Meetings

Let's look at each element more closely:

Expert Judgment   The concept behind expert judgment is to rely on individuals, or groups of individuals, who have training, specialized knowledge, or skills in the areas you're assessing. These individuals may be stakeholders, consultants, other experts in the organization, subject matter experts, the project management office (PMO), industry experts, or technical or professional organizations.

Data Gathering   There are several data-gathering techniques that can be used, and the *PMBOK® Guide* lists three: brainstorming, focus groups, and interviews.

>   **Brainstorming.** Brainstorming is a technique that helps form a list of ideas in a short period of time. It is typically done in a group setting led by a facilitator.

>   **Focus groups.** Focus groups bring together groups of subject matter experts and stakeholders to discuss success criteria, project risk, and other topics in an open forum.

>   **Interviews.** Interviews can be used to gather information for assumptions, constraints, or high-level requirements by talking directly to stakeholders.

Interpersonal and Team Skills   Project managers rely on people skills to help bring results to the project. This technique focuses on the interpersonal and team skills needed for project success. This may include, but isn't limited to, the following skills:

>   **Conflict management.** During a project there are certain periods of strife and interpersonal clash. Conflict management is a technique used to help bring stakeholders into a pool of shared meaning on objectives, success criteria, project description, and other elements.

>   **Facilitation.** Facilitation refers to the application of the project management processes through the use of brainstorming, meeting management, conflict resolution, and other techniques employed by the facilitators.

>   **Meeting management.** Meeting management includes the activities of agenda creation, ensuring stakeholder representation, and preparing and sending minutes and action items.

Meetings   During the creation of the charter, meetings are a key activity for identifying objectives, success criteria, deliverables, requirements, milestones, and other information as needed.

In addition, you should be familiar with who is considered to be a key stakeholder. Key project stakeholders include the following individuals:

Project Manager   The project manager is the person who assumes responsibility for the success of the project. The project manager should be identified as early as possible in the project and ideally should participate in writing the project charter. The following are examples of what the role of project manager entails:

- Project planning and managing the overall work of the project
- Setting the standards and policies for the projects on which they work

- Establishing and communicating the project procedures to the project team and stakeholders
- Identifying activities and tasks, resource requirements, project costs, project requirements, performance measures, and more
- Keeping all stakeholders and other interested parties informed

Project Sponsor   The project sponsor is usually an executive in the organization who has the power and authority to make decisions and settle disputes or conflicts regarding the project. The sponsor takes the project into the limelight, gets to call the shots regarding project outcomes, and funds the project. The project sponsor should be named in the project charter and identified as the final authority and decision maker for project issues.

Project Champion   The project champion is usually someone with a great deal of technical expertise or industry knowledge regarding the project who helps focus attention on the project from a technical perspective. Unlike the sponsor, the project champion doesn't necessarily have a lot of authority or executive powers.

Functional Managers   Project managers must work with and gain the support of functional managers in order to complete the project. Functional managers fulfill the administrative duties of the organization, provide and assign staff members to projects, and conduct performance reviews for their staff.

Outputs of the Develop Project Charter Process

The Develop Project Charter process results in two outputs: the project charter and assumption log.

Project Charter   According to the *PMBOK® Guide*, a useful and well-documented project charter should include at least these elements:

- Purpose or justification for the project
- Project objectives that are measurable
- High-level list of requirements
- High-level description of the project
- High-level list of risks
- Summary milestone schedule
- Summary budget
- List of key stakeholders known
- Criteria for project approval
- Name of the project manager and their authority levels
- Name of the sponsor (or authorizer of the project) and their authority levels

Assumption Log   The business case typically identifies high-level assumptions, both at a strategic and at an operational level. The assumption log is a tool used to record all assumptions and constraints throughout the project life cycle, especially as they evolve to more lower-level activity and task assumptions.

Exam Essentials

Be able to list the Develop Project Charter inputs. The inputs for Develop Project Charter are business documents, agreements, enterprise environmental factors, and organizational process assets.

Be able to describe the purpose of the business case. The purpose of a business case is to understand the business need for the project and determine whether the investment in the project is worthwhile.

Obtaining Project Charter Approval

The project charter isn't complete until sign-off has been received from the project sponsor, senior management, and key stakeholders. Sign-off indicates that the document has been read by those signing it and that they agree with the contents and are on board with the project. The signature signifies the formal authorization of the project. Acceptance of the charter is also important to formalize the assignment of the project manager and their level of authority.

The last step in this process is publishing the charter. Publishing, in this case, simply means distributing a copy of the project charter to the key stakeholders, the customer, the management team, and others who might be involved with the project. Publication can take several forms, including printed format or electronic format distributed via the company email system or the company intranet.

Exam Essentials

Be able to describe the importance of the project charter. The project charter is the document that officially recognizes and acknowledges that a project exists. The charter authorizes the project to begin. It authorizes the project manager to assign resources to the project and documents the business need and justification. The project charter describes the customer's requirements and ties the project to the ongoing work of the organization.

Performing Key Stakeholder Analysis

Identifying stakeholders and performing analysis on key stakeholders is an important part of setting the stage for a successful project outcome. Stakeholder analysis is carried out through the Identify Stakeholders process and involves the use of brainstorming, interviewing, and several data-gathering techniques.

By performing stakeholder identification and analysis, the project manager can better document stakeholder expectations and ensure that the expectations are aligned with the project objectives. It also serves as a way of gaining project support.

> Project stakeholders are those people or organizations who have a vested interest in the outcome of the project. They have something to either gain or lose as a result of the project, and they have the ability to influence project results.

Identify Stakeholders is the first process of the Project Stakeholder Management Knowledge Area and part of the Initiating process group. This process involves identifying and documenting all the stakeholders on the project, including their interests, impact, and potential negative influences on the project. Stakeholder identification should occur as early as possible in the project and continue throughout its life cycle.

Figure 2.14 shows the inputs, tools and techniques, and outputs of the Identify Stakeholders process.

FIGURE 2.14 Identify Stakeholders process

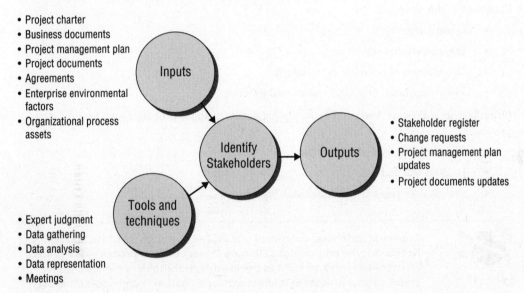

- Project charter
- Business documents
- Project management plan
- Project documents
- Agreements
- Enterprise environmental factors
- Organizational process assets

Inputs

Identify Stakeholders

Outputs

- Stakeholder register
- Change requests
- Project management plan updates
- Project documents updates

Tools and techniques

- Expert judgment
- Data gathering
- Data analysis
- Data representation
- Meetings

> For more detailed information on the Identify Stakeholders process, see Chapter 2 of *PMP®: Project Management Professional Exam Study Guide, Ninth Edition.*

Inputs of the Identify Stakeholders Process

There are seven inputs within the Identify Stakeholders process:

Project Charter   Within this process, the project charter provides the list of stakeholders along with other individuals or organizations that are affected by the project.

Business Documents   The benefits management plan and business case help inform about who are project stakeholders.

Project Management Plan   While the project management plan is not available during initial stakeholder identification, once the project management plan is developed, it can be helpful for this process, specifically the communications management plan and the stakeholder engagement plan.

Project Documents   Since stakeholder identification occurs throughout the project, project documents like the change and issue log can be an input to this process.

Agreements   The parties to any agreement can be stakeholders, and therefore, agreements serve as an input to this process.

Enterprise Environmental Factors   The following enterprise environmental factors are utilized within this process:

- Company culture
- Organizational structure
- Governmental or industry standards
- Local, regional, or global trends and practices

Organizational Process Assets   The following organizational process assets pertain to this process:

- Stakeholder register templates
- Lessons learned
- Stakeholder register from previous projects

In several instances, outputs of one process become inputs to another. Notice that the output of the Develop Project Charter process—the project charter—becomes an input to the Identify Stakeholders process. Understanding how processes interact with one another is an important aspect of the exam.

Tools and Techniques of the Identify Stakeholders Process

The tools and techniques of Identify Stakeholders are expert judgment, data gathering, data analysis, data representation, and meetings.

Expert Judgment   Expert judgment is used in combination with stakeholder analysis to ensure that stakeholder identification is comprehensive. This may involve interviewing key stakeholders that are already identified and senior management, subject matter experts, or other project managers.

Data Gathering Data gathering for this process would focus on, but is not limited to, the use of questionnaires, surveys, and brainstorming.

Data Analysis Data analysis techniques used for this process include but are not limited to the following:

Stakeholder Analysis During stakeholder analysis, you'll want to identify the influences stakeholders have in regard to the project and understand their expectations, needs, and desires. From there, you'll derive more specifics regarding the project goals and deliverables. Stakeholders are often concerned with their own interests and what they have to gain or lose from the project.

According to the *PMBOK® Guide*, two steps are involved in stakeholder analysis:

1. Identify all potential stakeholders and capture general information about them, such as the department they work in, contact information, knowledge levels, and influence levels.

2. Assess the reaction or responses of the stakeholder to various situations. This will assist the project manager in managing the stakeholders.

Document Analysis Document analysis assesses available project documentation, as well as lessons learned from previous projects, to help inform potential project stakeholders.

Data Representation This technique may be used in the Identify Stakeholder process and includes, but is not limited to, stakeholder mapping and representation, identifying the potential impact or support each stakeholder may have on the project, and then classifying them according to impact so that you can devise a strategy to deal with them. The *PMBOK® Guide* lists four classification models for classifying the power and influence of each stakeholder on a simple four-square grid:

- Power/interest grid, power/influence grid, or impact/influence grid
- Stakeholder cube
- Directions of influence/impact grid
- Salience model (which charts stakeholder power, urgency, and legitimacy)

Meetings Meetings are often used as a mechanism for performing stakeholder analysis. Project managers often gather and analyze information on roles, positions, and interests of stakeholders through meetings.

Outputs of the Identify Stakeholders Process

The Identify Stakeholders process has four outputs: stakeholder register, change requests, project management plan updates, and project documents updates.

Stakeholder Register A stakeholder register captures all of the information about the stakeholders in one place. This general information includes things like the department they work in, contact information, knowledge levels, and influence levels. In addition, the stakeholder register contains at least the following:

Identifying Information   This includes items like contact information, department, role in the project, and so on.

Assessment Information   This includes elements regarding influence, expectations, key requirements, and when the stakeholder involvement is most critical.

Stakeholder Classification   Stakeholders can be classified according to their relationship to the organization and, more important, whether they support the project, are resistant to the project, or have no opinion.

Change Requests   Early in the project there aren't likely to be any change requests. However, as the project progresses and stakeholder identification continues, new information about stakeholders may result in a change request to the product, project management plan, or project documents.

Project Management Plan Updates   Similar to change requests, there are not likely to be any updates at the beginning of the project. As stakeholder identification continues throughout the project, updates to the project management plan documents are likely, including to the following documents:

- Requirements management plan
- Communications management plan
- Risk management plan
- Stakeholder engagement plan

Project Documents Updates   This process may result in updating project documents such as the following:

- Assumption log
- Issue log
- Risk register

Exam Essentials

Understand the Identify Stakeholders process.   The purpose of this process is to identify the project stakeholders, assess their influence and level of involvement, devise a plan to deal with potential negative impacts, and record stakeholder information in the stakeholder register.

Bringing the Processes Together

As a recap, the Initiating process group kicks off the project and results in the creation of the project charter and the stakeholder register. This phase acknowledges that a new project or phase should begin.

But before a project formally exists, several scenarios may unfold:

1. First, needs and demands surface within an organization, demonstrating the need for a project to be initiated.

2. The potential project may then go through a feasibility study to determine whether the project and end result of the project are viable and whether there is an opportunity for success.

3. A project may also go through a selection process. We looked at mathematical models and benefit measurement methods as two categories of project selection methods.

After a project is selected, a project charter is created (using the Develop Project Charter process) and signed, formally authorizing the project. By the end of the Develop Project Charter process, the project charter contains several documented elements, including the justification for the project, high-level requirements and description, summary milestone schedule and budget, and the sponsor and project manager (if already selected).

Once the project charter is generated, project stakeholders can be identified. This occurs in the Identify Stakeholders process. You learned that stakeholders, along with their interests and levels of influence, are important to identify and define early on within the project. As a result, a stakeholder register, which identifies, assesses, and classifies the individual stakeholders, is created.

Figure 2.15 shows the potential path of a new project, from its inception and through the initiating phase.

FIGURE 2.15   Initiating a project

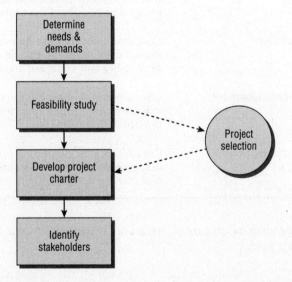

In this chapter, we also covered the ten Project Management Knowledge Areas, which are summarized in Table 2.11.

TABLE 2.11 Project Management Knowledge Areas summary

Knowledge Area	Description
Project Integration Management	Concerned with coordinating all the aspects of the project management plan to accomplish the project objectives
Project Scope Management	Concerned with managing the project scope and defining and controlling what is (and isn't) included within the project
Project Time Management	Concerned with completing the project on time
Project Schedule Management	Concerned with completing the project within budget
Project Quality Management	Concerned with ensuring that the project satisfies the needs for which it was undertaken
Project Resource Management	Concerned with organizing, developing, and managing the project team and physical resources
Project Communications Management	Concerned with connecting people and information together to result in successful communications throughout the project
Project Risk Management	Concerned with increasing the probability and impact of positive events and decreasing the probability and impact of adverse events
Project Procurement Management	Concerned with managing the purchasing activities of the project and the life cycle of the procurement contracts
Project Stakeholder Management	Concerned with identifying project stakeholders, assessing their needs and expectations, and managing their engagement

With the initiating phase taken care of, we are ready to move into the next phase of the project's life cycle: Planning.

Review Questions

1. Identify Stakeholders, Plan Stakeholder Engagement, and Monitor Stakeholder Engagement are all processes of which Knowledge Area?

    A. Project Integration Management

    B. Project Stakeholder Management

    C. Project Resource Management

    D. Project Procurement Management

2. Ron is the project manager of a pharmaceutical company that develops multiple products to help fight diseases affecting children. There are currently two new drugs that the company is planning to develop within the next two years. Ron has been tasked with determining which of the two drugs has the greatest opportunity for success in today's marketplace. This is an example of:

    A. A business need

    B. A demand

    C. A project selection method

    D. A feasibility study

3. Your manager has recently given you the responsibility of selecting the next project, which you will manage as the project manager. There are currently three projects on hold to choose from. Using the weighted scoring models method, you determine that Project A has a weighted score of 16, Project B has a weighted score of 14, and Project C has a weighted score of 17. Which project do you choose?

    A. Project A

    B. Project B

    C. Project C

    D. None of the prospects are good selections.

4. What type of project selection method is multi-objective programming?

    A. Benefit measurement method

    B. Constrained optimization method

    C. Decision model

    D. Scoring model

5. What is $5,525 four years from now worth today given a 10 percent interest rate?

    A. $3,773.65

    B. $5,022.73

    C. $5,525.00

    D. $6,077.50

6. Which of the following *best* describes the characteristics of the product, service, or result of the project?

    A. Strategic plan

    B. Product scope description

    C. Agreement

    D. Project charter

7. All of the following are inputs to the Develop Project Charter process *except*:

    A. Agreements

    B. Business documents

    C. Organizational process assets

    D. Project charter

8. Maryann has just wrapped up the final draft of the project charter and emailed a copy to the appropriate individuals. A kick-off meeting in two days has already been scheduled to complete the project charter, with all those involved having accepted the meeting invitation. What will Maryann need done during the kick-off meeting to complete the project charter?

    A. Have the charter published

    B. Confirm that the sponsor, senior management, and all key stakeholders have read and understand the charter

    C. Gather excitement and buy-in for the project among the key stakeholders

    D. Obtain sign-off of the project charter from the sponsor, senior management, and key stakeholders

9. All of the following are inputs to the Identify Stakeholders process *except*:

    A. Agreements

    B. Project charter

    C. Project statement of work

    D. Enterprise environmental factors

10. The stakeholder register can *best* be described as:

    A. A document that captures all information about the stakeholders in one place

    B. The documented approach used to minimize negative impacts or influences that stakeholders may have throughout the life of the project

    C. A list of potential strategies for redirecting the support of stakeholders

    D. A classification method that classifies all stakeholders according to their influence, expectations, key requirements, and when the stakeholder involvement is most critical

11. Polly is a project manager tasked with leading a project that will establish business continuity management practices for a major retail coffee chain. With the guidance of the sponsor, she drafts a document that authorizes her to begin assigning resources to the project once signed. What process will Polly likely perform next?

    A. Identify Stakeholders

    B. Develop Project Management Plan

    C. Develop Project Charter

    D. Plan Resource Management

12. Power/interest grid, salience model, and influence/impact grid are all examples of which of the following techniques?

    A. Expert judgment

    B. Data representation

    C. Stakeholder strategy

    D. Stakeholder register

13. All of the following are processes of the Project Scope Management Knowledge Area *except*:

    A. Collect Requirements

    B. Create WBS

    C. Validate Scope

    D. Control Requirements

14. Beans by the Dozen is a company that ships precooked beans to restaurants in the Western United States. Recently, the company has decided to expand their operation to the northern regions of the country. A business case was developed, citing market demand, and a project manager informally assigned to formalize and kick off the project. What is the project manager likely to do first?

    A. Obtain sign-off of the business case and celebrate

    B. Form a project team to begin planning out the project work

    C. Develop the project charter and obtain sign-off

    D. Develop the project management plan and obtain sign-off

15. Which of the following options best defines project scope?

    A. It addresses the features and functionality that characterize the product, service, or result of the project.

    B. It describes how the scope will be defined, developed, monitored, controlled, and verified.

    C. It contains a list of potential strategies for redirecting the support of stakeholders.

    D. It identifies the work that needs to be accomplished to deliver a product, service, or result with the specified features and functionality.

16. Product scope is measured against the product specifications whereas project scope is measured against:

    A. The project management plan

    B. The scope management plan

    C. Requirements documentation

    D. Requirements management plan

17. Beans by the Dozen is a company that ships precooked beans to restaurants in the Western United States. June is the project manager assigned to lead the expansion of the company's operation. As part of performing stakeholder analysis, she lists out all of the known stakeholders and includes various notes about each within a register. What is June likely to do next?

   A. Publish a stakeholder register for the project team to reference

   B. Identify the potential impact or support each may have on the project

   C. Document the stakeholder details within a project charter

   D. Obtain sign-off from the sponsor of the stakeholder register

18. Life-cycle costing is defined as:

   A. A technique that looks for alternative product ideas to make certain the team is applying the lowest cost for the same or better-quality results

   B. A technique that compares the cost to produce the product, service, or result of the project with the benefit that the organization will receive

   C. A decision model that employs various forms of analysis and comparative approaches to make project decisions

   D. An economic evaluation technique that determines the total cost of a product

19. Which of the following Knowledge Areas is responsible for linking the processes across the project management process groups?

   A. Project Integration Management

   B. Project Scope Management

   C. Project Stakeholder Management

   D. Project Quality Management

20. Polly is a project manager tasked with leading a project that will establish business continuity management practices for a major retail coffee chain. With the guidance of the sponsor, she drafts a document that authorizes her to begin assigning resources to the project once signed. What process is Polly performing?

   A. Identify Stakeholders

   B. Develop Project Management Plan

   C. Develop Project Charter

   D. Plan Human Resource Management

Chapter 3

Planning Project Scope and Schedule Management

THE PMP® EXAM CONTENT FROM THE PLANNING PERFORMANCE DOMAIN COVERED IN THIS CHAPTER INCLUDES THE FOLLOWING:

✓ Review and assess detailed project requirements, constraints, and assumptions with stakeholders based on the project charter, lessons learned, and by using requirement gathering techniques in order to establish the project deliverables.

✓ Develop a scope management plan, based on the approved project scope and using scope management techniques, in order to define, maintain, and manage the scope of the project.

✓ Develop the project schedule based on the approved project deliverables and milestones, scope, and resource management plans in order to manage timely completion of the project.

Planning is the second of five project management process groups and includes the largest number of processes, 24 in total. For this reason, coverage of these processes has been split between four chapters. In this chapter, we will cover processes that belong to the following Knowledge Areas: Project Scope Management and Project Schedule Management.

According to the *PMBOK® Guide*, processes belonging to the Planning process group are "required to establish the scope of the project, refine the objectives, and define the course of action required to attain the objectives that the project was undertaken to achieve." Throughout the Planning processes, these objectives are defined and refined, and a course of action is mapped out to successfully complete the project objectives as outlined by the project scope. Several key project documents are created within this process group, including the project management plan and its collection of subsidiary plans and baselines, which will guide the project management activities. Because the subsidiary plans and baselines come together to produce the project management plan, we will cover those processes first, and wrap up the Planning process group review by addressing the plan as the finale for Chapter 6, "Planning Stakeholder Engagement and Obtaining Project Plan Approval."

The Planning process group accounts for 24 percent of the questions on the Project Management Professional (PMP)® exam.

The process names, inputs, tools and techniques, outputs, and descriptions of the project management process groups and related materials and figures in this chapter are based on content from *A Guide to the Project Management Body of Knowledge (PMBOK® Guide), Sixth Edition* (PMI®, 2017).

Developing a Scope Management Plan

The Project Scope Management Knowledge Area is kicked off through a process that develops two key plans that will guide the identification of requirements as well as the development, validation, and management of the project's scope. These plans, referred to as the scope management plan and requirements management plan, are subsidiary documents of an overarching plan called the project management plan.

Understand Project Scope Management

The scope management plan is the culmination of the processes needed to guarantee that the project includes all the work required to complete the project successfully. It also works to make sure that the project focuses only on the work required to complete the project and does not include unneeded tasks. As you learned in Chapter 2, "Initiating the Project," the Project Scope Management Knowledge Area consists of six processes, but only four of them are a part of the Planning process group. The four processes used in the Planning process group are Plan Scope Management, Collect Requirements, Define Scope, and Create WBS.

Plans not created out of a formal process are considered to be generated out of the Develop Project Management Plan process, which is a high-level planning process that will be covered in Chapter 6. Figure 3.1 shows the inputs, tools and techniques, and outputs of the Plan Scope Management process.

FIGURE 3.1 Plan Scope Management process

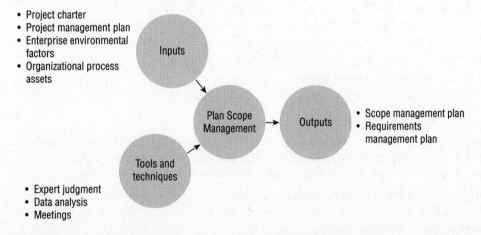

In addition to being familiar with the two plans emerging from this process, it is important to understand the difference between product scope and project scope. According to the *PMBOK® Guide*, product scope refers to the features and functions that characterize a product, service, or result, while project scope refers to work performed to deliver a product, service, or result with the specified features and functions. The project scope is measured against the project management plan, while product scope is measured against the product requirements.

Plan Scope Management

The Plan Scope Management process is the first process from within the Project Scope Management Knowledge Area. The purpose of the process is to generate the scope management plan, which contains the following information or explanations:

- The process used to prepare the project scope statement
- A process for creating the work breakdown structure (WBS)

- A definition of how the deliverables will be validated for accuracy and the process used for accepting deliverables

- A description of the process for controlling scope change requests, including the procedure for requesting changes and obtaining a change request form

Keep in mind that throughout the Project Scope Management Knowledge Area, the scope management plan serves as a guide for documenting and controlling the scope of the project.

Inputs of Plan Scope Management

Know the following four inputs of the Plan Scope Management process:

Project Charter   The project charter communicates the high-level goals, business needs, assumptions, and constraints. It is used in this process to align the scope management plan with stakeholder expectations.

Project Management Plan   The project management plan more closely defines what the project is intended to accomplish. This plan, with all of its approved subsidiary plans, is used to help create the scope management plan. In particular, the following components of the project management plan are referenced:

- Quality management plan

- Project life cycle description

- Development approach

Enterprise Environmental Factors   Several enterprise environmental factors can influence the Plan Scope Management process, including but not limited to the organization's culture, its infrastructure, marketplace conditions, and personnel administration.

Organizational Process Assets   Policies, procedures, and historical information, including a lessons learned knowledge base, are a few of the organizational process assets that help shape the scope management plan.

Tools and Techniques of Plan Scope Management

The three tools and techniques that the Plan Scope Management process uses are expert judgement, data analysis, and meetings:

Expert Judgment   Input that is received from experienced team members and those who are knowledgeable about the project area provide what is considered to be expert judgment. Be sure that you look to all corners of your organization for any person or group with specialized education or training, or who might possess knowledge, skills, and/or experience in helping to develop the scope management plan.

Data Analysis   Alternatives analysis is a helpful data analysis technique that can be used to develop the scope and requirements management plans. The plans often document the various types of techniques that will be used to collect requirements and develop scope.

Meetings   In the course of developing the scope management plan, members of project teams may attend meetings to facilitate information exchange and decision making. Depending on the meeting, the following members might be a part of the discussion: project manager, project sponsor, selected project team members, and anyone having responsibility in this particular area.

Outputs of Plan Scope Management

For the exam, know the outputs of the Plan Scope Management process. This includes, naturally, the scope management plan, as well as the requirements management plan.

Scope Management Plan   The components of the scope management plan include processes for the following activities:

- Preparing a detailed project scope statement
- Creating a WBS from the detailed project scope statement
- Establishing how the WBS will be maintained and approved
- Specifying how formal acceptance will be obtained for completed project deliverables
- Controlling and handling change requests to the detailed project scope statement

Remember that a scope management plan can be tailored to your needs; it can be formal or informal and may be highly detailed or broadly framed.

Requirements Management Plan   The requirements management plan defines how the requirements will be analyzed, documented, and managed throughout all phases of the project. The type of phase relationship used to manage the project will determine how requirements are managed throughout the project. A requirements management plan includes the following components:

- How planning, tracking, and reporting of requirements activities will occur
- How changes to the requirements will be requested, tracked, and analyzed along with other configuration management activities
- How requirements will be prioritized
- Which metrics will be used to trace product requirements
- Which requirements attributes will be documented in the traceability matrix
- The structure that will be used to help create the traceability matrix

Collect Requirements

During the early stages of planning, requirements will need to be collected, documented, and assessed. This is carried out through the Collect Requirements process (one of the 49 project management processes). This tends to be an iterative process because requirements often need to be refined as the project moves forward.

> Requirements are typically conditions that must be met or criteria that the product or service of the project must possess to satisfy the objectives of the project. Requirements quantify and prioritize the wants, needs, and expectations of the project sponsor and stakeholders. According to the *PMBOK® Guide*, you must be able to measure, trace, and test requirements. It's important that they be complete and accepted by your project sponsor and key stakeholders.

As covered in Chapter 2, high-level requirements are documented within the project charter. Based on this document and lessons learned from past projects, detailed requirements will need to be gathered and assessed with the stakeholders. This is necessary to establishing the project deliverables. Detailed requirements can be gathered through the use of several requirement-gathering techniques that will produce a comprehensive list of requirements and that are needed to later establish the project deliverables. Collect Requirements is the third process within the Planning process group, following the creation of the scope management plan, and the second process in the Project Scope Management Knowledge Area. The primary purpose of the Collect Requirements process is to define and document the project sponsors', customers', and stakeholders' expectations and needs for meeting the project objectives. This can be done through the use of lessons learned from previous projects, information from within the project charter and stakeholder register, and several requirement-gathering techniques. By the end of this process, the project will include a plan that defines how the requirements will be documented and managed throughout all phases of the project.

Figure 3.2 shows the inputs, tools and techniques, and outputs of the Collect Requirements process.

FIGURE 3.2   Collect Requirements process

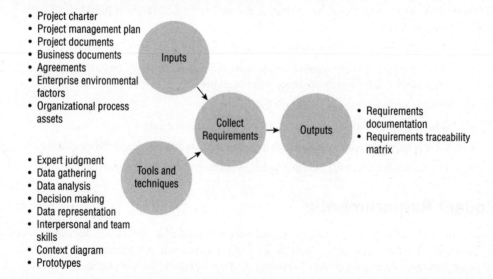

For more detailed information on the Collect Requirements process, see Chapter 3, "Developing the Project Scope Statement," of *PMP®: Project Management Professional Exam Study Guide, Ninth Edition* (Sybex, 2017).

Inputs of Collect Requirements

Know the following inputs of the Collect Requirements process:

Project Charter   In this process, the high-level project requirements and product description are used from within the project charter.

Project Management Plan   The project management plan contains the scope, requirements, and stakeholder engagement plans, which are useful for gathering requirements.

> **Scope Management Plan**   The scope management plan provides direction on how members of the project pick the type of requirements that need to be collected for the project.
>
> **Requirements Management Plan**   The requirements management plan helps define and document the stakeholders' wants and needs.
>
> **Stakeholder Engagement Plan**   We will cover the stakeholder engagement plan in Chapter 6. For the Collect Requirements process, the stakeholder engagement plan is used to document the stakeholder communication requirements and their level of engagement. This will help the project team adjust the requirements activities to the level of stakeholder participation that is needed.

Project Documents   In this process, the stakeholder register is used as a way of determining who can provide the necessary information on the project and product requirements. In addition to this document, the assumption log and lessons learned register are helpful in identifying requirements.

Business Documents   The business case can offer insight and criteria for meeting business needs.

Agreements   When agreements exist, they are key since they often contain project and/or product requirements.

Enterprise Environmental Factors   Enterprise environmental factors applicable to collecting requirements include things like organizational culture, marketplace conditions, infrastructure, and personnel administration.

Organizational Process Assets   Historical information from past similar projects can be very useful, such as archived requirements documentation. Lessons learned, policies, and procedures are other types of assets that can be used.

Tools and Techniques of Collect Requirements

Know the following tools and techniques that can be used during the Collect Requirements process:

- Expert judgment
- Data gathering

- Data analysis
- Decision making
- Data representation
- Interpersonal and team skills
- Context diagrams
- Prototypes

Expert Judgment   Subject matter experts and experienced project participants can impart a lot of information, particularly in topics such as business analysis, requirements elicitation and analysis, and facilitation.

Data Gathering   There are several data gathering techniques that can be used to collect requirements. The *PMBOK® Guide* highlights the following:

Brainstorming   Brainstorming involves getting together to generate ideas and gather the project requirements.

Interviews   Interviews are a way of collecting information from subject matter experts quickly. The following are characteristics of interviews:

- Typically structured as a one-on-one conversation with stakeholders
- Can be formal or informal
- Consist of questions prepared ahead of time

Focus Groups   Focus groups are usually conducted by a trained moderator. The key to this tool lies in picking the subject matter experts and stakeholders to participate in the focus group. The participants then engage in discussion and conversation as a way of imparting their feedback about a project's end result.

Questionnaires and Surveys   Questionnaires and surveys allow you to query a group of participants and apply statistical analysis to the results as needed. This tool is considered to be a quick way of obtaining feedback from a large number of stakeholders.

Benchmarking   Ever wish to see how you measure up against other organizations or internal projects? Benchmarking compares actual or planned practices against comparable organizations to measure performance, to glean new ideas to be used to improve your organization, and to identify best practices.

Data Analysis   Another technique used in the identification of requirements is document or data analysis, where existing documentation is reviewed to see if there is information relevant to completing the requirements. According to the *PMBOK® Guide*, a variety of documents can be scrutinized, including but not limited to the following:

- Business plans
- Marketing materials
- Contractual agreements

- Requests for proposals
- Business processes or interface documentation
- Use cases
- Problem/issues logs
- Policies and procedures
- Regulatory documents

Decision Making   Throughout the requirements gathering process, decisions will need to be made. There are a variety of techniques that can be used to aid decision making, such as voting and multicriteria decision analysis.

Voting   According to the *PMBOK® Guide*, several methods of reaching a decision can be used. The four methods mentioned are as follows:

Unanimity, where everyone agrees on the resolution or course of action

Majority, where more than 50 percent of the members support the resolution

Plurality, where the largest subgroup within the group makes the decision if a majority is not reached

Autocratic, where one person makes the decision on behalf of the group

Multicriteria Decision Analysis   With multicriteria decision analysis, a decision matrix is used for establishing criteria for a systematic analytical approach.

Data Representation   Data representation techniques referenced by the *PMBOK® Guide* as examples for collecting requirements include mind mapping and affinity diagrams.

Idea/Mind Mapping   In idea/mind mapping, participants use a combination of brainstorming and diagramming techniques to record their ideas.

Affinity Diagrams   Affinity diagrams sort ideas into related groups for further analysis and review.

Interpersonal and Team Skills   Several interpersonal and team skills are needed to collect requirements, such as the nominal group technique, observation and conversation, and facilitation.

Nominal Group Technique   Nominal group technique works to engage all participants through an idea-gathering or structured brainstorming session and ranking process.

Observation/Conversation   Observation and conversation consists of a one-on-one experience where an observer sits side by side with the participant to observe how the participant interacts with the product or service. This technique is also known as job shadowing; it can also involve participant observers who perform the job themselves to ascertain requirements, or the observation of a group of participants performing a job function. Observations are particularly useful when stakeholders have a difficult time verbalizing requirements.

Facilitation   Cross-functional stakeholders come together in a facilitated workshop to discuss and define requirements that affect more than one department. The following are characteristics of facilitated workshops:

- All the participants of the workshops understand the various project needs.

- The workshops provide a facilitated forum to discuss and resolve the participants' issues.

- A consensus is reached more easily than through other methods

- Some additional examples of facilitation include joint application design/development (JAD), quality function deployment (QFD), and user stories.

Context Diagrams   Use of context diagrams helps to visually represent the product scope by mapping a business system with the people and other systems that interact with that business system. This is done by displaying the business system inputs and user roles and then depicting the inputs, outputs, and user roles for those who receive the output.

Prototypes   Prototyping is a technique involving constructing a working model or mock-up of the final product for participants to experiment with. The prototype does not usually contain all the functionality the end product does, but it gives participants enough information that they can provide feedback regarding the mock-up. This is an iterative process where participants experiment and provide feedback, the prototype is revised, and the cycle starts again. Prototypes are a great way of getting feedback during the early stages of a project's life cycle.

Focus groups and facilitated workshops are different. Focus groups are gatherings of prequalified subject matter experts and stakeholders where the intention is to gather feedback from these individuals. Facilitated workshops consist of cross-functional stakeholders who work together to define cross-functional requirements.

Outputs of Collect Requirements

For the exam, know the outputs of the Collect Requirements process, which are as follows:

Requirements Documentation   This output involves recording the requirements in a requirements document. Requirements can be progressively elaborated, meaning that they start out as high-level requirements, then are specified in greater detail as more is known. Examples of what may be captured are as follows:

- Business need for the project and why it was undertaken

- Objectives of the project and the business objectives the project hopes to fulfill

- Stakeholder requirements, including impacts to other organizational areas

- Functional requirements

- Nonfunctional requirements

- Quality requirements
- Acceptance criteria
- Business rules
- Organizational areas and outside entities impacted
- Support and training requirements
- Assumptions and constraints
- Signatures of the key stakeholders

The *PMBOK® Guide* highlights the fact that requirements can be grouped into classifications. Examples of classifications are business requirements, stakeholder requirements, solution requirements (such as functional and nonfunctional requirements), transition and readiness requirements, project requirements, and quality requirements.

Requirements Traceability Matrix   The traceability matrix links requirements to business needs and project objectives and also documents the following:

- Where the requirement originated
- What the requirement will be traced to
- Status updates all the way through delivery or completion

According to the *PMBOK® Guide*, the requirements traceability matrix helps ensure that business value is realized when the project is complete because each requirement is linked to a business and project objective.

Table 3.1 shows a sample traceability matrix with several attributes that identify the requirement.

TABLE 3.1   Requirements traceability matrix

Unique ID	Description of Requirement	Source	Priority	Test Scenario	Test Verification	Status
001	Requirement one	Project objective and stakeholder	B	User acceptance		Approved
002	Requirement two	Project kickoff meeting	A	User acceptance		Approved

Here are the characteristics of a traceability matrix:

- Each requirement should have its own unique identifier.
- A brief description includes enough information to easily identify the requirement.

- The source column refers to where the requirement originated.

- Priority refers to the priority of the requirement.

- The test scenario records how the requirement will be tested or during which project phase, and test verification indicates if it passes or fails the test.

- Status may capture information about the requirement that refers to whether or not the requirement has been approved to be included in the project. Examples include added, deferred, and canceled.

Exam Essentials

Understand the purpose of collecting requirements.   Requirements are collected to define and document the project sponsors', customers', and stakeholders' expectations and needs for meeting the project objective.

Know the outputs of the Collect Requirements process.   The outputs of the Collect Requirements process include requirements documentation and requirements traceability matrix.

After requirements have been gathered, the next step is to begin breaking down and documenting the project and product's scope. The end result will be a work breakdown structure (WBS), which is a deliverable-oriented, high-level decomposition of the project work. But before the WBS can be generated, a few additional steps must be addressed:

- The creation and sign-off of the project scope statement

- The creation of a scope baseline

The project scope statement is an output of the Define Scope process and is where the project deliverables are documented along with the constraints and assumptions of the project. Once the project scope statement, WBS, and another output called the WBS dictionary are created, they become part of a scope baseline.

Define Scope

The result and main objective of the Define Scope process is the creation of the project scope statement. The project scope statement is used to develop and document a detailed description of the deliverables of the project and the work needed to produce them. This process addresses the project objectives, requirements, constraints, assumptions, and other elements of writing the project scope statement and is progressively elaborated as more detail becomes known.

Figure 3.3 shows the inputs, tools and techniques, and outputs of the Define Scope process.

FIGURE 3.3   Define Scope process

- Project charter
- Project management plan
- Project documents
- Enterprise environmental factors
- Organizational process assets

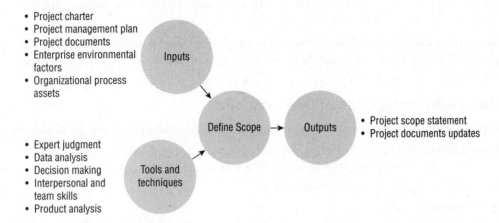

- Project scope statement
- Project documents updates

- Expert judgment
- Data analysis
- Decision making
- Interpersonal and team skills
- Product analysis

For more detailed information on the Define Scope process, see Chapter 3 of *PMP®: Project Management Professional Exam Study Guide, Ninth Edition* (Sybex, 2017).

Inputs of Define Scope

The Define Scope process has five inputs you should know:

Project Charter   From within the project charter, this process primarily utilizes the project objectives. Objectives are quantifiable criteria used to measure project success. They describe what the project is trying to do, accomplish, or produce. Quantifiable criteria should at least include the following items:

- Schedule
- Cost
- Quality measures
- Business measures or quality targets (sometimes)

Project Management Plan   The primary document utilized from within the project management plan is the scope management plan. The scope management plan outlines how the Define Scope process is to be carried out.

Project Documents   Project documents typically used to define scope include the assumption log, requirements documentation, and the risk register. In particular, the requirements documentation includes elements such as functional and nonfunctional characteristics, quality metrics, and acceptance criteria. For a more detailed description, see "Outputs of Collect Requirements" earlier in this chapter.

Enterprise Environmental Factors   Enterprise environmental factors that apply to the Define Scope process typically include the organizational culture, infrastructure, marketplace conditions, and personnel administration.

Organizational Process Assets   This process uses historical information from within the organizational process assets as well as policies, procedures, and project scope statement templates.

Tools and Techniques of Define Scope

Know the following tools and techniques that you will use during the Define Scope process:

Expert Judgment   Expert judgment plays an important role in the definition of scope. Sources of expert judgment used in this process include the following sources:

- Subject matter experts or consultants
- Stakeholders
- Industry groups and associations
- Other departments or units internal to the organization

Data Analysis   Alternatives analysis is a data analysis technique used for discovering different methods or ways of accomplishing the work of the project. Examples of alternatives analysis are brainstorming and lateral thinking.

Lateral thinking is a process of separating problems, looking at them from angles other than their obvious presentation, and encouraging team members to come up with ways to solve problems that are not apparently obvious or look at scope in a different way. This can also be described as out-of-the-box thinking.

Decision Making   An example of a decision-making technique noted earlier in this chapter that can be used to define scope is multicriteria decision analysis.

Interpersonal and Team Skills   Facilitation, a form of interpersonal and team skills, involves stakeholders coming together to discuss and define requirements that affect more than one department.

Product Analysis   Product analysis is a method for converting the product description and project objectives into deliverables and requirements. According to the *PMBOK® Guide*, product analysis might include performing the following to further define the product or service:

- Value analysis
- Functional analysis
- Requirements analysis
- Systems-engineering techniques
- Systems analysis
- Product breakdown
- Value-engineering techniques

Outputs of Define Scope

Know the following outputs of the Define Scope process:

Project Scope Statement   The purpose of the project scope statement is to document the project objectives, deliverables, and the work required to produce the deliverables so that it can be used to direct the project team's work and as a basis for future project decisions. The project scope statement is an agreement between the project organization and the customer that states precisely what the work of the project will produce.

> The project scope statement guides the work of the project team during the Executing processes, and all change requests will be evaluated against the scope statement. The criteria outlined will also be used to determine whether the project was completed successfully.

According to the *PMBOK® Guide*, the project scope statement should include all of the following:

- Product scope description
- Acceptance criteria
- Project deliverables
- Project exclusions

Product Scope Description   The product scope description describes the characteristics of the product, service, or result of the project.

Acceptance Criteria   Acceptance criteria include the process and criteria that will be used to determine whether the deliverables and the final product, service, or result of the project is acceptable and satisfactory.

Project Deliverables   Deliverables are measurable outcomes, measurable results, or specific items that must be produced to consider the project or project phase completed. Deliverables should be specific, unique, and verifiable and may include supplementary outcomes.

Deliverables vs. Requirements

Deliverables describe the components of the goals and objectives in a quantifiable way. Requirements are the specifications of the deliverables. Select deliverables and requirements are sometimes referred to as *critical success factors*. Critical success factors are those elements that must be completed for the project to be considered complete.

Project Exclusions   Project exclusions are anything that isn't included as a deliverable or work of the project. Project exclusions should be noted in the project scope statement for stakeholder management purposes.

Project Documents Updates   Project documents encompass those documents from within the project that are not plans or baselines. There may be several common updates and changes to project documents resulting from this process:

- Assumption log
- Stakeholder register
- Requirements documentation
- Requirements traceability matrix

> In practice, the Define Scope process is performed before the Collect Requirements process. Deliverables must be identified before their detailed requirements are documented.

Create WBS

The Create WBS process takes the well-defined deliverables and requirements and begins the process of breaking down the work via a WBS. WBS stands for work breakdown structure, which defines the scope of the project and breaks down the deliverables into smaller, more manageable components of work that can be scheduled and estimated as well as easily assigned, monitored, and controlled. The WBS should detail the full scope of work needed to complete the project.

Figure 3.4 shows the inputs, tools and techniques, and outputs of the Create WBS process.

FIGURE 3.4   Create WBS process

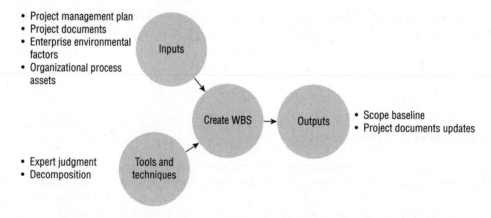

Inputs of Create WBS

For the exam, know the following inputs of the Create WBS process:

Project Management Plan   The scope management plan, which is a component of the project management plan, is a planning tool that documents how the project team will define project scope, how changes to scope will be maintained and controlled, and how scope will be verified.

Project Documents   Project documents used as part of this process typically include the project scope statement and the requirements documentation. The project scope statement contains information valuable to creating the WBS, most notably the list of project deliverables. The requirements documentation describes how the requirements meet the business needs of the project.

Enterprise Environmental Factors   In addition to enterprise environmental factors that have already been discussed, there may be industry-specific WBS standards that are relevant to the type of project that you are undertaking. If so, that information may serve as an additional reference to the creation of the WBS.

Organizational Process Assets   This process uses historical information from within the organizational process assets as well as policies, procedures, and WBS templates.

For more detailed information on the Create WBS process, see Chapter 3 of *PMP®: Project Management Professional Exam Study Guide, Ninth Edition* (Sybex, 2017).

Tools and Techniques of Create WBS

The Create WBS process has two tools and techniques: expert judgment and decomposition.

Expert Judgment   For creating the WBS, expert judgment is routinely used to start breaking down project deliverables by analyzing the information available. Don't forget that expert judgment can also come in the form of predefined templates, which provide instructions on how to effectively break down common deliverables. Templates can come from the industry you are working in, or they can be created by your organization as a result of experience gained from performing similar projects.

Decomposition   Decomposition involves breaking down the project deliverables into smaller, more manageable components of work that can be easily planned, executed, monitored and controlled, and closed out.

The project manager typically decomposes the work with the help of the project team, whose members have expert knowledge of the work. Benefits of team involvement include a more realistic decomposition of the work and getting team buy-in.

Decomposition provides a way of managing the scope of the project and also does the following:

- Improves estimates
- More easily assigns performance measures and controls
- Provides a baseline to compare against throughout the project or phase
- Ensures that assignments go to the proper parties

According to the *PMBOK® Guide*, decomposition consists of the following five-step process:

1. Identify the deliverables and work.
2. Organize the WBS.
3. Decompose the WBS components into lower-level components.
4. Assign identification codes.
5. Verify the WBS.

Outputs of Create WBS

The Create WBS process has two outputs:

- Scope baseline
- Project documents updates

Scope Baseline The scope baseline for the project is the approved project scope statement, the WBS, and the WBS dictionary. These documents together describe in detail all the work of the project. The documents allow managers to carry out the following activities:

- Document schedules
- Assign resources
- Monitor and control the project work

Work Breakdown Structure (WBS) The following are various ways of organizing the WBS:

Major Deliverables The major deliverables of the project are used as the first level of decomposition in this structure.

Subprojects Another way to organize the work is by subprojects. Each of the subproject managers will develop a WBS for their subproject that details the work required for that deliverable.

Project Phases Many projects are structured or organized by project phases. Each phase listed here would be the first level of decomposition, and its deliverables would be the next level.

The following is a general description of the various levels within the WBS:

Level 1 According to the *PMBOK® Guide*, Level 1 of the WBS is the project level. The first level of decomposition, however, may be the second level of the WBS, which could include deliverables, phases, and subprojects—see Figure 3.5 for an example.

FIGURE 3.5   WBS Level 1 and Level 2

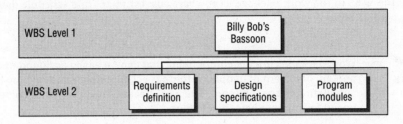

Level 2   Level 2 and levels that follow show more and more detail. Each of these breakouts is called a level in the WBS. See Figure 3.6 and Figure 3.7 for examples.

FIGURE 3.6   WBS Levels 1 through 3

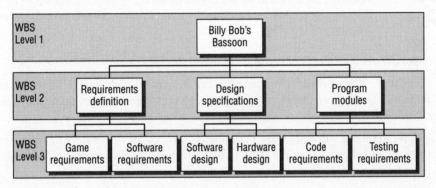

FIGURE 3.7   WBS Levels 1 through 4

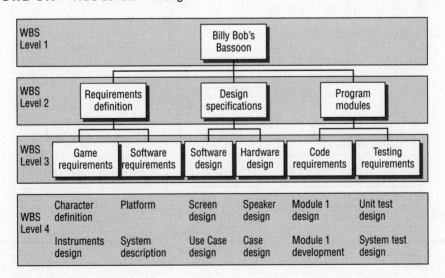

Lowest Level   The lowest level of any WBS is called the work package level. The goal is to construct the WBS to the work package level where cost estimates and schedule dates can be estimated reliably and easily.

> Work packages are the components that can be easily assigned to one person, or a team of people, with clear accountability and responsibility for completing the assignment. The work package level will later be decomposed further into lists of activities.

Collectively, all the levels of the WBS roll up to the top so that all the work of the project is captured. According to the *PMBOK® Guide*, this is known as the 100 percent rule.

> For more information on WBS, and for industry-specific examples of WBS templates, refer to the *Practice Standard for Work Breakdown Structures, Second Edition* (PMI®, 2006).

Here are the other elements of the WBS that you should know:

WBS Templates   Work breakdown structures can be constructed using WBS templates or the WBS from a similar completed project. Although every project is unique, many companies and industries perform the same kind of projects repeatedly.

Rolling Wave Planning   Rolling wave planning is a process of elaborating deliverables, project phases, or subprojects in the WBS to differing levels of decomposition depending on the expected date of the work.

Unique WBS Identifiers   Each element at each level of the WBS is generally assigned a unique identifier according to the *PMBOK® Guide*. Figure 3.8 shows what a WBS with unique identifiers displayed might look like.

FIGURE 3.8   Unique WBS identifiers

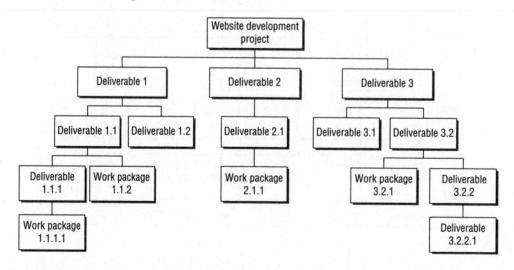

WBS Dictionary   The WBS dictionary is where work component descriptions are documented. According to the *PMBOK® Guide*, the WBS dictionary should include the following elements for each component of the WBS:

- Code of accounts identifier
- Description of the work of the component
- Organization responsible for completing the component
- List of schedule milestones
- Schedule activities associated with the schedule milestones
- Required resources
- Cost estimates
- Quality requirements
- Criteria for acceptance
- Technical references
- Contract information

Project Documents Updates   The following documents may need to be updated as a result of this process:

- Requirements documentation
- Assumption log
- Any other project documents that should reflect approved changes to the project scope statement

---

Exam Essentials

Understand the purpose of the project scope statement.   The project scope statement serves as a common understanding of project scope among the stakeholders. The project objectives and deliverables and their quantifiable criteria are documented in the project scope statement and are used by the project manager and the stakeholders to determine whether the project was completed successfully. It also serves as a basis for future project decisions.

Be able to describe the purpose of the scope management plan.   The scope management plan has a direct influence on the project's success and describes the process for determining project scope, facilitates creating the WBS, describes how the product or service of the project is verified and accepted, and documents how changes to scope will be handled. The scope management plan is a subsidiary plan of the project management plan.

Be able to define a WBS and its components.   The WBS is a deliverable-oriented hierarchy. It uses the deliverables from the project scope statement or similar documents and decomposes them into logical, manageable units of work. The lowest level of any WBS is called a work package.

> Don't forget that the Project Scope Management Knowledge Area has two more processes: Validate Scope and Control Scope. Look for a discussion of these processes in Chapter 8, "Monitoring and Controlling the Project."

Developing a Project Schedule

Like most Knowledge Areas, the Project Schedule Management Knowledge Area also has a plan that guides the processes within it: the schedule management plan. A good tip to remember is that there is a pattern to the logic regarding a standard and consistent methodology in each of the Knowledge Areas described in this chapter, namely that each Knowledge Area leads with a process to develop the plan for that area of management. In this chapter, that process is called Plan Schedule Management.

Developing a schedule consists of six processes, each carried out through a formal planning process:

- Plan Schedule Management, which is similar to processes in other Knowledge Areas, sets the policies, procedures, and documentation used in the planning, creation, managing, executing, and controlling of the project schedule.

- Define Activities, which breaks down the work packages of the WBS into detailed work (activities) to be carried out by project team members.

- Sequence Activities, which places the activities into a logical order based on existing dependencies.

- Estimate Activity Resources, which estimates the type and quantity of resources needed to carry out each activity.

- Estimate Activity Durations, which estimates how long each activity will take.

- Develop Schedule, which produces an accepted and signed-off project schedule.

Through the use of the planning processes noted, the project management team builds a schedule that is based on the project's timeline, scope, and resource plan to arrive at the timely completion of the project. The accepted and signed-off version of the project schedule becomes the schedule baseline.

> Although estimating activity resources is covered in this section, the process that produces these estimates is actually a part of another Knowledge Area that will be covered in Chapter 5, the Project Resource Management Knowledge Area. Since the process, called Estimate Activity Resources, is an essential step in the schedule development process, it makes more sense to cover it here.

Figure 3.9 shows the inputs, tools and techniques, and outputs of the Plan Schedule Management process.

FIGURE 3.9   Plan Schedule Management process

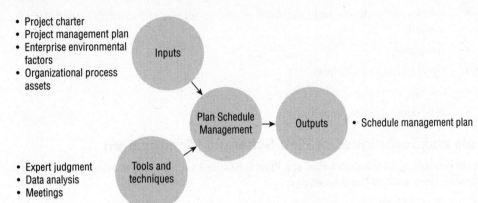

- Project charter
- Project management plan
- Enterprise environmental factors
- Organizational process assets

Inputs

Plan Schedule Management

Outputs

- Schedule management plan

- Expert judgment
- Data analysis
- Meetings

Tools and techniques

Understand Plan Schedule Management

The schedule management plan should be created early within the planning stages of a project. The plan is responsible for guiding the creation, management, and control of the project schedule.

Inputs of Plan Schedule Management

Similar to the Plan Scope Management process, you will need to know the following four inputs of the Plan Schedule Management process:

Project Charter   In this process, the project charter is used to define the summary milestone schedule and the requirements to obtain project approval as it relates to managing the project schedule.

Project Management Plan   To help inform what the project is intended to accomplish, the project management plan with all of its approved subsidiary plans is used to help create the schedule management plan. Specifically, the scope management plan provides information on how scope will be defined, which can aid in the process for defining the schedule itself. The project management plan also contains a summary of the development approach, which is an important input for determining how the schedule should be approached.

Enterprise Environmental Factors   Several enterprise environmental factors can influence the Plan Schedule Management process, including but not limited to the organization's culture, its infrastructure, project management software that provides the scheduling tool and schedule alternative generation, published commercial information, and organizational work systems.

Organizational Process Assets   Quite a few process assets influence the Plan Schedule Management process, including but not limited to these:

- The use of monitoring and reporting tools
- Schedule control tools

- Historical information
- Policies, procedures, and guidelines related to formal and informal schedule control
- Templates
- Project closure guidelines
- Change control procedures
- Risk control procedures

Tools and Techniques of Plan Schedule Management

The three tools and techniques that the Plan Schedule Management process uses are expert judgment, data analysis, and meetings:

Expert Judgment Expert judgment brings invaluable perspective about prior similar projects attempted as well as the existing environment that will affect the project. This can also be useful in considering how to combine methods of schedule planning and how to best resolve differences between those methods.

Data Analysis Most analytical techniques used here involve picking between different options, and it is no different for this process. Plan schedule management might require you to pick between strategic options to estimate and schedule the project, like the scheduling methodology, which scheduling tools and techniques to use, estimating approaches, formats, and project management software. As the project progresses, the schedule management plan might require analysis to determine options that fast-track or crash the project schedule. Remember that these options may introduce risk to the project, so don't forget to update the risk register.

Meetings In the course of developing the schedule management plan, members of project teams may attend schedule development meetings. Depending on the meeting, the following members might be included: the project manager, project sponsor, selected project team members, and anyone having responsibility in this area.

Outputs of Plan Schedule Management

The primary output of the Plan Schedule Management process is the schedule management plan. According to the *PMBOK® Guide*, the components of this plan establish the following:

- Project schedule model development, which specifies the methodology and tools to be used
- Level of accuracy, which sets the tolerances used to determine realistic activity duration estimates and the amount needed for contingencies
- Units of measure, which could be vital depending on the industry the project is in and whether the project involves multiple countries
- Organizational procedure links, as provided by the framework of the WBS

- Project schedule model maintenance, or a model for updating status and progress of the project

- Control thresholds, which establish the variance thresholds for monitoring schedule performance and define the amount of variation the project can sustain before some action must be performed

- Rules of performance measurement, where physical measurement, rules of performance measurement, or earned value measurement rules are set

- Reporting formats and frequency of reports

- Process descriptions for each of the schedule management processes

 Remember that a schedule management plan can be tailored to your needs, meaning that it can be formal or informal and might be highly detailed or broadly framed.

Define Activities

The purpose of the Define Activities process is to decompose the work packages into schedule activities where the basis for estimating, scheduling, executing, and monitoring and controlling the work of the project is easily supported and accomplished. This process documents the specific activities needed to fulfill the deliverables detailed in the WBS. By the end of this process, the project team will have defined a list of activities, their characteristics, and a milestones list.

Figure 3.10 shows the inputs, tools and techniques, and outputs of the Define Activities process.

FIGURE 3.10   Define Activities process

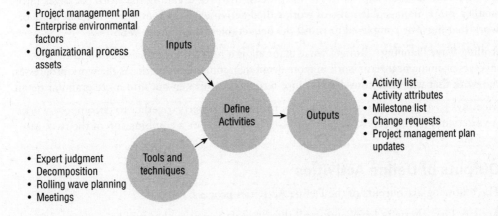

For more detailed information on the Define Activities process, see Chapter 4, "Creating the Project Schedule," of *PMP®: Project Management Professional Exam Study Guide, Ninth Edition* (Sybex, 2017).

Inputs of Define Activities

You should know the following inputs of the Define Activities process:

Project Management Plan   The critical input from this plan is the defined level of detail needed to manage the work. This is taken from the schedule management plan. The scope baseline, another essential input from the project management plan, takes into account the following:

- Work packages, from within the WBS
- Deliverables, constraints, and assumptions, from within the project scope statement

Enterprise Environmental Factors   Enterprise environmental factors include the project management information system; the organizational culture and structure; and published, commercially available information.

Organizational Process Assets   The organizational process assets provide existing guidelines and policies, historical project documents (such as partial activity lists from previous projects), and a lessons-learned knowledge base, all of which are used for defining the project activities.

Tools and Techniques of Define Activities

You can use the following four tools and techniques in the Define Activities process:

Expert Judgment   Expert judgment helps define activities and involves project team members with prior experience developing project scope statements and WBSs.

Decomposition   Decomposition in this process involves breaking the work packages into smaller, more manageable units of work called activities. Activities are individual units of work that must be completed to fulfill the deliverables listed in the WBS.

Rolling Wave Planning   Rolling wave planning is a form of progressive elaboration that involves planning near-term work in more detail than future-term work. As the work progresses, the work that was once considered future-term is then broken out into more granular detail.

Meetings   Meetings can be a useful tool for getting experts together to decompose work. A variety of meeting types, such as virtual, face to face, or a combination of the two, can be used.

Outputs of Define Activities

The following are outputs of the Define Activities process:

Activity List   Activity lists contain all the schedule activities that will be performed for the project. The list includes a scope-of-work description for each activity and a unique identifier so that team members understand what the work is and how it is to be completed.

The schedule activities are individual elements of the project schedule.

Activity Attributes   Activity attributes describe the characteristics of the activities and are an extension of the activity list. Activity attributes will change over the life of the project, as more information is known.

During the early stages of the project, activity attributes typically consist of the following:

- Activity ID
- WBS identification code it's associated with
- Activity name

As the project progresses, the following activity attributes may be added:

- Predecessor and successor activities
- Logical relationships
- Leads and lags
- Resource requirements
- Constraints and assumptions associated with the activity

Milestone List   Milestones are major accomplishments of the project and mark the completion of major deliverables or some other key event in the project. The milestone list does several things:

- Records the accomplishments
- Documents whether a milestone is mandatory or optional
- Becomes part of the project management plan
- Helps develop the project schedule

Change Requests   Change requests become applicable after the project scope and schedule have been baselined and progressive elaboration occurs. As a result, new activities may be defined over time.

Project Management Plan Updates   Just as with change requests, updates to the project management plan may be required after the project has been baselined and new work is identified through progressive elaboration. As change requests are approved through the formal change control process, updates to the plan will be necessary. Typically, this includes updates to the schedule baseline and cost baseline.

    In practice, the Define Activities process and Sequence Activities process may be combined into one process or step.

Sequence Activities

The Sequence Activities process takes the identified schedule activities from the Define Activities process, sequences them in logical order, and identifies any dependencies that exist among the activities. The interactivity of logical relationships must be sequenced correctly in order to facilitate the development of a realistic, achievable project schedule. The end of this process results in the creation of project schedule network diagrams, which visually show the sequence of activities and their dependencies.

Figure 3.11 shows the inputs, tools and techniques, and outputs of the Sequence Activities process.

FIGURE 3.11   Sequence Activities process

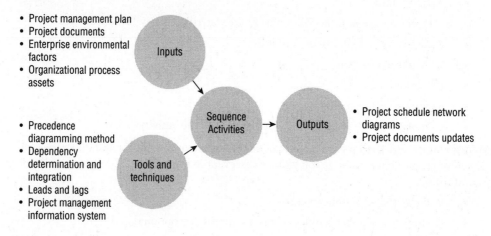

* Project management plan
* Project documents
* Enterprise environmental factors
* Organizational process assets

Inputs

* Precedence diagramming method
* Dependency determination and integration
* Leads and lags
* Project management information system

Tools and techniques

Sequence Activities

Outputs

* Project schedule network diagrams
* Project documents updates

 NOTE   For more detailed information on the Sequence Activities process, see Chapter 4 of *PMP®: Project Management Professional Exam Study Guide, Ninth Edition* (Sybex, 2017).

Inputs of Sequence Activities

Within the Sequence Activities process, you will use the following inputs:

* Project management plan
* Project documents
* Enterprise environmental factors
* Organizational process assets

Project Management Plan   The schedule management plan, a component of the project management plan, clarifies the tools and methods to be used in scheduling, which informs activity sequencing. The scope baseline can also be used when sequencing activities and identifying dependencies. Through this baseline, the deliverables, constraints, and assumptions are considered.

Project Documents   To sequence activities, there are several project documents that may be useful, such as the activity list, activity attributes, milestone list, and assumption log.

Activity List   The first document utilized tends to be the activity list. The activity list includes the activities along with their identifiers and a description of the work's scope.

Activity Attributes   Activity attributes may reveal information on the sequencing of activities, such as through predecessor or successor relationships.

Milestone List   Milestone lists may contain milestones with scheduled dates. These dates might impact the sequencing of activities.

Assumption Log   Assumptions recorded in this log may influence how activities need to be sequenced as well as any leads or lags necessary.

Enterprise Environmental Factors   Sequence activities may be influenced by enterprise environmental factors such as government or industry standards, the project management information system, schedule tool, and any company work authorization systems.

Organizational Process Assets   The project files found within the corporate knowledge base are used from within the organizational process assets for scheduling purposes. Templates and lessons learned, in particular, can be very useful, as well as any other documented policies or procedures that exist for sequencing activities.

Tools and Techniques of Sequence Activities

You will need to be familiar with the following tools and techniques of the Sequence Activities process:

- Precedence diagramming method (PDM)
- Dependency determination and integration
- Leads and lags
- Project management information system

Precedence Diagramming Method   The PDM uses boxes or rectangles to represent the activities (called nodes). The nodes are connected with arrows showing the dependencies between the activities. This method is also called activity on node (AON). PDM uses only one-time estimates to determine duration.

The following information is displayed on a node:

- Activity name (required)
- Activity number (optional)
- Start and stop dates (optional)
- Due dates (optional)
- Slack time (optional)
- Any additional or relevant information (optional)

Figure 3.12 shows a general example of a PDM, or AON.

FIGURE 3.12   Precedence diagramming method (PDM)

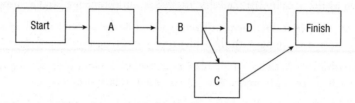

The PDM is further defined by the following four types of dependencies, also known as logical relationships:

Finish-to-Start   The finish-to-start (FS) relationship is the most frequently used relationship. In this relationship, the predecessor activity must finish before the successor activity can start.

Start-to-Finish   In the start-to-finish (SF) relationship, the predecessor activity must start before the successor activity can finish. This logical relationship is seldom used.

Finish-to-Finish   In the finish-to-finish (FF) relationship, the predecessor activity must finish before the successor activity finishes.

Start-to-Start   In the start-to-start (SS) relationship, the predecessor activity must start before the successive activity can start.

Day of the Exam

Memorize a diagram of the precedence diagramming methods like activity on node (AON) to add to your scratch paper at the start of the exam.

Dependency Determination and Integration   Dependencies are relationships between the activities in which one activity is dependent on another to complete an action, or perhaps an activity is dependent on another to start an action before it can proceed. Dependency determination is a matter of determining where those dependencies exist.

The following are four types of dependencies defined by their characteristics:

Mandatory Dependencies   Mandatory dependencies, also known as hard logic or hard dependencies, are defined by the type of work being performed. The nature of the work itself dictates the order in which the activities should be performed.

Discretionary Dependencies   Discretionary dependencies are defined by the project team. Discretionary dependencies are also known as preferred logic, soft logic, or preferential logic. These are usually process- or procedure-driven or best-practice techniques based on past experience.

External Dependencies   External dependencies are external to the project. The *PMBOK® Guide* points out that even though the dependency is external to the project (and therefore a non-project activity), it impacts project activities.

Internal Dependencies   Internal dependencies are internal to the project. These dependencies involve a precedence relationship between project activities that are within the project team's ability to control.

Arrow Diagramming Method   The arrow diagramming method (ADM) technique isn't used nearly as often as PDM. ADM is visually the opposite of the PDM. The arrow diagramming method places activities on the arrows, which are connected to dependent activities with nodes. This method is also called activity on arrow (AOA). Characteristics of the ADM technique are as follows:

- ADM allows for more than one-time estimates to determine duration and uses only the finish-to-start dependency.

- Dummy activities may be plugged into the diagram to accurately display the dependencies.

Figure 3.13 shows a general example of the ADM method.

FIGURE 3.13   Arrow diagramming method (ADM)

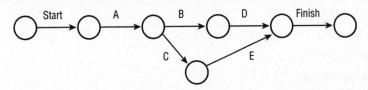

The information in Figure 3.14 can help you remember the difference between PDM and ADM for the exam.

FIGURE 3.14   PDM versus ADM

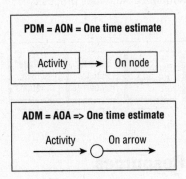

Leads and Lags   Consider applying leads and lags when determining dependencies:

Leads   Leads speed up the successor activities and require time to be subtracted from the start date or the finish date of the activity you're scheduling.

Lags   Lags delay successor activities (those that follow a predecessor activity) and require time added either to the start date or to the finish date of the activity being scheduled.

Project Management Information System   Tools such as scheduling software are often used to assist in developing the schedule.

Outputs of Sequence Activities

There are two outputs of the Sequence Activities process that you should be familiar with:

Project Schedule Network Diagrams   The project schedule network diagram provides a visual view of the activities within the schedule, including the existing sequence, dependencies, leads, and lags. Like the WBS, the project schedule network diagrams might contain all the project details or contain only summary-level details, depending on the complexity of the project. Summary-level activities are a collection of related activities also known as *hammocks*. Hammocks are a group of related activities rolled up into a summary heading that describes the activities likely to be contained in that grouping.

Project Documents Updates   The following project documents may require updates as a result of this process:

- Activity lists
- Activity attributes
- Assumption log
- Milestone list

Figure 3.15 shows the position of the Sequence Activities process in relation to the other related processes that produce the schedule.

FIGURE 3.15   Order of Sequence Activities process

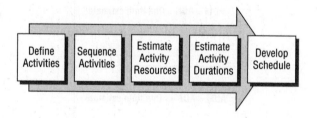

Estimate Activity Resources

After the activities are sequenced, the next steps involve estimating the resources required for completion and the duration of each activity so that they can be plugged into the project schedule. The Estimate Activity Resources process, which is part of the Project Resource Management Knowledge Area, is concerned with determining the types and quantities of resources (both human and material) needed for each schedule activity within a work package.

The term *resource* refers to all the physical resources required to complete the project. The *PMBOK® Guide* defines resources as people, equipment, and materials.

Figure 3.16 shows the inputs, tools and techniques, and outputs of the Estimate Activity Resources process.

FIGURE 3.16   Estimate Activity Resources process

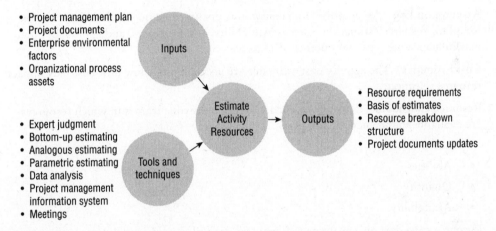

For more detailed information on the Estimate Activity Resources process, see Chapter 4 of *PMP®: Project Management Professional Exam Study Guide, Ninth Edition* (Sybex, 2017).

Inputs of Estimate Activity Resources

You should know the following inputs for the Estimate Activity Resources process:

- Project management plan
- Project documents
- Enterprise environmental factors
- Organizational process assets

Project Management Plan   Two elements of the project management plan provide inputs for this activity. The resource management plan assists in determining the resources to be estimated. This plan documents how this estimating process is to be carried out and includes the methods used to quantify resources needed.

The scope baseline captures the project and product scope required to achieve project objectives. This information helps identify what resources will be needed.

Project Documents   Among the various project documents that are generated within a project, the following can be used to help estimate resources: activity list, activity attributes, assumption log, cost estimates, resource calendars, and risk register.

Activity List   The activity list is necessary to know which activities will need resources.

Activity Attributes   The activity attributes provide the details necessary to estimate the resources needed per activity.

Assumption Log   Assumptions and constraints documented may include information useful for resource estimation, such as availability, cost estimates, and approaches that may influence the type and number of resources.

Cost Estimates   The activity cost estimates are necessary to know how cost may impact resource selection.

Resource Calendars   Resource calendars describe the time frames in which resources are available and include the following:

- Skills
- Abilities
- Quantity
- Availability

Resource calendars also examine the quantity, capability, and availability of equipment and material resources that have a potential to impact the project schedule.

Risk Register   Risks documented within the risk register may influence resource estimates. The risk register helps inform how risk events can disrupt resource selection and availability.

Remember that the Estimate Activity Resources process belongs to the Project Resource Management Knowledge Area. Because it is a key step to the schedule development process, it is covered in detail here.

Enterprise Environmental Factors   Information on the resource availability and skills can be obtained through enterprise environmental factors.

Organizational Process Assets   Information from previous similar projects and policies and procedures relating to staffing and equipment purchase and rental are used from within the organizational process assets.

Tools and Techniques of Estimate Activity Resources

The tools and techniques within the Estimate Activity Resources process include the following:

- Expert judgment
- Bottom-up estimating
- Analogous estimating
- Parametric estimating
- Data analysis
- Project management information system (PMIS)
- Meetings

Expert Judgment   Individuals with experience and knowledge of resource planning and estimating can be tapped for information and guidance used within this process.

Bottom-Up Estimating   Bottom-up estimating is used when an activity cannot be confidently estimated. With the help of experts, the activity is broken down into smaller components of work for estimating purposes and then rolled back up to the original activity level. This is an accurate means of estimating, but it can be time-consuming and costly.

Analogous Estimating   Analogous estimating involves using information from past similar projects to calculate estimates for the existing project. This is useful when minimal information is known (it is not as precise a method) or estimates are needed quickly.

Parametric Estimating   Parametric estimates use information from past similar projects and other variables to calculate an estimate that is considered to be a relatively good confidence level. For example, if past experience tells you that three testers are needed to test 500 lines of code, then you may assume six testers are needed for 1,000 lines of code within a similar time frame.

Data Analysis   Alternatives analysis, a form of data analysis, helps to make decisions about the possible resource types (such as expert or novice) and methods that are available to accomplish the activities. Make-or-buy analysis can also be used for decisions regarding resources.

Project Management Information System   Within this process, project management software can help in the following ways:

- Plan, organize, and estimate resource needs
- Document resource availability
- Create resource breakdown structures
- Create resource rates
- Create resource calendars

Meetings   Meetings are commonly used to bring experts together during the estimation process.

Outputs of Estimate Activity Resources

Four outputs result from carrying out the Estimate Activity Resources process:

Resource Requirements   Resource requirements describe the types of resources and the quantity needed for each activity associated with a work package. The description should include the following:

- How estimates were determined
- Information used to form the estimate
- Assumptions made about the resources and their availability

 NOTE   Work package estimates are derived by taking a cumulative total of all the schedule activities within that particular work package.

Basis of Estimates   Basis of estimates captures the additional information associated to the estimates developed. This may include things such as the following items:

- Any known constraints or assumptions
- Range of estimates
- Confidence level
- Methods used to develop the estimates
- Who produced the estimates
- Any risks associated with the estimates

Resource Breakdown Structure   The resource breakdown structure (RBS) is a hierarchical structure that lists resources by category and type. Figure 3.17 illustrates a basic example of what an RBS may look like.

FIGURE 3.17   Resource breakdown structure

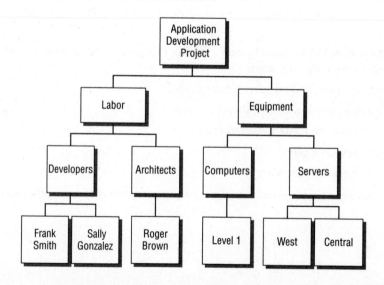

Here are some examples of categories:

- Labor
- Hardware
- Equipment
- Supplies

Here are some examples of types:

- Skill levels
- Quality grades
- Cost

Project Documents Updates   Project documents updates include updates to the following items:

- Activity attributes
- Assumption log
- Lessons learned register

Estimate Activity Durations

The Estimate Activity Durations process attempts to estimate the work effort, resources, and number of work periods needed to complete each activity. These are quantifiable estimates expressed as the number of work periods needed to complete a schedule activity. Estimates are progressively elaborated, typically starting at a fairly high level, and as more and more details are known about the deliverables and their associated activities, the estimates become more accurate.

When estimating activity durations, the project manager must consider a variety of factors. The *PMBOK® Guide* names the following considerations:

- Law of diminishing returns
- Number of resources
- Advances in technology
- Motivation of staff

When it comes to staff motivation, know the concepts of student syndrome and Parkinson's Law. Student syndrome is where team members will procrastinate and tackle the work as a deadline nears; Parkinson's Law is where team members expand the work and fill up the time allotted for the activity's completion, even if the full amount of time was not needed.

Figure 3.18 shows the inputs, tools and techniques, and outputs of the Estimate Activity Durations process.

FIGURE 3.18   Estimate Activity Durations process

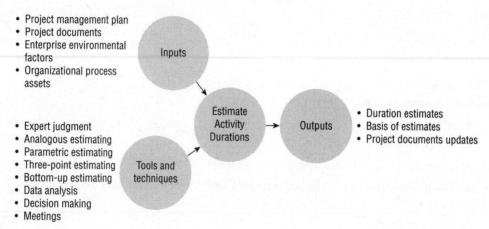

- Project management plan
- Project documents
- Enterprise environmental factors
- Organizational process assets

- Expert judgment
- Analogous estimating
- Parametric estimating
- Three-point estimating
- Bottom-up estimating
- Data analysis
- Decision making
- Meetings

Inputs

Tools and techniques

Estimate Activity Durations

Outputs

- Duration estimates
- Basis of estimates
- Project documents updates

For more detailed information on the Estimate Activity Durations process, see Chapter 4 of *PMP®: Project Management Professional Exam Study Guide*, Ninth Edition (Sybex, 2017).

Inputs of Estimate Activity Durations

You should be familiar with four major inputs of the Estimate Activity Durations process:

- Project management plan

- Project documents

- Enterprise environmental factors

- Organizational process assets

Project Management Plan   There are two key inputs used that are part of the project management plan: the schedule management plan and the scope baseline. The schedule management plan sets the approach used and the level of accuracy required to estimate activity durations, including the project update cycle.

Project Documents   Several documents can be referenced and used to help pull together the estimated duration of activities, such as those noted below:

Activity List   The list of activities is necessary to estimate the activity durations.

Activity Attributes   Information included within the activity attributes will influence the activity duration estimates.

Resource Requirements   The availability of the assigned resources will impact the duration of the activities.

Resource Calendars Information from the resource calendars that influences this process is as follows:

- Type, availability, and capability of human resources
- Type, availability, capability, and quantity of equipment and material resources

Assumption Log Constraints and assumptions are considered when estimating activity durations.

Milestone List The list of scheduled dates for specific milestones is necessary to estimate the activity durations.

Risk Register The list of risks is necessary, along with the results of risk analysis and risk response planning.

Resource Breakdown Structure The resource breakdown structure provides a hierarchical view of the identified resources. This then provides key information that will help estimate activity durations.

Project Team Assignments Team assignments include those assignments that have already been officially made, along with the named resources.

Lessons Learned Register Lessons learned captured throughout the project can help estimate durations as the estimates are progressively elaborated.

Enterprise Environmental Factors Enterprise environmental factors used include the following items:

- Internal reference data for estimating durations
- External reference data available commercially
- Defined productivity metrics

Organizational Process Assets The following organizational process assets are used:

- Historical information from previous similar projects, including duration information, project calendars, and lessons learned
- Scheduling methodology
- Any existing policies and procedures for developing estimates

Tools and Techniques of Estimate Activity Durations

The eight tools and techniques of the Estimate Activity Durations process are as follows:

- Expert judgment
- Analogous estimating
- Parametric estimating
- Three-point estimating
- Bottom-up estimating
- Data analysis
- Decision making
- Meetings

Expert Judgment   Expert judgment used includes staff members who will perform the activities and is based on their experience with past similar activities. When estimating durations, experts should consider the following:

- Resource levels
- Resource productivity
- Resource capability
- Risks
- Any other factors that can impact estimates

Analogous Estimating   Analogous estimating is commonly used when little detail is available on the project. For a complete description of analogous estimating, see "Tools and Techniques of Estimate Costs" in Chapter 4.

Parametric Estimating   Parametric estimating is a quantitatively based estimating method that multiplies the quantity of work by the rate. It is considered to be a quick and low-cost estimating technique, with a good level of accuracy when used with actual historical data and current market conditions that take inflation or other factors into consideration. The best way to describe it is with an example:

> **Activity:** Install 15 10×10 drapes.
>
> **Average time** to install one 10×10 drape, based on previous experience: 30 minutes.
>
> **Estimate:** Therefore, installing 15 drapes at an average 30-minute installation time per drape results in an estimated duration of 7.5 hours.

> The *PMBOK® Guide* states that parametric estimating can also be used to determine time estimates for the entire project or portions of the project.

Three-Point Estimating   Three-point estimating uses the average of the following three estimates to result in a final estimate:

Most Likely (ML)   The estimate assumes there are no disasters and the activity can be completed as planned.

Optimistic (O)   This represents the fastest time frame in which your resource can complete the activity.

Pessimistic (P)   The estimate assumes the worst happens and it takes much longer than planned to get the activity completed.

There are two formulas that can be used with these three estimates: beta distribution and triangular distribution. Triangular distribution calculates a simple average of these three variables, as depicted in the following formula:

$$t_E = \frac{t_O + t_{ML} + t_P}{3}$$

Beta distribution uses a weighted average, assigning a greater weight to the most likely estimate. The concept of the beta distribution comes from the Program Evaluation and Review Technique (PERT), which uses the following formula to determine the weighted average using the three duration estimates:

$$t_E = \frac{t_O + 4t_{ML} + t_P}{6}$$

In the following example, the most likely (ML) estimate = 15, the optimistic (O) estimate = 11, and the pessimistic (P) estimate = 25.

$$Estimate = \frac{(11 + (4 \times 15) + 25)}{6}$$

Thus, the activity duration = 16.

Day of the Exam

The beta distribution formula will be helpful to add to scratch paper before you begin the exam:

$$\frac{(Optimistic + (4 \times Most\ Likely) + Pessimistic)}{6}$$

The purpose in creating a key on your scratch paper is perhaps it frees your mind to focus entirely on the problem you are attempting to solve and does not introduce further stress caused by trying to remember equations.

Bottom-Up Estimating   Bottom-up estimating involves calculating estimates at a granular level and then aggregating all of the estimates up to the work package level. This is helpful when it is difficult to come up with an estimate. In these cases, breaking up an activity into smaller pieces of work may allow the team to come up with an estimate at a higher degree of confidence.

Data Analysis   Data analysis often includes the use of the alternatives analysis and reserve analysis techniques.

Alternatives analysis compares resource capability or skills as well as schedule compression techniques.

Reserve time—also called buffer/time reserves or contingency reserve in the *PMBOK® Guide*—is the portion of time added to the activity to account for schedule risk or uncertainty. To make sure the project schedule is not impacted, a reserve time of the original estimate is built in to account for the problems that may be encountered.

Original activity duration to install 15 10×10 drapes: 7.5 hours.

10 percent reserve time added: 45 minutes.

Estimate: Therefore, the new activity duration is adjusted to include the reserve, resulting in an estimated duration of 8.25 hours.

Decision Making   It is helpful to have multiple alternatives for future actions when estimating activity durations. Decision making is an assessment process that delivers those alternatives. By engaging team members, it improves estimate accuracy and commitment to the emerging estimates. This has the by-product of helping to win the hearts and minds of those contributing to the project.

Meetings   Meetings help bring team experts together during the estimating process. Meetings are used in combination with other estimating techniques.

Outputs of Estimate Activity Durations

There are three outputs of the Estimate Activity Durations process you should know:

- Duration estimates
- Basis of estimates
- Project documents updates

Duration Estimates   Activity duration estimates are estimates of the required work periods needed to complete the activity. This is a quantitative measure usually expressed in hours, weeks, days, or months.

Final estimates should contain a range of possible results, such as X hours ±10 hours. Percentages also may be used to express the range.

Original activity duration to install 15 10×10 drapes: 7.5 hours.

Final estimate: 7.5 hours ±1 hour. Therefore, the activity may take as little as 6.5 hours or as much as 8.5 hours.

Final estimate example using a percentage range: 7.5 hours ± 10%. Therefore, the activity may take as little as 6.75 hours or as much as 8.25 hours.

Basis of Estimates   Basis of estimates includes all of the information and details used to develop the duration estimates. It is important to capture and archive this information for future use and reference. Examples of what may be captured include how the estimates were developed, the assumptions made, known constraints, the range of possible estimates, the confidence level for each estimate, and the identified risks.

Project Documents Updates   The following information might need to be revisited and updated as a result of this process:

- Activity attributes
- Assumptions made regarding resource availability and skill levels

Develop Schedule

The purpose of the Develop Schedule process is to create the project schedule. Here, start and finish dates are created, activity sequences and durations are finalized, and the critical path is determined. The Develop Schedule process cannot be completed until the following processes of project planning have occurred:

- Collect Requirements
- Define Scope
- Create WBS
- Define Activities
- Sequence Activities
- Estimate Activity Resources
- Estimate Activity Durations
- Plan Resource Management

Figure 3.19 shows the inputs, tools and techniques, and outputs of the Develop Schedule process.

FIGURE 3.19   Develop Schedule process

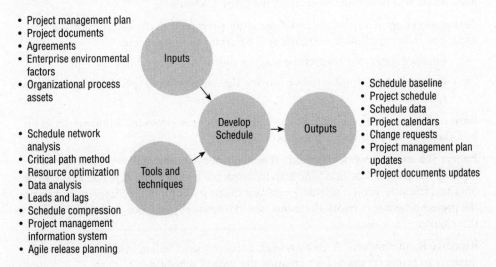

- Project management plan
- Project documents
- Agreements
- Enterprise environmental factors
- Organizational process assets

Inputs

- Schedule network analysis
- Critical path method
- Resource optimization
- Data analysis
- Leads and lags
- Schedule compression
- Project management information system
- Agile release planning

Tools and techniques

Develop Schedule → Outputs

- Schedule baseline
- Project schedule
- Schedule data
- Project calendars
- Change requests
- Project management plan updates
- Project documents updates

For more detailed information on the Develop Schedule process, see Chapter 4 of *PMP®: Project Management Professional Exam Study Guide, Ninth Edition* (Sybex, 2017).

Inputs of Develop Schedule

The Develop Schedule process has five inputs you should be familiar with:

- Project management plan
- Project documents
- Agreements
- Enterprise environmental factors
- Organizational process assets

Project Management Plan   The scheduling method and tools used to create the schedule and a description of how the schedule is formulated are identified through the schedule management plan. In addition to this plan, the scope baseline is a key input to assembling the schedule. Both these elements are part of the project management plan.

Project Documents   There are several documents used and referenced to develop the schedule. Some of these are outputs of the other scheduling processes covered thus far.

Activity List   Developing the project schedule requires the project activities, which are obtained from the activity list developed in the Define Activities process.

Activity Attributes   Activity attributes provide the necessary details of the project activities, which will be utilized in creating the project schedule.

Assumption Log   Constraints and assumptions recorded in the assumption log are used. The following time constraints are important to this process:

- Imposed dates that restrict the start or finish date of activities
- Key events/major milestones to ensure the completion of specific deliverables by a specific date

Basis of Estimates   If needed, the basis of estimates can provide additional detail on how duration estimates were developed.

Project Schedule Network Diagram   The sequence of events will be important in creating the project schedule. The activity sequence and existing dependencies can be obtained from the project schedule network diagram. For a more complete description of the project schedule network diagrams, see "Outputs of Sequence Activities" earlier in this chapter.

Resource Requirements   Activity resource requirements will provide the types and quantity of resources needed for creating the project schedule.

Resource Calendars   Resource calendars display availability of project team members and other resources, which will help to avoid schedule conflicts.

Duration Estimates   Activity duration estimates will provide the time to complete each activity that is needed to assign start and finish dates.

Lessons Learned Register   As the project progresses, lessons learned are captured. These aid in carrying out this process as it occurs throughout future phases of the project.

Milestone List   The milestone list provides specific dates for documented milestones, which are important in assembling the schedule.

Risk Register   Developing the project schedule requires the details of all identified risks and their characteristics that will affect the schedule model.

Project Team Assignments   Developing the project schedule requires the project staff assignments, which specify resource assignments for each activity.

Agreements   If vendors are engaged within the project, schedule information such as date commitments made by vendors is typically captured within the vendor's agreement.

Enterprise Environmental Factors   Existing holidays and other external information that could impact the project schedule may be used from within the enterprise environmental factors. Government or industry standards might also apply and should be referenced.

Organizational Process Assets   Within the organizational process assets, project calendars may exist that provide information on working days and shifts that can be used in this process.

Tools and Techniques of Develop Schedule

The Develop Schedule process has several tools and techniques you can use:

- Schedule network analysis
- Critical path method
- Resource optimization
- Data analysis
- Leads and lags
- Schedule compression
- Project management information system
- Agile release planning

Schedule Network Analysis   Schedule network analysis involves calculating early and late start dates and early and late finish dates for project activities to generate the project schedule. In short, it generates the schedule through the use of the following analytical techniques and methods:

- Critical path method
- Critical chain method
- Modeling techniques
- Resource optimization techniques

 NOTE   Calculations are performed without taking resource limitations into consideration, so the dates are theoretical. Resource limitations and other constraints are taken into consideration during the outputs of this process.

Critical Path Method The critical path method (CPM), a schedule network analysis technique, determines the amount of float, or schedule flexibility, for each of the network paths by calculating the earliest start date, earliest finish date, latest start date, and latest finish date for each activity. This technique relies on sequential networks and a single duration estimate for each activity. PDM can be used to perform CPM. Here is some information related to CPM that you should know:

Critical Path The critical path (CP) is generally the longest full path on the project. Any project activity with a float time that equals zero is considered a critical path task. The critical path can change under the following conditions:

- When activities become tasks on the critical path as a result of having used up all their float time
- When a milestone on the critical path is not met

Float There are two types of float time, also called slack time:

- Total float (TF) is the amount of time you can delay the earliest start of a task without delaying the ending of the project
- Free float (FF) is the amount of time you can delay the start of a task without delaying the earliest start of a successor task

Calculating the Forward and Backward Pass A forward pass is used to calculate the early start and early finish date of each activity on a network diagram. To calculate a forward pass, follow these steps:

1. Begin with the first activity.
2. The calculation of the first activity begins with an early start date of one. Add the duration of the activity and then subtract one to determine the early finish. This is based on the concept of calendar days.
3. The early start date of the next activity is the early finish date of the previous activity plus one. Continue calculating the early start and early finish dates forward through all the network paths while following the existing dependencies.
4. When an activity has two connecting predecessors, the early start date would be the early finish of the predecessor that finishes last, plus one. (For example, suppose activity A has an early finish of 4 and activity B has an early finish of 5. If activities A and B both converge at activity C, then activity C would have an early start date of 6.)

A backward pass is used to calculate the late start and late finish date of each activity on a network diagram. To calculate a backward pass, follow these steps:

1. Begin with the last activity. The late finish date will be the same as the early finish date.
2. Subtract the duration of the activity from the end date and add one to calculate late start. Take this number and subtract one to calculate the late finish of its predecessors.
3. Continue calculating the latest start and latest finish dates moving backward through all of the network paths.

4. When an activity has two connecting predecessors, the late finish date would be the late start minus one of the activities that follows. (For example, if activity C has a late start of 7 and both activity A and activity B connect to activity C, the late finish of both activity A and B would be 7.)

Figure 3.20 summarizes a forward and backward pass.

FIGURE 3.20   Forward and backward pass

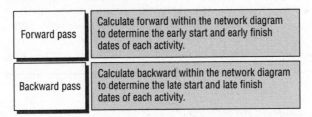

| Forward pass | Calculate forward within the network diagram to determine the early start and early finish dates of each activity. |
| Backward pass | Calculate backward within the network diagram to determine the late start and late finish dates of each activity. |

Calculating the Critical Path   A critical path task is any task that cannot be changed without impacting the project end date. By definition, these are all tasks with zero float. Float can be calculated for each activity by subtracting either the early start from the late start or early finish from the late finish (both will give you the same answer). To determine the CP duration of the project, add the duration of every activity with zero float.

Another way to determine the critical path is by determining the longest path within the network diagram. This can be done by adding the duration of all the activities within each path of the network.

Using Table 3.2, set up a network diagram using the activity number, activity description, dependency, and duration. Next, practice calculating the early start, early finish, late start, and late finish dates. Check your answers against the dates shown on the chart and by referencing Figure 3.21. In this example, the bottom path, or the following activity path, would be your critical path: 1, 4, 5, 6, 7, 8, 9 totally 101 days.

TABLE 3.2   CPM calculation

Activity number	Activity description	Dependency	Duration	Early start	Early finish	Late start	Late finish	Float/ Slack
1	Project Deliverables	—	12	4/1	4/12	4/1	4/12	0
2	Procure Hardware	1	2	4/13	4/14	6/19	6/20	67
3	Test Hardware	2	8	4/15	4/22	6/21	6/28	67
4	Procure Software Tools	1	10	4/13	4/22	4/13	4/22	0
5	Write Programs	4	45	4/23	6/6	4/23	6/6	0

TABLE 3.2 CPM calculation *(continued)*

Activity number	Activity description	Dependency	Duration	Early start	Early finish	Late start	Late finish	Float/ Slack
6	Test and Debug	5	22	6/7	6/28	6/7	6/28	0
7	Install	3, 6	8	6/29	7/6	6/29	7/6	0
8	Training	7	3	7/7	7/9	7/7	7/9	0
9	Acceptance	8	1	7/10	7/10	7/10	7/10	0

FIGURE 3.21 Critical path diagram

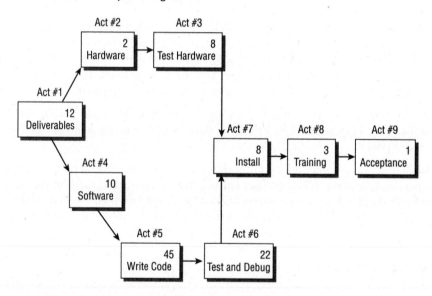

Calculating Expected Value Using PERT PERT and CPM are similar techniques: CPM uses the most likely duration to determine project duration, whereas PERT uses what's called expected value (or the weighted average). Expected value is calculated using the three-point estimates for activity duration.

 For an explanation of how to calculate three-point estimates, see the tools and techniques of the Estimate Activity Durations process.

Calculating Standard Deviation   The formula for standard deviation is as follows:

$$\frac{Pessimistic - Optimistic}{6}$$

For data that fits a bell curve, the following is true:

- Work will finish within ± 3 standard deviations 99.73 percent of the time.
- Work will finish within ± 2 standard deviations 95.44 percent of the time.
- Work will finish within ± 1 standard deviation 68.27 percent of the time.

Standard Deviation

The higher the standard deviation is for an activity, the higher the risk. Since standard deviation measures the difference between the pessimistic and the optimistic times, a greater spread between the two, which results in a higher number, indicates a greater risk. Conversely, a low standard deviation means less risk.

One standard deviation gives you a 68 percent (rounded) probability, and two standard deviations give you a 95 percent (rounded) probability. For an example of calculating date ranges for project durations, see Chapter 4 of *PMP®: Project Management Professional Exam Study Guide, Ninth Edition* (Sybex, 2017).

Critical Chain Method   The critical chain method is a schedule network analysis technique that will modify the project schedule by accounting for limited or restricted resources. The modified schedule is calculated, and it often changes the critical path as a result of adding duration buffers, which are nonworking activities added to help manage the planned activity durations. The new critical path showing the resource restrictions is called the critical chain.

Critical chain uses both deterministic (step-by-step) and probabilistic approaches. The following are steps in the critical chain process:

1. Construct the schedule network diagram using activity duration estimates (you'll use nonconservative estimates in this method).
2. Define dependencies.
3. Define constraints.
4. Calculate the critical path.
5. Enter resource availability into the schedule.
6. Recalculate for the critical chain.

A project buffer is placed at the end of the critical chain to help keep the finish date from slipping. After the buffers are added, the planned activities are then scheduled at their latest start and finish dates.

Resource Optimization   Resource optimization techniques are used when the supply and demand of resources necessitate an adjustment to the schedule model. They attempt to smooth out the peaks and valleys of total resource usage through strategic consumption of float while also addressing any overcommitment of individual resources through rescheduling or reassignment. Examples include but are not limited to the following:

Resource Leveling   Resource leveling attempts to smooth out the resource assignments to get tasks completed without overloading the resources and while trying to keep the project on schedule. This typically takes the form of allocating resources to critical path tasks first.

Here are some examples of resource leveling:

- Delaying the start of a task to match the availability of a key team member
- Adjusting the resource assignments so that more tasks are given to team members who are underallocated
- Requiring the resources to work mandatory overtime

Resource Smoothing   Resource smoothing is a technique that adjusts the schedule model by arranging the activities so that the requirements for resources do not exceed the constraints of the project. The key difference between resource smoothing and resource leveling is that, with resource smoothing, the critical path of the project remains unchanged. The ability to delay an activity is limited by the amount of an activity's free and total float.

   Resource leveling can cause the original critical path to change.

Data Analysis   There are multiple types of modeling techniques that a project manager can use in developing the schedule. Two examples that you should be familiar with for the exam include what-if scenario analysis and simulation.

What-If Scenario Analysis   What-if scenario analysis evaluates different scenarios in order to predict their positive or negative effect on project objectives. According to the *PMBOK® Guide*, this is an analysis of the question, What if the situation represented by scenario X happens? To support this effort, a schedule network analysis is performed using the schedule to calculate different scenarios, like the delay of a deliverable or a major weather event for a construction project.

Simulation   Taking different sets of activity assumptions, simulation calculates multiple project duration models using probability distributions constructed from three-point estimates to account for uncertainty. Simulation techniques such as Monte Carlo analysis use a range of probable activity durations for each activity, and those ranges are then used to calculate a range of probable duration results for the project itself. Monte Carlo runs the possible activity durations and schedule projections many, many times to come up with the schedule projections and their probability, critical path duration estimates, and float time.

Leads and Lags   A lead accelerates the start date of an activity by the number of days specified, whereas a lag delays the start date of an activity. Leads and lags were first used in the Sequence Activities process, discussed earlier in this chapter.

Schedule Compression   Schedule compression is a form of mathematical analysis that's used to shorten the project schedule without changing the project scope. To be effective, work compressed must be based on those activities that fall on the critical path. There are two types of schedule compression techniques:

Crashing   Crashing is a compression technique that looks at cost and schedule trade-offs. This involves adding resources to critical path tasks in order to shorten the length of the tasks and therefore the length of the project. Crashing the schedule can lead to increased risk, increased costs, and a change in the critical path.

Fast-Tracking   Fast-tracking is performing two tasks in parallel that were previously scheduled to start sequentially. Fast-tracking can increase project risk and cause the project team to have to rework tasks, and it only works for activities that can be overlapped.

Project Management Information System   The scheduling tools used are typically in the form of project management software programs. They will automate the mathematical calculations and perform resource-leveling functions.

Agile Release Planning   When using Agile, this technique provides the release schedule and the number of iterations or sprints within the release, based on the product road map and product vision.

Outputs of Develop Schedule

Know the following outputs of the Develop Schedule process:

- Schedule baseline
- Project schedule
- Schedule data
- Project calendars
- Change requests
- Project management plan updates
- Project documents updates

Schedule Baseline   The schedule baseline can be described as the final, approved version of the project schedule with baseline start and baseline finish dates and resource assignments. The *PMBOK® Guide* notes that the schedule baseline is a designated version of the project schedule that's derived from the schedule network analysis. The approved project schedule becomes a part of the project management plan.

Exam Note

For the exam, remember that the project schedule is based on the timeline (derived from the activity), the scope document (to help keep track of major milestones and deliverables), and resource plans.

Project Schedule The project schedule details the start and finish dates for each project activity as well as the resource assignments. In *PMBOK® Guide* terms, the project schedule is considered preliminary until resources are assigned. The following are additional elements of the project schedule:

- The project schedule should be approved and signed off by stakeholders and functional managers.

- For functional organizations, confirmation that resources will be available as outlined in the schedule should be obtained.

- The schedule cannot be finalized until approval and commitment for the resource assignments outlined in it are received.

- Once approved, the schedule becomes the schedule baseline for the remainder of the project.

The following are various ways of displaying the project schedule:

Bar Charts Also known as Gantt charts, these tools are commonly used to display schedule activities. They may show activity sequences, activity start and end dates, resource assignments, activity dependencies, and the critical path. Figure 3.22 shows a simple example that plots various activities against time.

FIGURE 3.22 Gantt chart

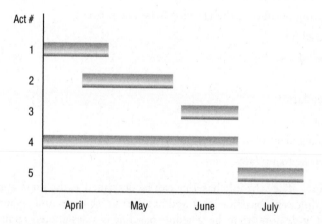

Project Schedule Network Diagrams Project schedule network diagrams usually show the activity dependencies and critical path. They will work as schedule diagrams when the start and finish dates are added to each activity.

Milestone Charts Milestone charts mark the completion of major deliverables or some other key events in the project. They can be displayed in a bar chart form, similar to a Gantt chart, or in a simple table format, as shown in Table 3.3. As the milestones are met, the Actual Date column within the table is filled in.

TABLE 3.3   Milestone chart

Milestone	Scheduled Date	Actual Date
Sign-off on deliverables	4/12	4/12
Sign-off on hardware test	4/22	4/25
Programming completed	6/06	
Testing completed	6/28	
Acceptance and sign-off	7/10	
Project closeout	7/10	

Schedule Data   The schedule data refers to documenting the supporting data for the schedule. At least the following elements must be included within the schedule data:

- Milestones
- Schedule activities
- Activity attributes
- Assumptions
- Constraints
- Any other information that doesn't fit into the other categories
- Resource requirements by time period, often in the form of resource histograms (suggested by the *PMBOK® Guide*)

Project Calendars   A project calendar is a template of sorts that clarifies the working days and shifts that are available for scheduling activities.

Change Requests   After the project is baselined, changes may come about as a result of progressive elaboration. Changes to the schedule may also result from approved changes to the scope of the project.

Project Management Plan Updates   Updates may be made to the schedule baseline, the cost baseline, and/or the schedule management plan.

Project Documents Updates   Updates may be made to the following project documents:

- Resource requirements
- Activity attributes
- Assumption log
- Duration estimates
- Lessons learned register
- Risk register

Exam Essentials

Know the difference between the precedence diagramming method (PDM) and the arrow diagramming method (ADM).   PDM uses boxes or rectangles to represent the activities (called *nodes*) that are connected with arrows showing the dependencies between the activities. ADM places activities on the arrows (called *activity on arrow*), which are connected to dependent activities with nodes.

Be able to describe the purpose of the Estimate Activity Resources process.   The purpose of Estimate Activity Resources is to determine the types and quantities of resources (human, equipment, and materials) needed for each schedule activity within a work package.

Be able to name the tools and techniques of Estimate Activity Durations.   The tools and techniques of Estimate Activity Durations are expert judgment, analogous estimating, parametric estimating, three-point estimating, bottom-up estimating, decision making, data analysis, and meetings.

Be able to define the difference between analogous estimating, parametric estimating, and bottom-up estimating.   Analogous estimating is a top-down technique that uses expert judgment and historical information. Parametric estimating multiplies the quantity of work by the rate. Bottom-up estimating performs estimates for each work item and rolls them up to a total.

Be able to calculate the critical path.   The critical path includes the activities whose durations add up to the longest path of the project schedule network diagram. The critical path is calculated using the forward pass, backward pass, and float calculations.

Be able to define a critical path task.   A critical path task is a project activity with zero float.

Be able to describe and calculate beta distribution.   This is a weighted average technique that uses three estimates: optimistic, pessimistic, and most likely. The formula is as follows:

$$\frac{Optimistic + (4 \times Most\ Likely) + Pessimistic}{6}$$

Be able to name the schedule compression techniques.   The schedule compression techniques are crashing and fast-tracking.

Be able to describe a critical chain.   The critical chain is the new critical path in a modified schedule that accounts for limited resources.

Be able to name the outputs of the Develop Schedule process.   The outputs are project schedule, schedule baseline, schedule data, change requests, project calendars, project management plan updates, and project documents updates.

Bringing the Processes Together

This chapter covered a tremendous amount of information within the Planning process group, and there is still much ground that remains to be covered in the next three chapters. The Planning process group is the largest project management process group. In addition to understanding each process individually, you'll need to know how the processes work together. Understanding that bigger picture will help you with situational exam questions as well as using the project management processes in a real-world setting.

With this big picture in mind, let's go back and review what you've learned thus far about each of the project management Knowledge Areas within this chapter; we'll fill in the remaining gaps in the chapter that follows. You'll find that what goes on within each Knowledge Area is connected on a high level and is structured in a logical format.

Project Scope Management Knowledge Area Review

You may recall that the project scope defines the work to be completed during the project, providing the project with boundaries. Figure 3.23 illustrates the process and inputs used to create the work breakdown structure. (Remember that the WBS is a decomposition of the project deliverables, down to the work package level.) The WBS becomes part of the scope baseline, as is the project scope statement and the WBS dictionary. The scope baseline is necessary input for activities in the next Knowledge Area, Project Schedule Management.

FIGURE 3.23   Project Scope Management Knowledge Area process interaction

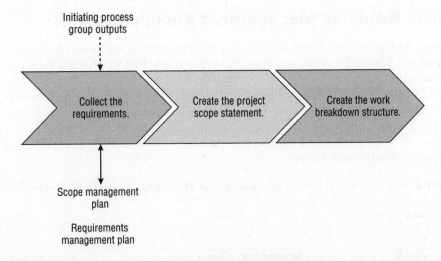

Project Schedule Management Knowledge Area Review

Figure 3.24 reflects, step-by-step, how the project schedule is developed. The flow of the Planning processes within the Project Schedule Management Knowledge Area is extremely clear. It's important to understand the following points:

- The scope baseline is central to creating the initial list of project activities; creating the list is the first step toward developing the project schedule.

- The project budget can influence the number and type of resources the project can use.
- Clearly defining the resources needed to carry out the project activities is key to planning resources and procurements.

FIGURE 3.24 Project Schedule Management Knowledge Area process interaction

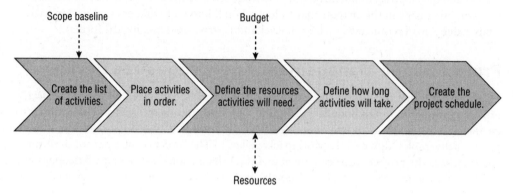

Project Resource Management Knowledge Area

Although we didn't fully address the planning processes within the Project Resource Management Knowledge Area, we covered a key process within this Knowledge Area that plays an important role in developing the schedule: Estimate Activity Resources.

The Estimate Activity Resources process may occur after sequencing activities and before estimating activity durations, which are both processes belonging to the Project Schedule Management Knowledge Area, or it may occur in parallel for smaller projects.

Figure 3.25 highlights where the Estimate Activity Resources process falls in relation to the schedule development process.

FIGURE 3.25 Project Schedule Management Knowledge Area process interaction

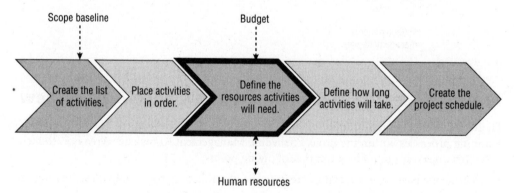

Review Questions

1. All of the following are subsidiary elements of the project management plan *except*:
   A. Quality management plan
   B. Risk management plan
   C. Project scope statement
   D. Scope baseline

2. Which of the following *best* describes a focus group?
   A. Gathering of prequalified subject matter experts and stakeholders who provide feedback
   B. One-on-one conversations with stakeholders
   C. Group of subject matter experts who participate anonymously
   D. Group of cross-functional stakeholders who can define cross-functional requirements

3. Sam is currently in the planning stages of a project and is working on developing the project scope statement. As part of converting the product scope description into deliverables, he has used the product breakdown and systems analysis techniques. Which of the following tools and techniques of the Define Scope process is Sam currently using?
   A. Expert judgment
   B. Product analysis
   C. Data analysis
   D. Interpersonal and team skills

4. The following are included within the WBS dictionary *except*:
   A. Code of accounts identifiers
   B. Cost estimates
   C. Description of the work of the component
   D. Activity list

5. While sequencing activities, a project manager decides to use the precedence diagramming method to show existing dependencies between activities. Which of the logical relationships is the project manager *most likely* to use?
   A. Finish-to-start
   B. Start-to-finish
   C. Finish-to-finish
   D. Start-to-start

6. The scope management plan should contain the following information *except*:
   A. The process used to prepare the project scope statement
   B. The definition of how deliverables will be checked for accuracy and the process for accepting deliverables
   C. The list of all the requirements to be included in the scope
   D. The process used to create the WBS

7. Which of the following is the purpose of collecting requirements?

    A. Creating a clear billing structure for project reimbursement

    B. Documenting stakeholder expectations for meeting the project objective

    C. Establishing the order in which activities should be conducted

    D. Determining the total budget that will be needed for the project

8. What is the *correct* definition of a project constraint?

    A. Project constraints limit the options of the project team.

    B. Project constraints are conditions presumed to be true.

    C. Project constraints do not affect project outcomes.

    D. Project constraints never change during the project.

9. Using the following table, calculate the total float of activity B.

Activity Name	Predecessor	Duration
A	None	5
B	A	2
C	A	6
D	A	3
E	B, C, D	1

    A. 4

    B. 2

    C. 1

    D. 0

10. Calculate the triangular distribution using the following values:

    Optimistic estimate of 12

    Most likely estimate of 23

    Pessimistic estimate of 38

    A. 12

    B. 38

    C. 23

    D. 24

Chapter

4

Planning Project Cost and Quality Management

THE PMP® EXAM CONTENT FROM THE PLANNING PERFORMANCE DOMAIN COVERED IN THIS CHAPTER INCLUDES THE FOLLOWING:

✓ Develop the cost management plan based upon the project scope, schedule, resources, approved project charter-and other information, using estimating techniques, in order to manage project costs.

✓ Develop the quality management plan and define the quality standards for the project and its products, based on the project scope, risks, and requirements in order to prevent the occurrence of defects and reduce the cost of quality.

As noted in Chapter 3, Planning is the second of five project management process groups and includes the largest number of processes—24 in total. In this chapter, we will cover processes that belong to the following Knowledge Areas: Project Cost Management and Project Quality Management.

The process names, inputs, tools and techniques, outputs, and descriptions of the project management process groups and related materials and figures in this chapter are based on content from *A Guide to the Project Management Body of Knowledge (PMBOK® Guide), Sixth Edition* (PMI®, 2017).

Developing a Cost Management Plan

The purpose of the cost management plan is, naturally, to create, monitor, and control the project costs. This plan is based on the project scope and documents the estimating techniques that will be used as well as how the cost-related processes will be carried out.

The project budget is created by carrying out three planning processes:

- Plan Cost Management, which is primarily focused on the costs of resources to complete the project

- Estimate Costs, which estimates how much each activity will cost

- Determine Budget, which aggregates the total cost estimates plus contingency reserves to create the project budget

The project budget is referred to as the cost baseline, which, along with the cost management plan, becomes a part of the project management plan.

Figure 4.1 shows the inputs, tools and techniques, and outputs of the Plan Cost Management process.

FIGURE 4.1   Plan Cost Management process

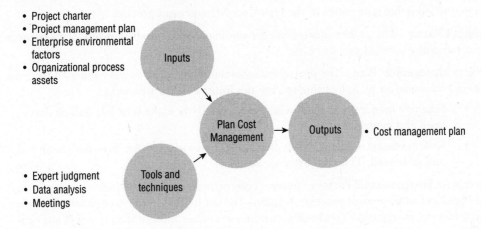

- Project charter
- Project management plan
- Enterprise environmental factors
- Organizational process assets

- Expert judgment
- Data analysis
- Meetings

- Cost management plan

Understand the Cost Management Plan

The cost management plan plays an important role within all of the Project Cost Management Knowledge Area processes. The cost management plan is created during the Plan Cost Management process and is a subsidiary plan of the project management plan (as all subplans are). Using the preceding components, the cost management plan will guide the project management team in carrying out the three cost-related processes.

Plan Cost Management

The cost management plan contains the following information:

- Level of accuracy
- Units of measure
- Organizational procedures links
- Control thresholds
- Rules of performance measurement
- Reporting formats
- Process descriptions

Keep in mind that throughout the Project Cost Management Knowledge Area, the cost management plan serves as a guide for documenting and controlling the budget of the project.

Inputs of Plan Cost Management

Know the following four inputs of the Plan Cost Management process:

Project Charter   The project charter has the summary budget, which provides a key input for creating the detailed project costs.

Project Management Plan   The project management plan contains elements used to create the cost management plan, focusing on, but not limited to, the following:

- Schedule management plan, which helps clarify how the schedule will be developed and managed.
- Risk management plan, which documents how risks will be identified, analyzed, and addressed. This can influence costs.

Enterprise Environmental Factors   Several enterprise environmental factors can influence the Plan Cost Management process, including but not limited to the organization's culture and structure, marketplace conditions, currency exchange rates (if the project is multinational), published commercial information such as resource cost rate information, and the project management information system.

Organizational Process Assets   Financial controls procedures; historical information, including a lessons learned knowledge base; financial databases; and existing formal and informal cost estimating and budgeting-related policies, procedures, and guidelines are a few of the organizational process assets that help shape the Plan Cost Management process.

Tools and Techniques of Plan Cost Management

The three tools and techniques that the Plan Cost Management process uses are expert judgement, data analysis, and meetings.

Expert Judgment   Expert judgment brings invaluable perspective about prior similar projects attempted, as well as the existing environment that will affect the project. This can also be key in considering whether to combine methods of cost planning and how to best resolve differences between those methods.

Data Analysis   You may have many strategic options to consider when developing the cost management plan. Those options include self-funding, funding with equity, or funding with debt. Financial options will be influenced by the organization's policies and procedures, including but not limited to payback period, return on investment, internal rate of return, discounted cash flow, and net present value.

Meetings   In the course of developing the cost management plan, members of project teams may attend meetings to help with information exchange and decision making. Depending on the meeting, the following members might be a part of the discussion: the project manager, the project sponsor, selected project team members, and anyone having responsibility in this area.

Outputs of Plan Cost Management

For the exam, know that the output of the Plan Cost Management process is the cost management plan.

Cost Management Plan   The cost management plan should establish the following:

- Units of measure, such as quantity and time measures, and currency to be used

- Level of precision, which is the degree to which activity cost estimates will be rounded up or down

- Level of accuracy, which is the acceptable range used in determining contingencies and realistic activity cost estimates

- Organizational procedures links, where the WBS provides the framework for the cost management plan to help foster consistency with estimates, budgets, and controls

- Control thresholds, which document the identified variation that can occur before some action needs to be taken

- Rules of performance measurement, like the rules for earned value management (EVM), and which techniques to use

> For more detailed information on earned value management, see *Practice Standard for Earned Value Management, Second Edition* (PMI®, 2011).

- Reporting formats defining the form and frequency of various cost reports

- Process descriptions for the other cost management processes

- Additional details such as explanations of strategic funding choices, how to deal with currency exchange rate fluctuations, and the procedure for project cost recording

Estimate Costs

The purpose of the Estimate Costs process is to develop cost estimates for resources, both human and material, required for all schedule activities and the overall project. This includes weighing alternative options and examining risks and trade-offs. The cost-related processes are governed by the cost management plan, which establishes the format and conditions used to plan for project costs. It also outlines how you will estimate, budget, and control project costs.

Figure 4.2 shows the inputs, tools and techniques, and outputs of the Estimate Costs process.

FIGURE 4.2   Estimate Costs process

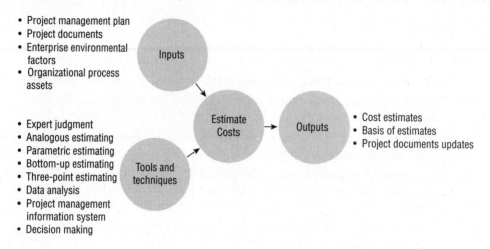

- Project management plan
- Project documents
- Enterprise environmental factors
- Organizational process assets

- Expert judgment
- Analogous estimating
- Parametric estimating
- Bottom-up estimating
- Three-point estimating
- Data analysis
- Project management information system
- Decision making

Inputs

Estimate Costs

Outputs

Tools and techniques

- Cost estimates
- Basis of estimates
- Project documents updates

For more detailed information on the Estimate Costs process, see Chapter 5, "Developing the Project Budget," of *PMP®: Project Management Professional Exam Study Guide, Ninth Edition* (Sybex, 2017).

Inputs of Estimate Costs

You should be familiar with these four inputs of the Estimate Costs process:

- Project management plan

- Project documents

- Enterprise environmental factors

- Organizational process assets

Project Management Plan   There are three primary inputs used from within the project management plan: cost management plan, quality management plan, and scope baseline.

Cost Management Plan   The cost management plan is a key input that specifies how project costs will be managed and controlled, including the method to be used and level of accuracy targets required to estimate cost activity.

Quality Management Plan   For the purposes of the Estimate Costs process, the quality management plan documents the activities and resources needed to meet the quality objectives.

Scope Baseline   The following are included within the scope baseline and are used in creating cost estimates:

- Project scope statement (key deliverables, funding constraints, and other financial assumptions)

- WBS, which serves as the basis for estimating costs (project deliverables, control accounts)

- WBS dictionary

> Scope definition is a key component of determining the estimated costs and should be completed early within the project.

Project Documents   There are four project documents that are typically referenced for estimating costs: the project schedule, resource requirements, risk register, and lessons learned register.

Project Schedule and Resource Requirements   Activity resource requirements and activity duration estimates are used from within the project schedule and serve as key inputs when estimating costs.

Risk Register   From within the risk register, the cost of mitigating, avoiding, or transferring risks will be used for estimating costs, particularly when the risks have negative impacts to the project.

Lessons Learned Register   The lessons learned register can provide insight into future phases, where cost estimates have yet to be developed.

Enterprise Environmental Factors   According to the *PMBOK® Guide*, the following enterprise environmental factors should be considered in this process:

- Market conditions, which help you to understand the materials, goods, and services available in the market and what terms and conditions exist to procure those resources.
- Published commercial information, which refers to resource cost rates. These are obtained from commercial databases or published seller price lists.
- Exchange rates and inflation.

Organizational Process Assets   The organizational process assets include historical information and lessons learned on previous projects of similar scope and complexity. Also useful are cost-estimating worksheets from past projects as templates for the current project.

Tools and Techniques of Estimate Costs

The following list includes the tools and techniques of the Estimate Costs process:

- Expert judgment
- Analogous estimating
- Parametric estimating
- Bottom-up estimating
- Three-point estimating
- Data analysis
- Project management information system
- Decision making

Expert Judgment   Cost estimates from individuals who have had previous experience in the past on similar projects can be used. Information from those who have experience in performing the activities becomes valuable for calculating accurate estimates.

Analogous Estimating   Analogous estimating, also called top-down estimating, is a form of expert judgment. This technique uses actual costs of a similar activity completed on a previous project to determine the cost estimate of the current activity. It can be used when the previous activities being compared are similar to the activities being estimated. Analogous estimating may also be useful when detailed information about the project is not yet available. Top-down estimating techniques are also used to estimate total project cost to look at the estimate as a whole. Although analogous estimating is considered to be a quick and low-cost estimating technique, it is low in accuracy.

The *PMBOK® Guide* states that analogous estimating can also be used to determine overall project duration and cost estimates for the entire project (or phases of the project).

Parametric Estimating   Parametric estimating uses historical information and statistical data to calculate cost estimates. For a complete description of parametric estimating, see "Tools and Techniques of Estimate Activity Durations" in Chapter 3.

Bottom-Up Estimating   This technique estimates costs associated with every activity individually by decomposing an activity into smaller pieces of work until the cost of the work can be confidently estimated. The costs of the activity are then rolled up to the original activity level.

Three-Point Estimating   Three-point estimates are used in this process when the project team is attempting to improve estimates and account for risk by estimating uncertainty. The concept and formulas are similar to those used to estimate activity durations. The most likely, optimistic, and pessimistic estimates are captured. From there, a triangular distribution can be calculated (simple average) or a beta distribution (weighted average):

$$\text{Triangular distribution: } c_E = \frac{c_O + c_{ML} + c_P}{3}$$

$$\text{Beta distribution: } c_E = \frac{c_O + (4 \times c_{ML}) + c_P}{6}$$

Data Analysis   Data analysis techniques typically used to develop cost estimates include alternatives analysis, reserve analysis, and cost of quality.

During this process, cost reserves (or contingencies) and management reserves are added. Cost contingencies can be aggregated and assigned to a schedule activity or a WBS work package level. Contingency reserve is added to account for existing known risk, whereas management reserves are added to account for unknown risk.

The cost of quality (COQ) is the total cost to produce the product or service of the project according to the quality standards. You can find additional information on cost of quality in "Tools and Techniques of Plan Quality Management" later in this chapter.

Vendor bid analysis, a type of alternatives analysis, involves gathering information from vendors to help establish cost estimates. This can be accomplished by requesting bids or quotes or working with some of the trusted vendor sources for estimates.

Project Management Information System   The project management software tool can help quickly determine estimates given different variables and alternatives.

Decision Making   In this assessment process, an evaluation of multiple alternatives is performed to determine the results future actions might bring. Decision-making techniques are valuable in improving estimate accuracy and commitment to the determined estimates.

Outputs of Estimate Costs

The following are three outputs that result from the Estimate Costs process:

- Cost estimates
- Basis of estimates
- Project documents updates

Cost Estimates   Cost estimates are quantitative amounts that reflect the cost of the resources needed to complete the project activities. The following resources are commonly needed:

- Human resources
- Material
- Equipment
- Information technology needs
- Any contingency reserve amounts and inflation factors

Basis of Estimates   Basis of estimates is the supporting detail for the activity cost estimates and includes any information that describes how the estimates were developed, what assumptions were made during the Estimate Costs process, and any other details needed. According to the *PMBOK® Guide*, the basis of estimates should include the following as a minimum:

- Description of how the estimate was developed or the basis for the estimate
- Description of the assumptions made about the estimates or the method used to determine them
- Description of the constraints
- Range of possible results
- Confidence level regarding the final estimates

Project Documents Updates   Updates to project documents, as a result of determining cost estimates, commonly include the following to account for cost variances and refined estimates:

- Lessons learned register
- Risk register
- Assumption log

Determine Budget

The Determine Budget process is primarily concerned with determining the cost baseline, which represents the project budget. This process aggregates the cost estimates of activities and establishes a cost baseline for the project that is used to measure performance of the project throughout the remaining process groups. By the end of this process, the project schedule and the project budget will both have been created.

Figure 4.3 shows the inputs, tools and techniques, and outputs of the Determine Budget process.

FIGURE 4.3   Determine Budget process

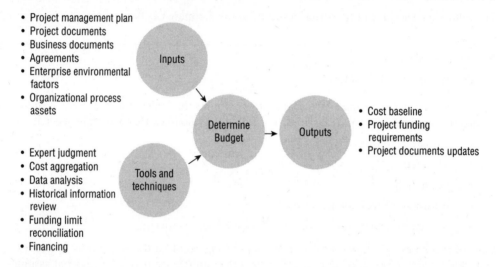

- Project management plan
- Project documents
- Business documents
- Agreements
- Enterprise environmental factors
- Organizational process assets

- Expert judgment
- Cost aggregation
- Data analysis
- Historical information review
- Funding limit reconciliation
- Financing

Inputs

Determine Budget → Outputs

Tools and techniques

- Cost baseline
- Project funding requirements
- Project documents updates

For more detailed information on the Determine Budget process, see Chapter 5 of *PMP®: Project Management Professional Exam Study Guide, Ninth Edition* (Sybex, 2017).

Inputs of Determine Budget

The Determine Budget process contains six inputs:

- Project management plan

- Project documents

- Business documents

- Agreements

- Enterprise environmental factors

- Organizational process assets

Project Management Plan   As we have seen earlier in the chapter, the cost management plan lays out how project costs will be managed and controlled. This is a key document used from within the project management plan. Others include the scope baseline and resource management plan. When determining the budget, the following is used within the scope baseline:

- Project scope statement (describes the constraints of the project)
- WBS (shows how the project deliverables are related to their components and typically provides control account information)
- WBS dictionary

Project Documents   The following documents are used to develop the budget: cost estimates, basis of estimates, project schedule, and risk register.

Cost Estimates   Activity cost estimates are determined for each activity within a work package and then summed to determine the total estimate for a work package.

Basis of Estimates   Basis of estimates contains all the supporting details regarding the estimates. Assumptions regarding indirect costs and whether they will be included in the project budget should be considered. Indirect costs cannot be directly linked to any one project but are allocated among several projects.

Project Schedule   The schedule contains information that is helpful in developing the budget, such as start and end dates for activities, milestones, and so on. Based on the information in the schedule, budget expenditures for calendar periods can be determined.

Risk Register   When determining the budget, a review of the risk register will help to compile the costs for risk response.

Business Documents   Business documents referenced during the budget development process include the business case and the benefits management plan. Both document success factors and metrics that the project has set out to achieve.

Agreements   Agreements, such as contracts, include cost information that should be included in the overall project budget.

Enterprise Environmental Factors   Exchange rates (considered to be an enterprise environmental factor) are important to reference when developing the budget.

Organizational Process Assets   The organizational process assets used include the following items:

- Cost budgeting tools
- Policies and procedures of the organization regarding budgeting exercises
- Reporting methods

Outputs from other planning processes, including Create WBS, Develop Schedule, and Estimate Costs, must be completed prior to working on Determine Budget because some of them become the inputs to this process.

Tools and Techniques of Determine Budget

Know the following tools and techniques of the Determine Budget process for the exam:

- Expert judgment
- Cost aggregation
- Data analysis
- Historical information review
- Funding limit reconciliation
- Financing

Expert Judgment   Expert judgment in calculating the project budget will include information from those with past experience in conducting similar projects.

Cost Aggregation   Cost aggregation is the process of tallying the schedule activity cost estimates at the work package level and then totaling the work package levels to higher-level WBS component levels. All costs can then be aggregated to obtain a total project cost.

Data Analysis   In this process, reserve analysis outlines contingency reserves for unplanned project scope and unplanned project costs. Contingency reserves are included as part of the cost baseline, whereas management reserves are not.

Historical Information Review   Analogous estimates and parametric estimates can be used to help determine total project costs. Actual costs from previous projects of similar size, scope, and complexity are used to estimate the costs for the current project. This is helpful when detailed information about the project is not available or it's early in the project phases and not much information is known.

 Remember that parametric estimates are more precise than analogous estimates. Analogous estimates tend to be quicker and less costly to develop.

Funding Limit Reconciliation   Funding limit reconciliation involves reconciling the amount of funds to be spent with the amount of funds budgeted for the project. The organization or the customer sets these limits. Reconciling the project expenses will require adjusting the schedule so that the expenses can be smoothed. This can be done by placing imposed date constraints on work packages or other WBS components in the project schedule.

Financing   Financing refers to securing funds for the project. This may be from within the organization or through external funding sources.

Outputs of Determine Budget

There are three outputs of the Determine Budget process:

Cost Baseline   The cost baseline provides the basis for measurement, over time, of the expected cash flows (or funding disbursements) against the requirements. Adding the costs of the WBS elements by time periods develops the cost baseline. This is also known as the project's time-phased budget. Most projects span some length of time, and most organizations time the funding with the project.

Cost baselines can be displayed graphically, as shown in Figure 4.4.

FIGURE 4.4   Cost baseline

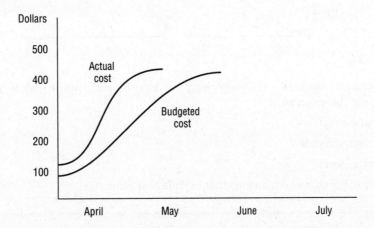

The cost baseline should contain the costs for all of the expected work on the project as well as the contingency reserves set aside to account for known risks. Large projects may have more than one cost performance baseline.

 Cost baselines are displayed as an S curve. The reason for this is that project spending starts out slowly, gradually increases over the project's life until it reaches a peak, and then tapers off again as the project wraps up.

Project Funding Requirements   Project funding requirements describe the need for funding over the course of the project and are derived from the cost performance baseline. Funding requirements can be expressed in monthly, quarterly, or annual increments or other increments that are appropriate for your project.

Figure 4.5 shows the cost baseline, the funding requirements, and the expected cash flows plotted on the S curve. This example shows a negative amount of management reserve. The difference between the funding requirements and the cost performance baseline at the end of a project is the management reserve. Management reserves are set aside to deal with unknown risks.

FIGURE 4.5   Cost baseline, funding requirements, and cash flow

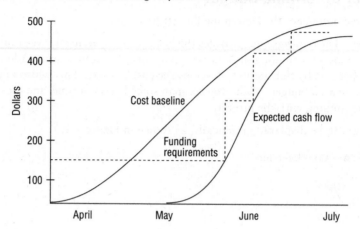

Project Documents Updates   The following project documents require updates as a result of carrying out this process:

- Cost estimates
- Project schedule
- Risk register
- Any other project documents that include cost estimates

> Don't forget that the Project Cost Management Knowledge Area has one more process: Control Costs. Look for a discussion of this process in Chapter 8 when we discuss the Monitoring and Controlling process group.

Exam Essentials

Be able to identify and describe the primary output of the Estimate Costs process.   The primary output of Estimate Costs is cost estimates. These estimates are quantitative amounts—usually stated in monetary units—that reflect the cost of the resources needed to complete the project activities.

Be able to identify the tools and techniques of the Estimate Costs process.   The tools and techniques of Estimate Costs are expert judgment, analogous estimating, parametric estimating, bottom-up estimating, three-point estimating, data analysis, project management information system, and decision making.

Be able to identify the tools and techniques of the Determine Budget process.   The tools and techniques of Determine Budget are expert judgment, cost aggregation, data analysis, historical information review, funding limit reconciliation, and financing.

Be able to describe the cost baseline.   The cost baseline is the authorized, time-phased cost of the project when using budget-at-completion calculations. The cost baseline is displayed as an S curve.

Be able to describe project funding requirements.   Project funding requirements are an output of the Determine Budget process. They detail the funding requirements needed on the project by time period (monthly, quarterly, or annually).

Developing a Quality Management Plan

Preventing the occurrence of defects and reducing the cost of quality can be critical to a project's success. To this end, a quality management plan is created out of the Plan Quality Management process and is responsible for guiding the project management team in carrying out the three quality-related processes. This plan should be based on the project scope and requirements.

In addition to creating the quality management plan, the Plan Quality Management process is responsible for creating the process improvement plan. This plan measures the effectiveness of and improves the project management processes. Continuous improvement is a recurring theme throughout the *PMBOK® Guide* and is an important element of modern quality theories. The ideas, concepts, and theories from key quality theorists (such as Deming, Juran, and Crosby) played an important role in shaping the Project Quality Management Knowledge Area processes.

The Plan Quality Management process is concerned with targeting quality standards that are relevant to the project at hand and devising a plan to meet and satisfy those standards. The quality management plan is the result of the Plan Quality Management process, which describes how the quality policy will be implemented by the project management team. The result of this process also produces the process improvement plan, which documents the actions for analyzing processes to ultimately increase customer value.

Figure 4.6 shows the inputs, tools and techniques, and outputs of the Plan Quality Management process.

FIGURE 4.6   Plan Quality Management process

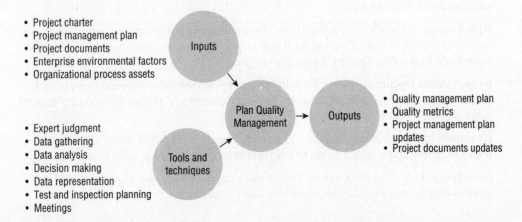

- Project charter
- Project management plan
- Project documents
- Enterprise environmental factors
- Organizational process assets

Inputs

- Expert judgment
- Data gathering
- Data analysis
- Decision making
- Data representation
- Test and inspection planning
- Meetings

Tools and techniques

Plan Quality Management → Outputs

- Quality management plan
- Quality metrics
- Project management plan updates
- Project documents updates

For more detailed information on the Plan Quality Management process, see Chapter 7 of *PMP®: Project Management Professional Exam Study Guide, Ninth Edition* (Sybex, 2017).

Inputs of Plan Quality Management

The Plan Quality Management process contains the following inputs:

- Project charter
- Project management plan
- Project documents
- Enterprise environmental factors
- Organizational process assets

Project Charter   The project charter provides a high-level description of the project and the product's characteristics. In addition to this, the charter may include success criteria and project objectives that will need to be measured through the quality management processes.

Project Management Plan   The following are used from within the project management plan:

- Scope baseline, including the project scope statement, which defines the project deliverables, objectives, and threshold and acceptance criteria, all of which are used within the quality processes; the WBS; and the WBS dictionary

- Other management plans that might influence the overall project quality, such as the risk management plan, requirements management plan, and stakeholder engagement plan

Project Documents   Several project documents may be used to help plan quality. According to the *PMBOK® Guide*, the following are typically referenced: the stakeholder register, risk register, requirements documentation, requirements traceability matrix, and assumption log.

Stakeholder Register   A list of stakeholders is used in this process to understand the expectations of all stakeholders. Quality has been achieved when the expectations of all stakeholders have been met.

Risk Register   The risk register outlines the documented information pertaining to risk, including the list of risks. Dealing with risk is tied into quality and should therefore be considered in the Plan Quality Management process.

Requirements Documentation   To help ensure that stakeholder expectations are met, requirements documentation becomes a key instrument to help plan how quality control will function on the project.

Requirements Traceability Matrix   The requirements traceability matrix links requirements to deliverables, which helps to ensure that requirements are fully tested.

Assumption Log   The assumption log provides the documented assumptions and constraints that relate to quality requirements and compliance.

Enterprise Environmental Factors   The project manager should consider any standards, regulations, guidelines, quality policies, or rules that exist concerning the work of the project when writing the quality plan. In addition to this, organizational structure and culture should be considered, as well as geographic distribution, marketplace conditions, and others as needed.

Organizational Process Assets   The quality policy is included from within the organizational process assets and used in this process. The quality policy is a guideline published by executive management that describes what quality policies should be adopted for projects the company undertakes.

Standards and Regulations

A standard is something that's approved by a recognized body and that employs rules, guidelines, or characteristics that should be followed. According to the *PMBOK® Guide*, the Project Quality Management Knowledge Area is designed to be in alignment with the ISO standards.

A regulation is mandatory. Governments or institutions almost always impose regulations, although organizations might also have their own, self-imposed regulations.

Tools and Techniques of Plan Quality Management

Know the following tools and techniques of the Plan Quality Management process:

- Expert judgment
- Data gathering
- Data analysis
- Decision making
- Data representation
- Test and inspection planning
- Meetings

Expert Judgment   Experts typically play an important role in quality management planning activities, particularly in identifying what the appropriate tools and metrics are for measuring quality adherence.

Data Gathering   Various techniques are used to gather data that aids in the quality management processes. Examples noted next include benchmarking, brainstorming, and interviews.

Benchmarking   Benchmarking is a process of comparing previous similar activities to the current project activities to provide a standard against which to measure performance.

Brainstorming   Brainstorming is used to generate ideas within a large group and as a creative method for pulling ideas out for team members. A brainstorming session can also use and review information obtained using the nominal group technique.

Interviews   Conducting interviews is a method of identifying quality needs and expectations from participants and other stakeholders. Interviews can be conducted one on one or in other formats and help to create an environment of comfort, trust, and confidentiality.

Data Analysis   Two data analysis techniques that are important to know for the exam are cost-benefit analysis and cost of quality.

Cost-Benefit Analysis   In the case of quality management, cost of quality trade-offs should be considered from within cost-benefit analysis. The benefits of meeting quality requirements are as follows:

- Stakeholder satisfaction is increased.
- Costs are lower.
- Productivity is higher.
- There is less rework.

Cost of Quality   The cost of quality (COQ) is the total cost to produce the product or service of the project according to the quality standards. Costs are broken into two categories: cost of conformance, which is money spent during the project to avoid failures, and cost of nonconformance, which is money spent during and after the project because of failures. Four costs are associated with the cost of quality: prevention costs and appraisal costs (conformance) and internal and external failure costs (nonconformance).

> **Prevention Costs:** Prevention costs are the costs associated with satisfying customer requirements by producing a product without defects.
>
> **Appraisal Costs:** Appraisal costs are the costs expended to examine the product or process and make certain the requirements are being met.
>
> **Failure Costs:** Failure costs are what it costs when things don't go according to plan. Failure costs are also known as cost of poor quality. Two types of failure costs exist:

- Internal failure costs
- External failure costs

There are two categories of costs within COQ, as listed in Table 4.1.

TABLE 4.1   Cost of conformance and nonconformance

Conformance Costs	Nonconformance Costs
Prevention costs	Internal failure costs
Appraisal costs	External failure costs

Quality must be planned into the project, not inspected after the fact, to ensure that the product or service meets stakeholders' expectations.

Decision Making   Decision making for quality planning purposes may include multicriteria decision analysis, where criteria are prioritized and weighted and then applied to issues and alternatives are identified. This can help to develop quality metrics.

Data Representation   There are several data representation techniques that are used as part of the Plan Quality Management process. Examples noted within the *PMBOK® Guide* include the following:

> **Flowcharts** show the relationships between the process steps. In regard to quality planning, flowcharting helps the project team identify quality issues before they occur.
>
> **Logical data models** are a way of depicting an organization's data as a visual representation. This helps the project team identify where quality issues can arise when it comes to data integrity or other issues.
>
> **Matrix diagrams** help identify relationships between multiple factors, particularly when several options or alternatives are available.
>
> **Mind mapping** can be used to group and organize thoughts and facts; it can also be used in conjunction with brainstorming.

Test and Inspection Planning   As part of developing the quality plan, the project team will determine how to test and inspect the product, service, or deliverable to ensure that it meets the specified needs of stakeholders.

Meetings   Meetings are used by the project team to assemble the quality management plan using a mixture of the tools and techniques described earlier in this section.

Quality theorists and quality techniques are responsible for the rise of the quality management movement and the theories behind the cost of quality. Figure 4.7 highlights four quality theorists, along with their ideas, with whom you should be very familiar for the exam.

FIGURE 4.7   Quality theorists

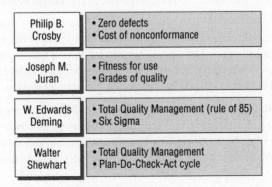

Philip B. Crosby   Philip B. Crosby is known for devising the zero defects practice, which means to do it right the first time. If the defect is prevented from occurring in the first place, costs are lower, conformance to requirements is easily met, and the cost measurement for quality becomes the cost of nonconformance rather than the cost of rework.

Joseph M. Juran   Joseph M. Juran is known for the fitness for use premise, which means the stakeholders' and customers' expectations are met or exceeded and reflects their views of quality. Juran proposed that there could be grades of quality.

 Grade is a category for products or services that are of the same type but have differing technical characteristics. *Quality* describes how well the product or service (or characteristics of the product or service) fulfills the requirements. *Low quality* is usually not an acceptable condition, whereas *low grade* might be.

W. Edwards Deming   W. Edwards Deming suggested that as much as 85 percent of the cost of quality is management's responsibility, which came to be known as the 85 percent rule, or rule of 85. He believed that workers need to be shown what acceptable quality is and that they need to be provided with the right training so that quality and continuous improvement become natural elements of the working environment. Deming was also a major contributor to the modern quality movement and theories, which emphasize a more proactive approach to quality management (prevention over inspection). For example, he documented 14 points that summarize how management can transform their organization to one that is effective. This and his body of work have been credited for launching the Total Quality Management (TQM) movement. He also popularized the Plan-Do-Check-Act cycle, also referred to as the Deming Cycle, which focuses on continuous improvement.

Six Sigma is a measurement-based strategy that focuses on process improvement and variation reduction by applying Six Sigma methodologies to the project. There are two Six Sigma methodologies:

- DMADV (define, measure, analyze, design, and verify) is used to develop new processes or products at the Six Sigma level.
- DMAIC (define, measure, analyze, improve, and control) is used to improve existing processes or products.

Walter Shewhart   According to some sources, Walter Shewhart is the grandfather of statistical quality control and the Plan-Do-Check-Act model, which was further popularized by Deming. Shewhart developed statistical tools to examine when a corrective action must be applied to a process. He is also known for the control chart techniques.

Kaizen Approach   The Kaizen approach—*kaizen* means improvement in Japanese—is a technique in which all project team members and managers should be constantly watching for quality improvement opportunities. The Kaizen approach states that the quality of the people should be improved first and then the quality of the products or service.

Outputs of Plan Quality Management

There are four outputs of the Plan Quality Management process:

- Quality management plan
- Quality metrics
- Project management plan updates
- Project documents updates

Quality Management Plan   The project manager in cooperation with the project staff writes the quality management plan. The plan, which is part of the overarching project management plan, should be based on the project scope and requirements to successfully prevent defects, thus reducing the cost of quality.

The quality management plan includes the following elements:

- Quality standards and objectives, along with a description of how the project management team will carry out the quality policy
- Quality roles and responsibilities, as well as resources needed to carry out the quality plan
- Quality tools used for the project
- List of project deliverables and processes that might go through a quality review
- All the processes and procedures the project team and organization should use to satisfy quality requirements, including the following items:
  - Quality control
  - Quality assurance techniques
  - Continuous improvement processes

Quality Metrics   A quality metric, also known as operational definition, describes what is being measured and how it will be measured during the Control Quality process. Examples of quality metrics provided by the *PMBOK® Guide* include percentage of tasks completed on time, cost performance measured by CPI, failure rate, number of defects identified per day, and errors found per line of code.

Project Management Plan Updates   Updates made to the project management plan as a result of carrying out this process include the risk management plan and scope baseline.

Project Documents Updates   The following project documents may need to be updated:

- Stakeholder register
- Risk register
- Requirements traceability matrix
- Lessons learned register

As with previous knowledge areas, the Quality Management Knowledge Area has other processes not included in the Planning process group: Manage Quality is in the Executing process group, and Control Quality is in the Monitoring and Controlling process group. Look for these processes in Chapters 7 and 8 of this book.

Exam Essentials

Be able to identify the benefits of meeting quality requirements. The benefits of meeting quality requirements include increased stakeholder satisfaction, lower costs, higher productivity, and less rework, and they are discovered during the Plan Quality process.

Be able to define the cost of quality (COQ). The COQ is the total cost to produce the product or service of the project according to the quality standards. These costs include all the work necessary to meet the product requirements for quality. The three costs associated with cost of quality are prevention, appraisal, and failure costs (also known as cost of poor quality).

Be able to name four people associated with COQ and some of the techniques they helped establish. They are Crosby, Juran, Deming, and Shewhart. Some of the techniques they helped to establish are TQM, Six Sigma, cost of quality, and continuous improvement. The Kaizen approach concerns continuous improvement and specifies that people should be improved first.

Be able to name the tools and techniques of the Plan Quality Management process. The tools and techniques of the Plan Quality Management process consist of expert judgment, data gathering, data analysis, decision making, data representation, test and inspection planning, and meetings.

Bringing the Processes Together

This chapter covered additional information within the Planning process group, and there is still more to come!

With this additional information in mind, let's go back and review what you've learned thus far about each of the project management Knowledge Areas within this chapter. Remember that Chapters 5 and 6 will continue to cover additional material that belongs to the Planning process group.

Project Cost Management Knowledge Area Review

Figure 4.8 shows the key process steps for creating the project budget. The scope baseline is necessary for determining estimates for the cost of each activity. The cost management plan comes into play and governs how the activity costs are estimated and how the project budget is created.

FIGURE 4.8   Project Cost Management Knowledge Area process interaction

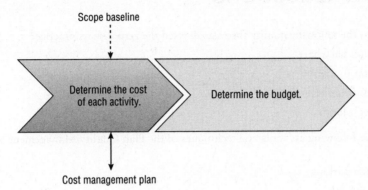

Project Quality Management Knowledge Area Review

The single planning step within the Project Quality Management Knowledge Area results in several key items in the quality management processes. Figure 4.9 shows how the information resulting from scope, cost, time, and risk planning processes is necessary for carefully planning project quality. This first step in defining project quality produces the following:

- Method for planning, carrying out, and controlling quality activities
- Metrics used to measure project quality
- Methods the project management team can use to approach and then carry out quality management activities

FIGURE 4.9   Project Quality Management Knowledge Area process interaction

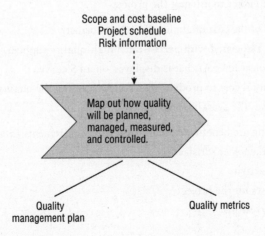

Review Questions

1. Which of the following quality theorists devised the zero defects practice?

   A. Walter Shewhart

   B. Philip B. Crosby

   C. W. Edwards Deming

   D. Joseph Juran

2. All of the following are tools and techniques of the Plan Quality Management process *except*:

   A. Benchmarking

   B. Flowcharts

   C. Meetings

   D. Operational definition

3. What is the *correct* definition of a critical path task?

   A. A critical path task must be done before all other project activities.

   B. A critical path task does not affect the project schedule.

   C. A critical path task is a project activity with schedule flexibility.

   D. A critical path task is a project activity with zero float.

4. What is the cost baseline?

   A. The total budget allocated to the project

   B. The authorized, time-phased cost of the project

   C. The source of all project funding

   D. The barrier to entry to attempt the project

5. Which definition of the cost of quality (COQ) is correct?

   A. COQ is cost associated with parts from a high-quality supplier.

   B. COQ is a project forecast that is displayed on an S curve.

   C. COQ is the total cost to produce the product meeting the quality standards.

   D. COQ increases the overall budget of the project.

6. All of the following are benefits of meeting quality requirements *except*:

   A. Increased stakeholder satisfaction

   B. Higher productivity

   C. Increased costs for the project

   D. Reduction in rework

7. Megan is a project manager for a data center consolidation project. During a recent planning meeting, she collected estimates for how long it would take to configure all of the switches within the new location. Ron, who will be the lead for performing the activity, noted that if all goes well, it would take the team 15 hours, although he noted most likely closer to 20 hours. In a worst case, it would take the team 50 hours, provided that multiple issues arise. Based on Ron's estimates, what is the estimate that Megan will use as the duration of the activity if she were to calculate it based on a beta distribution?

   A. 24 hours

   B. 20 hours

   C. 28 hours

   D. Insufficient information

8. Using the table provided below, calculate the late start of activity C.

Activity Name	Predecessor	Duration
A	None	5
B	A	2
C	A	6
D	A	3
E	D	1

   A. 11

   B. 10

   C. 6

   D. 5

9. Using the table provided below, calculate the early finish of activity D.

Activity Name	Predecessor	Duration
A	None	5
B	A	2
C	A	6
D	A	3
E	B, C, D	1

   A. 6

   B. 8

   C. 3

   D. 11

10. Using the table provided below, calculate the duration of the critical path.

Activity Name	Predecessor	Duration
A	None	5
B	A	2
C	A	6
D	A	3
E	B, C, D	1

A. 8
B. 24
C. 12
D. 6

Chapter

5

Planning Project Resource, Communication, Procurement, Change, and Risk Management

THE PMP® EXAM CONTENT FROM THE PLANNING PERFORMANCE DOMAIN COVERED IN THIS CHAPTER INCLUDES THE FOLLOWING:

✓ Develop the human resource management plan by defining the roles and responsibilities of the project team members in order to create a project organizational structure and provide guidance regarding how resources will be assigned and managed.

✓ Develop the communications management plan based on the project organizational structure and stakeholder requirements in order to define and manage the flow of project information.

✓ Develop the procurement management plan based on the project scope, budget, and schedule in order to ensure that the required project resources will be available.

✓ Develop the change management plan by defining how changes will be addressed and controlled in order to track and manage change.

✓ Plan for risk management by developing a risk management plan; identifying, analyzing, and prioritizing project risk; creating the risk register; and defining risk response strategies in order to manage uncertainty and opportunity throughout the project life cycle.

In this chapter, we continue to address content that belongs to the Planning process group and related exam domain. Specifically, we will address the following Knowledge Areas: Project Resource Management, Project Communications Management, Project Procurement Management, and Project Risk Management.

Planning is by far the largest process group when it comes to the number of project management processes. In the chapter that follows, Chapter 6, we will finalize our review of the Planning process group.

The process names, inputs, tools and techniques, outputs, and descriptions of the project management process groups and related materials and figures in this chapter are based on content from *A Guide to the Project Management Body of Knowledge (PMBOK ® Guide), Sixth Edition* (PMI®, 2017).

Developing a Resource Management Plan

The project manager creates a resource management plan by carrying out a process called Plan Resource Management. Through this process, roles and responsibilities of the project team members are defined and the strategies for using and managing the project team, equipment, and inventory are documented. The high-level purpose of the plan itself is to create an effective project organization structure.

The Plan Resource Management process is responsible for defining how to estimate, acquire, manage, and use physical and human resources; it documents the roles and responsibilities of individuals or groups for various project elements and then documents the reporting relationships for each. Reporting relationships can be assigned to groups as well as to individuals, and the groups or individuals might be internal or external to the organization or a combination of both. This process will result in the creation of the resource management plan, which considers factors such as the availability of resources, skill levels, training needs, and more.

For more detailed information on the Plan Resource Management process, see Chapter 7, "Planning Project Resources," of *PMP®: Project Management Professional Exam Study Guide, Ninth Edition* (Sybex, 2017).

Figure 5.1 shows the inputs, tools and techniques, and outputs of the Plan Resource Management process.

FIGURE 5.1 Plan Resource Management process

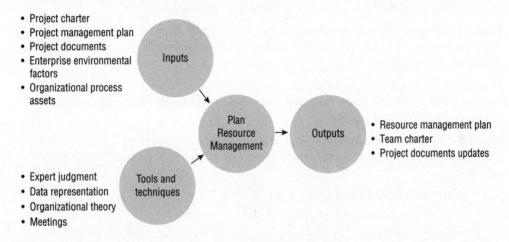

- Project charter
- Project management plan
- Project documents
- Enterprise environmental factors
- Organizational process assets

Inputs

Plan Resource Management

Outputs

- Resource management plan
- Team charter
- Project documents updates

- Expert judgment
- Data representation
- Organizational theory
- Meetings

Tools and techniques

Inputs of Plan Resource Management

Inputs of the Plan Resource Management process you should know are as follows:

- Project charter

- Project management plan

- Project documents

- Enterprise environmental factors

- Organizational process assets

Project Charter   The project charter includes high-level details about the project, which can provide useful information for establishing how resources will be identified and managed. Information utilized from within the charter can include key stakeholder list, summary milestones, any preapproved or assigned resources, and a high-level description of the project.

Project Management Plan   The resource management plan borrows several elements from the project management plan, including but not limited to the following:

- Quality management plan that aids in identifying resources needed for quality activities

- Scope baseline, which contains the deliverables that will be produced and then managed

- The project life cycle and the processes that will be applied to each phase
- Definition of how work will be performed to meet project objectives
- A change management plan that documents the monitoring and controlling of changes
- A configuration management plan that documents how configuration management will be performed
- The maintenance of project baselines
- Needs and methods of communicating with stakeholders

Project Documents   Resources are needed to perform and complete the activities outlined in the project schedule. During the Plan Resource Management process, these resources are defined in further detail.

In addition to the schedule, other project documents that are useful in planning how resources will be identified and managed include the requirements documentation, risk register, and stakeholder register.

Enterprise Environmental Factors   Enterprise environmental factors play a key role in determining resource roles and responsibilities. The following is a list of factors that are used:

- Organizational factors
- Existing human resources and marketplace conditions
- Personnel policies
- Technical factors
- Interpersonal factors
- Location and logistics
- Political factors
- Organizational structures
- Collective bargaining agreements
- Economic conditions

Organizational Process Assets   The following elements of the organizational process assets are used in this process:

- Organizational processes and standardized role descriptions
- Safety and security policies
- Templates and checklists
- Historical information
- Escalation procedures for handling issues within the team

Tools and Techniques of Plan Resource Management

The following are tools and techniques of the Plan Resource Management process that you should be familiar with:

- Expert judgment
- Data representation
- Organizational theory
- Meetings

Expert Judgment   Expert judgment helps inform the resource management plan as follows:

- Listing the preliminary requirements for the required skills
- Assessing the roles required for the project based on standardized role descriptions
- Determining number of resources and level of effort needed to meet project objectives
- Determining reporting relationships
- Providing guidelines for lead time required for staffing
- Identifying risks associated with staff acquisition, retention, and release plans
- Using programs for complying with contracts, with both government and unions

Data Representation   Charts are a data representation technique that can be useful in documenting the resource plan. Information is presented in the following types of organization charts and position descriptions:

Hierarchical Charts   Hierarchical charts, like a WBS, are designed in a top-down format. Two types of hierarchical charts that can be used are OBS and RBS:

- Organization breakdown structure (OBS), which displays departments, work units, or teams in an organization and their respective work packages
- Resource breakdown structure (RBS), which breaks down the work of the project according to the types of resources needed

Matrix-Based Charts   Matrix-based charts are used to show the type of resource and the responsibility that resource has in the project. You can use a couple of types of matrix-based charts:

- Responsibility assignment matrix (RAM) is displayed as a chart with resource names listed in each column and project phases or WBS elements listed as the rows. Indicators in the intersections show where the resources are needed.
- A RACI chart is a type of RAM. Table 5.1 shows a sample portion of an RACI chart for a software development team. In this example, the RACI chart shows the roles and expectations of each participant.

TABLE 5.1 Sample RAM

	Olga	Rae	Jantira	Nirmit
Design	R	A	C	C
Test	I	R	C	A
Implement	C	I	R	A

R = Responsible, A = Accountable, C = Consult, I = Inform

The letters in the acronym RACI are the designations shown in Table 5.1.

R = Responsible for performing the work

A = Accountable, the one who is responsible for producing the deliverable or work package and approving or signing off on the work

C = Consult, someone who has input to the work or decisions

I = Inform, someone who must be informed of the decisions or results

Text-Oriented Formats   Text-oriented formats are used when there is a significant amount of detail to record. These are also called position descriptions or role-responsibility-authority forms. Text-oriented formats typically provide the following information:

- Role
- Responsibility
- Authority of the resource

Organizational Theory   Organizational theory refers to all the theories that attempt to explain what makes people, teams, and work units behave.

Meetings   Meetings help in the planning of human resources and allow team members to reach consensus on the human resource management plan.

Outputs of Plan Resource Management

There are three outputs of the Plan Resource Management process:

- Resource management plan
- Team charter
- Project documents updates

Resource Management Plan   The resource management plan documents how human and physical resources should be defined, obtained or staffed, managed, controlled, and released from the project when their activities are complete. This plan is meant to clearly outline the roles and responsibilities of the project team and to create an effective project organization structure. As a result, guidance is provided on how resources are to be used and managed throughout the project. In some cases, the resource management plan may be broken out into two separate plans—one for managing human resources, sometimes called the team management plan, and another for managing the physical resources.

This output captures the methods for identifying, quantifying, and acquiring resources, as well as the following additional components:

Roles and Responsibilities   The roles and responsibilities component includes the list of roles and responsibilities for the project team. It can take the form of the RAM or RACI, or the roles and responsibilities can be recorded in text format. The following key elements should be included in the roles and responsibilities documentation:

> *Role* describes which part of the project the individuals or teams are accountable for. This should also include a description of authority levels, responsibilities, and what work is not included as part of the role.

> *Authority* describes the amount of authority the resource has to make decisions, dictate direction, and approve the work.

> *Responsibility* describes the work required to complete the project activities.

> *Competency* describes the skills and ability needed to perform the project activities.

Project Organizational Charts   The project organizational charts display project team members and their reporting relationships in the project.

Project Team Resource Management   The resource management plan documents how and when resources are introduced to the project and the criteria for releasing them. The plan should be updated throughout the project. The following elements should be considered and included in the plan:

- Staff acquisition describes how team members are acquired, where they're located, and the costs for specific skills and expertise.

- Resource calendars describe the time frames in which the resources will be needed on the project and when the recruitment process should begin.

- Staff release plan describes how project team members will be released at the end of their assignment, including reassignment procedures.

- Training needs describe any training plans needed for team members who don't have the required skills or abilities to perform project tasks.

- Recognition and rewards describe the systems used to reward and reinforce desired behavior.

- Compliance details regulations that must be met and any human resource policies the organization has in place that deal with compliance issues.

- Safety includes safety policies and procedures that are applicable to the project or industry and should be included in the staffing management plan.

Don't forget that the Project Resource Management Knowledge Area has five more processes: Estimate Activity Resources, Acquire Resources, Develop Team, Manage Team, and Control Resources. We've already reviewed Estimate Activity Resources in Chapter 3. Look for a discussion of the other processes in Chapter 7 when we discuss the Executing process group.

Team Charter   According to the *PMBOK® Guide*, the team charter documents the team values, agreements, and operating guidelines. It typically includes the following:

- Team values
- Team agreements
- Communication and meeting guidelines
- Conflict resolution process

Project Documents Updates   The assumption log and risk register might require updates as a result of carrying out this process.

Exam Essentials

Be able to define the purpose of the Plan Resource Management process.   Plan Resource Management involves defining how to estimate, acquire, manage, and use resources; it is where roles and responsibilities for the project are determined.

Developing a Communications Management Plan

Communications plays an important role in effectively and efficiently carrying out a project—with successful results! Like other plans, the communications management plan should be as detailed as needed for the project at hand and should be based on the project organization structure and stakeholder requirements. This plan is responsible for managing the flow of project information and is created out of the Plan Communications Management process.

Keep in mind that, according to PMI®, a good project manager spends up to 90 percent of their time communicating. Therefore, the communications management plan should be well thought out and clearly documented.

The Plan Communications Management process involves determining the communication needs of the stakeholders by defining the types of information needed, the format for communicating the information, how often it's distributed, and who prepares it. All of this is documented in the communications management plan, which is an output of this process. The total number of existing communication channels is also calculated in this process.

Figure 5.2 shows the inputs, tools and techniques, and outputs of the Plan Communications Management process.

FIGURE 5.2   Plan Communications Management process

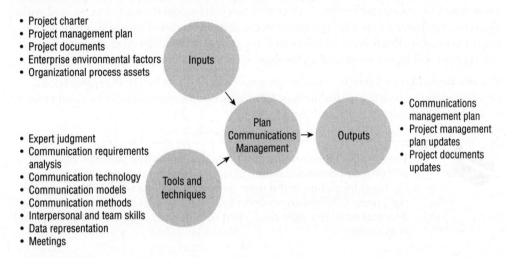

- Project charter
- Project management plan
- Project documents
- Enterprise environmental factors
- Organizational process assets

Inputs

- Expert judgment
- Communication requirements analysis
- Communication technology
- Communication models
- Communication methods
- Interpersonal and team skills
- Data representation
- Meetings

Tools and techniques

Plan Communications Management → Outputs

- Communications management plan
- Project management plan updates
- Project documents updates

For more detailed information on the Plan Communications Management process, see Chapter 5 of *PMP®: Project Management Professional Exam Study Guide, Ninth Edition* (Sybex, 2017).

Inputs of Plan Communications Management

Know the following inputs of the Plan Communications Management process:

- Project charter
- Project management plan
- Project documents
- Enterprise environmental factors
- Organizational process assets

Project Charter   The project charter captures the list of key stakeholders, which can be useful in planning out how communications are to occur throughout the project.

Project Management Plan   The project management plan will provide direction on how information on the project will be executed, monitored, controlled, and closed. In particular, the resource management plan and stakeholder engagement plan should be referenced.

Project Documents   The stakeholder register is a list of all the project stakeholders and contains additional information, including their potential influence on the project and their classifications. This and the requirements documentation are key project documents that should be referenced when developing the communications management plan.

Enterprise Environmental Factors   All enterprise environmental factors can be used within the Plan Communications Management process. Special attention should be given to the organizational structure and culture as well as external stakeholder requirements. This information will be key to managing the flow of the project's information.

Organizational Process Assets   All the elements described previously as organizational process assets can be used in this process. Particular consideration should be given to lessons learned and historical information.

The *PMBOK® Guide* notes that there is a difference between effective and efficient communication. Effective communication refers to providing the information in the right format for the intended audience at the right time. Efficient communication refers to providing the appropriate information at the right time—that is, only the information that's needed at the time.

Tools and Techniques of Plan Communications Management

The Plan Communications Management process includes the following tools and techniques:

- Expert judgment
- Communication requirements analysis
- Communication technology
- Communication models
- Communication methods
- Interpersonal and team skills
- Data representation
- Meetings

Expert Judgment   Tapping into experts when developing any of the subsidiary plans is important. In this process, experts can help properly shape how efficient and effective communication should occur for the project; they also participate actively in utilizing other tools and techniques used in this process.

Communication Requirements Analysis   Communication requirements analysis involves analyzing and determining the communication needs of the project stakeholders. According to the *PMBOK® Guide*, there are several sources of information you can examine to help determine these needs:

- Company and departmental organizational charts

- Stakeholder responsibility relationships

- Other departments and business units involved in the project

- The number of resources involved in the project and where they're located in relation to project activities

- Internal needs that the organization may need to know about the project

- External needs that organizations such as the media, government, or industry groups might have that require communication updates

- Stakeholder information (documented in the stakeholder register and stakeholder management strategy outputs of Identify Stakeholders)

The preceding list goes through analysis to make certain that information that is valuable to the stakeholders is being supplied. It is important to know the number of communication channels, also known as lines of communication, that exist. Figure 5.3 shows an example of a network model with six stakeholders included.

FIGURE 5.3   Network communication model

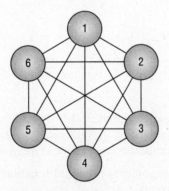

Nodes = participants
Lines = lines of communication
between participants

The nodes are the participants, and the lines show the connection between them all. The formula for calculating the lines of communication is as follows (where *n* represents total participants):

$$\frac{n \times (n-1)}{2}$$

Let's consider six participants. When you plug the total participants into the formula, the result is a total of 15 communication channels, as noted in the following example:

$$\frac{6 \times (6-1)}{2} = 15$$

Day of the Exam

This is another formula that would be helpful to add to scratch paper before you begin the exam:

Lines of communication $= \dfrac{n \times (n-1)}{2}$

Communication Technology Communication technology examines the methods (or technology) used to communicate the information to, from, and among the stakeholders. This tool and technique examines the technology elements that might affect project communications.

The following are examples of methods used when communicating:

- Written
- Spoken
- Email
- Formal status reports
- Meetings
- Online databases
- Online schedules

Communication Models Communication models depict how information is transmitted from the sender and how it's received by the receiver. According to the *PMBOK® Guide*, the key components of a communication model are as follows:

Encode Encoding the message means to put information or thoughts into a language that the receiver will understand.

Message and Feedback Message The result or output of the encoding.

Medium The method used to communicate, such as written, oral, or email.

Noise Anything that keeps the message from being either transmitted or understood.

Decode The receiver translates the information that was sent by the sender.

The sender is responsible for encoding the message, selecting the medium, and decoding the feedback message. The receiver is responsible for decoding the original message from the sender and encoding and sending the feedback message. Figure 5.4 shows this dynamic through the basic communication model.

FIGURE 5.4 Communication model

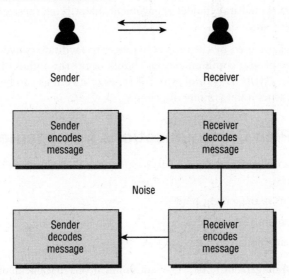

Communication Methods   Communication methods refer to how the project information is shared among the stakeholders. According to the *PMBOK® Guide*, there are three classifications of communication methods:

Interactive Communication   Interactive communication involves multidirectional communication where two or more parties must exchange thoughts or ideas. This method includes videoconferencing, phone or conference calls, and meetings.

Push Communications   Push communications refers to sending information to intended receivers. It includes methods such as letters, memos, reports, emails, voicemails, and so on. This method ensures that the communication was sent but is not concerned with whether it was actually received or understood by the intended receivers.

Pull Communications   The likely recipients of the information access the information themselves using methods such as websites, e-learning sites, knowledge repositories, shared network drives, and so on.

Interpersonal and Team Skills   When planning communications, there are various interpersonal and team skills that can be used:

- Communication styles assessment, where the communication style of various stakeholders is considered
- Political awareness, where the project environment is considered and planned against
- Cultural awareness, where stakeholder cultures, as well as the organizational culture, are considered

Data Representation   Stakeholder engagement assessment matrices can be useful in identifying gaps in the expected stakeholder engagement. Identifying these gaps early and iteratively can help fill or reduce them.

Meetings   Meetings are used by the project manager to facilitate conversations with the project team on how project communications should occur throughout the life of the project. According to the *PMBOK® Guide*, various types of meetings can be used, many of which help resolve issues and facilitate decisions.

Outputs of Plan Communications Management

The following three outputs result from carrying out the Plan Communications Management process:

- Communications management plan
- Project management plan updates
- Project documents updates

Communications Management Plan   The communications management plan documents the following:

- Types of information needs the stakeholders have
- When the information should be distributed
- How the information will be delivered

According to the *PMBOK® Guide*, the communications management plan typically describes the following elements:

- The communication requirements of each stakeholder or stakeholder group
- Purpose for communication
- The information to be communicated
- Frequency of communications, including time frames for distribution
- Name of the person responsible for communicating information, the individual that authorizes the communication, and recipients
- Individuals assigned to communications-related activities
- Format of the communication, communication flow charts, and method of transmission
- Any communication constraint, including those resulting from laws, technology, or policies
- Method for updating the communications management plan
- Glossary of common terms

The information that will be shared with stakeholders and the distribution methods are based on the following items:

- Needs of the stakeholders
- Project complexity
- Organizational policies

Project Management Plan Updates   The communications management plan may trigger updates to any other plan that exists.

Project Documents Updates   The following updates may be required as a result of performing this process:

- Project schedule
- Stakeholder register

Don't forget that the Project Communications Management Knowledge Area has two more processes: Manage Communications (a part of the Executing process group) and Monitor Communications (a part of the Monitoring and Controlling process group). Look for a discussion of these processes in Chapter 7 and Chapter 8.

Exam Essentials

Be able to describe the purpose of the communications management plan.   The communications management plan determines the communication needs of the stakeholders. It documents what information will be distributed, how it will be distributed, to whom it will be distributed, and the timing of the distribution.

Developing a Procurement Management Plan

In many cases, some resources will need to be obtained externally (meaning outside of the project's organization). When this is the case, a procurement management plan will be needed. This plan is created out of the Plan Procurement Management process, which is also responsible for producing other key procurement documents.

The procurement management plan should be based on the project's scope and schedule and is responsible for guiding the procurement-related processes and ensuring that the required project resources will be available when and as needed.

Plan Procurement Management is a process of identifying what goods or services will be purchased from outside the organization. This process addresses the make-or-buy decision and when acquired goods or services will be needed. By the end of this process, a procurement management plan will have been created, make-or-buy decisions will have been made, and a contract statement of work will have been drafted.

Figure 5.5 shows the inputs, tools and techniques, and outputs of the Plan Procurement Management process.

FIGURE 5.5   Plan Procurement Management process

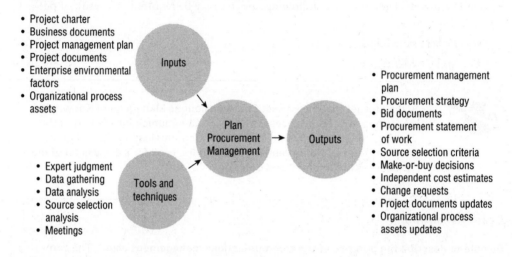

- Project charter
- Business documents
- Project management plan
- Project documents
- Enterprise environmental factors
- Organizational process assets

Inputs

Plan Procurement Management

Outputs

- Expert judgment
- Data gathering
- Data analysis
- Source selection analysis
- Meetings

Tools and techniques

- Procurement management plan
- Procurement strategy
- Bid documents
- Procurement statement of work
- Source selection criteria
- Make-or-buy decisions
- Independent cost estimates
- Change requests
- Project documents updates
- Organizational process assets updates

For more detailed information on the Plan Procurement Management process, see Chapter 7 of *PMP®: Project Management Professional Exam Study Guide, Ninth Edition* (Sybex, 2017).

Inputs of Plan Procurement Management

You should be familiar with these inputs to the Plan Procurement Management process:

- Project charter

- Business documents

- Project management plan

- Project documents

- Enterprise environmental factors

- Organizational process assets

Project Charter   The project charter provides a high-level summary of the project as well as other information that may aid the procurement planning activities, such as a summary milestone and any preapproved financial resources.

Business Documents   Business documents referenced as part of this process include the business case and benefits management plan. The business case helps ensure alignment of the procurement strategy, while the benefits management plan may end up driving some of the procurement details, such as procurement dates and contract language.

Project Management Plan   The Plan Procurement Management process uses several components of the project management plan:

- Scope management plan, which documents how the scope performed by contractors will be managed.

- Quality management plan, which may reveal industry standards and codes impacting the project that have already been documented.

- Resource management plan, which notes how purchased or leased resources will be managed.

- Scope baseline, which contains the project scope statement, WBS, and WBS dictionary. These may be useful in drafting the statement of work and terms of reference.

Project Documents   Multiple documents are used to plan procurements, including the following:

Milestone List   The milestone list is key in determining when deliverables are due by sellers.

Project Team Assignments   Team assignments also capture the skills and capabilities of assigned team members as well as their availability to participate in the procurement process.

Requirements Documentation   The requirements documentation established the details of the project requirements. For a more detailed description, see "Outputs of Collect Requirements" in Chapter 3.

Requirements Traceability Matrix   The requirements traceability matrix links product requirements to the deliverables that satisfy them.

Resource Requirements   The availability of the assigned resources affects the procurement process and will aid in make-or-buy decisions.

Risk Register   The risk register guides the project team in determining the types of services or goods needed for risk management. It also identifies which procurement decisions are driven as a result of a risk response, such as acquiring insurance or other services to transfer liability to a third party.

Stakeholder Register   The stakeholder register shows details on the participants in the project and their interest in the outcomes.

Enterprise Environmental Factors   Marketplace conditions are the key element of enterprise environmental factors used within this process. Other factors include products, services, and results available in the marketplace; unique local requirements; any contract management systems or financial accounting and contract payment systems that exist within the organization, as well as legal advice; and industry-specific typical terms and conditions.

Organizational Process Assets   The organization's guidelines, policies, and procedures (including any procurement policies and guidelines) are the elements of the organizational process assets used in this process. Legal contractual relationships are another component to organizational process assets for the Plan Procurement Management process and include any existing preapproved seller lists. Contracts will generally fall into three general categories: fixed-price, cost reimbursable, and time and materials.

A contract is a compulsory agreement between two or more parties and is used to acquire products or services from outside the organization. Contracts are enforceable by law and require an offer and an acceptance, with money typically exchanged for goods or services. As reflected in Figure 5.6, there are different types of contracts for different purposes.

FIGURE 5.6   Contract types

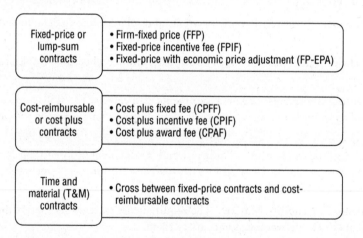

The *PMBOK® Guide* divides contracts into three categories:

Fixed-Price or Lump-Sum Contracts   Fixed-price contracts (also referred to as lump-sum contracts) either can set a specific, firm price for the goods or services rendered (known as a firm fixed-price contract) or can include incentives for meeting or exceeding certain contract deliverables. There are three types of fixed-price contracts:

- In a firm fixed-price (FFP) contract, the buyer and seller agree on a well-defined deliverable for a set price. In this kind of contract, the biggest risk is borne by the seller. The seller assumes the risks of increasing costs, nonperformance, or other problems.

- Fixed-price incentive fee (FPIF) contracts are another type of fixed-price contract. The difference is that the contract includes an incentive—or bonus—for early completion or for some other agreed-upon performance criterion that meets or exceeds contract specifications. Some of the risk is borne by the buyer as opposed to the firm fixed-price contract, where most of the risk is borne by the seller.

- A fixed-price with economic price adjustment (FP-EPA) contract allows for adjustments due to changes in economic conditions, like cost increases or decreases, inflation, and so on. These contracts are typically used when the project spans many years. This type of contract protects both the buyer and the seller from economic conditions that are outside their control.

Cost-Reimbursable or Cost Plus Contracts   With cost-reimbursable contracts, the allowable costs associated with producing the goods or services are charged to the buyer. All the costs the seller takes on during the project are charged back to the buyer; thus, the seller is reimbursed. Cost-reimbursable contracts carry the highest risk for the buyer because the total costs are uncertain and are used most often when the project scope contains a lot of uncertainty or for projects that have large investments early in the project life. The following list includes three types of cost-reimbursable contracts:

- Cost plus fixed fee (CPFF) contracts charge back all allowable project costs to the seller and include a fixed fee upon completion of the contract. The fee is always firm in this kind of contract, but the costs are variable. The seller doesn't necessarily have a lot of motivation to control costs with this type of contract.

- Cost plus incentive fee (CPIF) is the type of contract in which the buyer reimburses the seller for the seller's allowable costs and includes an incentive for meeting or exceeding the performance criteria laid out in the contract. A possibility of shared savings between the seller and buyer exists if performance criteria are exceeded.

- Cost plus award fee (CPAF) is the riskiest of the cost plus contracts for the seller. In a CPAF contract, the seller will recoup all the costs expended during the project, but the award fee portion is subject to the sole discretion of the buyer.

Time and Material (T&M) Contracts   T&M contracts are a cross between fixed-price and cost-reimbursable contracts. The full amount of the material costs is not known at the time the contract is awarded. T&M contracts are most often used when human resources with specific skills are needed and when the scope of work needed for the project can be quickly defined. Time and material contracts include the following characteristics:

- This type of contract resembles a cost-reimbursable contract because the costs will continue to grow during the contract's life and are reimbursable to the contractor. The buyer bears the biggest risk in this type of contract.

- This type of contract resembles fixed-price contracts when unit rates are used. Unit rates might be used to preset the rates of certain elements or portions of the project.

The project manager and the project team will be responsible for coordinating all the organizational interfaces for the project, including technical, human resource, purchasing, and finance.

Tools and Techniques of Plan Procurement Management

Know these five tools and techniques of the Plan Procurement Management process:

- Expert judgment
- Data gathering
- Data analysis
- Source selection analysis
- Meetings

Expert Judgment   Expert judgment can be used within the Plan Procurement Management process to aid in procurement and purchasing activities, to determine what contract type or documents are needed, and to provide information on regulation or compliance items that impact procurements.

Data Gathering   With market research, an examination is conducted of industry- and vendor-specific capabilities. This effort can be conducted with information obtained at industry conferences, by evaluating online reviews, and by using a variety of sources to identify market capabilities.

Data Analysis   Make-or-buy analysis is concerned with whether it is more cost-effective to buy or lease the products and services or more cost-effective for the organization to produce the goods and services needed for the project. Costs should include both direct costs and indirect costs. Other considerations in make-or-buy analysis are as follows:

- Capacity issues
- Skills
- Availability
- Trade secrets

 Make-or-buy analysis is considered a general management technique and concludes with the decision to do one or the other.

Source Selection Analysis   According to the *PMBOK® Guide*, the competing demands and priorities of the project should first be evaluated before selection criteria or methods can be determined. Typical selection methods are as follows:

- Least cost
- Qualifications only
- Quality-based / technical proposal score

- Quality and cost-based
- Sole source
- Fixed budget

Meetings   As a complement to the effort of market research, meetings with potential bidders may be conducted to help augment the interchange of information. This approach can be mutually beneficial to both the purchaser and the supplier.

Outputs of Plan Procurement Management

Know the following outputs of the Plan Procurement Management process:

- Procurement management plan
- Procurement strategy
- Bid documents
- Procurement statement of work
- Source selection criteria
- Make-or-buy decisions
- Independent cost estimates
- Change requests
- Project documents updates
- Organizational process assets updates

Procurement Management Plan   The procurement management plan details how the procurement process will be managed. According to the *PMBOK® Guide*, it includes the following information:

- Types of contracts to use
- Timetable of procurement activities
- Authority of the project team
- How the procurement process will be integrated with other project processes
- Where to find standard procurement documents (provided your organization uses standard documents)
- How many vendors or contractors are involved and how they'll be managed
- How the procurement process will be coordinated with other project processes, such as performance reporting and scheduling
- How the constraints and assumptions might be impacted by purchasing
- How multiple vendors or contractors will be managed
- Coordination of purchasing lead times with the development of the project schedule
- Schedule dates that are determined in each contract

- Identification of prequalified sellers (if known)
- Risk management issues
- Procurement metrics for managing contracts and for evaluating sellers
- Directions to sellers regarding the development and maintenance of the WBS
- Setting the form and format of statements of work
- Selection of prequalified sellers to be used, if there are any
- Identification of procurement metrics to be used to manage contracts and evaluate sellers
- Prequalified sellers

As with other plans, the procurement management plan can be highly detailed or broadly stated and can be formal or informal based on the needs of the project.

Procurement Strategy   After procurement decisions are made, a procurement strategy document is pulled together and documents the following:

- Delivery methods
- Contract payment types
- Procurement phases

Bid Documents   Procurement documents are used to solicit vendors and suppliers to bid on procurement needs. These documents are prepared by the buyer to ensure as accurate and complete a response as possible from all potential bidders. Examples of procurement documents include the following:

- Request for proposal (RFP)
- Request for information (RFI)
- Invitation for bid (IFB)
- Request for quotation (RFQ)

Procurement documents typically include the following information:

- Clear description of the work requested
- Contract SOW
- Explanation of how sellers should format and submit their responses
- Any special provisions or contractual needs

The following words are used during the procurement process:

- When the decision will be based primarily on price, the words *bid* and *quotation* are used, as in IFB or RFQ.
- When considerations other than price (such as technology or specific approaches to the project) are the deciding factor, the word *proposal* is used, as in RFP.

Procurement documents are posted or advertised according to the buyer's organizational policies. This might include ads in newspapers and magazines or ads/posts on the Internet.

Procurement Statement of Work   A procurement statement of work (SOW) contains the details of the procurement item in clear, concise terms. It includes the following elements:

- Project objectives
- Description of the work of the project and any post-project operational support needed
- Concise specifications of the product or services required
- Project schedule, time period of services, and work location

The procurement SOW is prepared by the buyer and is developed from the project scope statement and the WBS and WBS dictionary. The seller uses the SOW to determine whether they are able to produce the goods or services as specified. It will undergo progressive elaboration as the procurement processes occur.

Source Selection Criteria   The term *source selection criteria* refers to the method the buyer's organization will use to choose a vendor from among the proposals received. The criteria might be subjective or objective.

Here are some examples of criteria used:

- Purchase price
- Scoring models
- Rating models

The following list includes some of the criteria for evaluating proposals and bids:

- Comprehension of the needs of the project as documented in the contract SOW
- Cost
- Technical ability of the vendor and their proposed team
- Technical approach
- Risk
- Experience on projects of similar size and scope, including references
- Project management approach
- Management approach
- Financial stability and capacity
- Production capacity
- Reputation, references, and past performance
- Intellectual and proprietary rights

Make-or-Buy Decisions   The make-or-buy decision is a document that outlines the decisions made during the process regarding which goods and/or services will be produced by the organization and which will be purchased. This can include any number of items:

- Services
- Products

- Insurance policies
- Performance
- Performance bonds

Independent Cost Estimates   In some cases, a project team may elect to have an independent cost estimate prepared for the work being procured. This may include having the internal project team develop these estimates or having an external professional estimator produce the estimates. Independent estimates can serve as a benchmark or proposed response to seller bids.

Change Requests   As a result of going through this process, changes to the project management plan may be required due to vendor capability, availability, cost, quality considerations, and so on. Change requests must be processed through the Perform Integrated Change Control process.

Project Documents Updates   According to the *PMBOK® Guide*, the list of project documents that may be updated includes but is not limited to the following items:

- Lessons learned register
- Milestone list
- Requirements documentation
- Requirements traceability matrix
- Risk register
- Stakeholder register

Organizational Process Assets Updates   Organizational process assets may need to be updated as a result of carrying out this process. This may include archiving information on qualified sellers.

Don't forget that the Project Procurement Management Knowledge Area has three more processes: Conduct Procurements (a part of the Executing process group), and Control Procurements (a part of the Monitoring and Controlling process group). Look for a discussion of these processes in Chapter 8, Chapter 6, and Chapter 7.

Exam Essentials

Be able to define the purpose of the Plan Procurement Management process.   The purpose of the Plan Procurement Management process is to identify which project needs should be obtained from outside the organization. Make-or-buy analysis is used as a tool and technique to help determine this.

Be able to identify the contract types and their usage.   Contract types are a tool and technique of the Plan Procurement Management process and include fixed-price and cost-reimbursable contracts. Use fixed-price contracts for well-defined projects with a high value to the company, and use cost-reimbursable contracts for projects with uncertainty and large investments early in the project life. The three types of fixed-price contracts are FFP, FPIF, and FP-EPA. The three types of cost-reimbursable contracts are CPFF, CPIF, and CPAF. Time and material contracts are a cross between fixed-price and cost-reimbursable contracts.

Be able to name the outputs of the Plan Procurement Management process. The outputs of Plan Procurement Management are a procurement management plan, procurement strategy, bid documents, procurement statement of work, source selection criteria, make-or-buy decisions, independent cost estimates, change requests, project documents updates, and organizational process assets updates.

Developing a Change Management Plan

Managing changes is important to successfully managing a project overall. Scope creep is often the result of a poorly documented scope and poorly documented change control procedures. To ensure that changes are managed appropriately, a change management plan should be created. It should be noted that there isn't a formal documented process that creates this plan.

The change management plan should document the following:

- How changes will be monitored and controlled
- Detailed processes for managing change to a project
- How change requests are to be documented and managed
- Process for approving changes
- How to document and manage the final recommendation for the change requests

Once created and approved, the change management plan becomes part of the overarching project management plan.

Developing a Risk Management Plan

The first official step in performing risk management is creating a risk management plan. This is done by carrying out the Plan Risk Management process, which is the first official process of the Project Risk Management Knowledge Area. Five of the seven processes that fall in this Knowledge Area belong to the Planning process group.

The risk management plan is created to manage uncertainty throughout the project life cycle, which allows the project management team to control the outcome of the project to the extent possible. Like other plans, it plays an important role in guiding the rest of the processes that fall within its respective Knowledge Area. Without the risk management plan, a project management team cannot effectively identify and manage risks because this plan ensures that everyone is on the same page when it comes to assessing, prioritizing, responding to, and managing risks.

Aside from the Plan Risk Management process, the following risk-related processes fall within the Planning process group: Identify Risks, Perform Qualitative Risk Analysis, Perform Quantitative Risk Analysis, and Plan Risk Responses. Remember that there are two other processes within this Knowledge Area: Implement Risk Responses, which is part of the Executing process group, and Monitor Risks, which is a part of the Monitoring and Controlling process group.

Plan Risk Management

The Plan Risk Management process determines how the project team will conduct risk management activities. The risk management plan, which will be developed during this process, guides the project team in carrying out the risk management processes and also ensures that the appropriate amount of resources and time is dedicated to risk management. By the end of this process, the project team will have developed a common understanding for evaluating risks throughout the remainder of the project.

Figure 5.7 shows the inputs, tools and techniques, and outputs of the Plan Risk Management process.

FIGURE 5.7 Plan Risk Management process

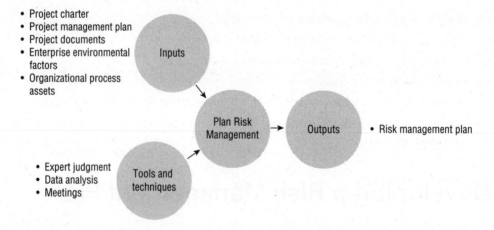

For more detailed information on the Plan Risk Management process, see Chapter 6, "Risk Planning," of *PMP®: Project Management Professional Exam Study Guide, Ninth Edition* (Sybex, 2017).

Inputs of Plan Risk Management

You should know the following inputs of the Plan Risk Management process:

- Project charter
- Project management plan
- Project documents
- Enterprise environmental factors
- Organizational process assets

Project Charter   From the project charter, various inputs can be gleaned, including risks, project descriptions, and requirements, all at a high level.

Project Management Plan   For the purposes of risk management planning, it is necessary to consider all other approved subsidiary management plans and baselines. The project management plan sets the baseline for all risk-affected areas, especially scope, schedule, and cost.

Project Documents   The stakeholder register provides details related to the project stakeholder, including an overview of their roles.

Enterprise Environmental Factors   One of the key elements of the enterprise environmental factors to consider in this process is the risk tolerance levels of the organization and the stakeholders. This is important for evaluating and ranking risk.

Organizational Process Assets   Organizational process assets include policies and guidelines that might already exist in the organization. The following should be considered when developing the risk management plan:

- Risk categories
- Risk statement formats
- Risk management templates tailored to the needs of the project
- Defined roles and responsibilities
- Authority levels of the stakeholders and project manager

Tools and Techniques of Plan Risk Management

The Plan Risk Management process has three tools and techniques: expert judgment, data analysis, and meetings.

- Expert judgment
- Data analysis
- Meetings

Expert Judgment   In the creation of a comprehensive risk management plan, judgment and expertise should be considered from those with specialized training or knowledge in the subject area, including but not limited to the following:

- Senior management
- Other project managers who have performed similar work efforts
- Subject matter experts in the field
- Project stakeholders
- Industry groups and consultants
- Technical and professional associations

Data Analysis   To create and communicate the overall risk management context of the project, analytical techniques are used. The risk management context combines the strategic risk exposure of a given project with the stakeholders' attitude on risk. These assessments will inform the project team on the appropriate resource allocation and allow the team to focus on risk management activities.

Meetings   During these meetings, the fundamental plans for performing risk management activities will be discussed and determined and then documented in the risk management plan.

Outputs of Plan Risk Management

The output of the Plan Risk Management process is the risk management plan. The risk management plan describes how you will define, respond to, and monitor risks throughout the project. It also details how risk management processes will be implemented and managed. According to the *PMBOK® Guide*, the risk management plan should include the following elements:

Risk Strategy   The risk strategy captures the general approach to how risks will be managed in the project.

Methodology   Methodology is a description of how you'll perform risk management, including elements such as methods and tools, and how you'll determine where you might find risk data that you can use in the later processes.

Roles and Responsibilities   The risk management plan should include descriptions of the people who are responsible for managing the identified risks and their responses and the people responsible for each type of activity identified in the plan.

Funding   The budget for risk management activities is included in the plan as well. In this section, you'll assign resources and estimate the costs of risk management activities and methods. These costs are then included in the cost performance baseline.

Timing   Timing refers to how often and at what point in the project life cycle risk management processes will occur. You may also include protocols designed to establish contingency schedule reserves.

Stakeholder Risk Appetite   As the project proceeds through the risk management processes, risk appetite will change. This is documented in the risk management plan. Risk management should be carried out according to stakeholder risk appetite.

Reporting Formats   In the reporting formats section, you'll describe the content and format of the risk register. You should also detail how risk management information will be maintained, updated, analyzed, and reported to project participants.

Tracking   This includes a description of how you'll document the history of the risk activities for the current project and how the risk processes will be audited.

Risk Categories   Risk categories are a way of systematically identifying risks and providing a foundation for understanding. Risk categories should be identified during this process and documented in the risk management plan.

There are multiple ways of displaying risk categories, such as through a simple list or by constructing a risk breakdown structure (RBS), which lists the categories and subcategories. Figure 5.8 shows a sample of an RBS.

FIGURE 5.8   Risk breakdown structure

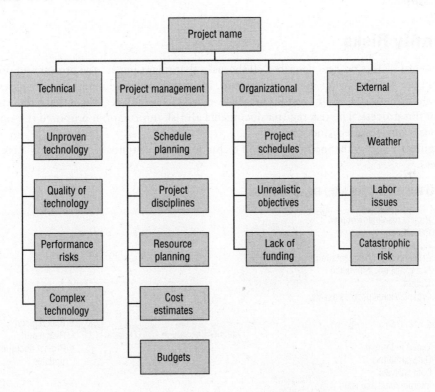

The following list includes some examples of the categories you might consider during this process:

- Technical/quality/performance risks
- Project management risks
- Organizational risks
- External risks

Definitions of Risk Probability and Impacts   The definitions for probability and impact are documented in the risk management plan as they relate to potential positive or negative risk events and their impacts on project objectives.

- Probability describes the potential for the risk event occurring.
- Impact describes the effects or consequences the project will experience if the risk event occurs.

Probability and Impact Matrix   A probability and impact matrix prioritizes the combination of probability and impact scores and helps determine which risks need detailed risk response plans.

Identify Risks

The Identify Risks process describes all the risks that might impact the project and documents their characteristics in the risk register. Identify Risks is an iterative process that continually builds on itself as additional risks emerge. The risk register is created at the end of this process. The risk register documents all risk information, proposed responses, responses implemented, and status.

Figure 5.9 shows the inputs, tools and techniques, and outputs of the Identify Risks process.

FIGURE 5.9   Identify Risks process

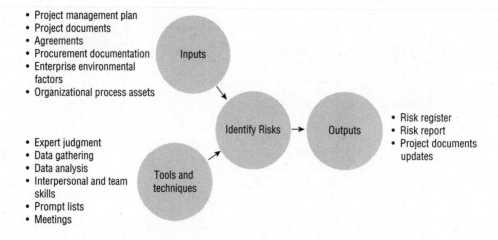

For more detailed information on the Identify Risks process, see Chapter 6 of *PMP®: Project Management Professional Exam Study Guide, Ninth Edition* (Sybex, 2017).

Inputs of Identify Risks

You should be familiar with the following inputs of the Identify Risks process:

- Project management plan
- Project documents
- Agreements
- Procurement documentation
- Enterprise environmental factors
- Organizational process assets

Project Management Plan   Several subsidiary plans and baselines are used from within the project management plan to identify risk, including the following:

Risk Management Plan   In this process, the roles and responsibilities section of the risk management plan will be used, as well as the budget and schedule set aside for risk activities.

Cost Management Plan, Schedule Management Plan, Quality Management Plan, Resource Management Plan, Requirements Management Plan   An understanding of these subsidiary plans is necessary for identifying risks. A thorough review of these documents should be carried out to identify risks associated with them.

Baselines   The project scope statement, part of the scope baseline, contains a list of project assumptions, which are issues believed to be true. The assumptions about delivery times are reexamined, and it is determined if they are still valid.

Project Documents   Multiple project documents will be used when carrying out the Identify Risks process. Below are examples:

Assumption Log   Noted assumptions and constraints from within the log may generate risks associated with them.

Cost Estimates   Activity cost estimates may provide insight into the identification of risks if the estimates are found to be insufficient to complete the activity.

Duration Estimates   Activity duration estimates may reveal existing risks in relation to the time that has been allotted for completing an activity or the project as a whole.

Issue Log   As with the assumption log, issues captured within the issue log may generate risk.

Lessons Learned Register   Since the identification of risks is an iterative process, the lessons learned register should be reviewed regularly to guide future risk identification activities.

Requirements Documentation and Resource Requirements   The project team should inspect the list of requirements and resources for any associated risks.

Stakeholder Register   Understanding stakeholder influence is essential to risk management. The stakeholder register provides a list of stakeholders and may list levels of influence.

Agreements   If the project includes procurement activities, the agreements should be inspected for any risks associated with the contract type chosen, acceptance criteria used within the agreement, or milestone dates to which vendors will be held accountable.

Procurement Documentation   When a project requires the use of external procurement of resources, procurement documents are an influential input to the Identify Risks process.

Enterprise Environmental Factors   The enterprise environmental factors include aspects from outside the project that might help determine or influence project outcomes. Industry information or academic research that might exist for your application areas regarding risk information is especially relevant.

Organizational Process Assets   Historical information, such as from previous project experiences and project team knowledge, is used from within the organizational process assets. Risk register templates can also be used from past similar projects.

Tools and Techniques of Identify Risks

The Identify Risks process includes the following tools and techniques:

- Expert judgment
- Data gathering
- Data analysis
- Interpersonal and team skills
- Prompt lists
- Meetings

Expert Judgment   For risk identification purposes, experts can include individuals with the following experience:

- Experience with similar projects
- Experience in the business area for which the project was undertaken
- Industry-specific experience

The bias of experts regarding the project or potential risk events should be considered when using this technique.

Data Gathering   Data-gathering techniques referenced by the *PMBOK® Guide* for risk identification includes brainstorming, checklists, and interviews.

Brainstorming   Simply bringing team members together for brainstorming sessions is a creative way to help the team initially identify risks. Many times, brainstorming can yield a comprehensive list of risks and allow the team to categorize them.

Checklists   Checklists used during the Identify Risks process are usually developed based on historical information and previous project team experience. The lowest level of the RBS or a list of risks from previous similar projects may be used. The WBS can also be used as a checklist.

Interviews   Interviews can capture risks from a broad list of participants. This aids in capturing risks in a way that can promote confidentiality, trust, and unbiased feedback.

Data Analysis   Data analysis techniques used to identify risks include root cause analysis, assumption and constraint analysis, SWOT analysis, and document analysis.

Root Cause Analysis   Two types of diagramming techniques are used in the Identify Risks process that aid in root cause analysis:

Cause-and-Effect   Cause-and-effect diagrams show the relationship between the effects of problems and their causes. This diagram depicts every potential cause and subcause of a problem and the effect that each proposed solution will have on the problem. This diagram is also called a fishbone diagram or Ishikawa diagram after its developer, Kaoru Ishikawa. Figure 5.10 shows a sample cause-and-effect diagram.

FIGURE 5.10   Cause-and-effect diagram

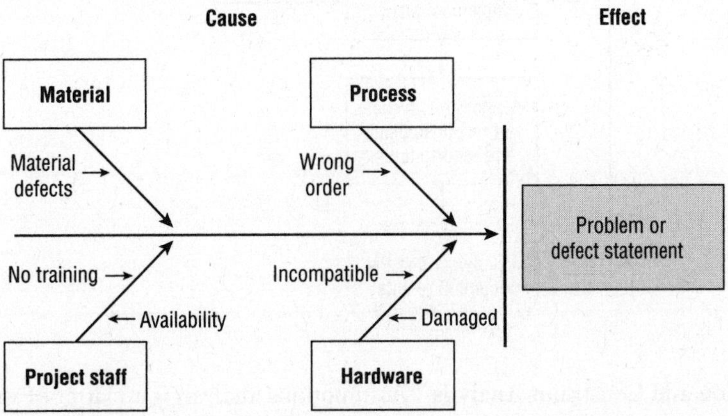

System or Process Flowcharts   The system or process flowcharts show the logical steps needed to accomplish an objective, how the elements of a system relate to each other, and which actions cause which responses. Figure 5.11 shows a flowchart to help determine whether risk response plans should be developed for the risk.

FIGURE 5.11   Flowchart diagram

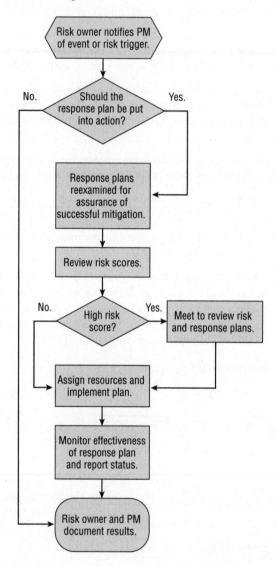

Assumption and Constraint Analysis   Assumptions analysis is a matter of validating the assumptions identified and documented during the course of the project planning processes. Assumptions should be accurate, complete, and consistent. All assumptions are tested against two factors:

- Strength of the assumption or the validity of the assumption
- Consequences that might impact the project if the assumption turns out to be false

SWOT Analysis   Strengths, weaknesses, opportunities, and threats (SWOT) analysis is a technique that examines the project from each of these viewpoints and from the viewpoint of the project itself. SWOT should also be used to examine project management processes, resources, the organization, and so on to identify risks to the project, including risks that are generated internally. SWOT analysis uncovers the following:

- Negative risks, which are typically associated with the organization's weaknesses
- Positive risks, which are typically associated with the organization's strengths

SWOT analysis also determines whether any of the organization's strengths can be used to overcome its weaknesses.

Document Analysis   Documentation reviews involve reviewing project plans, assumptions, and historical information from previous projects from a total project perspective as well as from an individual deliverables and activities level. This review helps the project team identify risks associated with the project objectives.

Interpersonal and Team Skills   With many of the techniques listed within this process, facilitation will be required. Facilitation is a form of interpersonal and team skills and may be carried out by a professional facilitator, the project manager, or other skilled team member.

Prompt Lists   According to the *PMBOK® Guide*, a prompt list is a predetermined list of risk categories that may identify project risks or overall sources of project risk.

Meetings   Meetings or workshops are a common way of bringing the team together in combination with other techniques to identify risks.

Outputs of Identify Risks

There are three outputs of the Identify Risks process:

- Risk register
- Risk report
- Project documents updates

There will be other risk-related planning processes that will continue to add information to the risk register.

Risk Register   The risk register contains the following elements:

- List of identified risks
- List of potential responses
- Potential risk owners

List of Identified Risks Risks are all the potential events and their subsequent consequences that could occur as identified during this process. A list provides a means of tracking risks and their occurrence and responses. The list should contain the following items:

- All potential risks
- Tracking number
- Potential cause or event
- Potential impact
- Responses implemented

List of Potential Responses While you're identifying risks, you may identify a potential response at the same time. If this is the case, these potential responses are documented.

Table 5.2 shows a sample template for a risk register.

TABLE 5.2 Risk register template

ID	Risk	Trigger	Event	Cause	Impact	Owner	Response Plan
1	Infrastructure team is not available when needed.	Predecessor tasks are/ were not completed on time.	Operating system upgrade is/ was delayed.	Equipment was not delivered on time.	Schedule delay	Brown	Compress the schedule by beginning tasks in the next milestone while working on operating system upgrade.

Potential Risk Owners Along with risks identified and potential responses, potential risk owners may also be documented while carrying out this process. Risk owners will not be confirmed until the Perform Qualitative Risk Analysis process is carried out.

Risk Report The focus of the risk report is at the project level. The risk report documents information on the sources of overall project risk and typically includes the following:

- Sources of overall risk
- Summary of risks identified, including the number of threats, opportunities, and risks across the risk categories

Project Documents Updates As risks are identified, the following project documents might require an update:

- Assumption log
- Issue log
- Lessons learned register

Perform Qualitative Risk Analysis

The Perform Qualitative Risk Analysis process involves determining what impact the identified risks will have on the project objectives and the probability that they will occur. It also ranks the risks in priority order according to their effect on the project objectives. The purpose of this process is to determine risk event probability and risk impact. By the end of this process, updates will have been made to the risk register.

Figure 5.12 shows the inputs, tools and techniques, and outputs of the Perform Qualitative Risk Analysis process.

FIGURE 5.12   Perform Qualitative Risk Analysis process

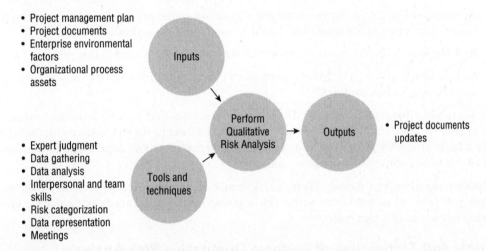

- Project management plan
- Project documents
- Enterprise environmental factors
- Organizational process assets

Inputs

Perform Qualitative Risk Analysis

Outputs

- Project documents updates

- Expert judgment
- Data gathering
- Data analysis
- Interpersonal and team skills
- Risk categorization
- Data representation
- Meetings

Tools and techniques

For more detailed information on the Perform Qualitative Risk Analysis process, see Chapter 6 of *PMP®: Project Management Professional Exam Study Guide, Ninth Edition* (Sybex, 2017).

Inputs of Perform Qualitative Risk Analysis

Know the following inputs of the Perform Qualitative Risk Analysis process and how they apply:

- Project management plan
- Project documents
- Enterprise environmental factors
- Organizational process assets

Project Management Plan   The project management plan contains the risk management plan, which is the primary subsidiary plan referenced when performing qualitative risk

analysis. The risk management plan documents the following, which are used when prioritizing risks:

- Roles and responsibilities of risk team members
- Budget and schedule factors for risk activities
- Stakeholder risk tolerances
- Definitions for probability and impact
- Probability and impact matrix

Project Documents   There are three key documents used to perform this process: the
assumption log, risk register, and stakeholder register.

Assumption Log   Assumptions captured may influence the priority of individual project
risks. Assumptions and constraints should be monitored throughout the project.

Risk Register   The list of risks from within the risk register is used in this process.

Stakeholder Register   The list of stakeholders is helpful for reference as decisions are
made regarding risk owners.

Enterprise Environmental Factors   As with other processes that we have examined earlier,
enterprise environmental factors provide insight and context to the risk assessment, including studying industry projects of a similar nature and exploring risk databases that may be
available from industry or proprietary sources.

Organizational Process Assets   Historical information, lessons learned, and risk databases
from past projects are used from within the organizational process assets as a guide for prioritizing the risks for this project.

Tools and Techniques of Perform Qualitative Risk Analysis

The following tools and techniques are used in the Perform Qualitative Risk Analysis
process:

- Expert judgment
- Data gathering
- Data analysis
- Interpersonal and team skills
- Risk categorization
- Data representation
- Meetings

Expert Judgment   Expert judgment is used to determine the probability, impact, and other
information derived to date from this process. Interviews and facilitated workshops are two
techniques used in conjunction with expert judgment to perform this process.

Data Gathering   Interviews, a data-gathering technique, can be used when assessing the
probability and impact of individual project risks. As noted previously, interviews promote
a sense of confidentiality, trust, and unbiased feedback.

Data Analysis There are three data analysis techniques used in this process: risk data quality assessment, risk probability and impact assessment, and the assessment of other risk parameters.

Risk Data Quality Assessment The risk data quality assessment involves determining the usefulness of the data gathered to evaluate risk. The data must be unbiased and accurate. Elements such as the following are used when performing this tool and technique:

- Quality of the data used
- Availability of data regarding the risks
- How well the risk is understood
- Reliability and integrity of the data
- Accuracy of the data

Risk Probability and Impact Assessment This tool and technique assesses the probability that the risk events identified will occur and determines the effect (or impact) they have on the project objectives:

Probability: Probability is the likelihood that an event will occur.

Impact: Impact is the amount of pain or gain that the risk event poses to the project. The following are two types of scales used to assign a value to risk:

- The risk impact scale, also known as an ordinal scale, can be a relative scale that assigns values such as high, medium, or low.
- Cardinal scale values are actual numeric values assigned to the risk impact. Cardinal scales are expressed as values from 0.0 to 1.0 and can be stated in equal (linear) or unequal (nonlinear) increments.

Table 5.3 shows a typical risk impact scale for cost, time, and quality objectives based on a high-high to low-low scale.

TABLE 5.3 Risk impact scale

Objectives	Low-Low	Low	Medium	High	High-High
	0.05	0.20	0.40	0.60	0.80
Cost	No significant impact	Less than 6% increase	7%–12% increase	13%–18% increase	More than 18% increase
Time	No significant impact	Less than 6% increase	7%–12% increase	13%–18% increase	More than 18% increase
Quality	No significant impact	Few components impacted	Significant impact requiring customer approval to proceed	Unacceptable quality	Product not usable

The idea behind both probability and impact values is to develop predefined measurements that describe which value to place on a risk event. Assumptions used to arrive at these determinations should also be documented in this process.

Assessment of Other Risk Parameters   Risk urgency assessment determines how soon the potential risks might occur and quickly determines responses for those risks that could occur in the near term. The following play a role in determining how quickly a risk response is needed:

- Risk triggers
- Time to develop and implement a response
- Overall risk rating

In addition to urgency, the following are other characteristics that may be assessed, as noted by the *PMBOK® Guide*:

- Proximity
- Dormancy
- Manageability
- Controllability
- Detectability
- Connectivity
- Strategy impact
- Propinquity

Probability and Impact Matrix   The outcome of a probability and impact matrix is an overall risk rating for each of the project's identified risks. The following are characteristics of the probability and impact matrix:

- The combination of probability and impact results in a classification usually expressed as high, medium, or low.
- Values assigned to the risks determine how the Plan Risk Responses process is carried out later on during the risk-planning processes.
- Values for the probability and impact matrix (and the probability and impact scales) are determined prior to the start of this process.
- The impact and probability matrix is documented in the risk management plan.

Hierarchical Charts   In addition to showing risks based on a probability and impact matrix, hierarchical charts can be used. An example of this type of chart is a bubble chart, which can reflect multiple dimensions of data.

In several countries, it is common for high risks to be reflected as a red condition within the probability and impact matrix, medium risks as a yellow condition, and low risks as a green condition. This type of ranking is known as an *ordinal scale* because the values are ordered by rank from high to low.

Interpersonal and Team Skills   Facilitation is a form of interpersonal and team skills used to carry out this process. This may include a trained facilitator, a skilled team member, or the project or risk manager.

Risk Categorization   Risk categorization is used to determine the effects risk has on the project. This involves grouping risks in multiple ways to determine what areas within the project are the most exposed. Examples of how risks can be categorized include areas affected, RBS components, WBS components, and risk categories.

Data Representation   Data representation techniques that you should be familiar with include the probability and impact matrix and hierarchical charts.

Meetings   Risk workshops are often held to bring team members together to carry out several of the techniques discussed within this process.

Outputs of Perform Qualitative Risk Analysis

The output of the Perform Qualitative Risk Analysis process delivers project documents updates, including updates to the risk register, issue log, risk report, and assumption log.

According to the *PMBOK® Guide*, the risk register will receive the following updates, which are added as new entries:

- Risk ranking (or priority) for the identified risks

- Risks grouped by categories

- Causes of risk

- List of risks requiring near-term responses

- List of risks that need additional analysis and response

- Watch list of low-priority risks

- Trends in qualitative risk analysis results

The assumption log will receive updates as new information is made available through the qualitative risk assessment. Assumptions could be incorporated in the project scope statement or in a separate log.

Perform Quantitative Risk Analysis

The Perform Quantitative Risk Analysis process evaluates the impacts of risk prioritized during the Perform Qualitative Risk Analysis process and quantifies risk exposure for the project by assigning numeric probabilities to each risk and determining their impacts on project objectives. The purpose of this process is to perform the following:

- Quantify the project's possible outcomes and probabilities.

- Determine the probability of achieving the project objectives.

- Identify risks that need the most attention by quantifying their contribution to overall project risk.

- Identify realistic and achievable schedule, cost, or scope targets.

- Determine the best project management decisions possible when outcomes are uncertain.

Figure 5.13 shows the inputs, tools and techniques, and outputs of the Perform Quantitative Risk Analysis process.

FIGURE 5.13   Perform Quantitative Risk Analysis process

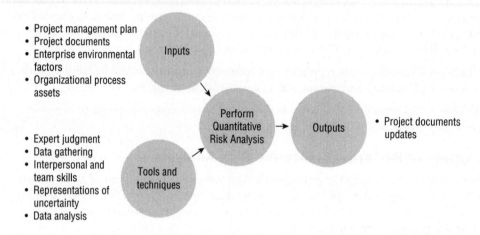

- Project management plan
- Project documents
- Enterprise environmental factors
- Organizational process assets

- Expert judgment
- Data gathering
- Interpersonal and team skills
- Representations of uncertainty
- Data analysis

Inputs

Perform Quantitative Risk Analysis

Tools and techniques

Outputs

- Project documents updates

For more detailed information on the Perform Quantitative Risk Analysis process, see Chapter 6 of *PMP®: Project Management Professional Exam Study Guide, Ninth Edition* (Sybex, 2017).

Inputs of Perform Quantitative Risk Analysis

Know the following inputs of the Perform Quantitative Risk Analysis process:

- Project management plan
- Project documents
- Enterprise environmental factors
- Organizational process assets

Project Management Plan   The risk management plan, a component of the project management plan, guides the project team in carrying out the risk processes. The following key elements are used from within the risk management plan:

- Roles and responsibilities
- Risk management activities
- Guidelines for setting aside contingency reserves
- RBS
- Stakeholder tolerances

All project baselines (scope, cost, schedule) are considered when performing quantitative risk analysis. Baselines provide a starting point against which to measure uncertainty.

Project Documents   The risk register contains a list of identified risks as well as any other documented information on risks to date. In addition to the risk register, there are several other documents that may prove useful in quantifying risks:

- Assumption log
- Basis of estimates
- Cost estimates
- Cost forecasts
- Duration estimates
- Milestone list
- Resource requirements
- Risk report
- Schedule forecasts

Enterprise Environmental Factors   Enterprise environmental factors contribute insight and context to the risk analysis. Two factors to consider are industry studies of similar projects that are conducted by risk specialists and a review of risk databases available from the industry or through proprietary sources.

Organizational Process Assets   The organizational process assets include historical information from previous projects.

Tools and Techniques of Perform Quantitative Risk Analysis

Five tools and techniques are used in the Perform Quantitative Risk Analysis process:

- Expert judgment
- Data gathering
- Interpersonal and team skills
- Representations of uncertainty
- Data analysis

Expert Judgment   Experts can come from inside or outside the organization and should have experience that's applicable to the project. When performing quantitative risk analysis, experts can also assist in validating the data and tools used and translating information on individual project risks.

Data Gathering   Data-gathering and representative techniques used primarily consist of interviews. Project team members, stakeholders, and subject matter experts are typical interview subjects. Oftentimes, three-point estimates are gathered from the experts to quantify the probability and impact of risks on project objectives. The following interview topics are common:

- Experiences on past projects
- Experiences working with the types of technology or processes used during this project

Interpersonal and Team Skills   As with other risk management processes, facilitation is a key interpersonal and team skill used in combination with other techniques described within the Perform Quantitative Risk Analysis process.

Representations of Uncertainty   Continuous probability distributions (particularly beta and triangular distributions) are commonly used in Perform Quantitative Risk Analysis. According to the *PMBOK® Guide*, the following probability distributions are often used:

- Normal and lognormal
- Triangular
- Beta
- Uniform distributions
- Discrete distributions

Distributions are graphically displayed and represent both the probability and time or cost elements.

Data Analysis   Data analysis techniques referenced by the *PMBOK® Guide* include simulation, sensitivity analysis, decision tree analysis, and influence diagrams.

Simulation   Modeling and simulation techniques are often used for schedule risk analysis and cost analysis. Simulation techniques compute the project model using various inputs, such as cost or schedule duration, to determine a probability distribution for the variable chosen. Modeling and simulation techniques examine the identified risks and their potential impacts to the project objectives from the perspective of the whole project.

Monte Carlo analysis is an example of a simulation technique. It is replicated many times, typically using cost or schedule variables. Every time the analysis is performed, the values for the variable are changed with the output plotted as a probability distribution. This type of information helps the risk management team determine the probability of completing the project on time and/or within budget.

Sensitivity Analysis   Sensitivity analysis is a quantitative method of analyzing the potential impact of risk events on the project and determining which risk event (or events) has the greatest potential for impact by examining all the uncertain elements at their baseline values. Figure 5.14 shows a sample tornado diagram, which is one of the ways that sensitivity analysis data can be displayed.

FIGURE 5.14   Tornado diagram

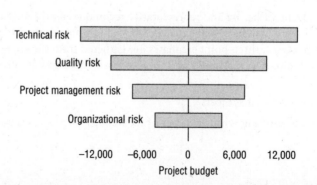

Decision Tree Analysis   Expected monetary value (EMV) analysis is a statistical technique that calculates the average, anticipated future impact of the decision. EMV is calculated by multiplying the probability of the risk by its impact and then adding them together:

- Positive results generally indicate an opportunity within the project.
- Negative results generally indicate a threat to the project.

EMV is used in conjunction with the decision tree analysis technique. Decision trees are diagrams that show the sequence of interrelated decisions and the expected results of choosing one alternative over the other. Typically, more than one choice or option is available in response to a decision. The available choices are depicted in tree form, starting at the left with the risk decision branching out to the right with possible outcomes. Decision trees are usually used for risk events associated with time or cost. Figure 5.15 shows a sample decision tree using EMV as one of its inputs.

FIGURE 5.15   Decision tree

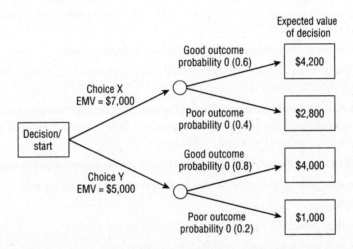

Influence Diagramming   Influence diagramming typically shows the causal influences among project variables, the timing or time ordering of events, and the relationships among other project variables and their outcomes. Figure 5.16 shows an influence diagram for a product introduction decision.

FIGURE 5.16   Influence diagram

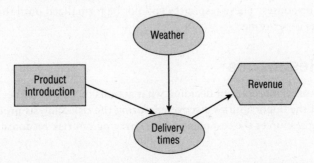

Outputs of Perform Quantitative Risk Analysis

Like the process before it, the Perform Quantitative Risk Analysis process contains one output, project documents updates, including updates to the risk register and risk report.

The following risk register updates occur as a result of this process:

- Probabilistic analysis of the project
- Probability of achieving the cost and time objectives
- Prioritized list of quantified risks
- Trends in Perform Quantitative Risk Analysis results
- Recommended risk responses

Probabilistic Analysis of the Project   Probabilistic analysis of the project is the forecasted results of the project schedule and costs as determined by the outcomes of risk analysis. The following are characteristics of probabilistic analysis:

- Results include projected completion dates and costs along with a confidence level associated with each.
- The output is often expressed as a cumulative distribution.
- Results are used along with stakeholder risk tolerances to quantify the time and cost contingency reserves.

Probability of Achieving the Cost and Time Objectives   The probability of achieving the cost and time objectives of the project are documented based on the results of performing the quantitative risk analysis tools and techniques.

Prioritized List of Quantified Risks   The prioritized list of risks includes the following items:

- Risks that present the greatest threat or opportunity to the project
- Risk impacts
- Risks that present the greatest opportunities to the project
- Risks that are most likely to impact the critical path
- Risks with the largest cost contingency

Trends in Perform Quantitative Risk Analysis Results   Trends in Perform Quantitative Risk Analysis appear as the process is repeated. Trends are documented for further analysis and for use in developing risk response plans.

Recommended Risk Responses   As part of the risk report, recommendations may be captured on risk responses. These responses will not be formalized until the Plan Risk Responses process is performed.

Plan Risk Responses

Plan Risk Responses is a process of deciding what actions to take to reduce threats and take advantage of the opportunities discovered during the risk analysis processes. This includes assigning resources the responsibility of carrying out risk response plans outlined in this process. By the end of this process, the risk register will be updated to include a risk response plan for all risks that require some form of action.

Figure 5.17 shows the inputs, tools and techniques, and outputs of the Plan Risk Responses process.

FIGURE 5.17   Plan Risk Responses process

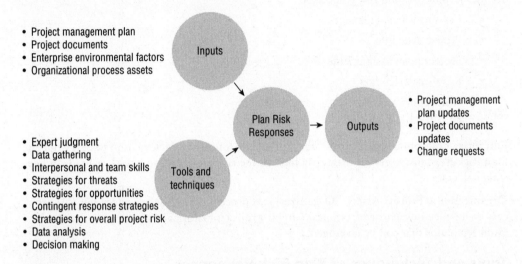

- Project management plan
- Project documents
- Enterprise environmental factors
- Organizational process assets

Inputs

- Expert judgment
- Data gathering
- Interpersonal and team skills
- Strategies for threats
- Strategies for opportunities
- Contingent response strategies
- Strategies for overall project risk
- Data analysis
- Decision making

Tools and techniques

Plan Risk Responses

Outputs

- Project management plan updates
- Project documents updates
- Change requests

For more detailed information on the Plan Risk Responses process, see Chapter 6 of *PMP®: Project Management Professional Exam Study Guide, Ninth Edition* (Sybex, 2017).

Inputs of Plan Risk Responses

The Plan Risk Responses process contains four inputs that you should be familiar with. Be sure you know how they are used during the process. They are as follows:

- Project management plan
- Project documents
- Enterprise environmental factors
- Organizational process assets

Project Management Plan   The following are used from within the risk management plan in carrying out this process:

- Roles and responsibilities that pertain to risk
- Definitions of risk analysis
- Risk thresholds
- Time and budget requirements allotted for risk activities

In addition to the risk management plan, the resource management plan and cost baseline are used as part of the project management plan input. The cost baseline contains information on the contingency fund that will be needed to respond to risks.

Project Documents   All of the information included within the risk register to date will be used in developing risk responses. In addition to the risk register, the following documents are useful in developing risk responses:

- Lessons learned register
- Project schedule
- Project team assignments
- Resource calendars
- Risk report
- Stakeholder register

Enterprise Environmental Factors   Enterprise environmental factors used to carry out the Plan Risk Responses process primarily include the risk appetite and risk thresholds of key stakeholders.

Organizational Process Assets   Organizational process assets used to carry out this process include lessons learned from past similar projects, historical databases, and any relevant templates that can be leveraged.

Tools and Techniques of Plan Risk Responses

Tools and techniques of the Plan Risk Responses process that you should know are as follows:

- Expert judgment
- Data gathering
- Interpersonal and team skills
- Strategies for threats
- Strategies for opportunities
- Contingent response strategies
- Strategies for overall project risk
- Data analysis
- Decision making

Expert Judgment   Expert judgment is used in developing risk responses, including feedback and guidance from risk management experts and those internal to the project qualified to provide assistance in this process. Experts are key in providing feedback and information on response strategies used.

Data Gathering   Interviews are a useful data-gathering technique to gain feedback and information from key stakeholders on risk response strategies in an environment that provides trust and confidentiality and protects against bias.

Interpersonal and Team Skills Facilitation is used in combination with other techniques to develop risk response strategies.

Strategies for Threats As Figure 5.18 shows, strategies for threats include escalate, avoid, transfer, mitigate, and accept.

FIGURE 5.18 Strategies for threats

Strategies for Threats

- Escalate
- Avoid
- Transfer
- Mitigate
- Accept

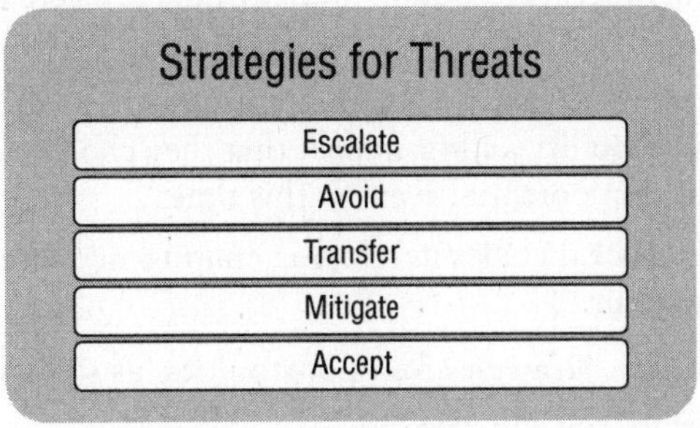

Escalate Escalate is a risk response strategy used for threats when the threat goes beyond the authority level of the project manager or is outside of the project, such as within a program or portfolio. It is then up to the program or portfolio manager to lead the response strategy.

According to the *PMBOK® Guide*, after a risk has been escalated, it is no longer monitored further by the project team. The project team, however, may choose to log it within the risk register as information.

Avoid To avoid a risk means to evade it altogether, eliminate the cause of the risk event, or change the project plan to protect the project objectives from the risk event.

Here are some examples of avoiding risk:

- Improving communications
- Refining requirements
- Assigning additional resources to project activities
- Refining the project scope to avoid risk events

Transfer The purpose of risk transfer is to transfer a risk and its consequences to a third party. This strategy will impact the project budget.

Here are some examples of transferring risk:

- Insurance
- Contracting
- Warranties
- Guarantees
- Performance bonds

Mitigate To mitigate a risk means to reduce the probability of a risk event and its impacts to an acceptable level. According to the *PMBOK® Guide*, the purpose of mitigation is to reduce the probability that a risk will occur and reduce the impact of the risk to an acceptable level.

Accept The acceptance strategy is used when the project team isn't able to eliminate all the threats to the project. Acceptance of a risk event is a strategy that can be used for risks that pose either threats or opportunities to the project. There are two forms of acceptance:

- Passive acceptance occurs when the project team has assessed the risk as low enough in probability and/or impact that they choose to do no additional planning for that potential event at this time.

- Active acceptance includes developing contingency reserves to deal with risks should they occur.

Strategies for Opportunities Strategies for opportunities, as shown in Figure 5.19, include escalate, exploit, share, enhance, and accept.

FIGURE 5.19 Strategies for opportunities

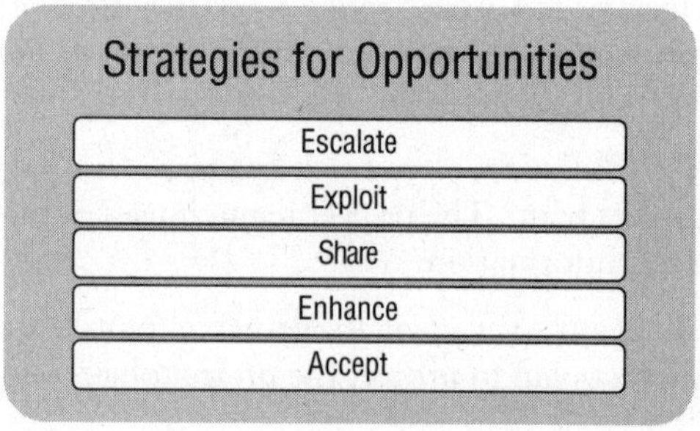

Escalate As with threats, responses to opportunities that are either outside the authority level of the project manager or outside the project's scope are escalated to the appropriate parties. If opportunities are under the jurisdiction of a program or portfolio, then the risk is escalated to the program manager or portfolio manager. respectively.

Exploit Exploiting a risk event is to look for opportunities for positive impacts. This is the strategy of choice when opportunities have been identified and the project team wants to make certain the risk will occur within the project. An example of exploiting a risk would be reducing the amount of time to complete the project by bringing on more qualified resources.

Share The share strategy is similar to transferring because risk is assigned to a third-party owner who is best able to bring about the opportunity the risk event presents. An example of sharing a risk would be a joint venture.

Enhance   The enhance strategy involves closely watching the probability or impact of the risk event to ensure that the organization realizes the benefits. This entails watching for and emphasizing risk triggers and identifying the root causes of the risk to help enhance impacts or probability.

Accept   This is similar to the accept strategies used for threats.

Contingent Response Strategies   Contingent response strategies, also known as contingency planning, involves planning alternatives to deal with the risks should they occur. Contingency planning recognizes that risks may occur and that plans should be in place to deal with them.

The following contingency responses are common:

- Contingency reserves, which include project funds that are held in reserve to offset any unavoidable threats that might occur to project scope, schedule, cost, or quality. Also includes reserving time and resources to account for risks.
- Fallback plans, which are developed for risks with high impact or for risks with identified strategies that might not be the most effective at dealing with the risk.

Strategies for Overall Project Risk   Strategies for addressing overall project risk are similar to those used for threats or opportunities. The only difference is that they respond to overall project risk versus individual project risks.

Risk strategies are as follows:

- Avoid/exploit
- Transfer/share
- Mitigate/enhance
- Accept

Data Analysis   Data analysis techniques refer to alternative analysis and cost-benefit analysis. These techniques are used when weighing options that exist in responding to identified risks.

Decision Making   Multicriteria decision analysis is a form of a decision-making technique used to develop risk responses. This type of analysis uses a decision matrix to develop criteria that is then used to prioritize risk response strategies. Sample criteria provided by the *PMBOK® Guide* include things such as the likely effectiveness of a response, cost of response, timing constraints, and the introduction of secondary risks.

Outputs of Plan Risk Responses

Here are the three outputs of the Plan Risk Responses process:

- Project management plan updates
- Project documents updates
- Change requests

Project Management Plan Updates   The following documents within the project management plan may require updates to reflect the changes in process and practice that are driven by the risk responses:

- Any and all of the management plans, including the schedule management plan, cost management plan, quality management plan, procurement management plan, and resource management plan

- Any and all of the project baselines, including the scope baseline, schedule baseline, and cost baseline

Project Documents Updates   There are several project document updates, with the key update occurring to the risk register. Elements to the risk register can include but are not limited to the following items:

- List of identified risks, including their descriptions, what WBS element they impact (or area of the project), categories (RBS), root causes, and how the risks impact the project objectives

- Risk owners and their responsibility

- Outputs from the Perform Qualitative Analysis process

- Agreed-upon response strategies

- Actions needed to implement response plans

- Risk triggers

- Cost and schedule activities needed to implement risk responses

- Contingency plans

- Fallback plans, which are risk response plans that are executed when the initial risk response plan proves to be ineffective

- Contingency reserves

- Residual risk, which is a leftover risk that remains after the risk response strategy has been implemented

- Secondary risks, which are risks that come about as a result of implementing a risk response

Other project documents, such as the risk report, technical documentation, and the assumptions documented in the assumption log, may require an update after performing this process.

Change Requests   Change requests may be required as a result of carrying out this process due to the risk responses selected, which may call for altering an approach noted within a plan, or impact a baseline.

Don't forget that the Project Risk Management Knowledge Area has one more process: Monitor Risks. Look for a discussion of this process in Chapter 8 when we discuss the Monitoring and Controlling process group.

Exam Essentials

Be able to define the purpose of the risk management plan.   The risk management plan describes how you will define, monitor, and control risks throughout the project. It details how risk management processes (including Identify Risks, Perform Qualitative Risk Analysis, Perform Quantitative Risk Analysis, Plan Risk Responses, Implement Risk Responses, and Monitor Risks) will be implemented, monitored, and controlled throughout the life of the project. It describes how you will manage risks but does not attempt to define responses to individual risks.

Be able to define the purpose of the Identify Risks process.   The purpose of the Identify Risks process is to identify all risks that might impact the project, document them, and identify their characteristics.

Be able to define the risk register and some of its primary elements.   The risk register is an output of the Identify Risks process, and updates to the risk register occur as an output of every risk process that follows this one. By the end of the Plan Risk Responses process, the risk register contains these primary elements: identified list of risks, risk owners, risk triggers, risk strategies, contingency plans, and contingency reserves.

Be able to define the purpose of the Perform Qualitative Risk Analysis process.   Perform Qualitative Risk Analysis determines the impact the identified risks will have on the project and the probability they'll occur, and it puts the risks in priority order according to their effects on the project objectives.

Be able to define the purpose of the Perform Quantitative Risk Analysis process.   Perform Quantitative Risk Analysis evaluates the impacts of risks prioritized during the Perform Qualitative Risk Analysis process and quantifies risk exposure for the project by assigning numeric probabilities to each risk and determining their impact on project objectives.

Be able to define the purpose of the Plan Risk Responses process.   Plan Risk Responses is the process where risk response plans are developed using strategies such as escalate, avoid, transfer, mitigate, accept, exploit, share, enhance, develop contingent response strategies, and apply expert judgment. The risk response plan describes the actions to take should the identified risks occur. It should include all the identified risks, a description of the risks, how they'll impact the project objectives, and the people assigned to manage the risk responses.

Bringing the Processes Together

This chapter covered additional information on processes that belong to the Planning process group. Although there is a lot of material to take in within the Planning process group alone, you are nearly there! Chapter 6 will wrap up our overview of this process group.

As we have done in previous chapters, let's go back and review what you've learned thus far about each of the project management Knowledge Areas covered in this chapter. Remember that activity that occurs within each Knowledge Area is connected on a high level and is structured in a logical format.

Project Resource Management Knowledge Area Review

Figure 5.20 depicts the two planning processes within the Project Resource Management Knowledge Area. Key to the first process of the Knowledge Area is developing the resource management plan, which will guide the rest of the processes relating to resources, including hiring, developing, and managing the project team. The second process, Estimate Activity Resources, which was covered in detail within Chapter 3, is key to developing the schedule.

FIGURE 5.20   Project Resource Management Knowledge Area process interaction

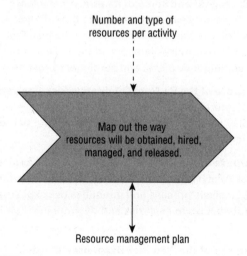

Number and type of
resources per activity

Map out the way
resources will be obtained, hired,
managed, and released.

Resource management plan

Project Communications Management Knowledge Area Review

As you learned in this chapter, meeting stakeholder needs, requirements, and expectations is essential to a successful project. Project communications play a big role in meeting these objectives. Figure 5.21 depicts the only planning-related step within the Project Communications Management Knowledge Area. This step determines how project communications will be managed and defines stakeholder communication requirements. The result is the communications management plan. To define the communication needs and requirements of stakeholders, you need the following result of the Initiating process group: stakeholder register.

FIGURE 5.21   Project Communications Knowledge Area process interaction

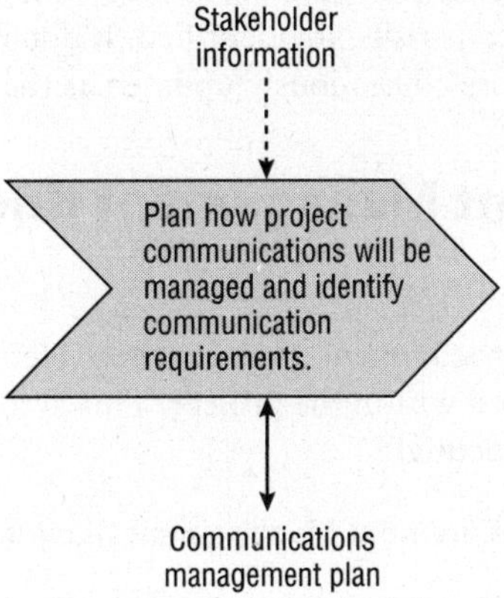

Stakeholder
information

Plan how project
communications will be
managed and identify
communication
requirements.

Communications
management plan

Project Risk Management Knowledge Area Review

Risk management planning begins as early as the project begins. The first step, which creates the risk management plan, is carried through early on during the planning phase of the project. Project plans, such as the cost management plan, the schedule management plan, and the communications management plan, are used to develop the risk management plan. The project scope statement is also used.

As depicted in Figure 5.22, the steps within risk management planning are very intuitive. First, you plan how to manage, assess, and deal with risks. Then, you identify the risks and prioritize them. Analyzing the risks comes next. As you may recall, this can include qualitative risk analysis and quantitative risk analysis.

FIGURE 5.22   Project Risk Management Knowledge Area process interaction

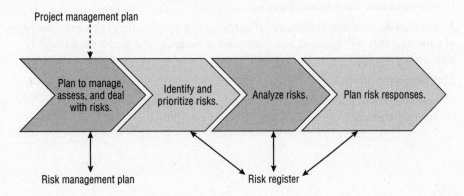

Project management plan

Plan to manage,
assess, and deal
with risks.

Identify and
prioritize risks.

Analyze risks.

Plan risk responses.

Risk management plan

Risk register

With the existing information at hand, you can now plan how you will respond to risks that call for action. As you can see in Figure 5.22, the risk register is a living document, updated throughout the project as risks are identified. It documents all of the information about these risks and is therefore continuously updated as the processes are carried out.

Project Procurement Management Knowledge Area Review

Figure 5.23 shows the single procurement-planning step. Here you plan how procurements will be carried out and managed within the project. This activity also determines which products or services will be procured.

FIGURE 5.23   Project Procurement Management Knowledge Area process interaction

The results include the following items:

- A plan that lays out the guidelines for carrying out procurement activities, the types of contracts that will be used, and how vendor progress and performance will be measured

- Make-or-buy decisions

- Several key procurement-related documents, including make-or-buy decisions, the procurement statement of work, and source selection criteria

Review Questions

1. Rodrigo is in the Plan Communications Management process of a new systems component project. He has determined that there are 32 stakeholders in the project. How many communication channels exist?

   A. 496

   B. 512

   C. 32

   D. 31

2. What is the purpose of the Perform Qualitative Risk Analysis process?

   A. To determine how the project team will plan for risks

   B. To identify and gather all potential risks within the project

   C. To determine the impact and probability of identified risks and prioritize them

   D. To evaluate the impact of risks prioritized and determine the risk exposure

3. Which type of contract carries the highest risk for the buyer?

   A. Fixed-price contracts

   B. Lump-sum contracts

   C. Cost-reimbursable contracts

   D. Time and material contracts

4. All of the following are determined by the Plan Resource Management process *except*:

   A. Project communication needs for stakeholders

   B. Project roles and responsibilities

   C. Reporting relationships for the project

   D. Project team resource management

5. All of the following are outputs of the Plan Procurement Management process *except*:

   A. Procurement statement of work

   B. Make-or-buy analysis

   C. Procurement documents

   D. Source selection criteria

6. All of the following define the purpose of the Identify Risks process *except*:

   A. Identify all risks that might impact the project.

   B. Document all risks that might impact the project.

   C. Control all risks that might impact the project.

   D. Identify all characteristics of identified risks.

7. Hierarchical charts and matrix-based charts are what type of tool and technique?

    A. Data representation

    B. Data gathering

    C. Expert judgment

    D. Data analysis

8. Emails, letters, and voicemails are forms of what communication method?

    A. Interactive communication

    B. Push communication

    C. Pull communication

    D. Multidirectional communication

9. Which type of contract carries the least amount of risk for the seller?

    A. Lump-sum

    B. Cost plus

    C. Time and material

    D. Cost-reimbursable

10. What technique allows the project manager to gather information from stakeholders in a way that encourages unbiased feedback as well as an environment of trust?

    A. Brainstorming

    B. Focus groups

    C. Interviews

    D. Checklists

Chapter

6

Planning Stakeholder Engagement and Obtaining Project Plan Approval

---

THE PMP® EXAM CONTENT FROM THE PLANNING PERFORMANCE DOMAIN COVERED IN THIS CHAPTER INCLUDES THE FOLLOWING:

✓ Develop the stakeholder engagement plan by analyzing needs, interests, and potential impact in order to effectively manage stakeholders' expectations and engage them in project decisions.

✓ Present the project management plan to the relevant stakeholders according to applicable policies and procedures in order to obtain approval to proceed with project execution.

✓ Conduct kick-off meeting, communicating the start of the project, key milestones, and other relevant information in order to inform and engage stakeholders and gain commitment.

As we covered in Chapter 3, Chapter 4, and Chapter 5, planning is an essential part of project management, regardless of what methodology or project life cycle you choose to use. In this chapter, we will cover the remaining project management processes that fall within the Planning process group, wrapping up coverage of this exam domain.

The process names, inputs, tools and techniques, outputs, and descriptions of the project management process groups and related materials and figures in this chapter are based on content from *A Guide to the Project Management Body of Knowledge (PMBOK® Guide), Sixth Edition* (PMI®, 2017).

Developing a Stakeholder Engagement Plan

The primary reason that a project is undertaken is to satisfy the expectations of the project stakeholders. Clearly, it is important to ensure efforts are made to identify, work with, and communicate with the appropriate stakeholders. Within the Planning process group, the Plan Stakeholder Engagement process is the key work effort for the Project Stakeholder Management Knowledge Area. The purpose of the process is to develop approaches to involve stakeholders based on their needs, expectations, interests, and potential impact on the project.

Figure 6.1 shows the inputs, tools and techniques, and outputs of the Plan Stakeholder Engagement process.

For more detailed information on the Plan Stakeholder Engagement process, see Chapter 5 of *PMP®: Project Management Professional Exam Study Guide, Ninth Edition* (Sybex, 2017).

FIGURE 6.1   Plan Stakeholder Engagement process

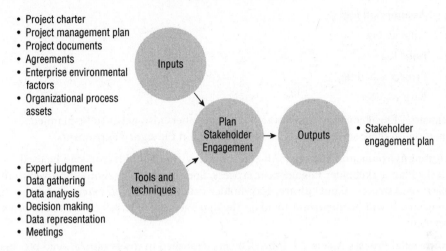

- Project charter
- Project management plan
- Project documents
- Agreements
- Enterprise environmental factors
- Organizational process assets

Inputs

- Expert judgment
- Data gathering
- Data analysis
- Decision making
- Data representation
- Meetings

Tools and techniques

Plan Stakeholder Engagement

Outputs

- Stakeholder engagement plan

Inputs of Plan Stakeholder Engagement

Know the following inputs of the Plan Stakeholder Engagement process:

- Project charter
- Project management plan
- Project documents
- Agreements
- Enterprise environmental factors
- Organizational process assets

Project Charter   The project charter provides high-level information on the project's purpose, objectives, and success criteria. When planning activities are carried out, this document is frequently reviewed.

Project Management Plan   According to the *PMBOK® Guide*, to develop the stakeholder engagement plan you can use the following information from the project management plan:

- Resource management plan, which captures roles and responsibilities of the project team as well as other information regarding resource management
- Communications management plan, which documents the communication strategies selected
- Risk management plan, which details the risk thresholds and risk attitudes of stakeholders

Project Documents   Information that is needed to plan engagement with project stakeholders is provided from the stakeholder register. This is a key document, as it captures additional information about individual stakeholders, including their levels of influence, authority, and interest in the project.

In addition to the stakeholder register, the following other documents may be useful:

- Assumption log
- Change log
- Issue log
- Project schedule
- Risk register

Agreements   Engagement with contractors and suppliers also needs to be planned. Information on these stakeholders can be found within the signed agreements.

Enterprise Environmental Factors   All enterprise environmental factors can be used within the Plan Stakeholder Engagement process. Special attention should be given to the organizational structure and culture, stakeholder risk appetites, and external stakeholder requirements. It will be important to adapt the management of stakeholders to the project environment.

Organizational Process Assets   All the elements described in the organizational process assets can be used in this process. Particular consideration should be given to lessons learned and historical information.

Tools and Techniques of Plan Stakeholder Engagement

The Plan Stakeholder Engagement process includes the following tools and techniques:

- Expert judgment
- Data gathering
- Data analysis
- Decision making
- Data representation
- Meetings

Expert Judgment   Using the project objectives as a guide, a project manager should apply expert judgment when considering the level of engagement required for each stakeholder. It may be necessary to adjust the level of engagement, considering the different phases of the project. In the creation of the stakeholder engagement plan, a project manager can look to the following groups, depending on specialized training or subject matter expertise these individuals might possess:

- Senior management and other identified key stakeholders
- Project team members
- Other functional units or individuals
- Project managers who have completed similar projects
- Subject matter experts in the business or project areas
- Industry groups and consultants
- Professional and technical associations

Data Gathering   Benchmarking is a useful data gathering technique for developing a stakeholder engagement plan. Benchmarking involves comparing information from other, similar projects or with other projects from other organizations.

Data Analysis   According to the *PMBOK® Guide*, data analysis techniques used in this process include, but are not limited to, the following three examples:

- Assumption and constraint analysis, used to tailor engagement strategies
- Root cause analysis, used to identify underlying reasons for existing levels of support
- SWOT analysis, used to evaluate current and possible future positions of key stakeholders

Decision Making   When developing stakeholder engagement strategies, the stakeholder requirements may need to be prioritized and ranked. This is a form of a decision-making technique.

Data Representation   A stakeholder engagement assessment matrix allows for a comparison between current and desired engagement levels. The current engagement level of all stakeholders should be compared to the planned levels of engagement to ensure project success. This is a critical process that needs to be performed throughout the life cycle of the project to help ensure satisfied stakeholders. According to the *PMBOK® Guide*, the level of engagement with stakeholders can be classified as follows:

> **Unaware,** where the stakeholder is unaware of the project and potential impacts
>
> **Resistant,** where the stakeholder is aware of the project but is resistant to change
>
> **Neutral,** where the stakeholder is aware but is neither supportive nor resistant
>
> **Supportive,** where the stakeholder is aware of the project and is supportive of change
>
> **Leading,** where the stakeholder is actively engaged in ensuring that the project is a success

Table 6.1 shows how current engagement can be documented using the stakeholder engagement assessment matrix, where C indicates the current level of engagement and D indicates the desired level of engagement.

TABLE 6.1   Sample stakeholder engagement assessment matrix

STAKEHOLDER	Unaware	Resistant	Neutral	Supportive	Leading
Stakeholder 1				D C	
Stakeholder 2	C		D		
Stakeholder 3		C		D	

Aside from the stakeholder engagement assessment matrix, mind mapping is yet another type of data representation technique that aids in the development of stakeholder engagement strategies. Mind mapping involves organizing information about stakeholders together and their relationship to each other and the organization.

Meetings   The stakeholder management strategy defines the level of participation needed for each stakeholder.

Outputs of Plan Stakeholder Engagement

There is one output that results out of the Plan Stakeholder Engagement process:

Stakeholder Engagement Plan   This component of the project management plan identifies the management strategies necessary to effectively engage stakeholders. Adding to the information provided by the stakeholder register, the stakeholder engagement plan often provides the following information:

- Desired and current engagement levels of key stakeholders
- Scope and impact of change to stakeholders
- Interrelationships and potential overlap of stakeholders
- Method for updating and refining this plan as the project advances

Remember that the Project Stakeholder Management Knowledge Area has three additional processes: Identify Stakeholders, a part of the Chapter 2 discussion of the Initiating process group; Manage Stakeholder Engagement, which will be covered in Chapter 7 as part of the Executing process group; and Monitor Stakeholder Engagement. Look for a discussion of this last process in Chapter 8 when we discuss the Monitoring and Controlling process group.

Exam Essentials

Be able to describe the purpose of the stakeholder engagement plan.   The stakeholder engagement plan identifies the management strategies necessary to effectively engage stakeholders.

Obtaining Project Management Plan Approval

With the subsidiary plans and baselines created, it's time to bring them all together into a project management plan. The project management plan consists of a compilation of these plans and baselines and is an output of the Develop Project Management Plan process. This primary plan is presented to key stakeholders for sign-off (if required). Once the plan is approved, the team can move forward to execute it.

Develop Project Management Plan is the first process in the Planning process group, and it's part of the Project Integration Management Knowledge Area. Although listed as the first Planning process within the *PMBOK® Guide*, as you can see, it is not technically the first process carried out in practice. This process defines, coordinates, and integrates all the various subsidiary project plans and baselines. The result is a project management plan document that describes how the project outcomes will be executed, monitored, and controlled as the project progresses and how the project will be closed out once it concludes.

Throughout the project, the project management plan will be updated to reflect approved project changes. It will be used as an input to many of the project management processes, and as a result of approved changes, it will also become an output of several processes.

Figure 6.2 shows the inputs, tools and techniques, and outputs of the Develop Project Management Plan process.

FIGURE 6.2   Develop Project Management Plan process

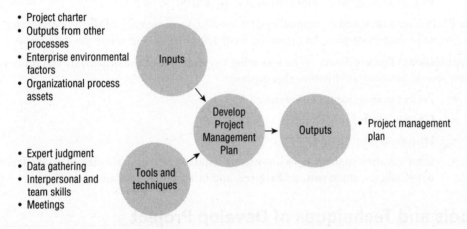

- Project charter
- Outputs from other processes
- Enterprise environmental factors
- Organizational process assets

- Expert judgment
- Data gathering
- Interpersonal and team skills
- Meetings

Inputs

Develop Project Management Plan

Tools and techniques

Outputs

- Project management plan

For more detailed information on the Develop Project Management Plan process, see Chapter 3 of *PMP®: Project Management Professional Exam Study Guide, Ninth Edition* (Sybex, 2017).

Inputs of Develop Project Management Plan

Know the following inputs of the Develop Project Management Plan process:

- Project charter

- Outputs from other processes

- Enterprise environmental factors

- Organizational process assets

Project Charter   Based on the high-level scope outlined in the project charter, the project team can start determining which project management processes will be most beneficial for this particular project.

Outputs from Other Processes   Outputs from other project management processes are used to develop the project management plan. In particular, the following outputs from the planning processes may be helpful inputs to develop the project management plan:

- Any processes used that produce a baseline
- Any processes that produce a subsidiary management plan

Enterprise Environmental Factors   The following key elements of the environmental factors should be considered when choosing the processes to perform for this project:

- Standards and regulations (both industry and governmental)
- Company culture and organizational structure
- Personnel administration
- Project management information system (PMIS)

The PMIS is an automated or manual system used to document the subsidiary plans and the project management plan, facilitate the feedback process, and revise the documents.

Organizational Process Assets   The following key elements of the organizational process assets should be considered within this process:

- Project management plan template
- Change control procedures
- Historical information
- Configuration management knowledge database that contains the official company policies, standards, procedures, and other project documents

Tools and Techniques of Develop Project Management Plan

There are several tools and techniques used to carry out the Develop Project Management Plan process:

- Expert judgment
- Data gathering
- Interpersonal and team skills
- Meetings

Expert Judgment   The following types of expert judgment are needed to complete this process:

- Tailoring techniques
- Understanding technical and management details that need to be included in the project management plan

- Determining resources and assessing skill levels needed for project work
- Determining and defining the amount of configuration management to apply on the project
- Developing additional components of the plan as needed, based on the project
- Prioritizing the work of the project to ensure appropriate resource allocation

Data Gathering   The following data gathering techniques are used to formulate ideas and solutions for what the project approach should be:

- Brainstorming
- Checklists
- Focus groups
- Interviews

Interpersonal and Team Skills   Conflict management, facilitation, and meeting management are examples of interpersonal and team skills used to develop the project management plan. These various techniques help bring together diverse stakeholders and help them reach mutual understanding and get buy-in.

Meetings   Meetings are often used to bring experts together, whether for workshops to develop the plan together or to hold a kick-off meeting to mark the end of planning and start of execution. Look for additional information on the kick-off meeting within this chapter.

Output of Develop Project Management Plan

The output of the Develop Project Management Plan process is the project management plan.

> The purpose of most processes is to produce an output. Outputs are usually a report or document of some type, a deliverable, or an update to a set of documents.

To put it simply, the project management plan contains all of the subsidiary management plans and baselines discussed thus far. In more detailed terms, the project management plan addresses and includes the following elements:

- Processes used to perform each phase of the project
- Life cycle used for the project and for each phase of the project when applicable
- Tailoring of results the project team defines
- Methods for executing the work of the project to fulfill the objectives
- Change management plan describing methods for monitoring and controlling change
- Configuration management

- Methods for determining and maintaining the validity of performance baselines
- Communication needs of the stakeholders and techniques to fulfill those needs
- Management reviews of content, issues, and pending decisions

The project management plan also contains multiple subsidiary plans and baselines, as described in Table 6.2. Figure 6.3 depicts a high-level view of the contents that make up the plan.

TABLE 6.2   Project management plan summary

Subsidiary plan or document	Description
Requirements management plan	This plan documents how the project requirements will be managed throughout the life of the project. It also addresses how the requirements will be analyzed and documented.
Scope management plan	This plan describes how scope will be identified, decomposed, validated, and monitored throughout the project.
Schedule management plan	This plan identifies the scheduling format, tool, and methodology that will be used for creating and managing the project schedule.
Cost management plan	This plan defines the criteria for planning, budgeting, estimating, and managing the costs of the project. It also identifies the cost-related formats and tools that will be used in the project.
Quality management plan	This plan describes how the organization's quality policies will be implemented and addresses the following items: quality assurance, quality control, and process improvement.
Resource management plan	This plan documents how human resources should be defined, staffed, managed and controlled, and released from the project.
Communications management plan	This plan guides the communication for the project. It defines the communication requirements of the stakeholders as well as the format, type, frequency, and methods for project reports. It also lists report recipients and anything else pertinent to project communication.
Risk management plan	This plan defines how risk management activities will be carried out. It also outlines the budget and time allotted for risk activities, risk roles and responsibilities, risk categories, and how risks will be defined and assessed.

Subsidiary plan or document	Description
Procurement management plan	This plan describes how procurements will be managed, from make-or-buy decisions all the way through contract closure.
Stakeholder engagement plan	This plan identifies the management strategies necessary to effectively engage stakeholders.
Schedule baseline	This baseline is an approved version of the project schedule that will be used to compare and measure the planned schedule against the actual schedule.
Cost baseline	This baseline contains an approved budget that is used to measure, monitor, and control the planned budget against the actual amount of funds used.
Scope baseline	This baseline provides scope boundaries for the project and consists of the project scope statement, the work breakdown structure (WBS), and the WBS dictionary.

FIGURE 6.3   High-level view of project management plan contents

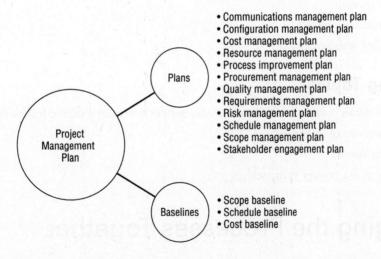

 Subsidiary and component plans may be detailed or simply a synopsis, depending on the project needs. As the project progresses and more and more processes are performed, the subsidiary plans and the project management plan itself may change.

Exam Essentials

Be able to state the purpose of the Develop Project Management Plan process. The project management plan defines how the project is executed, monitored and controlled, and closed, and it documents the processes used during the project.

Conducting a Kick-off Meeting

A kick-off meeting typically occurs at the end of the Planning process, prior to beginning the project work. The purpose of the kick-off meeting is to ensure that everyone is aware of the project details and their role within the project and to announce that the project work is ready to begin. This is a great opportunity to review project milestones and other important information with key stakeholders.

Meeting Attendees

Those who attend a kick-off meeting include, but are not limited to, the following individuals:

- Project manager
- Project team members
- Customer
- Project sponsor
- Department managers
- Other key stakeholders

Meeting Topics

Discussions within a kick-off meeting include, but are not limited to, the following topics:

- Introductions of attendees
- Meeting agenda
- Review of the project management plan

Bringing the Processes Together

This chapter, along with Chapter 3, Chapter 4, and Chapter 5, covered a lot of ground, and you have now officially learned about all of the processes that make up the Planning process group. The outputs of all of these deliverables culminated in the project management plan. As you saw when reviewing the inputs of the various processes, the project management plan is a key input and is regularly updated throughout the project. Keep in mind that after it is approved and the project is baselined, changes must go through a formal change control process. Understanding that bigger picture will help you with situational exam questions as well as using the project management processes in a real-world setting.

Now that you have a strong grasp of how the outputs from various processes become the inputs for other processes, you understand why some processes must occur before others can move forward. For example, to create the project management plan, the results of the Initiating process group are required. Figure 6.4 shows this interaction between the Initiating process group and the Planning process group, the first two stages of the project's life cycle. The relationship between the project management plan and the rest of the planning processes is just as interactive, if not more dynamic.

FIGURE 6.4   Planning process group interaction

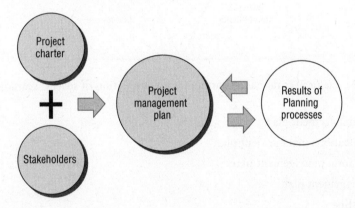

The project management plan is used in Planning processes across nine of the ten Knowledge Areas. (The remaining Knowledge Area generates the project management plan.) The results of these planning processes are fed back into the project management plan as updates. The updates might, in turn, impact several of the other planning processes. For example, the project management plan contains the cost management plan. Any changes that are approved in the cost management plan become updates to the project management plan. As a result, these approved and updated changes could impact other planning processes that might *also* require that updates and changes be made.

By now, it should be clear that the project management plan is the heart of the project and that much of the project's success can be based on the processes of the Planning process group. A common motto in the project management industry is, "A well-planned project makes for a successful project." Figure 6.5 illustrates how the project management plan remains at the center of the Planning process group.

FIGURE 6.5   Planning process group triangle

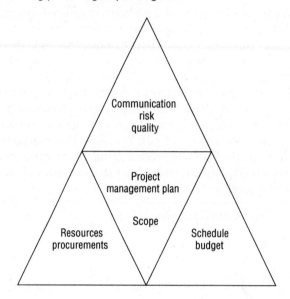

In summary, the project management plan is a compilation of several subsidiary plans and baselines:

- Change management plan
- Communications management plan
- Configuration management plan
- Cost management plan
- Cost baseline
- Resource management plan
- Process improvement plan
- Procurement management plan
- Quality management plan
- Requirements management plan
- Risk management plan
- Stakeholder engagement plan
- Schedule baseline
- Schedule management plan
- Scope baseline
- Scope management plan

The change management plan, which was not previously addressed, describes how you will document and manage change requests, the process for approving changes, and how to document and manage the final recommendation for the change requests. Configuration management changes deal with the components of the product of the project, such as functional ability or physical attributes, rather than the project process itself.

Scope is also a critical element within planning because it defines the boundaries of the project and what it is that the project has set out to achieve. The project schedule and the project budget are part of the project's foundation. These project elements play a big role in measuring and monitoring the progress of the project. The resources and purchased services and/or products complete the project's foundation. Without the human resources, as well as the external project teams, the project could not move forward.

Guiding the project from above are communications management, quality management, and risk management—all critical elements of the project that influence and guide the project toward success. As you can see, all of these project elements are intertwined and build on one another.

Keeping the broader picture in mind, let's go back and review what you've learned thus far about each of the project management Knowledge Areas covered in this chapter. You'll find that what goes on within each Knowledge Area is connected on a high level and is structured in a logical format.

Project Stakeholder Management Knowledge Area Review

The Project Stakeholder Management Knowledge Area is concerned with identifying all of the stakeholders associated with the project, both internal and external to the organization. These processes also assess stakeholder needs, expectations, and involvement on the project and seek to keep the lines of communication with stakeholders open and clear. The definition of a successful project is one where the stakeholders are satisfied. These processes ensure that stakeholder expectations are met and that their satisfaction is a successful deliverable of the project. Figure 6.6 depicts the only planning step in the Project Stakeholder Management Knowledge Area.

FIGURE 6.6   Project Stakeholder Management Knowledge Area process interaction

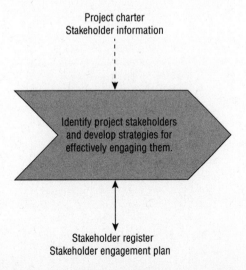

Project charter
Stakeholder information

Identify project stakeholders and develop strategies for effectively engaging them.

Stakeholder register
Stakeholder engagement plan

As you can see, the planning processes within each Knowledge Area are highly interactive. The processes interact not just within their own respective Knowledge Areas but among the other planning processes.

Each project carries different needs, and not all of the processes will be necessary for every project. We previously touched on the fact that some processes can be combined to tailor management for a particular project to the needs of that individual project. But, as you've also seen, some process outputs are critical as inputs to other processes. The project management plan, which lies at the core of the Planning process group, is one of those critical outputs.

Review Questions

1. What type of risk response strategy is a project team likely to use for risks containing a low probability and impact, where no contingency is needed?

   A. Passive acceptance

   B. Active acceptance

   C. Mitigation

   D. Acceptance

2. Unaware, resistant, neutral, supportive, and leading are ways stakeholders can be classified using what data representation tool?

   A. Stakeholder engagement assessment matrix

   B. SWOT analysis

   C. Stakeholder engagement strategies

   D. Stakeholder engagement plan

3. Antwon is a system analyst on a critical project of Data Systems United, a technology consulting firm. Antwon has recently had a difficult conversation with another team member and, in frustration, asks the project manager where he can reference the team values to share with his colleague. To what document is the project manager likely to point Antwon?

   A. Stakeholder engagement plan

   B. Resource management plan

   C. Stakeholder register

   D. Team charter

4. All of the following are tools and techniques used to compile the project management plan *except*:

   A. Interviews

   B. Outputs from other processes

   C. Checklists

   D. Interpersonal and team skills

5. What tool computes the project model using various inputs, such as cost or schedule duration, to determine a probability distribution for the variable chosen?

   A. Sensitivity analysis

   B. Decision tree analysis

   C. Simulation

   D. Influence diagram

6. Frankfort Data Center Migration is a project that belongs to a large program responsible for the consolidation of European data centers into a single location located in Ireland. The project manager of the Frankfort project has just discovered a program-level risk that is affecting his project. What risk response strategy is he likely to use to address the threat?

    A. Avoid

    B. Accept

    C. Mitigate

    D. Escalate

7. All of the following are outputs of the Plan Procurement Management process *except*:

    A. Source selection analysis

    B. Make-or-buy decision

    C. Independent cost estimate

    D. Bid documents

8. Kaylee is a senior project manager of a technology startup company. After joining the company three months ago, she took on a major project with a large group of stakeholders. She has just finished facilitating a multi-day workshop to assemble risk responses for those risks identified to date. What process group is she in?

    A. Initiating

    B. Planning

    C. Executing

    D. Monitoring and Controlling

9. Data Systems United has just been acquired by Mega Data Consultants. The project manager for Mega Data Consultants responsible for integration activities has just finished the first wave of risk identification activities, producing the first iteration of the risk register. What is she likely to do next?

    A. Evaluate the impacts of risk prioritized and quantify risk exposure for the project

    B. Decide what actions to take to reduce threats and take advantage of opportunities discovered

    C. Describe the risks that might impact the project and document their characteristics in the risk register

    D. Determine what impact the identified risks will have on the project objectives and the probability that they will occur

10. A project manager is in the process of assembling the project management plan. What valid tool or technique are they likely to use to aid in successfully generating this plan?

    A. Interviews

    B. Project charter

    C. Organizational process assets

    D. Enterprise environmental factors

Chapter

7

Executing the Project

THE PMP® EXAM CONTENT FROM THE EXECUTING THE PROJECT PERFORMANCE DOMAIN COVERED IN THIS CHAPTER INCLUDES THE FOLLOWING:

✓ Obtain and manage project resources, including outsourced deliverables, by following the procurement plan in order to ensure successful project execution.

✓ Maximize team performance through leading, mentoring, training, and motivating team members.

✓ Execute the tasks as defined in the project plan in order to achieve the project deliverables within budget and schedule.

✓ Implement approved changes according to the change management plan in order to meet project requirements.

✓ Implement the quality management plan using the appropriate tools and techniques in order to ensure that work is being performed according to required quality standards.

✓ Implement approved actions and follow the risk management plan and risk register in order to minimize the impact of negative risk events on the project.

Executing is the third process group of the five project management process groups. The processes in this group are responsible for executing the work outlined in the project management plan, managing the project resources, and performing the work of the project. Within this process group, you will also see approved changes and actions implemented as well as re-planning and re-baselining as a result of implemented changes.

Executing also involves keeping the project in line with the original plan. The majority of the project budget and time will be spent in this process group, and the majority of conflicts will relate to the schedule. In addition, the product description will be finalized and contain more detail than it did in the Planning processes.

The Executing process group accounts for 30 percent of the questions on the Project Management Professional (PMP)® exam.

The process names, inputs, tools and techniques, outputs, and descriptions of the project management process groups and related materials and figures in this chapter are based on content from *A Guide to the Project Management Body of Knowledge (PMBOK® Guide), Sixth Edition* (PMI®, 2017).

Obtaining and Managing Resources

As mentioned previously, the Executing process group involves executing the project work. Naturally, this cannot be accomplished without first acquiring the resources needed to perform the project work. Obtaining resources occurs through the Acquire Resources process, which is part of the Project Resource Management Knowledge Area, and the Conduct Procurements process, which is a part of the Project Procurement Management Knowledge Area. The resource and procurement management plans play an important role in carrying out these processes because they outline how resources will be acquired, managed, and released throughout the project life cycle.

Acquire Resources

The Acquire Resources process involves acquiring and assigning resources, both internal and external, to the project. It is the project manager's responsibility to ensure that human resources are available and skilled in the project activities to which they're assigned. In addition to human resources, this process addresses acquiring physical resources, such as facilities, equipment, materials, supplies, and other physical resources needed to perform the work at hand. This process considers the following factors:

- The process of negotiation with individuals who can provide the needed resources

- The consequences of not obtaining the right resources

- Alternative resources should the planned resources not be available as a result of circumstances out of the project manager's control

Figure 7.1 shows the inputs, tools and techniques, and outputs of the Acquire Resources process.

FIGURE 7.1   Acquire Resources process

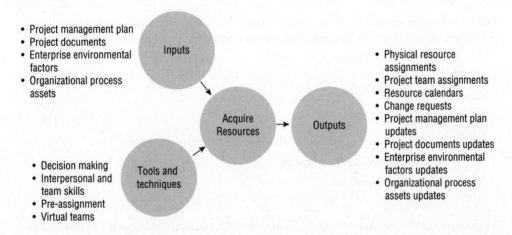

- Project management plan
- Project documents
- Enterprise environmental factors
- Organizational process assets

Inputs

Acquire Resources

Outputs

- Decision making
- Interpersonal and team skills
- Pre-assignment
- Virtual teams

Tools and techniques

- Physical resource assignments
- Project team assignments
- Resource calendars
- Change requests
- Project management plan updates
- Project documents updates
- Enterprise environmental factors updates
- Organizational process assets updates

For more detailed information on the Acquire Resources process, see Chapter 8, "Developing the Project Team," of *PMP®: Project Management Professional Exam Study Guide, Ninth Edition* (Sybex, 2017).

Inputs for Acquire Resources

Know the following inputs for the Acquire Resources process:

Project Management Plan   The project management plan is essential to this process. The following are utilized from within this plan:

- Resource management plan, which outlines the approach to acquiring resources for the project

- Procurement management plan, which outlines the approach to acquiring resources from outside the project, including spelling out how procurements will be integrated with other project work

- Cost baseline accounts for the overall budget assigned to project activities

The project management plan should detail how resources will be acquired.

Project Documents   Several project documents inform this process and can include, but are not limited to, the following:

- Project schedule, which outlines the project activities and includes their projected start and end dates
- Resource calendars, which document the availability of resources that will be needed
- Resource requirements, which outline the skills and experience needed for project resources
- Stakeholder register, which helps inform stakeholder needs or expectations for specific resources

Enterprise Environmental Factors   The enterprise environmental factors used in this process involve taking the following information into account before making assignments:

- Marketplace conditions
- Personal interests
- Cost rates
- Prior experience
- Availability of and information about potential team members
- Personnel administration policies
- Organizational structure
- Locations

Organizational Process Assets   The organizational process assets input refers to the standard processes, policies, procedures, and guidelines that the organization has in place. This includes policies around acquiring external resources. In particular, procurement practices should be taken into account.

Tools and Techniques for Acquire Resources

Be familiar with the following tools and techniques for the Acquire Resources process:

- Decision making
- Interpersonal and team skills
- Pre-assignment
- Virtual teams

Decision Making   Decision-making techniques used in this process include, but are not limited to, multi-criteria decision analysis. Multi-criteria decision analysis involves the use of selection criteria to make decisions on whether potential project team members are a fit. Criteria are typically assigned a weight based on their level of importance, and candidates are then rated against the criteria. Some examples of criteria used are availability, experience, ability, and cost.

Interpersonal and Team Skills   When working with shared resources, the use of interpersonal and team skills, specifically negotiation, is key. Project managers may use negotiation techniques when dealing with functional managers and other organizational department managers—and sometimes with a vendor to get some of their best people—for project resources and for the timing of those resources.

The following items are typically negotiated:

- Availability
- Competency level of the staff member assigned

Pre-assignment   Pre-assignment may take place when the project is put out for bid and specific team members or physical resources are promised as part of the proposal or when internal project team members are promised and assigned as a condition of the project. Pre-assignments are documented within the project charter.

Virtual Teams   According to the *PMBOK® Guide*, virtual teams are defined as groups of people with a shared goal who fulfill their roles with little or no time spent meeting face-to-face. The use of virtual teams makes it possible to draw in resources that wouldn't otherwise be available. It also reduces travel expenses by allowing teams to work from home. Virtual teams typically connect using technology tools, such as the Internet, email, and videoconferencing.

Communication becomes essential when functioning in a virtual structure. All team members should be made aware of the protocols for communicating in a virtual team environment, understand the expectations, and be clear on the decision-making processes.

Outputs of Acquire Resources

Know the following eight outputs of the Acquire Resources process:

Physical Resource Assignments   Physical resource assignments need to be documented, and the supplies, locations, material, and equipment should be recorded.

Project Team Assignments   Project team assignments are based on the results of negotiating and determining elements such as the roles and responsibilities and reviewing recruitment practices. This output also results in a published project team directory, which lists the names of all project team members and stakeholders.

Resource Calendars   Resource calendars show the team members' availability and the times they are scheduled to work on the project. A composite resource calendar includes availability information for potential resources as well as their capabilities and skills.

Change Requests   As a result of performing the Acquire Resources process, adjustments or preventative or corrective actions need to be documented in a change request. Change requests are then reviewed and disposed of through the Perform Integrated Change Control process.

Project Management Plan Updates   As a result of performing the Acquire Resources process, updates will be made to the resource management plan and the cost baseline.

Project Documents Updates   The Acquire Resources process will result in updates to the lessons learned register, resource breakdown structure, risk register, stakeholder register, project schedule, and resource requirements. There may also be other documents that will need to be updated depending upon the scope and nature of the project being performed.

Enterprise Environmental Factors Updates   The resource availability within the organization and the amount of consumable resources used are elements of enterprise environmental factors that may be updated through this process.

Organizational Process Assets Updates   At a minimum, documentation related to acquiring, assigning, and allocating resources may be updated through the Acquire Resources process.

Conduct Procurements

In some cases, resources will need to be procured externally. The Conduct Procurements process is concerned with obtaining responses to bids and proposals from potential vendors, selecting a vendor, and awarding the contract. This process is used only when goods or services are obtained from outside of the project's organization. After this process is conducted, sellers will have been selected, contracts awarded, and project documents updated to reflect the selected vendors.

Figure 7.2 shows the inputs, tools and techniques, and outputs of the Conduct Procurements process.

FIGURE 7.2   Conduct Procurements process

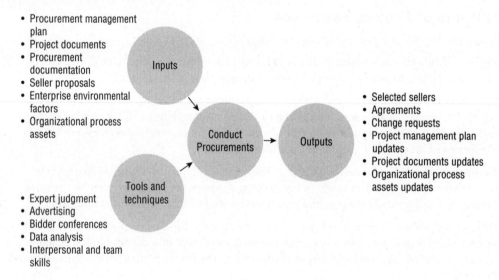

- Procurement management plan
- Project documents
- Procurement documentation
- Seller proposals
- Enterprise environmental factors
- Organizational process assets

Inputs

Conduct Procurements

Outputs

- Selected sellers
- Agreements
- Change requests
- Project management plan updates
- Project documents updates
- Organizational process assets updates

Tools and techniques

- Expert judgment
- Advertising
- Bidder conferences
- Data analysis
- Interpersonal and team skills

For more detailed information on the Conduct Procurements process, see Chapter 9, "Conducting Procurements and Sharing Information," in *PMP®: Project Manager Professional Exam Study Guide, Ninth Edition* (Sybex, 2017).

Inputs of Conduct Procurements

There are six inputs of the Conduct Procurements process that you should know:

- Project management plan
- Project documents
- Procurement documentation
- Seller proposals
- Enterprise environmental factors
- Organizational process assets

Project Management Plan   The project management plan elements used to guide the Conduct Procurement process may include, but are not limited to, the scope management plan, requirements management plan, communications management plan, risk management plan, procurement management plan, configuration management plan, and cost baseline.

Project Documents   Project documents typically used as an input to this process include the lessons learned register, project schedule, requirements documentation, risk register, and stakeholder register.

Procurement Documentation   The following procurement documents are typically utilized:

- Bid documents such as these:
  - Requests for proposals (RFPs)
  - Requests for information (RFIs)
  - Requests for quotations (RFQs)
- Procurement statement of work
- Independent cost estimates
- Source selection criteria

Seller Proposals   Seller proposals are literally the proposals submitted by sellers in response to a procurement document package. These proposals will be evaluated as part of this process.

Enterprise Environmental Factors   There are many enterprise environmental factors that could shape the Conduct Procurements process including, but not limited to, the following:

- Local laws and regulations
- Existing agreements

- Marketplace conditions
- Relevant experience with sellers, both good and bad
- Contract management systems.

Organizational Process Assets   Organizational process assets may contain information on sellers used, including a list of preferred sellers, organizational policies that influence seller selection, and relevant financial policies and procurements.

Tools and Techniques of Conduct Procurements

Know the following tools and techniques of the Conduct Procurements process:

- Expert judgment
- Advertising
- Bidder conferences
- Data analysis
- Interpersonal and team skills

Expert Judgment   Expert judgment may include experts from all areas of the organization when evaluating proposals and selecting vendors.

Advertising   Advertising lets potential vendors know that an RFP is available. It can be used as a way of expanding the pool of potential vendors, or it may be a requirement, such as in the case of government projects. Here are some examples of where advertising may appear:

- The company's Internet site
- Professional journals
- Newspapers

Bidder Conferences   Bidder conferences, also known as vendor conferences, prebid conferences, and contractor conferences, are meetings with prospective vendors or sellers that occur prior to the completion of their response proposal. Bidder conferences have the following characteristics:

- They allow all prospective vendors to meet with the buyers to ask questions and clarify issues they have regarding the project and the RFP.
- They are held once.
- They are attended by all vendors at the same time.
- They are held before vendors prepare their responses.

Data Analysis   There are several techniques that can be used to evaluate proposals. The types of goods and services you're trying to procure will dictate how detailed your evaluation criteria are. Depending on the complexity of the procurements, you may use one or more of the following techniques to evaluate and rate sellers:

- Use the source selection criteria process to rate and score proposals.
- When purchasing goods, request a sample from each vendor to compare quality (or some other criteria) against your need.

- Ask vendors for references and/or financial records.

- Evaluate the response itself to determine whether the vendor has a clear understanding of what you're asking them to do or provide.

After utilizing the necessary techniques, compare each proposal against the criteria, and rate or score each proposal for its ability to meet or fulfill these criteria. This can serve as your first step in eliminating vendors that don't match your criteria. The next step is to apply the tools and techniques of this process to further evaluate the remaining potential vendors.

Using a weighting system, you can assign numerical weights to evaluation criteria and then multiply them by the weights of each criteria factor to come up with total scores for each vendor. Screening systems and seller rating systems are also sometimes used.

Interpersonal and Team Skills   The primary interpersonal and team skill used for this process is negotiation. In procurement negotiations, both parties come to an agreement regarding the contract terms. At a minimum, deal points that may need negotiation in a contract should include the following items:

- Price

- Responsibilities

- Applicable regulations or laws that apply

- Overall approach to the project

Once agreement is reached and the negotiations are finished, the contract is signed by both buyer and seller and is executed.

Outputs of Conduct Procurements

The Conduct Procurements process contains the following six outputs:

- Selected sellers
- Agreements
- Change requests
- Project management plan updates
- Project documents updates
- Organizational process assets updates

Selected Sellers   Selected sellers are vendors that have been chosen to provide the goods or services requested by the buyer.

Agreements   A procurement agreement is a legally binding agreement between two or more parties, typically used to acquire goods or services. Agreements have several names:

- Memorandums of understanding (MOUs)

- Contracts

- Purchase orders

The type of contract awarded depends on the product or services being procured and on the organizational policies.

A contract's life cycle consists of four stages: requirement, requisition, solicitation, and award. In the requirement stage, the project and contract needs are established and requirements are defined within the statement of work (SOW). The requisition stage focuses on refining and confirming the project objectives and generating solicitation materials, such as the request for proposals (RFP), request for information (RFI), and request for quotations (RFQ). The solicitation stage is where vendors are asked to compete and respond to the solicitation materials. And last, the award stage is where the vendors are chosen and contracts awarded.

The contract should clearly address the following:

- Elements of the SOW
- Time period of performance
- Pricing and payment plan
- Acceptance criteria
- Warranty periods
- Dispute resolution procedures and penalties
- Roles and responsibilities

According to the *PMBOK® Guide*, a negotiated draft contract is one of the requirements of the selected sellers output. Also note that senior management signatures may be required on complex, high-risk, or high-dollar contracts. Be certain to check your organization's procurement policies regarding the authority level and amounts you are authorized to sign for.

Change Requests   Change requests may include changes to the project management plan and its subsidiary plans and components. These changes are submitted to the change control board for review.

Project Management Plan Updates   The following elements of the project management plan may need to be updated as a result of this process:

- Requirements management plan
- Quality management plan
- Procurement management plan
- Communications management plan
- Risk management plan
- Cost, scope, and schedule baselines

Project Documents Updates   The following documents may need to be updated as a result of this process:

- Lessons learned register
- Requirements documentation and requirements traceability matrix
- Resource calendars
- Risk register
- Stakeholder register

Organizational Process Assets Updates   The following organizational process assets may need to be updated as a result of this process:

- Listings of prospective and prequalified sellers
- Information on relevant experience with sellers, both good and bad

---

Exam Essentials

Be able to describe the purpose of the Acquire Resources process.   The Acquire Resources process involves acquiring and assigning physical and human resources, both internal and external, to the project.

Be able to describe the purpose of the Conduct Procurements process.   Conduct Procurements involves obtaining bids and proposals from vendors, selecting a vendor, and awarding a contract.

Be able to name the tools and techniques of the Conduct Procurements process.   The tools and techniques of the Conduct Procurements process are bidder conferences, advertising, data analysis, expert judgment, and interpersonal and team skills.

Be able to name the contracting life cycle stages.   The stages of the contracting life cycle are requirement, requisition, solicitation, and award.

Maximizing Team Performance

Maximizing team performance involves leading, mentoring, training, and motivating team members. The project manager leads these efforts with the guidance of the documented resource management plan. The processes used to achieve maximum team performance include Develop Team and Manage Team, which are both a part of the Project Resource Management Knowledge Area.

To be successful, project managers will need to be familiar with several leadership theories, the stages of team development, motivational theories, and leadership styles. Being familiar with and understanding conflict resolution techniques and types of power are also important when managing teams.

Develop Team

The Develop Team process is concerned with creating a positive environment for team members; developing the team into an effective, functioning, coordinated group; and increasing the team's competency levels. The proper development of the team is critical to a successful project. Since teams are made up of individuals, individual development becomes a critical factor to project success.

Figure 7.3 shows the inputs, tools and techniques, and outputs of the Develop Team process.

FIGURE 7.3   Develop Team process

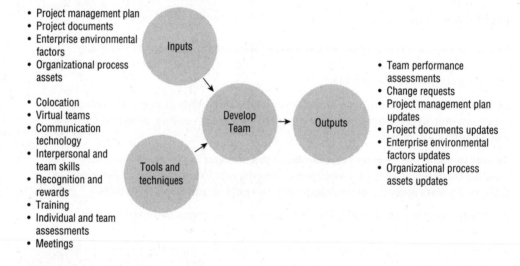

- Project management plan
- Project documents
- Enterprise environmental factors
- Organizational process assets

Inputs

- Colocation
- Virtual teams
- Communication technology
- Interpersonal and team skills
- Recognition and rewards
- Training
- Individual and team assessments
- Meetings

Tools and techniques

Develop Team

Outputs

- Team performance assessments
- Change requests
- Project management plan updates
- Project documents updates
- Enterprise environmental factors updates
- Organizational process assets updates

For more detailed information on the Develop Team process, see Chapter 8 of *PMP®: Project Management Professional Exam Study Guide, Ninth Edition* (Sybex, 2017).

Inputs of Develop Team

The Develop Team process includes the following inputs:

Project Management Plan   The project management plan, and specifically the resource management plan, provides guidance on providing the project team members with rewards, feedback, additional training, and disciplinary actions.

Project Documents   Project documents that serve as inputs to the Develop Team process include, but are not limited to, the lessons learned register, project schedule, resource calendars, project team assignments, and team charter.

Enterprise Environmental Factors   The Develop Team process is informed by the following enterprise environmental factors (among others):

- Human resource management policies

- Team member skills/specialized knowledge

- Geographic distribution of the team

Organizational Process Assets   Historical information and the lessons learned repository are the key organizational process assets that inform the Develop Team process.

Tools and Techniques of Develop Team

Before we review the tools and techniques of the Develop Team process, it is helpful to understand some key concepts and theories about leadership, management, and motivation.

Leadership vs. Management

Project managers need to use the traits of both leaders and managers at different times during a project. Therefore, it's important to understand the difference between the two.

Leaders display the following characteristics:

- Impart vision, motivate and inspire, and are concerned with strategic vision

- Have a knack for getting others to do what needs to be done

- Use and understand the following two techniques:

  - Power, which is the ability to get people to do what they wouldn't do ordinarily and the ability to influence behavior

  - Politics, which imparts pressure to conform regardless of whether people agree with the decision

- Have committed team members who believe in their vision

- Set direction and time frames and have the ability to attract good talent to work for them

- Are directive in their approach but allow for plenty of feedback and input

- Have strong interpersonal skills and are well respected

Managers display the following characteristics:

- Are generally task-oriented and concerned with issues such as plans, controls, budgets, policies, and procedures

- Are generalists with a broad base of planning and organizational skills

- Have a primary goal of satisfying stakeholder needs

- Possess motivational skills and the ability to recognize and reward behavior

There are four particularly notable theories regarding leadership and management:

Theory X & Y   Douglas McGregor defined two models of worker behavior, Theory X and Theory Y, that attempt to explain how different managers deal with their team members. Theory X managers believe the following statements to be true:

- Most people do not like work and will try to steer clear of it.
- People have little to no ambition and need constant supervision.
- People won't actually perform the duties of their job unless threatened.

As a result, Theory X managers are like dictators and impose very rigid controls over their employees. They believe people are motivated only by punishment, money, or position.

Theory Y managers have the following characteristics:

- Believe people are interested in performing their best given the right motivation and proper expectations
- Provide support to their teams
- Are concerned about their team members
- Are good listeners

Theory Y managers believe people are creative and committed to the project goals, that they like responsibility and seek it out, and that they are able to perform the functions of their positions with limited supervision.

Theory Z   Theory Z was developed by William Ouchi. This theory is concerned with increasing employee loyalty to their organization and results in increased productivity. Theory Z has the following characteristics:

- Puts an emphasis on the well-being of the employees both at work and outside of work
- Encourages steady employment
- Leads to high employee satisfaction and morale

Theory Z develops employee loyalty through group decision making, which also results in a sense of being valued and respected.

Figure 7.4 highlights the differences between a Theory X manager, a Theory Y manager, and a Theory Z manager.

Contingency Theory   The Contingency theory builds on a combination of Theory Y behaviors and the Hygiene theory. (The Hygiene theory is discussed shortly, in the section "Motivational Theories.") The Contingency theory says that people are motivated to achieve levels of competency and will continue to be motivated by this need even after competency is reached.

FIGURE 7.4   Theory X & Y and Theory Z

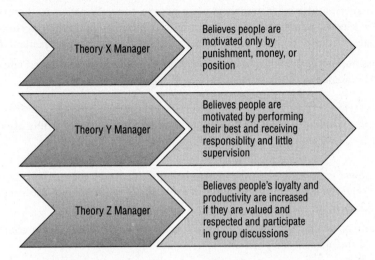

Situational Theory   Paul Hersey and Ken Blanchard developed the Situational Leadership theory during the mid-1970s. This theory's main premise is that the leadership style you use depends on the situation. Both Hersey and Blanchard went on to develop their own situational leadership models. Blanchard's model, Situational Leadership II, describes four styles of leadership that depend on the situation: directing, coaching, supporting, and delegating.

Leadership Styles

There are various leadership styles that a project manager may use, and in many cases, the appropriate leadership style is based on the situation. The following are examples of leadership styles:

Autocratic   All decisions are made by the leader.

Laissez-faire   The leader uses a hands-off approach and allows the team to drive the decisions.

Democratic   Leaders gather all facts and receive input from the team before reaching a decision.

Situational   Based on the Blanchard theory of situational leadership that uses four styles: directing, coaching, supporting, and delegating.

Transactional and Transformational   Developed by Bernard Bass. He described transactional leaders as activity-focused and autonomous; they use contingent reward systems and manage by exception. Transformational leaders are described as focusing on relationships rather than activities.

The Power of Leaders

Leaders, managers, and project managers use power to convince others to do tasks a specific way. The kind of power they use to accomplish this depends on their personality, their personal values, and the company culture. Here are five forms of power leaders may use:

- Punishment power, also known as *coercive* or *penalty power*, is exerted when employees are threatened with consequences if expectations are not met.

 Punishment power should be used as a last resort and only after all other forms have been exhausted.

- Expert power is exerted when the person being influenced believes the manager (or the person doing the influencing) is knowledgeable about the subject or has special abilities that make them an expert.

- Legitimate power, also known as *formal power*, is exerted when power comes about as a result of the influencer's position.

- Referent power is obtained by the influencer through a higher authority.

- Reward power is the ability to grant bonuses and incentives for a job well done.

Motivational Theories

There are many theories on motivation, and as a project manager, you should understand and tailor the recognition and rewards programs around the project team. The following are some important motivational theories to note:

Maslow's Hierarchy of Needs   Abraham Maslow theorized that humans have five basic sets of needs arranged in hierarchical order. The idea is that each set of needs must be met before a person can move to the next level of needs in the hierarchy. Once that need is met, they progress to the next level, and so on. Maslow's hierarchy of needs theory suggests that once a lower-level need has been met, it no longer serves as a motivator, and the next-higher level becomes the driving motivator in a person's life. Maslow theorized that humans are always in one state of need or another and they can move up and down the pyramid throughout their lives. The following is a brief review of the needs, as shown in Figure 7.5, starting with the highest level and ending with the lowest:

> **Self-actualization:** Highest level; performing at your peak potential
>
> **Self-esteem needs:** Accomplishment, respect for self, capability
>
> **Social needs:** A sense of belonging, love, acceptance, friendship
>
> **Safety and security needs:** Your physical welfare and the security of your belongings
>
> **Basic physical needs:** Lowest level; food, clothing, shelter

FIGURE 7.5   Maslow's hierarchy of needs

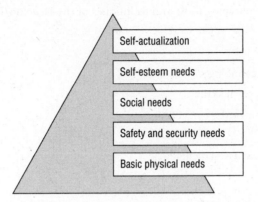

- Self-actualization
- Self-esteem needs
- Social needs
- Safety and security needs
- Basic physical needs

Hygiene Theory   Frederick Herzberg came up with the Hygiene theory, also known as the Motivation-Hygiene theory. He postulated that two factors contribute to motivation:

- Hygiene factors, which prevent dissatisfaction, deal with work environment issues and include factors such as pay, benefits, conditions of the work environment, and relationships with peers and managers.

- Motivators, which lead to satisfaction, deal with the substance of the work itself and the satisfaction one derives from performing the functions of the job. According to Herzberg, the ability to advance, the opportunity to learn new skills, and the challenges involved in the work are all motivators.

Expectancy Theory   The Expectancy theory, first proposed by Victor Vroom, says that the expectation of a positive outcome drives motivation. People will behave in certain ways if they think there will be good rewards for doing so and if they themselves value the reward. Also note that this theory says the strength of the expectancy drives the behavior. This means the expectation or likelihood of the reward is linked to the behavior. This theory also says that people become what you expect of them.

Achievement Theory   The Achievement theory, attributed to David McClelland, says that people are motivated by the need for three things:

- Achievement, as a result of a need to achieve or succeed
- Power, which involves a desire to influence the behavior of others
- Affiliation, as a result of a need to develop relationships with others

---

Day of the Exam

For the exam, you will need to memorize names of motivational and quality theories highlighted in this chapter, along with the individual(s) behind the theories. Don't forget to leverage mnemonic technique or other memory tricks to help you remember!

Tools and Techniques

You should know the following tools and techniques of the Develop Team process:

- Colocation
- Virtual teams
- Communication technology
- Interpersonal and team skills
- Recognition and rewards
- Training
- Individual and team assessments
- Meetings

Colocation   Colocation refers to basing team members out of the same physical location. Colocation enables teams to function more effectively than if they're spread out among different localities. One way to achieve colocation might be to set aside a common meeting room, sometimes called a war room, for team members who are located in different buildings or across town to meet and exchange information.

Virtual Teams   Through the use of technology, teams create online work environments that allow shared file storage, use of conversation threads or tools to communicate, and use of a team calendar.

Communication Technology   Communication technology helps in the Develop Team process for both collocated and virtual teams. Examples of this technology include video- and audioconferencing tools, use of a shared portal, and email/chat tools.

Interpersonal and Team Skills   Interpersonal skills, often referred to as soft skills, include things such as these:

- Leadership
- Influence
- Negotiation
- Communications
- Empathy
- Creativity

By possessing these skills, the project management team can reduce issues within the project team and better manage the team overall.

Team-Building Activities   Team-building activities are also important. Part of the project manager's job is to bring the team together, get its members headed in the right direction, and provide motivation, reward, and recognition. This is done using a variety of team-building techniques and exercises. Team building involves getting a diverse group of people to work together in the most efficient and effective manner possible.

Important to team-building activities are the theories behind team development. Authors Bruce Tuckman and Mary Ann Jensen developed a model that describes how teams develop and mature. According to Tuckman and Jensen, all newly formed teams go through the following five stages of development:

Forming   Forming occurs at the beginning stage of team formation, when team members are brought together, introduced, and told the objectives of the project. Team members tend to behave in a formal and reserved manner.

Storming   Storming is the stage when action begins. Team members tend to be confrontational with one another as they vie for position and control.

Norming   Norming is the stage when team members are comfortable with one another and begin to confront project concerns and issues.

Performing   Performing is the stage when the team becomes productive and effective. Trust among team members is high; this is considered to be the mature development stage.

Adjourning   The adjourning stage is when the team is released after the work is completed.

Figure 7.6 shows the stages of a team's development.

FIGURE 7.6   Stages of team development

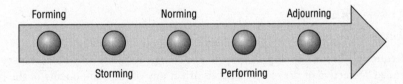

Recognition and Rewards   Recognition and rewards are an important part of team motivation. They are formal ways of recognizing and promoting desirable behavior and are most effective when carried out by the management team and the project manager. Criteria for rewards should be developed and documented, and rewards should be given to team members who go above and beyond the call of duty.

Motivation can be extrinsic or intrinsic:

- Extrinsic motivators are material rewards and might include bonuses, the use of a company car, stock options, gift certificates, training opportunities, extra time off, and so on.

- Intrinsic motivators are specific to the individual. Cultural and religious influences are forms of intrinsic motivators as well.

The recognition and rewards tool of this process is an example of an extrinsic motivator.

Training   Training is a matter of assessing the team members' skills and abilities, assessing the project needs, and providing the training necessary for the team members to carry out their assigned activities. Training can sometimes be a reward as well. Training needs may be incorporated into the staffing management plan or scheduled as they are assessed.

Individual and Team Assessments   Personnel and team assessment tools capture feedback obtained on the project team's level of effectiveness. The intention is to increase the probability of the team's success in achieving the project objectives through the increase of performance. Team performance is often measured against the following:

- Technical success
- Performance against the schedule
- Performance against the budget

Meetings   In the Develop Team process, meetings are used for, but not limited to, project orientation, team building, and team development.

Outputs of Develop Team

The following six outputs result from the Develop Team process:

Team Performance Assessments   Team performance assessments involve determining the project team's effectiveness. Assessing these characteristics helps to determine where (or whether) the project team needs improvements. The following indicators are among those assessed:

- Improvements in the team's skills
- Improvements in the team's competencies
- Lower staff attrition
- Greater level of team cohesiveness

Change Requests   In the Develop Team process, change requests may be necessary if recommended corrective or preventive actions affect any of the components of the project management plan or project documents.

Project Management Plan Updates   The resource management plan is one of the components of the project management plan that may be updated in this process.

Project Documents Updates   This process may include updates to multiple project documents including, but not limited to, the following:

- Lessons learned register
- Project schedule
- Resource calendars
- Project team assignments
- Team charter

Enterprise Environmental Factors Updates   Updates to the enterprise environmental factors typically include updates to team records regarding training and skill assessment and any personnel administration updates that resulted from carrying out this process.

Organizational Process Assets Updates   Updates to the organizational process assets include updates to the training requirements and personnel assessments.

Manage Team

The Manage Team process is concerned with tracking and reporting on the performance of individual team members. During this process, performance appraisals are prepared and conducted, issues are identified and resolved, and feedback is given to the team members. This process involves management skills that promote teamwork and result in high-performance teams.

Figure 7.7 shows the inputs, tools and techniques, and outputs of the Manage Team process.

FIGURE 7.7   Manage Team process

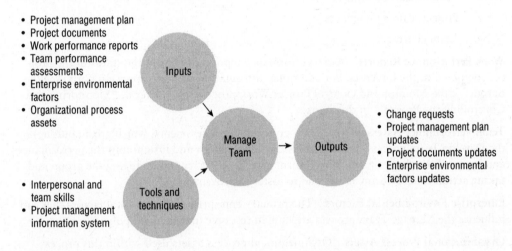

- Project management plan
- Project documents
- Work performance reports
- Team performance assessments
- Enterprise environmental factors
- Organizational process assets

Inputs

Manage Team

Outputs

- Change requests
- Project management plan updates
- Project documents updates
- Enterprise environmental factors updates

- Interpersonal and team skills
- Project management information system

Tools and techniques

For more detailed information on the Manage Team process, see Chapter 8 of *PMP®: Project Management Professional Exam Study Guide, Ninth Edition* (Sybex, 2017).

Inputs of Manage Project Team

There are six inputs to the Manage Team process:

- Project management plan
- Project documents
- Work performance reports
- Team performance assessments
- Enterprise environmental factors
- Organizational process assets

Project Management Plan   The primary, but not sole, input to the Manage Team process from the project management plan is the resource management plan. The resource management plan provides the following information that is utilized in this process:

- Staffing management plan
- Roles and responsibilities
- The project organization chart

Project Documents   Project documents that provide inputs into this process include, but are not limited to, the following:

- Issue log
- Lessons learned register
- Project team assignments
- Team charter

Work Performance Reports   Work performance reports document the status of the project compared to the forecasts. For additional information on performance reports, see the outputs of the Monitor and Control Project Work process in Chapter 8, "Monitoring and Controlling the Project," in this book.

Team Performance Assessments   Team performance assessments, which are an output of the Develop Team process, provide necessary information and insight into the performance and issues of the project team. This information is necessary for managing the group and taking action to resolve any issues and to foster improvement.

Enterprise Environmental Factors   The primary enterprise environmental factors that can influence the Manage Team process are human resource management policies.

Organizational Process Assets   Organizational process assets used within this process include any existing organizational perks and forms of recognition.

Tools and Techniques of Manage Team

Know the following tools and techniques of the Manage Team process:

- Interpersonal and team skills
- Project management information system

Interpersonal and Team Skills   There are five types of interpersonal and team skills used most often in this process:

- Conflict management
- Decision making
- Emotional intelligence
- Influencing
- Leadership

Of all these skills, conflict management deserves some specific focus. Conflict exists when the desires, needs, or goals of one party are incompatible with the desires, needs, or goals of another party (or parties). Conflict is the incompatibility of goals, which often leads to one party resisting or blocking the other party from attaining their goals. Conflict management is how an individual deals with these types of scenarios or issues.

The following six methods of conflict management are also shown in Figure 7.8:

FIGURE 7.8   Conflict resolution techniques

Conflict Resolution Techniques				
Forcing/Directing (win-lose)	Smoothing / Accommodating (lose-lose)	Compromising / Reconciling (lose-lose)	Collaborating / Problem Solving (win-win, *best* option)	Withdrawing / Avoiding (lose-lose, *worst* option)

Forcing/Directing   One person forces a solution on the other parties. This is an example of a win-lose conflict resolution technique.

Smoothing/Accommodating   Smoothing/accommodating is a temporary way to resolve conflict in which the areas of agreement are emphasized over the areas of difference, so the real issue stays buried. This is an example of a lose-lose conflict resolution technique because neither side wins.

Compromising/Reconciling   Compromise is achieved when each of the parties involved in the conflict gives up something to reach a solution. This is an example of a lose-lose conflict resolution technique because neither side gets what they wanted.

Collaborating/Problem Solving   Collaboration and problem solving are the *best* ways to resolve conflict. One of the key actions performed with this technique is a fact-finding mission. This is the conflict resolution approach project managers use most often and is an example of a win-win conflict resolution technique.

Withdrawing/Avoiding   An example of withdrawal/avoidance is when one of the parties gets up, leaves, and refuses to discuss the conflict. This is an example of a lose-lose conflict resolution technique because no solution is ever reached. This is considered to be the *worst* conflict resolution technique.

The following should also be noted about conflict and conflict resolution:

- In any situation, conflict should be dealt with as soon as it arises.
- According to the *PMBOK® Guide*, when you have successfully resolved conflict, it will result in increased productivity and better, more positive working relationships.

- Most conflicts are a result of schedule issues, availability of resources (usually the lack of availability), or personal work habits.

- Team members should be encouraged to resolve their own conflicts.

- Ground rules, established policies, and procedures help mitigate conflict before it arises.

Day of the Exam

Before starting your exam, consider noting down the conflict resolution types on your scratch sheet of paper, along with other items noted earlier in this book, such as formulas. Remember the best and worst conflict resolution type:

- *Best*: collaborating / problem solving

- *Worst*: avoiding / withdrawing

Project Management Information System   Scheduling or resource management software can be used for the management and coordination of team members.

Outputs of Manage Team

The Manage Team process includes the following outputs:

- Change requests
- Project management plan updates
- Project documents updates
- Enterprise environmental factors updates

Change Requests   Change requests may result from a change in staffing. Also included within change requests are corrective actions that may result from disciplinary actions or training needs and preventive actions, which may be needed to reduce potential issues among the project team.

Project Management Plan Updates   Project management plan updates may include changes that occurred in the resource management plan, schedule baseline, and cost baseline.

Project Documents Updates   The following project documents are typically updated as a result of carrying out this process:

- Issue log
- Lessons learned register
- Project team assignments

Enterprise Environmental Factors Updates   There are two components of the enterprise environmental factors that may need updating as a result of this process:

- Input to organizational performance appraisals from team members who have a high level of interaction with the project and one another
- Personnel skill updates

Exam Essentials

Be able to describe the purpose of the Develop Team process.   The Develop Team process is concerned with creating a positive environment for team members; developing the team into an effective, functioning, coordinated group; and increasing the team's competency levels.

Be able to name the five stages of group formation.   The five stages of group formation are forming, storming, norming, performing, and adjourning.

Be able to define Maslow's highest level of motivation.   Self-actualization occurs when a person performs at their peak and all lower-level needs have been met.

Be able to name the five types of power.   The five levels of power are reward, punishment, expert, legitimate, and referent.

Be able to identify the six styles of conflict resolution.   The six styles of conflict resolution are forcing, smoothing, compromising, confrontation, collaborating, and withdrawal.

Be able to name the tools and techniques of the Manage Team process.   The tools and techniques of Manage Team are interpersonal and team skills and the project management information system.

Executing the Project Management Plan

Executing the project management plan is carried out through the Direct and Manage Project Work process, which is a process that belongs to the Project Integration Management Knowledge Area. This is where the project work is carried out, according to the plan, as a way of producing the deliverables on time and on budget. The Direct and Manage Project Work process is also responsible for implementing changes that have been approved by the change control board. Typically, approved changes are implemented according to the change management plan as a way of meeting project requirements.

When implementing the plan, the project manager will need to be proactive in managing project communications. This includes distributing relevant project information in an efficient and effective manner. Managing stakeholder engagement is also important at this stage. Both of these objectives can be accomplished by carrying out the Manage Communications and Manage Stakeholder Engagement processes in accordance with the communications management plan and stakeholder engagement plan.

Direct and Manage Project Work

The Direct and Manage Project Work process is responsible for carrying out the project management plan. The project manager oversees the actual work, staying on top of issues and problems and keeping the work lined up with the plan. Coordinating and integrating all the elements of the project are among the most challenging aspects of this process.

According to the *PMBOK® Guide*, this process also requires implementing corrective actions to bring the work of the project back into alignment with the project management plan, preventive actions to reduce the probability of negative consequences, and repairs to correct product defects discovered during the quality management processes.

Figure 7.9 shows the inputs, tools and techniques, and outputs of the Direct and Manage Project Work process.

FIGURE 7.9   Direct and Manage Project Work process

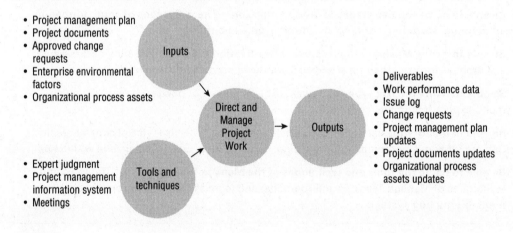

- Project management plan
- Project documents
- Approved change requests
- Enterprise environmental factors
- Organizational process assets

Inputs

- Expert judgment
- Project management information system
- Meetings

Tools and techniques

Direct and Manage Project Work

Outputs

- Deliverables
- Work performance data
- Issue log
- Change requests
- Project management plan updates
- Project documents updates
- Organizational process assets updates

For more detailed information on the Direct and Manage Project Work process, see Chapter 8 in *PMP®: Project Management Professional Exam Study Guide, Ninth Edition* (Sybex, 2017).

Inputs to Direct and Manage Project Work

Know the following inputs for the Direct and Manage Project Work process:

- Project management plan
- Project documents
- Approved change requests
- Enterprise environmental factors
- Organizational process assets

Project Management Plan   The project management plan documents the collection of outputs of the planning processes and describes and defines the work to be carried out and how the project should be executed, monitored, controlled, and closed.

Project Documents   The following project documents are typically considered as inputs for this process:

- Change log
- Lessons learned register
- Milestone list
- Project communications
- Project schedule
- Requirements traceability matrix
- Risk register
- Risk report

Approved Change Requests   Approved change requests come about as a result of the change request status updates output of the Perform Integrated Change Control process. Approved change requests are then submitted as inputs to the Direct and Manage Project Work process for implementation. Implementation of approved changes may also include the implementation of workarounds, which are unplanned responses to negative risks that have occurred.

Enterprise Environmental Factors   The following enterprise environmental factors are considered when performing the Direct and Manage Project Work process:

- Company culture and organizational structure
- Facilities available to the project team
- Personnel guidelines and hiring practices
- Risk tolerance levels
- Project management information systems

Organizational Process Assets   The following organizational process assets are utilized within the Direct and Manage Project Work process:

- Historical information from past projects
- Organizational guidelines and work processes
- Process measurement databases
- Issue and defect databases

Tools and Techniques of Direct and Manage Project Work

You should be familiar with the following tools and techniques of the Direct and Manage Project Work process:

Expert Judgment   Expert judgment is provided by the project manager and project team members as well as by the following sources:

- Industry and professional associations
- Consultants
- Stakeholders
- Other units within the company

Project Management Information System   As used in the Direct and Manage Project Work process, the project management information system (PMIS) provides the ability to connect to automated tools, such as scheduling software and configuration management systems, that can be utilized during project execution.

Meetings   Meetings are a key tool in managing the work of the project. According to the *PMBOK® Guide*, there are three types of meetings: information exchange, working sessions such as brainstorming and design, and decision making.

Outputs of Direct and Manage Project Work

These seven outputs result from carrying out the Direct and Manage Project Work process:

- Deliverables
- Work performance data
- Issue log
- Change requests
- Project management plan updates
- Project documents updates
- Organizational process assets updates

Deliverables   According to the *PMBOK® Guide*, a deliverable (see Figure 7.10) is defined as any unique and verifiable product, result, or capability to perform a service that is required to be produced to complete a process, phase, or project.

FIGURE 7.10   Definition of a deliverable

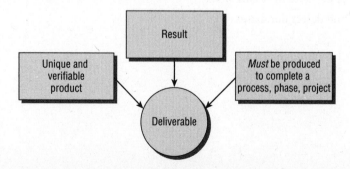

During the Direct and Manage Project Work process, the following information regarding the outcomes of the work is gathered and recorded:

- Activity completion dates
- Milestone completions
- Status of the deliverables
- Quality of the deliverables
- Costs
- Schedule progress and updates

 Although the *PMBOK® Guide* breaks up these processes for ease of explanation, several of the Executing and Monitoring and Controlling processes are performed together. Remember that the processes are iterative.

Work Performance Data   Work performance data involves gathering, documenting, and recording the status of project work. Here are types of information that may be gathered during this process:

- Schedule status and progress
- Status of deliverable completion
- Progress and status of schedule activities
- Adherence to quality standards
- Status of costs (those authorized and costs incurred to date)
- Schedule activity completion estimates for those activities started
- Percentage of schedule activities completed
- Lessons learned
- Resource consumption and utilization

Issue log   All project issues are recorded and tracked in a document known as the issue log. The following elements may be included on the issue log:

- Issue type
- Who raised the issue and when
- Description
- Priority
- Who is assigned to the issue
- Target resolution date
- Status
- Selected solution

Change Requests   Changes can come about from several sources, including stakeholder requests, external sources, and technological advances. Change requests may encompass changes to the following:

- Schedule
- Scope
- Requirement
- Resource changes

Implementation of change requests may incorporate the following actions:

Corrective Actions   Corrective actions are taken to get the anticipated future project outcomes to align with the project plan.

Preventive Actions   Preventive actions involve anything that will reduce the potential impacts of negative risk events should they occur. Contingency plans and risk responses are examples of preventive action.

Defect Repairs   Defects are project components that do not meet the requirements or specifications. Defect repairs are discovered during quality audits or when inspections are performed. A *validated defect repair* is the result of a reinspection of the original defect repair.

Project Management Plan Updates   The following project management plan updates may occur as a result of the Direct and Manage Project Work process:

- Subsidiary project plans
- Project baselines

Project Documents Updates   The following project documents may undergo updates as a result of the Direct and Manage Project Work process:

- Requirements documentation and project logs
- Lessons learned register
- Risk register
- Stakeholder register

Organizational Process Assets Updates   It is possible that any organizational process asset could be updated as a result of the Direct and Manage Project Work process.

Manage Communications

The Manage Communications process is responsible for getting information about the project to stakeholders in a timely manner. It describes how reports, and other information, are collected, stored, retrieved, and distributed and to whom. Executing the communications management plan also occurs during this process.

Figure 7.11 shows the inputs, tools and techniques, and outputs of the Manage Communications process.

FIGURE 7.11 Manage Communications process

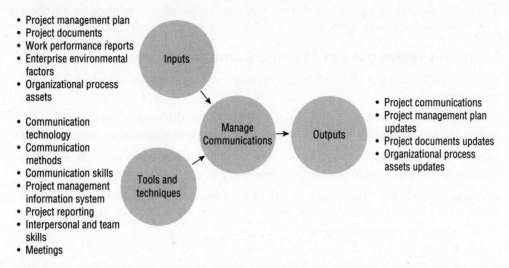

- Project management plan
- Project documents
- Work performance reports
- Enterprise environmental factors
- Organizational process assets

- Communication technology
- Communication methods
- Communication skills
- Project management information system
- Project reporting
- Interpersonal and team skills
- Meetings

- Project communications
- Project management plan updates
- Project documents updates
- Organizational process assets updates

 For more detailed information on the Manage Communications process, see Chapter 9 of *PMP®: Project Management Professional Exam Study Guide, Ninth Edition* (Sybex, 2017).

Inputs of Manage Communications

Know the following inputs of the Manage Communications process:

Project Management Plan The communications management plan, resource management plan, and stakeholder engagement plan are the primary components of the project management plan. The plan is put into action during this process.

Project Documents The following project documents are typically considered as inputs for this process:

- Change log
- Issue log
- Lessons learned register
- Quality report
- Risk report
- Stakeholder register

Work Performance Reports Work performance reports are utilized to distribute performance and status information to the appropriate individuals.

Enterprise Environmental Factors Enterprise environmental factors used through this process include the organizational culture and structure, any government- or industry-related standards, and the project management information system.

Organizational Process Assets   For this process, organizational process assets refer to any policies, procedures, and guidelines that the organization already has in place for distributing information and any existing documents and information that are relevant to the process.

Tools and Techniques of Manage Communications

The tools and techniques of the Manage Communications process include the following seven items:

Communication Technology   Technology is often used to disseminate information to stakeholders as appropriate and as described within the communications management plan.

Communication Methods   Choosing the appropriate communication methods will allow the message to be catered to the events and audience who need to receive the information.

Communication Skills   There are a variety of communication techniques that are used in the Manage Communications process, which include but are not limited to the following:

- Communication competence
- Feedback
- Nonverbal
- Presentations

Project Management Information System   The following information distribution tools are used to get the project information to the project team or stakeholders:

- Electronic tools, such as software, online-based tools, portals, etc.
- Electronic project management tools
- Social media management

Project Reporting   Project reporting refers to the actual collection and distribution of information, typically through the form of a project status report. This may include a diverse set of reports, from basic reporting to detailed and complex analysis of the project team's performance. Project reporting may also be communicated via progress metrics and forecasts.

Interpersonal and Team Skills   There are a number of interpersonal and team skills that can be used in the Manage Communications process. These include but are not limited to the following:

- Active listening
- Conflict management
- Cultural awareness
- Meeting management
- Networking
- Political awareness

Meetings   The communication model selected for managing communications should be based on the communication needs of the project.

Outputs of Manage Communications

Manage Communications results in four outputs that you should know: project communications, updates to the project management plan, updates to project documents, and updates to the organizational process assets.

Project Communications   *Project communications* refers to the actual communication produced, often by the project manager. Examples of project communications presented by the *PMBOK® Guide* include performance reports, deliverable status, schedule progress, and actual costs to date.

Project Management Plan Updates   Typical updates produced to the project management plan as a result of this process includes updates to the communications management plan, stakeholder management plan, and project baselines.

Project Documents Updates   Project documents updated as a result of carrying out this process often includes updates made to the issue log, schedule, and project funding requirements.

Organizational Process Assets Updates   There can be several updates to the organizational process assets as a result of carrying out this process. These updates are listed and described in Table 7.1.

TABLE 7.1   Organizational process assets updates

Update Item	Description
Stakeholder notifications	Notifications sent to stakeholders when solutions and approved changes have been implemented, the project status has been updated, issues have been resolved, and so on.
Project reports	The project status reports and minutes from project meetings, lessons learned, closure reports, and other documents from all the process outputs throughout the project.
Project presentations	Project information presented to the stakeholders and other appropriate parties when necessary.
Project records	Memos, correspondence, and other documents concerning the project.
Feedback from stakeholders	Feedback that can improve future performance on this project or future projects. The feedback should be captured and documented.
Lessons learned documentation	Information that is gathered and documented throughout the course of the project and can be used to benefit the current project, future projects, or other projects being performed by the organization.

Manage Stakeholder Engagement

The Manage Stakeholder Engagement process is responsible for satisfying the needs of the stakeholders by managing communications with them, resolving issues, improving project performance by implementing requested changes, and managing concerns in anticipation of potential problems.

Figure 7.12 shows the inputs, tools and techniques, and outputs of the Manage Stakeholder Engagement process.

> For more detailed information on the Manage Stakeholder Engagement process, see Chapter 9 of *PMP®: Project Management Professional Exam Study Guide, Ninth Edition* (Sybex, 2017).

FIGURE 7.12   Manage Stakeholder Engagement process

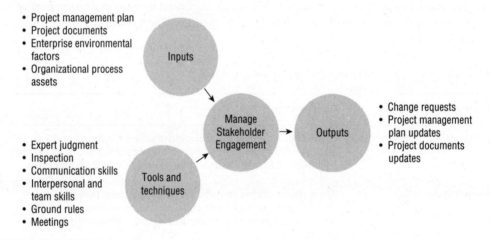

- Project management plan
- Project documents
- Enterprise environmental factors
- Organizational process assets

Inputs

- Expert judgment
- Inspection
- Communication skills
- Interpersonal and team skills
- Ground rules
- Meetings

Tools and techniques

Manage Stakeholder Engagement

Outputs

- Change requests
- Project management plan updates
- Project documents updates

Inputs of Manage Stakeholder Engagement

Know the following inputs of the Manage Stakeholder Engagement process:

- Project management plan
- Project documents
- Enterprise environmental factors
- Organizational process assets

Project Management Plan   The project management plan document contains several components useful in managing stakeholder expectations within the project. This includes, but is not limited to, the following components:

- Communications management plan
- Risk management plan

- Stakeholder engagement plan
- Change management plan

Project Documents   Project documents such as the change log, issue log, and lessons learned register can be inputs to the Manage Stakeholder Engagement process.

Enterprise Environmental Factors   Enterprise environmental factors used through this process include the organizational culture and structure, industry- or government-related standards, and the project management information system.

Organizational Process Assets   The following organizational process assets influence this process:

- Corporate policies and procedures governing social media, ethics, or security
- Issue management and change control procedures
- Organizational communication requirements
- Information from previous projects

According to the *PMBOK® Guide*, it's the project manager's responsibility to manage the engagement of stakeholders.

Tools and Techniques of Manage Stakeholder Engagement

Be familiar with the following six tools and techniques of the Manage Stakeholder Engagement process, and how they are used in this process:

Expert Judgment   Expert judgment may include input from experts or those with specialized knowledge on the following topics:

- Politics and power structures
- Environment and organizational culture
- Communication methods and strategies
- Management of requirements, vendors, and change management

Inspection   Project documentation and reports will need be inspected to enforce stakeholder engagement activities as originally designed or to make adjustments as needed.

Communication Skills   With guidance from the communications management plan, the project team uses feedback to assist in understanding stakeholder reaction to activities and decisions during the course of the project.

Interpersonal and Team Skills   Interpersonal and team skills were introduced in the Develop Team process. To manage stakeholder expectations and engagement, the project manager utilizes soft skills, such as building trust, conflict management, negotiation, establishing relationships, and listening.

Ground Rules   Defined in the team charter, ground rules set the behavioral expectations for team members and stakeholders.

Meetings   In the Management Stakeholder Engagement process, meetings provide a forum to discuss or address any issue or concern for communicating with stakeholders. This might include but is not limited to the following types of meetings:

- Project kick-off and status updates
- Decision making and issue resolution
- Lessons learned and retrospectives
- Sprint planning

Outputs of Manage Stakeholder Engagement

The Manage Stakeholder Engagement process results in the following outputs:

- Change requests
- Project management plan updates
- Project documents updates

Change Requests   The following change requests may emerge as a result of this process:

- Changes to the product or project
- Corrective actions
- Preventive actions

Project Management Plan Updates   Updates to the project management plan as a result of carrying out this process often involve updating the communications management plan and the stakeholder engagement plan.

Project Documents Updates   The stakeholder register, change log, lessons learned register, and issue log may all need updates as a result of carrying out this process.

Exam Essentials

Be able to identify the distinguishing characteristics of Direct and Manage Project Work.   Direct and Manage Project Work is where the work of the project is performed, and the majority of the project budget is spent during this process.

Be able to describe the purpose of the Manage Communications process.   The purpose of the Manage Communications process is to collect, retrieve, store, and get information to stakeholders about the project in a timely manner.

Be able to describe the purpose of the Manage Stakeholder Engagement process.   Manage Stakeholder Engagement concerns satisfying the needs of the stakeholders and successfully meeting the goals of the project by managing communications with stakeholders.

Implementing Approved Changes

As described in the previous section, the need for changes will emerge as the project work is executed. All change requests created to deal with this need must first be approved by the change control board before they can be implemented. This occurs through the Perform Integrated Change Control process, which is discussed in Chapter 8, "Monitoring and Controlling the Project," and must be managed according to the change management plan.

It's also important to keep in mind that the moment the work enters into the executing stage of the project, monitoring and controlling activities begin and continue concurrently as the work is progressing. Monitoring and controlling activities also identify the need for corrective and preventive actions as well as defect repairs. Once change requests are approved, they are implemented through the Direct and Manage Project Work process, discussed previously.

Exam Essentials

Be able to describe the various steps that a change request progresses through. Change requests are reviewed by the change control board through the Perform Integrated Change Control process. If approved, the changes are then implemented through the Direct and Manage Project Work process.

Implementing the Quality Management Plan

Implementing the quality management plan occurs throughout the Executing and Monitoring and Controlling process groups. During Executing, quality assurance activities take place. Quality assurance is responsible for auditing quality control activities and the effectiveness of the project management processes. These activities are carried out through the Manage Quality process.

The Manage Quality process involves performing systematic quality activities and uses quality audits to determine which processes should be used to achieve the project requirements and to ensure that they are performed efficiently and effectively. This process also brings about continuous process improvement through improved process performance and eliminating unnecessary actions. This is done by assessing whether the processes are efficient and whether they can be improved.

Figure 7.13 shows the inputs, tools and techniques, and outputs of the Manage Quality process.

FIGURE 7.13   Manage Quality process

- Project management plan
- Project documents
- Organizational process assets

- Data gathering
- Data analysis
- Decision making
- Data representation
- Audits
- Design for X
- Problem solving
- Quality improvement methods

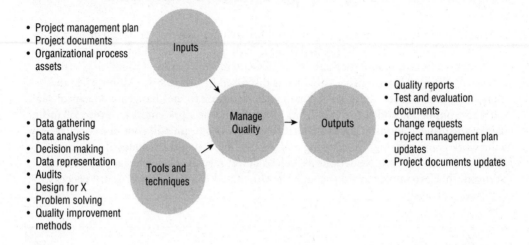

- Quality reports
- Test and evaluation documents
- Change requests
- Project management plan updates
- Project documents updates

For more detailed information on the Manage Quality process, see Chapter 9 of *PMP®: Project Management Professional Exam Study Guide, Ninth Edition* (Sybex, 2017).

Inputs of Manage Quality

Know the following three inputs of the Manage Quality process:

- Project management plan
- Project documents
- Organizational process assets

The project team members, project manager, and other stakeholders are all responsible for the quality assurance of the project.

Project Management Plan   The quality management plan is the primary, but not the only, component of the project management plan that can provide guidance for carrying out quality assurance activities through this process.

Project Documents   The following project documents are typically considered as inputs for this process:

- Lessons learned register
- Quality control measurements
- Quality metrics
- Risk report

Organizational Process Assets   The following organizational process assets influence this process:

- Organizational quality management system
- Quality templates
- Audit findings
- Lessons learned

Tools and Techniques for Manage Quality

You should be familiar with the following tools and techniques of the Manage Quality process:

Data Gathering   Checklists are a primary data-gathering technique used for this process. Checklists are structured tools that guide the specific steps to be performed to ensure that requirements are met.

Data Analysis   The following data analysis techniques can be used for this process:

- Alternatives analysis
- Process analysis
- Document analysis
- Root cause analysis

Decision Making   The primary, but not sole, decision-making technique used for this process is multicriteria decision analysis. When this technique is used, several criteria are considered while evaluating alternatives that impact project or product quality.

Data Representation   The Manage Quality process utilizes tools and techniques also used during the Plan Quality Management and Control Quality processes. Examples of tools used include, but aren't limited to, the following:

- Affinity diagrams
- Cause-and-effect diagrams
- Flowcharts
- Histograms
- Matrix diagrams
- Scatter diagrams

For a description of the tools and techniques also utilized in the Plan Quality Management process, see Chapter 4, "Planning Project Cost and Quality Management," in this book.

For a description of the tools and techniques also utilized in the Control Quality process, see Chapter 8, "Monitoring and Controlling the Project," in this book.

Audits   Audits are independent reviews performed by trained auditors or third-party reviewers, either on a regular schedule or at random. The purpose of an audit is to identify ineffective and inefficient activities or processes used on the project.

Quality improvements come about as a result of the audits, as shown in Figure 7.14.

Quality improvements are implemented by submitting change requests, which may entail taking corrective action.

FIGURE 7.14   Audit results

Benefits of Audits

Performing audits can confirm (or not) that the following items are true, or it can uncover faults preventing these items from being true. Conducting an audit and acting upon the findings can result in the following benefits:

- The product of the project is fit for use and meets safety standards.

- Applicable laws and standards are adhered to.

- Corrective action is recommended and implemented where necessary.

- The quality plan for the project is adhered to.

- Quality improvements are identified.

- The implementation of approved change requests, corrective actions, preventive actions, and defect repairs is confirmed.

Design for X   When inventing a specific product to meet a specific design aspect, design for X brings a set of technical guidelines to the product.

Problem Solving   Problem solving is the technique of searching for solutions for various issues or challenges. Using this tool effectively is a core piece of quality assurance and quality improvement.

Quality Improvement Methods   The Manage Quality process utilizes methods to improve quality based upon findings and recommendations from quality control processes, such as Plan-Do-Check-Act or Six Sigma.

Outputs of Manage Quality

The Manage Quality process results in the following five outputs:

- Quality reports
- Test and evaluation documents
- Change requests
- Project management plan updates
- Project documents updates

Quality Reports   Graphical, numerical, or qualitative reports can be used to direct corrective actions needed to fulfill the project quality expectations. These become an input to the Control Quality process.

Test and Evaluation Documents   Based upon organizational templates or industry needs, test and evaluation documents are used to evaluate the achievement of quality objectives. Dedicated checklists and detailed requirements traceability matrices are examples of these documents.

Change Requests   During this process, any recommended corrective actions, whether they are a result of a quality audit or process analysis, should be acted upon immediately. Change requests may involve corrective action, preventive action, or defect repair.

Project Management Plan Updates   As a result of this process, the quality management plan may need to be updated. The following documents may also require changes within the project management plan:

- Quality management plan
- Scope, schedule, and cost baselines

Project Documents Updates   Updates may include changes to the following project documents:

- Issue log
- Lessons learned register
- Risk register

Exam Essentials

Be able to describe the purpose of the Manage Quality process.   The Manage Quality process is concerned with making certain the project will meet and satisfy the quality standards of the project.

Implementing the Risk Management Plan

As the work of the project is executed, predefined risk triggers may occur and some risks will be realized, calling for the execution of risk response plans, contingency plans, and fallback plans. These responses are defined within the risk register and should be managed according to the risk management plan. The risk management plan is important in reducing the impact of negative risks on the project.

The risk responses documented within the risk register are executed as part of the Implement Risk Responses process, which is the only process within the Project Risk Management Knowledge Area that falls within the Executing process group.

Implement Risk Responses

The Implement Risk Responses process is responsible for implementing agreed-upon response plans so that overall risk exposure is managed and to minimize unique project threats and maximize opportunities. While listed in the Executing process group, managing risk responses can occur throughout the entire project.

Figure 7.15 shows the inputs, tools and techniques, and outputs of the Implement Risk Responses process.

For more detailed information on the Implement Risk Responses process, see Chapter 9 of *PMP®: Project Management Professional Exam Study Guide, Ninth Edition* (Sybex, 2017).

FIGURE 7.15 Implement Risk Responses process

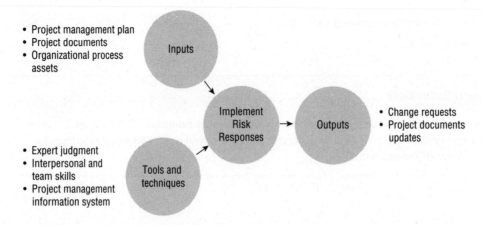

Inputs of Implement Risk Responses

Know the following inputs of the Implement Risk Responses process:

- Project management plan
- Project documents
- Organizational process assets

Project Management Plan   The primary, but not sole, component of the project management plan used in the Implement Risk Responses process is the risk management plan. The risk management plan helps to pair identified risks with an owner by listing the risk-related roles and responsibilities of the team. Additionally, this plan sets the precision, or level of detail, to be used for the risk management methodology. The risk management plan also lists risk thresholds for the project as defined by the stakeholders' risk appetite.

Project Documents   The following project documents are typically considered as inputs for this process:

- Lessons learned register
- Risk register
- Risk report

Organizational Process Assets   The lessons learned repository is the primary (but not only) organizational process asset that is used as an input to this process. Comparing risk responses from prior and similar projects can help guide the effectiveness of responses to risks.

Tools and Techniques of Implement Risk Responses

Be familiar with the following three tools and techniques of the Implement Risk Response process. Know how they are used in this process:

Expert Judgment   Expert judgment may include employing subject matter experts or those with specialized knowledge to validate or adjust risk responses.

Interpersonal and Team Skills   The primary interpersonal skill and team skill used is influencing. Projects often have external stakeholders who can have demands that compete with the goals of the project team.

Project Management Information System   The project management information system has cost, resource, and schedule information attached to agreed-upon risk response plans and their activities.

Outputs of Implement Risk Responses

The Implement Risk Responses process results in the following two outputs:

- Change requests
- Project documents updates

Change Requests   During this process, risk responses can have an impact on schedule and cost baselines and need to be processed as change requests through the Perform Integrated Change Control process.

Project Documents Updates   Updates may include, but are not limited to, changes to the following project documents:

- Issue log
- Lessons learned register
- Project team assignments
- Risk register
- Risk report

Exam Essentials

Be able to describe where risk response plans are documented and when they are executed.   Risk response plans, contingency plans, and fallback plans are documented within the risk register and are executed when predefined risk triggers occur.

Be able to describe the purpose of the Implement Risk Responses process.   The Implement Risk Responses process is responsible for implementing agreed-upon response plans so that overall risk exposure is managed and to minimize unique project threats and maximize opportunities.

Bringing the Processes Together

Let's briefly review the processes that were covered in this chapter and, more important, how these processes work together. You may recall that the primary objective of the Executing process group is to complete the work defined in the project management plan. In addition to this, we also coordinate and manage resources, implement approved changes, and manage communications.

As we went through the processes covered in this chapter, you may have noticed an ongoing theme: human resources. Whether these resources were internal to the organization or external, we covered a lot of information that dealt with the project team, including obtaining the resources and managing them. We also covered the management of stakeholder expectations and their engagement.

Figure 7.16 shows how people-centric the Executing Process Group really is. Within the realms of this figure, we see the following take place:

- The project information is planned.
- The planned information is handed off to the project team for execution of the project work.

- The project team's execution of the work generates results, which must be monitored and controlled.
- The results are fed back into the previous processes as necessary to improve the work and make changes and updates as needed.

FIGURE 7.16   The project team

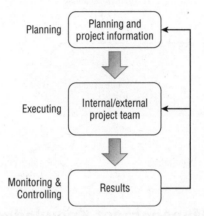

Clearly, a lot of behind-the-scenes effort goes into the executing stage. For example, the project team must be assembled and managed.

Altogether, we covered eight processes within this chapter, which make up the Executing process group. These processes spanned the following Knowledge Areas:

- Project Integration Management
- Project Quality Management
- Project Resource Management
- Project Risk Management
- Project Communications Management
- Project Procurement Management
- Project Stakeholder Management

Next, we will review the process interactions that occur within each Knowledge Area during the Executing process group.

Project Integration Management Knowledge Area Review

During the Executing process group, the Project Integration Management Knowledge Area covers the implementation of the project management plan through a single process known as the Direct and Manage Project Work process. As Figure 7.17 shows, the project management plan and the approved changes (which occur after the work has already been executed) are carried out through this process. As a result, deliverables and information on the work performance during the project are generated.

FIGURE 7.17   Process interaction—integration

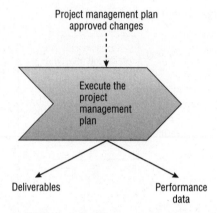

Project management plan
approved changes

Execute the
project
management
plan

Deliverables   Performance
data

Project Quality Management Knowledge Area Review

The Manage Quality process is the only quality-related process that falls within the Executing process group. As you may recall, this is where auditing takes place, which ultimately leads to implemented changes and continuous process improvement. The following items are among those that are audited:

▪   Quality requirements

▪   Results from quality control measurements

Figure 7.18 provides a glimpse into the information needed to perform the quality audits. Quality metrics, which were defined in the Planning process group, provide work performance data and quality measurements. These quality measurements are gathered while the project's quality is being monitored and controlled. You can see the level of interaction between the three quality processes throughout the life cycle of the project. The processes are iterative.

Project Resource Management Knowledge Area Review

Three of the six processes related to resources occur within the Executing process group. Remember that this process group involves coordinating and managing people, and you cannot implement the project work without a project team. Additionally, this process manages the physical assets needed for the project. Figure 7.19 shows, step-by-step, how the project team comes together so that the project work can be rolled out.

FIGURE 7.18   Process interaction—quality

FIGURE 7.19   Process interaction—human resource

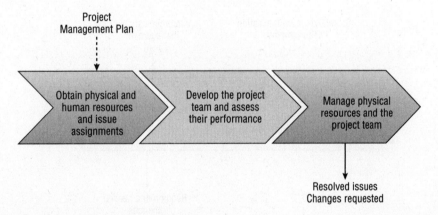

Here is an overview of these steps:

1. Using the project management plan as an information resource, bring the project team or resource on board and issue assignments.

2. Throughout project execution, assess the performance of the project team for developmental purposes. This includes enhancing the team's skills, monitoring the level of interaction among the group members, and improving the team's overall performance.

3. Use the performance assessment that was generated in the second step to manage the team. Here, issues are resolved and changes managed. The result? Recommend changes to resolve any staffing issues that may have emerged.

Project Communications Management Knowledge Area Review

As the project work is executed, communication becomes more important than ever. All of the planning behind how communication will take place within the project goes into effect. This is where knowing the communication needs and requirements of your stakeholders becomes particularly important. Be sure you place a great level of importance on knowing your stakeholders.

There is one communications-related process within the Executing process group, which makes project information available to stakeholders. As you can see in Figure 7.20, the stakeholder communication requirements must be developed before you can manage communications. After all, you cannot meet your team's communication needs if you do not know what they are. These communication needs and requirements are determined in the Initiating and Planning process groups.

FIGURE 7.20   Process interaction—communications

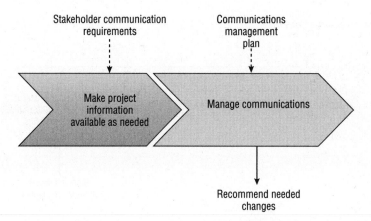

Figure 7.20 also shows how the management of the project stakeholder communications fits in with the communication processes. This step involves addressing any existing issues and recommending changes to resolve conflicts. It also involves the management of stakeholder engagement with the idea of unifying the project goals.

Project Risk Management Knowledge Area Review

Throughout the project, risk management becomes an important set of activities that project managers must be actively monitoring and engaging with. Beyond just the Executing process group, risks triggers will occur and risks will materialize. This means that risk response plans will need to be implemented.

The Project Risk Management Knowledge Area has only a single process that falls within the Executing process group, and that is the Implement Risk Responses process. It's through this process that the risk responses logged in the risk register are put into motion. Figure 7.21 provides a glimpse of the Implement Risk Responses process.

FIGURE 7.21   Process interaction—risk

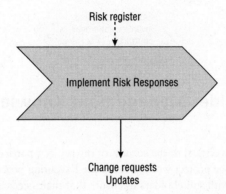

Risk register

Implement Risk Responses

Change requests
Updates

Project Procurement Management Knowledge Area Review

During the Executing process group, vendors are selected for work that will be handled externally. Conducting procurements is part of obtaining and hiring the resources needed to complete the project work. As you can see, much of project execution involves hiring and managing people resources—internal and external to the organization.

Figure 7.22 shows how the single procurement process that takes place during project execution results in the selection of the project's sellers and the issuance of procurement contracts. To arrive at this outcome, you will use several planned procurement items:

- Results of the make-or-buy decisions made during the planning phase
- List of qualified vendors (sellers) and their proposals
- Criteria that will be used to select the vendors
- Any agreements or documents impacting vendor selection
- Procurement management plan

FIGURE 7.22   Process interaction—procurement

Procurement management plan
Vendor information
Selection criteria
Purchase decisions

Select vendors and
award procurement
contracts

Project Stakeholder Management Knowledge Area Review

Stakeholder management is critical to the success of the project, particularly when the project team is actively executing the project work. During the Executing process group, the project manager actively engages with stakeholders to ensure that their needs and expectations are met.

Figure 7.23 shows how the Manage Stakeholder Engagement process interacts with other processes.

FIGURE 7.23   Process interaction—stakeholder

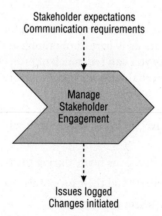

Stakeholder expectations
Communication requirements

Manage
Stakeholder
Engagement

Issues logged
Changes initiated

As you reflect on the Executing process group, always remember that the key purpose is to complete the project work.

Day of the Exam

Although the Executing process group consists of only 10 processes, remember that it makes up 30 percent of the exam. Be sure to memorize the key outputs of each of these processes.

Review Questions

1. Jon is gearing up for his upcoming project, which involves programming a complex system that will allow two programs to talk to each other. The project kicks off in one week, and he had been specifically requested by the customer. As a software architect, this assignment will be his most challenging project yet, and he has been looking forward to the assignment for months. Which of the following options *best* describes Jon's upcoming project role?

   A. Staff assignment

   B. Pre-assignment

   C. Project team member

   D. Acquisition

2. All of the following are benefits of virtual teams *except*:

   A. Access to resources otherwise unavailable

   B. Reduction in travel expenses

   C. Utilization of a war room

   D. Reduction in time spent commuting

3. At which stage of team development do employees compete for control?

   A. Forming

   B. Storming

   C. Norming

   D. Performing

4. Sally, a junior project manager for Project Red, is in the process of holding a status meeting for the project manager, who stepped out to deal with a procurement issue. The tension in the room has been high as a result of two critical resources who suddenly quit. John and Rick, both team members, have been arguing for five minutes over who will take over the tasks. Sally has tried to interject multiple times with no success. The side conversations don't make managing the meeting any easier. What is the *most likely* cause of the inefficient meeting?

   A. Absence of the project manager

   B. Poorly defined communications management plan

   C. Poor recognition and rewards

   D. Lack of ground rules

5. Which of the following levels within Maslow's hierarchy of needs describes the need to belong?

   A. Social needs

   B. Self-esteem needs

   C. Self-actualization

   D. Safety and security needs

6. Which of the following conflict management techniques is said to be the *best* strategy?

   A. Forcing

   B. Smoothing

   C. Collaborating

   D. Compromising

7. Meetings, email, videoconferences, and conference calls are all examples of which of the following options?

   A. Project management tools

   B. Communication models

   C. Communication methods

   D. Communication types

8. The project team of a new housing expansion project is in a state of frenzy because of a surprise quality audit that is being conducted today on the project. In three days, a major deliverable is due. The project manager explains to the team that the quality audit is important. What reasoning is the project manager likely to give the team for explaining why the quality audits are needed in a project?

   A. Quality audits look at problems experienced while conducting the project.

   B. Quality audits identify inefficiencies that exist within the processes and activities being performed.

   C. Quality audits ensure that the team members are doing their job and are necessary for documenting performance reviews.

   D. Conducting quality audits is a legal requirement.

9. Who is responsible for defining Theory X & Y?

   A. Douglas McGregor

   B. Frederick Herzberg

   C. Abraham Maslow

   D. Victor Vroom

10. The following are tools and techniques of the Manage Stakeholder Engagement process *except*:

   A. Project management plan

   B. Communication skills

   C. Interpersonal and team skills

   D. Inspection

11. Beans by the Dozen is a company that ships pre-cooked beans to restaurants in the western United States. Recently, the company has decided to expand their operation to the northern regions of the country. The project manager assigned to the project has just instituted a war room to bring project team members together and concluded a team-building session after collocating the team. What process is the project manager carrying out?

  A. Plan Resource Management

  B. Acquire Resources

  C. Develop Team

  D. Manage Team

12. Through which process group is the majority of the project budget consumed?

  A. Planning

  B. Executing

  C. Monitoring and Controlling

  D. Closing

13. Polly is a project manager tasked with leading a project that will establish business continuity management practices for a major retail coffee chain. She has just concluded planning efforts on the project and is gearing up to begin executing the work of the project. What is she likely to do first?

  A. Obtain resources

  B. Resolve team conflict

  C. Manage the project team

  D. Obtain funding

14. Which of the following tools and techniques provides an opportunity for prospective vendors to ask sellers questions about an RFP?

  A. Meetings

  B. Procurement negotiations

  C. Bidder conferences

  D. Market research

15. A deliverable can *best* be described as:

  A. Any unique and verifiable product, result, or capability to perform a service that is required to be produced in order to meet quality requirements

  B. A verifiable product, result, or capability to perform a service that is required to be produced to complete a project against the documented requirements

  C. A repeatable product that is required to be produced to complete a process, phase, or project

  D. Any unique and verifiable product, result, or capability to perform a service that is required to be produced to complete a process, phase, or project

16. A project manager has just gathered the status of project activities and calculated resource consumption to date. What process is the project manager carrying out?

    A. Manage Team

    B. Direct and Manage Project Work

    C. Manage Stakeholder Engagement

    D. Manage Quality

17. The issue log is first created as a result of which process?

    A. Manage Stakeholder Engagement

    B. Direct and Manage Project Work

    C. Manage Team

    D. Perform Quality Assurance

18. The following represent the results generated from carrying out the Direct and Manage Project Work process *except*:

    A. Project management plan updates

    B. Work performance information

    C. Deliverables

    D. Project documents updates

19. The following are inputs used to carry out the Manage Quality process *except*:

    A. Project management plan

    B. Organizational process assets

    C. Change requests

    D. Project documents

20. Polly is a project manager tasked with leading a project that will establish business continuity management practices for a major retail coffee chain. By facilitating quality audits, the project team recently discovered corrective action needed to bring the project into compliance with quality requirements. How will Polly process the corrective action?

    A. Process improvement plan update

    B. Organizational process assets update

    C. Project document update

    D. Change request

Chapter 8

Monitoring and Controlling the Project

THE PMP® EXAM CONTENT FROM THE MONITORING AND CONTROLLING PERFORMANCE DOMAIN COVERED IN THIS CHAPTER INCLUDES THE FOLLOWING:

✓ Measure project performance using appropriate tools and techniques in order to identify and quantify any variances and corrective actions.

✓ Manage changes to the project by following the change management plan in order to ensure that project goals remain aligned with business needs.

✓ Verify that project deliverables conform to the quality standards established in the quality management plan by using appropriate tools and techniques to meet project requirements and business needs.

✓ Monitor and assess risk by determining whether exposure has changed and evaluating the effectiveness of response strategies in order to manage the impact of risks and opportunities on the project.

✓ Review the issue log, update if necessary, and determine corrective actions by using appropriate tools and techniques in order to minimize the impact on the project.

✓ Capture, analyze, and manage lessons learned, using lessons learned management techniques in order to enable continuous improvement.

✓ Monitor procurement activities according to the procurement plan in order to verify compliance with project objectives.

Monitoring and Controlling is the fourth of the five project management process groups and accounts for 25 percent of the questions on the PMP exam. The processes in the Monitoring and Controlling process group concentrate on monitoring and measuring project performance to identify variances from the project management plan and get them back on track. Regularly monitoring project performance provides insight into the current state of the project and allows you to correct areas that are falling off track before they impact your project significantly. The Monitoring and Controlling process group is concerned not only with monitoring the project work but also with the project as a whole. In multiphase projects, this process group coordinates the project phases.

Measuring Project Performance

As the project work is carried out, it is important to monitor the project performance closely. This can be done by using various tools and techniques that assist in identifying and quantifying variances as well as determining the necessary corrective action. Monitoring project performance occurs through the Monitor and Control Project Work process, part of the Project Integration Management Knowledge Area.

Work performed by sellers (resources external to the organization) is monitored and controlled through the Control Procurements process. Control Procurements is a process that belongs to the Project Procurement Management Knowledge Area.

Monitor and Control Project Work

The Monitor and Control Project Work process involves monitoring all the processes in the Initiating, Planning, Executing, and Closing process groups to meet the performance objectives outlined in the project management plan. Collecting data, measuring results, and reporting on performance information are some of the activities performed during this process.

According to the *PMBOK® Guide*, the Monitor and Control Project Work process encompasses the following:

- Reporting and comparing actual project results against the project management plan
- Analyzing performance data and determining whether corrective or preventive action is needed

- Monitoring project risks

- Documenting all appropriate product information throughout the life of the project

- Gathering, recording, and documenting project information

- Providing forecasts on cost and schedule

- Monitoring approved change requests

- Reporting on project progress and status to program management, when appropriate

- Ensuring continued alignment with business needs

Figure 8.1 shows the inputs, tools and techniques, and outputs of the Monitor and Control Project Work process.

FIGURE 8.1   Monitor and Control Project Work process

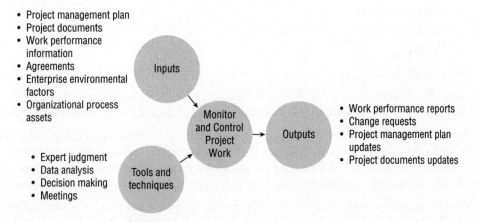

For more detailed information on the Monitor and Control Project Work process, see Chapter 10, "Measuring and Controlling Project Performance," in *PMP: Project Management Professional Exam Study Guide, Ninth Edition* (Sybex, 2017).

Inputs of Monitor and Control Project Work

Know the following inputs of the Monitor and Control Project Work process:

- Project management plan

- Project documents

- Work performance information

- Agreements

- Enterprise environmental factors

- Organizational process assets

Project Management Plan   The project management plan provides the information necessary to monitor the project work and determine whether the project is progressing as planned.

Project Documents   Several project documents inform this process and can include but are not limited to the following:

- Assumption log
- Basis of estimates
- Cost forecasts
- Issue log
- Lessons learned register
- Milestone list
- Quality reports
- Risk register
- Risk report
- Schedule forecasts

We have discussed the majority of this list in previous chapters, but for the purposes of the exam, there are two new concepts you will need to know: schedule forecasts and cost forecasts.

Schedule Forecasts   Schedule forecasts reflect whether the project is on track, ahead, or behind schedule, typically expressed in the form of schedule variance (SV) or schedule performance index (SPI). SV and SPI are calculated using earned value management (EVM) techniques. Schedule forecasts are an output of the Control Schedule process.

Cost Forecasts   Cost forecasts reflect whether the project is on, over, or under budget. Like schedule forecasts, cost forecasts may be calculated using EVM and expressed in the form of cost variance (CV) or cost performance index (CPI). In addition to CV and CPI, the estimate at completion (EAC) may also be calculated to determine whether forecasts are within a tolerable range from the planned budget. Cost forecasts are an output of the Control Costs process.

   Earned value management (EVM) is reviewed later within this chapter. EVM includes the calculation and explanation of schedule and cost forecasts.

Work Performance Information   Work performance information is produced as a result of carrying out various processes within the Monitoring and Controlling process group. It reflects performance data that has been analyzed and can therefore be used to make project decisions.

Agreements   Contractual terms and conditions are included in a procurement agreement and may offer other items the buyer specifies regarding the seller's product or service. When a project has outsourced part of the project work, the project manager would be responsible for overseeing the contractor's work.

Enterprise Environmental Factors   The enterprise environmental factors provide the following information utilized by this process:

- Project management information systems (scheduling, cost, resourcing tools, performance indicators, database, project records, and financials)

- Infrastructure

- Stakeholder expectations and risk tolerances

- Government or industry standards

Organizational Process Assets   The following organizational process assets are used as inputs:

- Communication requirements

- Procedures for financial controls, risk control, and problem solving

- Monitoring and reporting methods

- Issue and defect management procedures

- Organizational knowledge base, specifically the lessons learned repository

Tools and Techniques of Monitor and Control Project Work

The Monitor and Control Project Work process has four tools and techniques: expert judgment, data analysis, decision making, and meetings.

Expert Judgment   Expert judgment involves interpreting the information that results from this process and making key project decisions as a result of the information. Experts with specialized knowledge or training in the following topics should be consulted:

- Earned value analysis

- Interpretation and contextualization of data

- Techniques to estimate duration and costs

- Trend analysis

- Technical knowledge on the industry/project focus area

- Risk and contract management

Data Analysis   In the scope of this process, data analysis involves using various analytical techniques to forecast possible scenarios based on existing variables. The *PMBOK® Guide* provides the following examples:

- Alternatives analysis

- Cost-benefit analysis

- Earned value analysis

- Root cause analysis

- Trend analysis

- Variance analysis

Decision Making The key decision-making tool used for this process is voting. Whether making decisions based on unanimity, majority, or plurality, voting plays an important role in determining which direction to proceed.

Meetings This process involves a high degree of interaction and analysis by project experts. When used appropriately, meetings can be a powerful mechanism for project team members and other subject matter experts to discuss project performance and to make decisions. Meetings take many forms, including face-to-face, virtual, formal, and informal.

Outputs of Monitor and Control Project Work

The Monitor and Control Project Work process has four outputs.

Work Performance Reports As a result of assessing work performance information, work performance reports are compiled through this process; according to the *PMBOK® Guide*, work performance reports are physical or electronic representations of performance data. By documenting this information, it can be distributed to stakeholders and archived for future reference. Work performance reports can also be used as a means of increasing awareness and making decisions in relation to the project.

Change Requests As a result of assessing project performance and making decisions on how to proceed based on this information, changes may be required. Change requests typically include the following items:

- Corrective actions are intended to bring the project back on track with the plan.
- Preventive actions are intended to prevent the project from getting off track with the plan.
- Defect repairs are intended to address product or product components that do not conform to requirements.

Project Management Plan Updates Project management plan updates may include updates to one or more of the following:

- Schedule management plan
- Cost management plan
- Quality management plan
- Scope baseline
- Schedule baseline
- Cost baseline

Project Documents Updates Project documents updates may include updates to the following:

- Cost forecasts
- Issue log
- Lessons learned register
- Risk register
- Schedule forecasts

Control Procurements

The Control Procurements process is concerned with monitoring the vendor's performance and ensuring that all requirements of the contract are met. This process also manages the procurement relationships overall and makes changes and corrections as needed.

According to the *PMBOK® Guide*, you must integrate and coordinate the Direct and Manage Project Work, Control Quality, Perform Integrated Change Control, and Monitor Risks processes during the Control Procurements process.

Figure 8.2 shows the inputs, tools and techniques, and outputs of the Control Procurements process.

FIGURE 8.2   Control Procurements process

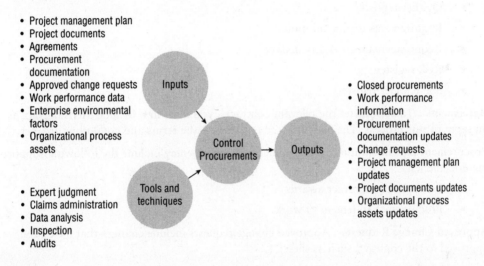

- Project management plan
- Project documents
- Agreements
- Procurement documentation
- Approved change requests
- Work performance data
- Enterprise environmental factors
- Organizational process assets

Inputs

Control Procurements

Outputs

- Expert judgment
- Claims administration
- Data analysis
- Inspection
- Audits

Tools and techniques

- Closed procurements
- Work performance information
- Procurement documentation updates
- Change requests
- Project management plan updates
- Project documents updates
- Organizational process assets updates

For more detailed information on the Control Procurements process, see Chapter 10 in *PMP: Project Management Professional Exam Study Guide, Ninth Edition* (Sybex, 2017).

Inputs of Control Procurements

Know the following inputs of the Control Procurements process:

- Project management plan

- Project documents

- Agreements

- Procurement documentation

- Approved change requests

- Work performance data

- Enterprise environmental factors

- Organizational process assets

Project Management Plan   The project management plan includes the procurement management plan, which guides the project management team in carrying out the procurement process. It also documents how the contracts will be managed through to closure. Other elements that serve as inputs to this process include the requirements management plan, risk management plan, change management plan, and schedule baseline.

Project Documents   Several project documents inform this process and can include but are not limited to the following:

- Assumption log
- Lessons learned register
- Milestone list
- Quality reports
- Requirements documentation
- Requirements traceability matrix
- Risk register
- Stakeholder register

Agreements   To administer the relevant contracts, you must first include each contract as an input to this process. The purpose is to ensure that the terms and conditions are met.

Procurement Documentation   Procurement documents may include the following supporting documents:

- Procurement contract awards
- Procurement statement of work

Approved Change Requests   Approved change requests include changes that have been approved to the contract, such as these:

- Modifications to deliverables
- Changes to the product or service of the project
- Changes in contract terms
- Termination for poor performance

Work Performance Data   Work performance data involves monitoring work results and examining the vendor's deliverables. This includes monitoring their work results against the project management plan and making sure that certain activities are performed correctly and in sequence.

Enterprise Environmental Factors   The enterprise environmental factors provide the following information utilized by this process:

- Contract change control system
- Marketplace conditions
- Financial management and accounts payable system
- Buying organization's code of ethics

Organizational Process Assets   Procurement policies are the primary, but not only, organizational process assets used as inputs.

Tools and Techniques of Control Procurements

Be familiar with the following tools and techniques of the Control Procurements process:

- Expert judgment
- Claims administration
- Data analysis
- Inspection
- Audits

Expert Judgment   Individuals or groups with specialized knowledge or training in the following areas should be consulted:

- Relevant functional areas such as finance, engineering, design, development, supply chain management, and other applicable areas
- Laws, regulations, and compliance requirements
- Claims administration

Claims Administration   Claims administration involves documenting, monitoring, and managing contested changes to the contract. Contested changes usually involve a disagreement about the compensation to the vendor for implementing the change. Here are some things to know about claims administration:

- Contested changes are also known as *disputes*, *claims*, or *appeals*.
- Claims can be settled directly between the parties themselves, through the court system, or by a process called arbitration.

According to the *PMBOK® Guide*, when the parties cannot reach an agreement themselves, they should use an alternative dispute-resolution process (ADR), like arbitration. Also note that the preferred method of settling disputes is negotiation.

Data Analysis   In the scope of this process, data analytical techniques can be used to monitor and control procurements. The *PMBOK® Guide* provides the following examples:

- Performance reviews for contracts measure, compare, and analyze quality, resource, schedule, and cost performance against the agreement.
- Earned value analysis (specifically schedule and cost variances) calculates indexes to determine the degree of variance from the target.
- Trend analysis can develop a forecast estimate at completion (EAC) to see if performance is improving or deteriorating.

Inspection   Inspections are structured reviews of work being performed by a contractor.

Audits   Audits are structured reviews of the procurement process.

Outputs of Control Procurements

Know the following seven outputs of the Control Procurements process:

- Closed procurements
- Work performance information
- Procurement documentation updates
- Change requests
- Project management plan updates
- Project documents updates
- Organizational process assets updates

Closed Procurements   After procured work has been completed, an authorized procurement administrator for the buyer provides the seller with formal written notice that the contract has been completed. A contract is closed when all deliverables have been completed and meet any technical or quality requirements, there are no outstanding claims or invoices, and all payments have been made.

Work Performance Information   Work performance information reflects performance data of the vendor that has been analyzed. The information will be used to make decisions about any corrective action or changes needed regarding the vendor's performance.

Procurement Documentation Updates   Procurement documentation may require updates as a part of this process. This would include updating the contract with all supporting schedules, requested unapproved contract changes, and approved change requests. Additionally, seller-developed technical documentations, deliverables, seller performance reports and warranties, financial documents, and the results of contract-related inspection may also be updated.

Change Requests   Change requests may result from performing the Control Procurements process and may include changes to plans and baselines. Changes may involve addressing any vendor-related performance issues or may even include requests for contract changes.

Change requests are submitted and processed through the project's change control system.

Project Management Plan Updates   Project management plan updates that may result from the Control Procurements process typically include updates to the procurement management plan and baselines. Other plans that may receive updates include the risk management plan as well as the cost and schedule baselines.

Project Documents Updates   Project documents typically updated as a result of carrying out this process include procurement documentation. Procurement documentation produced as part of this process includes but is not limited to the following:

- Lessons learned register
- Resource requirements
- Requirements traceability matrix
- Risk register
- Stakeholder register

Organizational Process Assets Updates   According to the *PMBOK® Guide*, organizational process assets updates typically include the following items:

Payment Schedules and Requests   Payment schedules and requests include information about paying the vendor on time and verifying that payment terms have been met and warrant payment.

Seller Performance Evaluation Documentation   Seller performance evaluation is a written record of the seller's performance on the contract and is prepared by the buyer. It should include information about whether the seller successfully met contract dates and fulfilled the requirements of the contract and/or contract statement of work and whether the work was satisfactory.

Prequalified Seller Lists Updates   Prequalified seller lists are lists of potential sellers who are preapproved to do work for a buyer. At the conclusion of a project, these lists are updated because sellers could be disqualified and removed from the lists due to sub-par performance. Additionally, the list should be updated when sellers meet or exceed expectations.

Lessons Learned Repository   To help improve procurements on future projects, the lessons learned should be updated with a comparison of the actual results to the original requests. This should state whether the project objectives were achieved and any reasons they were not.

Procurement File   A complete, indexed set of contract documentation, including the closed contract, is included in the final project files.

Exam Essentials

Name the outputs of the Monitor and Control Project Work process.   The outputs are work performance reports; change requests, which include corrective actions, preventive actions, and defect repair; project management plan updates; and project documents updates.

Name the processes that integrate with the Control Procurements process.   Direct and Manage Project Work, Control Quality, Perform Integrated Change Control, and Monitor Risks.

Managing Changes to the Project Scope, Schedule, and Costs

Managing the triple constraints is an important part of monitoring and controlling a project. This includes managing changes to the project scope, schedule, and costs, which requires that the project management plan be updated as needed. The Validate Scope,

Control Scope, Control Schedule, and Control Costs processes focus on managing these changes and uncovering existing variance to the plan. As the plan is updated with approved changes, these changes should be communicated to the team to ensure that revised project goals are met.

Validate Scope

Managing and reporting on project progress is the primary focus of the Monitoring and Controlling processes. One of the Monitoring and Controlling processes is Validate Scope. The primary purpose of the Validate Scope process is to formally accept completed deliverables and obtain sign-off that the deliverables are satisfactory and meet stakeholders' expectations. Validate Scope formalizes the acceptance of the project scope and is primarily concerned with the acceptance of work results.

Figure 8.3 shows the inputs, tools and techniques, and outputs of the Validate Scope process.

FIGURE 8.3   Validate Scope process

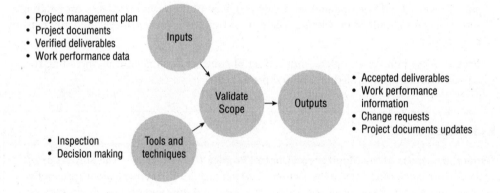

- Project management plan
- Project documents
- Verified deliverables
- Work performance data

Inputs

Validate Scope

Outputs

- Accepted deliverables
- Work performance information
- Change requests
- Project documents updates

- Inspection
- Decision making

Tools and techniques

For more detailed information on the Validate Scope process, see Chapter 11, "Controlling Work Results," in *PMP: Project Management Professional Exam Study Guide, Ninth Edition* (Sybex, 2017).

Inputs of Validate Scope

Know the following inputs of the Validate Scope process:

- Project management plan
- Project documents
- Verified deliverables
- Work performance data

Project Management Plan The scope management plan and scope baseline are used from the project management plan. The scope baseline includes the project scope statement, work breakdown structure (WBS), and WBS dictionary, all of which will be utilized by this process. The requirements management plan may also be consulted.

Project Documents To validate the scope of the project work, the project, product, technical requirements, and any others must be included as an input to this process. Several project documents inform this process, and can include but are not limited to the following:

- Lessons learned register
- Quality reports
- Requirements documentation
- Requirements traceability matrix

Verified Deliverables Verified deliverables include deliverables that have been verified through the Control Quality process. The quality team verifies that deliverables have been completed correctly.

Work Performance Data Work performance data reflects raw data relating to the deliverables, which is used to determine the degree of compliance against the requirements. This can include the number and severity of nonconformities and/or total validation cycles performed.

 You should perform Validate Scope even if the project is canceled, to document the degree to which the project was completed.

Tools and Techniques of Validate Scope

The Validate Scope process has two tools and techniques: inspection and group decision-making techniques.

Inspection According to the *PMBOK® Guide*, inspection is concerned with making sure the project work and deliverables meet the requirements and product acceptance criteria. This may include ensuring, examining, and validation activities.

Decision Making Voting, the primary form of decision making in this process, is used to reach a conclusion when validation is performed.

Outputs of Validate Scope

The Validate Scope process results in four outputs:

Accepted Deliverables The accepted deliverables output signifies that the deliverables have been formally accepted and signed off by the customer or sponsor. This output, along with related documentation, is then fed into the Close Project or Phase process at the appropriate time.

Work Performance Information Work performance information includes performance-related information relating to deliverables, such as which have been completed or accepted.

Change Requests   Change requests addresses deliverables that were rejected or not formally accepted. Remember, these deliverables may require a change request for defect repair.

Project Documents Updates   Project documents updates typically include updates to the following items:

- Lessons learned register
- Requirements documentation
- Requirements traceability matrix

Control Scope

The Control Scope process involves monitoring the status of both the project and the product scope, monitoring changes to the project and product scope, and monitoring work results to ensure that they match expected outcomes. Any modification to the agreed-upon WBS is considered a scope change. This means the addition or deletion of activities or modifications to the existing activities on the WBS constitutes a project scope change.

Figure 8.4 shows the inputs, tools and techniques, and outputs of the Control Scope process.

FIGURE 8.4   Control Scope process

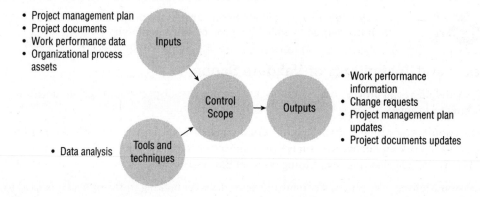

 For more detailed information on the Control Scope process, see Chapter 11 in *PMP: Project Management Professional Exam Study Guide, Ninth Edition* (Sybex, 2017).

Inputs of Control Scope

Know the following inputs of the Control Scope process:

- Project management plan
- Project documents

- Work performance data
- Organizational process assets

Project Management Plan   The following components of the project management plan are utilized in controlling scope:

- Scope management plan
- Requirements management plan
- Change management plan
- Configuration management plan
- Scope baseline
- Performance measurement baseline

Project Documents   Several project documents inform this process and can include but are not limited to the following:

- Lessons learned register
- Requirements documentation
- Requirements traceability matrix

Work Performance Data   Work performance data provides the status and progress of deliverables.

Organizational Process Assets   Organizational process assets utilized in this process include any policies, procedures, guidelines, and reporting methods that relate to scope control.

Tools and Techniques of Control Scope

The Control Scope process has one tool and technique: data analysis. Data analysis may include two components, variance analysis and trend analysis. Variance analysis includes reviewing project performance measurements to determine whether there are variances in project scope and whether any corrective action is needed as a result of existing variances. Trend analysis compares the project performance over time to determine if performance is improving or deteriorating.

 Unapproved or undocumented changes that sometimes make their way into the project are referred to as scope creep.

Outputs of Control Scope

The Control Scope process results in the following outputs:

- Work performance information
- Change requests

- Project management plan updates
- Project documents updates

Work Performance Information   Work performance information documents the results of comparing planned and actual scope performance. This information will be used when making scope-related decisions.

Change Requests   When scope changes are requested, all areas of the project should be investigated to determine what the changes would impact. Change requests typically involve the scope baseline or other components of the project management plan. Refer to the Perform Integrated Change Control process to make sure change requests are processed for review accordingly.

Project Management Plan Updates   Depending on the approved changes, updates to the project management plan may result in changes to the scope management plan as well as the scope, schedule, cost, and performance measurement baselines.

Project Documents Updates   Updates to project documents that occur as a result of this process typically include the lessons learned register, requirements documentation, and requirements traceability matrix.

Control Schedule

The Control Schedule process involves determining the status of the project schedule, determining whether changes have occurred or should occur, and influencing and managing schedule changes.

Figure 8.5 shows the inputs, tools and techniques, and outputs of the Control Schedule process.

FIGURE 8.5   Control Schedule process

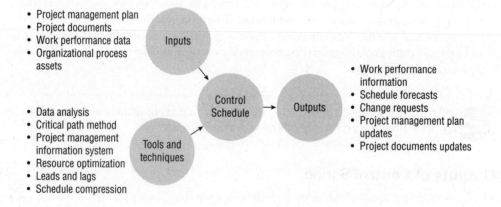

- Project management plan
- Project documents
- Work performance data
- Organizational process assets

Inputs

- Data analysis
- Critical path method
- Project management information system
- Resource optimization
- Leads and lags
- Schedule compression

Tools and techniques

Control Schedule

Outputs

- Work performance information
- Schedule forecasts
- Change requests
- Project management plan updates
- Project documents updates

For more detailed information on the Control Schedule process, see Chapter 11 in *PMP: Project Management Professional Exam Study Guide, Ninth Edition* (Sybex, 2017).

Inputs of Control Schedule

Know the following inputs of the Control Schedule process:

- Project management plan
- Project documents
- Work performance data
- Organizational process assets

Project Management Plan   The schedule management plan, schedule baseline, scope baseline, and performance measurement baseline are used to carry out the Control Schedule process from within the project management plan.

Project Documents   Several project documents inform this process and can include but are not limited to the following:

- Lessons learned register
- Project calendars
- Project schedule
- Resource calendars
- Schedule data

Work Performance Data   Work performance data provides status information on the schedule activities. This can include raw data, such as which activities have started, are in progress, or have finished.

Organizational Process Assets   The following organizational process assets are utilized in this process:

- Policies, procedures, guidelines, and reporting methods relating to schedule control
- Monitoring and reporting methods
- Schedule control tools

Tools and Techniques of Control Schedule

The Control Schedule process includes the following tools and techniques:

- Data analysis
- Critical path method
- Project management information system

- Resource optimization
- Leads and lags
- Schedule compression

Data Analysis   The following data analysis techniques can be used for this process:

- Earned value analysis encompasses schedule variance (SV) and schedule performance index (SPI), which can be used to determine the impact of the schedule variations and whether corrective action is necessary.

- Iteration burndown chart is a chart that is used to catalog the remaining work to be completed in the iteration backlog.

- Performance reviews in this process examine elements such as actual start and end dates for schedule activities and the remaining time to finish incomplete activities.

- Trend analysis examines the project performance over time.

- Variance analysis compares the actual start and finish dates to the planned dates, and also considers the actual/planned durations and float.

- What-if scenario analysis assesses possible scenarios as guided by the output from the Project Risk Management processes to bring the schedule model into alignment with the approved baseline.

Critical Path Method   This technique compares the process along the critical path to help determine schedule status.

Project Management Information System   Project management information systems, including scheduling software, can be used to track actual versus planned activity dates and the impact of any existing changes.

Resource Optimization   Resource optimization techniques can leverage techniques such as resource leveling and smoothing to better distribute the work among resources. It considers both resource availability and project time.

Leads and Lags   Leads and lags are adjusted during this process as a means of bringing the actual schedule back in line with the schedule baseline.

Schedule Compression   Schedule compression techniques, such as fast-tracking and crashing, are used to bring the actual schedule back in line with the planned schedule.

Outputs of Control Schedule

The Control Schedule process includes the following outputs:

- Work performance information
- Schedule forecasts
- Change requests
- Project management plan updates
- Project documents updates

Work Performance Information Work performance information typically includes the calculated schedule variance (SV) and schedule performance index (SPI) values. According to the *PMBOK® Guide*, SV and SPI are calculated for work packages and control accounts.

Schedule Forecasts Schedule forecasts are derived using the various tools and techniques described. Forecasts reflect the anticipated future performance of the project.

Change Requests Change requests generated as a result of this process typically include modifications to the schedule baseline. Aside from baseline changes, changes may come in the form of corrective or preventive actions as a means of getting the project back on track with the plan.

Project Management Plan Updates Project management plan updates typically include updates to the schedule baseline, cost baseline, schedule management plan, and performance measurement baseline.

Project Documents Updates The project documents updates output may require updates to the schedule data or the project schedule. Project documents updates typically include the following items:

- Assumption log
- Basis of estimates
- Lessons learned register
- Project schedule
- Resource calendars
- Risk register
- Schedule data

Control Costs

The Control Costs process monitors the project budget, manages changes to the cost baseline, and records actual costs. It's concerned with monitoring project costs to prevent unauthorized or incorrect costs from being included in the cost baseline. The following activities are among those included in this process:

- Monitoring changes to costs or the cost baseline and understanding variances from the baseline
- Monitoring change requests that affect cost and resolving them in a timely manner
- Informing stakeholders of approved changes and their costs

Figure 8.6 shows the inputs, tools and techniques, and outputs of the Control Costs process.

FIGURE 8.6   Control Costs process

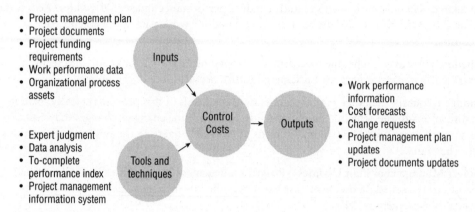

- Project management plan
- Project documents
- Project funding requirements
- Work performance data
- Organizational process assets

- Expert judgment
- Data analysis
- To-complete performance index
- Project management information system

Inputs

Control Costs

Outputs

Tools and techniques

- Work performance information
- Cost forecasts
- Change requests
- Project management plan updates
- Project documents updates

For more detailed information on the Control Costs process, see Chapter 11 in *PMP: Project Management Professional Exam Study Guide, Ninth Edition* (Sybex, 2017).

Inputs of Control Costs

Know the following inputs of the Control Costs process:

- Project management plan

- Project documents

- Project funding requirements

- Work performance data

- Organizational process assets

Project Management Plan   The project management plan includes the cost management plan, the cost baseline, and the performance measurement baseline, which will be utilized by this process. The cost management plan details how costs should be monitored and controlled throughout the life of the project. The cost baseline compares actual expenditures to date on the project to the baseline. The performance measurement baseline, when using the earned value analysis, is compared to actual results to decide if corrective or preventative action is needed.

Project Documents   Project documents include but are not limited to the lessons learned register.

Project Funding Requirements   Project funding requirements include the periodic and total project funding provided.

Work Performance Data   The work performance data input provides information about the project's progress, including authorized and incurred costs and project estimates.

Organizational Process Assets   The following organizational process assets are utilized by this process:

- Policies, procedures, guidelines, and reporting methods relating to cost
- Cost control tools

Tools and Techniques of Control Costs

You should be familiar with the following tools and techniques of the Control Costs process:

- Expert judgment
- Data analysis
- To-complete performance index (TCPI)
- Project management information system

Expert Judgment   Expert judgment in this process includes but is not limited to the following examples:

- Variance analysis
- Earned value analysis
- Forecasting
- Financial analysis

Data Analysis   Data analysis techniques that can be used to control costs include but are not limited to the following:

Earned Value Analysis (EVA)   Performance measurement analysis can be accomplished by using a technique called earned value management (EVM). EVM compares what you've received or produced to what you've spent and establishes the cause and impact of variances to determine necessary corrective action. It is the most often used performance measurement method.

EVM is performed on the work packages and the control accounts of the WBS. To perform the EVM calculations, the planned value (PV), earned value (EV), and actual cost (AC) are collected. They are defined in Table 8.1 along with other terms associated with the EVM technique.

TABLE 8.1   Earned value management definitions

Term	Definition
Planned value (PV)	The PV is the budgeted cost of work that has been authorized for a schedule activity or WBS component during a given time period or phase. These budgets are established during the Planning processes. All PVs add up to the budget at completion (BAC). PV is also known as budgeted cost of work scheduled (BCWS).

TABLE 8.1   Earned value management definitions *(continued)*

Term	Definition
Earned value (EV)	EV is measured as budgeted dollars for the work performed. EV is typically expressed as a percentage of the work completed compared to the budget. It is also known as budgeted cost of work performed (BCWP).
Actual cost (AC)	AC is the cost of completing the work component in a given time period. AC measures the costs (direct, indirect, or other) that were used to calculate the planned value. It is also known as actual cost of work performed (ACWP).
Cost variance (CV)	CV determines whether costs are higher or lower than budgeted. A negative CV means the project is over budget; a positive CV means the project is under budget.
Cost performance index (CPI)	CPI measures the value of the work completed against actual cost. A CPI of 1 means the project is on budget; a CPI > 1 means the project is under budget; a CPI < 1 means the project is over budget.
Schedule variance (SV)	SV determines whether the work is ahead of or behind the planned schedule. A positive SV means the project is ahead of schedule; a negative SV means the project is behind schedule.
Schedule performance index (SPI)	SPI measures the schedule progress to date against the planned progress. An SPI of 1 means the project is on schedule, an SPI of > 1 means the project is ahead of schedule, and an SPI of < 1 means the project is behind schedule.
Estimate at completion (EAC)	EAC is the expected total cost of a work component, a schedule activity, or the project at its completion.
Estimate to complete (ETC)	ETC is the amount of effort remaining based on completed and expected activities.
Budget at completion (BAC)	BAC is the sum of all the budgets (or PVs) established.
Variance at completion (VAC)	VAC is the difference between the budget at completion and the estimate at completion.

PV, AC, and EV measurements can be plotted graphically to show the variances between them. If there are no variances in the measurements, all lines on the graph remain the same, meaning that the project is progressing as planned. All of these measurements include a cost component. Costs are displayed in an S curve because spending is minimal in the beginning of the project, picks up steam toward the middle, and then tapers off at the end. This means your earned value measurements will also take on the S curve shape. Figure 8.7 shows an example that plots these three measurements.

FIGURE 8.7   Earned value

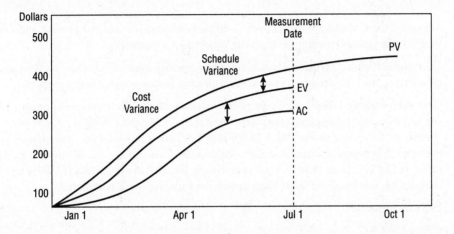

 It is important to understand the definition of the earned value management terms and how to interpret the results. As part of the exam, you may be asked to perform EVM calculations and answer questions based on the results.

Variance Analysis   Variance analysis calculates the difference between the budget at completion and the estimate at completion. To calculate this, use the variance at completion (VAC) formula:

$VAC = BAC - EAC$

Variance analysis works closely with the performance reviews technique. Aside from calculating VAC, variance analysis also focuses on the cause that led to a deviation from the baselines. By determining the cause of existing or potential variance, the project management team can then formulate an effective response through a change request.

Below is a further explanation of each type of variance analysis that might be conducted.

Cost Variance   Cost variance is one of the most popular variances that project managers use, and it tells you whether your costs are higher than budgeted (with a resulting negative number) or lower than budgeted (with a resulting positive number). It measures the actual performance to date or during the period against what's been spent.

Use this formula:

$CV = EV - AC$

Schedule Variance   Schedule variance, another popular variance, tells you whether the schedule is ahead of or behind what was planned for this period. This formula is most helpful when you've used the critical path methodology to build the project schedule.

Use this formula:

$SV = EV - PV$

Together, the CV and SV are known as efficiency indicators for the project and can be used to compare performance of all the projects in a portfolio.

Cost and schedule performance indexes are primarily used to calculate performance efficiencies, and they're often used to help predict future project performance.

Cost Performance Index   The cost performance index (CPI) measures the value of the work completed against actual cost. It is the most critical of all the EVM measurements according to the *PMBOK® Guide* because it tells you the cost efficiency for the work completed to date or at the completion of the project. As mentioned previously, if CPI is greater than 1, your spending is less than anticipated. If CPI is less than 1, you are spending more than anticipated for the work completed.

Use this formula:

$CPI = EV \div AC$

Schedule Performance Index   The schedule performance index (SPI) measures the progress to date against the progress that was planned. This formula should be used in conjunction with an analysis of the critical path activities to determine if the project will finish ahead of or behind schedule. As mentioned previously, if SPI is greater than 1, you are ahead of schedule. If SPI is less than 1, you are behind schedule.

Use this formula:

$SPI = EV \div PV$

Day of the Exam

Interpreting the results of EVM formulas is important. When interpreting CV and SV, remember that a positive number is good and a negative number is bad; when interpreting CPI and SPI, remember that > 1 is good and < 1 is bad.

What is bad when it comes to costs and schedule? Being *over* budget and *behind* schedule!

Trend Analysis   Trend analysis examines project performance over time to determine if performance is improving or deteriorating. Below is a further explanation of each type of trend analysis that might be conducted.

Forecasting   Forecasting uses the information gathered to date and estimates the future conditions or performance of the project based on what is known when the calculation is performed.

One of the forecasting formulas used is called estimate at completion (EAC). EAC estimates the expected total cost of a work component, a schedule activity, or the project at its completion. This is the probable final value for the work component (or project).

Use this formula:

EAC = AC + bottom-up ETC

The bottom-up estimate to complete (ETC) is the amount of effort remaining based on the activities completed to date and what is thought to occur in the future. Each estimate is summed to come up with a total ETC.

According to the *PMBOK® Guide*, there are four EAC forecasting formulas (see Table 8.2), which use budget at completion (BAC). BAC is the sum of all the budgets established for all the work in the work package, control account, schedule activity, or project. It's the total planned value for the work component or project. In addition to the bottom-up ETC, there is one other formula for calculating ETC that you should be aware of for the exam. This is also listed in Table 8.2.

TABLE 8.2   EAC and ETC forecasting

Forecast	Formula	Description
EAC	*EAC = AC + bottom-up ETC*	This is used if the initial plan is no longer valid
EAC	*EAC = AC + BAC – EV*	This formula calculates EAC based on the actual costs to date and the assumption that ETC work will be completed at the budgeted rate, thereby accepting previous performance (whether good or bad).
EAC	*EAC = BAC ÷ CPI*	This forecast assumes that future performance will be just like the past performance for the project.
EAC	*EAC = AC + ((BAC – EV) ÷ (CPI × SPI))*	This formula assumes there is a negative cost performance to date and the project schedule dates must be met.
ETC	*ETC = EAC – AC*	Use this formula when the work is expected to continue according to the plan.
ETC	*ETC = reestimate*	Use this formula for predicting future cost variances that will *not* be similar to the types of variances you've seen to date. It reestimates from the bottom up.

Reserve Analysis   Reserve analysis is used to monitor and manage the amount of funds within the contingency and management reserves. Reserve analysis is covered further later in this chapter as part of controlling risks.

To-Complete Performance Index   To-complete performance index (TCPI) is the projected performance level the remaining work of the project must achieve to meet the BAC or EAC. It's calculated by dividing the work that's remaining by the funds that are remaining.

The formula for TCPI when using the BAC is as follows:

$$TCPI = (BAC - EV) \div (BAC - AC)$$

If the result of calculating the TCPI is less than 1, future work does not have to be performed as efficiently as past performance.

When the BAC is no longer attainable, the project manager should calculate a new EAC, and this new estimate becomes the goal you'll work toward once it's approved by management. The formula for TCPI when EAC is your goal is as follows:

$$TCPI = (BAC - EV) \div (EAC - AC)$$

If cumulative CPI falls below 1, all future project work must be performed at the TCPI.

Project Management Information System (PMIS)   Project management information systems are used to monitor PV, EV, and AC. Table 8.3 shows the formulas used to calculate values.

TABLE 8.3   Earned value formula summary

Item	Formula	Comments
Cost variance (CV)	$CV = EV - AC$	
Schedule variance (SV)	$SV = EV - PV$	
Cost performance index (CPI)	$CPI = EV \div AC$	
Schedule performance index (SPI)	$SPI = EV \div PV$	
Estimate at completion (EAC)	$EAC = AC +$ bottom-up ETC	EAC using actual costs to date plus new budgeted rates based on expert feedback.

Item	Formula	Comments
Estimate at completion (EAC)	$EAC = AC + BAC - EV$	EAC using actual costs to date and future performance will be based on budgeted rate.
Estimate at completion (EAC)	$EAC = BAC \div CPI$	EAC assuming future performance will behave like past performance.
Estimate at completion (EAC)	$EAC = AC + [(BAC - EV) \div (CPI \times SPI)]$	EAC when cost performance is negative and schedule dates must be met.
Estimate to complete (ETC)	$ETC = EAC - AC$	When the work is expected to continue according to the plan.
Estimate to complete (ETC)	$ETC = reestimate$	When future cost variances will *not* be similar to the variances experienced to date and work must be reestimated from the bottom up.
To-complete performance index (TCPI)	$TCPI = (BAC - EV) \div (BAC - AC)$	This TCPI formula is used when employing BAC.
To-complete performance index (TCPI)	$TCPI = (BAC - EV) \div (EAC - AC)$	This TCPI formula is used when EAC is your goal.
Variance at completion (VAC)	$VAC = BAC - EAC$	Used to calculate the variance against the budget.

Day of the Exam

Don't forget to memorize formulas for the exam! EVM formulas are a great candidate to jot down on your scratch sheet of paper provided to you at the start of your exam. Expect to get a handful of EVM-related questions.

As a memorization technique, analyze the formulas provided in Table 8.3 and take note of similarities and differences. For example, notice the following:

- When calculating variance, you always subtract.
- When calculating index, you always divide.
- CV, SV, CPI, and SPI formulas all begin with EV.

Outputs of Control Costs

The Control Costs process results in the following outputs:

- Work performance information
- Cost forecasts
- Change requests
- Project management plan updates
- Project documents updates

Work Performance Information   Work performance information includes the calculated CV, SV, CPI, SPI, TCPI, and VAC values.

Cost Forecasts   Cost forecasts include the calculated EAC and ETC.

Change Requests   Change requests that result from this process typically involve a change to the cost baseline.

Project Management Plan Updates   Project management plan updates typically include updates to the cost baseline, performance measurement baseline, and cost management plan, which should reflect any approved changes.

Project Documents Updates   Project documents updates typically include the following items:

- Assumption log
- Basis of estimates
- Cost estimates
- Lessons learned register
- Risk register

Exam Essentials

Name the purpose of the Validate Scope process.   The purpose of Validate Scope is to determine whether the work is complete and whether it satisfies the project objectives.

Describe the purpose of the Control Costs process.   The Control Costs process is concerned with monitoring project costs to prevent unauthorized or incorrect costs from being included in the cost baseline.

Be able to describe earned value management techniques.   Earned value management (EVM) monitors the planned value (PV), earned value (EV), and actual cost (AC) expended to produce the work of the project. Cost variance (CV), schedule variance (SV), cost performance index (CPI), and schedule performance index (SPI) are the formulas used with the EVM technique.

Know the purpose of the Control Scope and Control Schedule processes.   The purpose of the Control Scope process is to monitor project and product scope and manage changes to the scope baseline. The purpose of the Control Schedule process is to monitor the status of the project's progress and to manage changes to the schedule baseline.

Be able to name the tools and techniques of the Control Costs process.   The tools and techniques of Control Costs are expert judgment, data analysis, to-complete performance index, and project management information systems.

Ensuring Adherence to Quality Standards

The Control Quality process is responsible for ensuring that project deliverables conform to the quality standards as laid out in the quality management plan. This inspection can be carried out by using several tools and techniques, such as control charts and testing, in order to satisfy customer requirements.

Control Quality

The Control Quality process identifies the causes of poor product quality or processes and makes recommendations to bring them up to the required levels. Quality control is practiced throughout the project to identify and remove the causes of unacceptable results.

According to the *PMBOK® Guide*, project management teams should have a working knowledge of statistical control processes in order to effectively analyze information as part of quality control activities. In particular, project management teams should understand the following:

- *Prevention versus inspection*. Prevention entails preventing errors from occurring, while inspection refers to catching and resolving defects before the product is released to the customer.

- *Attribute sampling versus variable sampling*. Attribute sampling refers to the measurements taken to determine whether they meet one of two options, conforming or nonconforming; variable sampling rates measurements on a continuous scale to measure the degree of conformance.

- *Tolerances versus control limits*. Tolerances refer to a range of acceptable results, while control limits identify boundaries of what is considered to be statistically stable within a process.

As noted within Chapter 4 of this book, quality management should be planned into the project, meaning that it is a proactive versus reactive activity. This helps to *prevent* errors from occurring in the first place rather than just resolving them by *inspecting* the product.

Figure 8.8 shows the inputs, tools and techniques, and outputs of the Control Quality process.

FIGURE 8.8 Control Quality process

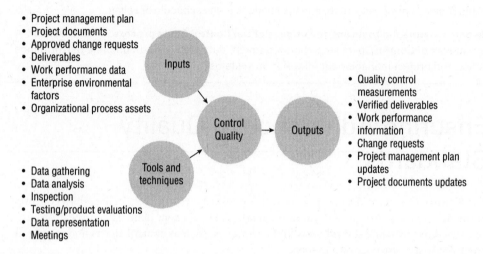

- Project management plan
- Project documents
- Approved change requests
- Deliverables
- Work performance data
- Enterprise environmental factors
- Organizational process assets

Inputs

- Quality control measurements
- Verified deliverables
- Work performance information
- Change requests
- Project management plan updates
- Project documents updates

Control Quality → Outputs

- Data gathering
- Data analysis
- Inspection
- Testing/product evaluations
- Data representation
- Meetings

Tools and techniques

> For more detailed information on the Control Quality process, see Chapter 11 in *PMP: Project Management Professional Exam Study Guide, Ninth Edition* (Sybex, 2017).

Inputs of Control Quality

Know the following inputs of the Control Quality process:

- Project management plan
- Project documents
- Approved change requests
- Deliverables
- Work performance data
- Enterprise environmental factors
- Organizational process assets

Project Management Plan   The project management plan contains the quality management plan, which is used to carry out the Control Quality process.

Project Documents   According to the *PMBOK® Guide*, project documents typically used as part of this process include lessons learned register, quality metrics, and test and evaluation documents.

Approved Change Requests   Approved change requests are requested changes that were approved through the Perform Integrated Change Control process and submitted as an input for implementation.

Deliverables   Part of achieving quality is ensuring that all deliverables are completed successfully. Deliverables will be verified as part of this process.

Work Performance Data   Work performance data allows the project team to evaluate actual versus planned progress in the areas of technical performance, schedule performance, and cost performance.

Enterprise Environmental Factors   The enterprise environmental factors provide the following information utilized by this process:

- Project management information system, specifically quality management software
- Government agency regulations
- Rules, standards, and guidelines pertaining to the project, product, or service

Organizational Process Assets   The following organizational process assets are utilized by this process:

- Standards, policies, and guidelines relating to quality standards
- Quality templates such as check sheets and checklists
- Procedures for reporting and communicating issues and defects

Tools and Techniques of Control Quality

Be familiar with the following tools and techniques of the Control Quality process and how they are utilized in this process:

- Data gathering
- Data analysis
- Inspection
- Testing/product evaluations
- Data representation
- Meetings

Exam Essentials

For the exam, be familiar with the tools used to control quality. This includes checklists, check sheets, statistical sampling, and questionnaires and surveys.

Data Gathering   The data gathering techniques that can be used for this process include but are not limited to the following:

- Checklists

- Check sheets

- Statistical sampling (Statistical sampling involves taking a sample number of parts from the whole population and examining them to determine whether they fall in acceptable variances. The quality management plan defines how to measure the results.)

- Questionnaires and surveys

Data Analysis   Performance reviews and root cause analysis (RCA) are the primary techniques used for data analysis.

Inspection   Inspection involves physically looking at, measuring, or testing results to determine whether they conform to the requirements or quality standards. Inspection will tell you where problems exist and gives you the opportunity to correct them, thus leading to quality improvements. Here's some additional information to know about inspections:

- Inspections might occur after the final product is produced or at intervals during the development of the product to examine individual components.

- Inspections are also known as *reviews* and *peer reviews*.

- Measurements that fall in a specified range are called tolerable results.

- One inspection technique uses measurements called attributes. Attribute sampling is used to verify conformance and nonconformance to predefined specifications.

Testing/Product Evaluations   Organized and constructed investigations to provide information about the quality of a product or service is called testing. For projects, the testing is conducted against the project requirements to attempt to find errors, defects, bugs, or other nonconformance problems. Testing can occur throughout the project as components are completed, as well as at the end when the product or service is completed.

Data Representation   Data representation techniques for this process can include cause-and-effect diagrams, control charts, histograms, and scatter diagrams. A more in-depth explanation of each of these elements is included below.

Cause-and-Effect Diagrams   Cause-and-effect diagrams, also known as *Ishikawa* or *fishbone diagrams*, help identify root causes of issues. The idea is to determine the possible issues or effects of various factors. A cause and its potential sub-causes are plotted on the diagram, which resembles the skeleton of a fish. Figure 8.9 shows what the cause-and-effect diagram may look like.

FIGURE 8.9 Cause-and-effect diagram

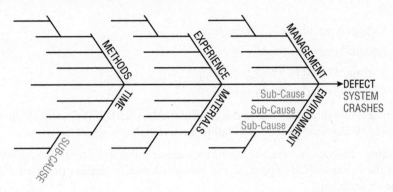

Control Charts Control charts measure the results of processes over time and display the results in graph form. They provide a way of measuring variances to determine whether process variances are in or out of control.

A control chart is based on sample variance measurements. From the samples chosen and measured, the mean and standard deviation are determined. Quality is usually maintained—or said to be in control—in plus or minus three standard deviations, also referred to as the upper and lower control limits.

Figure 8.10 illustrates a sample control chart.

FIGURE 8.10 Control chart

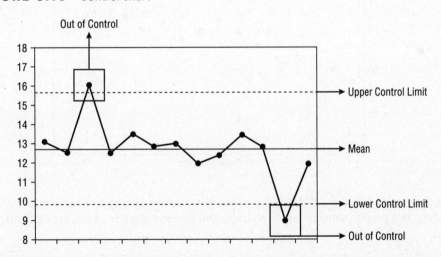

Out-of-control variances should be investigated to determine whether corrective action is needed.

For reference, know that standard deviation, or sigma, is equal to the following levels of quality:

± 1 sigma is equal to 68.27 percent.

± 2 sigma is equal to 95.46 percent.

± 3 sigma is equal to 99.73 percent.

± 6 sigma is equal to 99.99 percent.

If the process measurements fall in the control limits, then 99.73 percent (3 sigma) of the parts going through the process will fall in an acceptable range of the mean.

Histograms   Histograms are bar charts that depict the distribution of variables over time. In the Control Quality process, the histogram usually depicts the attributes of the problem or situation.

Scatter Diagrams   Scatter diagrams use two variables, one called an independent variable, which is an input, and one called a dependent variable, which is an output. Scatter diagrams display the relationship between these two elements as points on a graph. This relationship is typically analyzed to prove or disprove cause-and-effect relationships.

Figure 8.11 shows a sample scatter diagram.

FIGURE 8.11   Scatter diagram

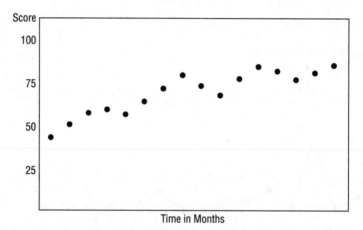

While not spelled out in the *PMBOK® Guide*, other control quality tools that one might encounter as a project manager are flowcharts and Pareto diagrams. They are explained below:

Flowcharts   Flowcharts are diagrams that show the logical steps that must be performed to accomplish an objective; they can also show how the individual elements of a system interrelate. Flowcharting helps identify where quality problems might occur on the project and how problems occur.

Pareto Diagrams   Pareto diagrams are named after Vilfredo Pareto, who is credited for discovering the theory behind them, which is based on the *80/20 rule*. The 80/20 rule as it applies to quality states that a small number of causes (20 percent) create the majority of the problems (80 percent). Pareto theorized that you get the most benefit by spending the majority of time fixing the most important problems.

The information shown in Table 8.4 is plotted on an example Pareto diagram shown in Figure 8.12.

TABLE 8.4   Frequency of failures

Item	Defect Frequency	Percent of Defects	Cumulative Percent
A	800	.33	.33
B	700	.29	.62
C	400	.17	.79
D	300	.13	.92
E	200	.08	1.0

FIGURE 8.12   Pareto diagram

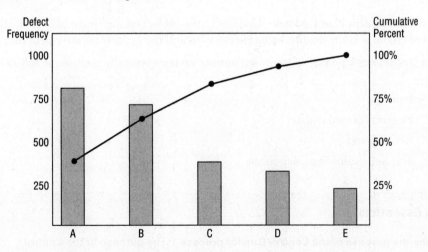

The problems are rank-ordered according to their frequency and percentage of defects. The defect frequencies in this figure appear as black bars, and the cumulative percentages of defects are plotted as circles. The rank ordering of these problems demonstrates where corrective action should be taken first.

Meetings   The primary types of meetings that may be used as a part of the Control Quality process are approved change requests review and retrospectives/lesson learned.

Outputs of Control Quality

The Control Quality process results in the following outputs:

- Quality control measurements
- Verified deliverables
- Work performance information
- Change requests
- Project management plan updates
- Project documents updates

Quality Control Measurements   Quality control measurements include the results of the quality control activities performed during this process.

Verified Deliverables   Verified deliverables are deliverables that have been taken through the tools and techniques of this process to determine if they are correct and accurate.

Work Performance Information   Work performance information reflects the performance data that has been gathered and analyzed using the various tools and techniques described as part of this process.

Change Requests   Change requests to the project management plan may result from carrying out this process and will be submitted to the Perform Integrated Change Control process.

Project Management Plan Updates   Updates to the project management plan typically consist of changes to the quality management plan and the process improvement plan.

Project Documents Updates   Project documents updates typically include the following items:

- Issue log
- Lessons learned register
- Risk register
- Test and evaluation documents

Exam Essentials

Describe the purpose of the Control Quality process.   The purpose of the Control Quality process is to monitor work results to see whether they comply with the standards set out in the quality management plan.

Updating the Risk Register

Identifying new risk, assessing old risks, and implementing the appropriate response strategies should occur as an integral part of monitoring and controlling activities. This is important to managing the impact of risks on the project and is carried out through the Monitor Risks process.

Monitor Risks

The Monitor Risks process should be carried out throughout the project life cycle. In addition to the activities just mentioned, this process is responsible for improving the risk management processes in a number of ways:

- Evaluating risk response plans that are put into action as a result of risk events

- Monitoring the project for risk triggers

- Reexamining existing risks to determine if they have changed or should be closed out

- Monitoring residual risks

- Reassessing project assumptions and determining validity

- Ensuring that policies and procedures are followed

- Ensuring that risk response plans and contingency plans are put into action appropriately and are effective

- Ensuring that contingency reserves (for schedule and cost) are updated according to the updated risk assessment

- Evaluating the overall effectiveness of the risk processes

Figure 8.13 shows the inputs, tools and techniques, and outputs of the Monitor Risks process.

FIGURE 8.13   Monitor Risks process

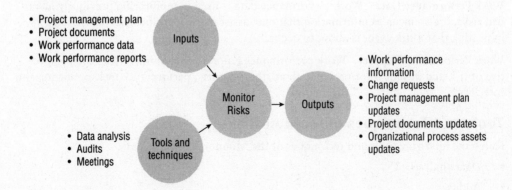

- Project management plan
- Project documents
- Work performance data
- Work performance reports

Inputs

Monitor Risks

Outputs

- Data analysis
- Audits
- Meetings

Tools and techniques

- Work performance information
- Change requests
- Project management plan updates
- Project documents updates
- Organizational process assets updates

For more detailed information on the Monitor Risks process, see Chapter 11 in *PMP: Project Management Professional Exam Study Guide, Ninth Edition* (Sybex, 2017).

Inputs of Monitor Risks

There are four inputs of the Monitor Risks process that you should know:

- Project management plan
- Project documents
- Work performance data
- Work performance reports

Project Management Plan   The project management plan includes the risk management plan, which provides the necessary information for carrying out this process.

Project Documents   Project documents considered as inputs for this process typically include the following:

- Issue log
- Lessons learned register
- Risk register
- Risk report

The risk register contains all of the documented information of the identified risks. It tracks and ranks individual risks, identifies the risk owner, describes risk triggers and residual risks, and lists the response plans and strategies you should implement in the event of an actual risk event. The risk register is fluid, meaning that additions, subtractions, and updates will be made throughout the project.

The risk report assesses the overall project risk exposure as well as agreed-upon risk response strategy.

Work Performance Data   Work performance data is used in monitoring previously identified risks. It also includes information that may assist in the identification of risk triggers, indicating that a risk event is about to occur.

Work Performance Reports   Work performance reports are examined from the perspective of risk and include information such as status reports, performance measurements, and forecasts.

Tools and Techniques of Monitor Risks

Know the following tools and techniques of the Monitor Risks process:

- Data analysis
- Audits
- Meetings

Data Analysis   Technical performance analysis and reserve analysis are the two primary techniques for this process.

Technical performance analysis compares the technical accomplishments of project milestones completed during the Executing processes to the technical milestones defined in the Planning processes. Variations may indicate risk.

Reserve analysis compares the amount of contingency reserve remaining to the amount of risk remaining in the project. The idea is to determine whether the contingency reserve is sufficient.

As part of data analysis, variance and trend analysis looks at the planned results in comparison with the actual results. Deviations may indicate risk.

Audits   Risk audits are specifically used to examine the implementation of response plans and their effectiveness at dealing with risks and their root causes. They are also used to determine the effectiveness of the risk management processes.

Meetings   Meetings, typically held in the form of status meetings, are used as a means of discussing risks with the project team. Risk reviews are important for this process and should examine and document the effectiveness of risk responses in dealing with overall and individual project risks.

Outputs of Monitor Risks

The Monitor Risks process produces the following five outputs:

- Work performance information
- Change requests
- Project management plan updates
- Project documents updates
- Organizational process assets updates

Work Performance Information   Work performance information reflects the risk-related information that has been gathered and analyzed as part of this process.

Change Requests   Recommended corrective actions or preventive actions may result from contingency plans or workarounds that were implemented as part of the Monitor Risks process. Change requests are submitted to the Perform Integrated Change Control process.

Project Management Plan Updates   The project management plan may include updates to the following documents, among others:

- Schedule management plan
- Cost management plan
- Quality management plan
- Procurement management plan
- Resource management plan

- WBS within the scope baseline
- Schedule baseline
- Cost baseline

Project Documents Updates   The result of carrying out this process typically includes the following items:

- Assumption log
- Issue log
- Lessons learned register
- Risk register
- Risk report

As noted earlier, the risk register is typically updated as a result of carrying out this process and typically results in the following:

- Addition of newly identified risks
- Updates to the probability and impact, priority, response plans, and ownership of previously identified risks
- Outcome of the project's risks and their risk responses

Organizational Process Assets Updates   The following updates are typically made to the organizational process assets:

- Risk management templates
- Risk breakdown structure (RBS)
- Lessons learned

Exam Essentials

Describe the purpose of the Monitor Risks process.   Monitor Risks involves identifying and responding to new risks as they occur. Risk monitoring and reassessment should occur throughout the life of the project.

Assessing Corrective Actions

As the need for corrective actions arise, the team may respond by submitting change requests. All change requests are reviewed by the change control board through the Perform Integrated Change Control process. The issue log should be assessed regularly for needed corrective action so that unresolved issues receive the appropriate follow-up. Responses to open issues should be made by using the necessary tools and techniques so that impact on the schedule, cost, and resources is minimized.

Perform Integrated Change Control

The Perform Integrated Change Control process, part of the Project Integration Management Knowledge Area, manages the project's change requests. This process approves or rejects changes and also manages changes to the deliverables. All change requests generated by other processes are submitted to the Perform Integrated Change Control process for review before implementation. Changes may involve corrective actions, preventive actions, and defect repair.

According to the *PMBOK® Guide*, the responsibilities of the Perform Integrated Change Control process are primarily as follows:

- Influencing the factors that cause change control processes to be circumvented

- Promptly reviewing and analyzing change requests as well as reviewing and analyzing corrective and preventive actions

- Coordinating and managing changes across the project

- Maintaining the integrity of the project baselines and incorporating approved changes into the project management plan and other project documents

- Documenting requested changes and their impacts

Figure 8.14 shows the inputs, tools and techniques, and outputs of the Perform Integrated Change Control process.

FIGURE 8.14   Perform Integrated Change Control process

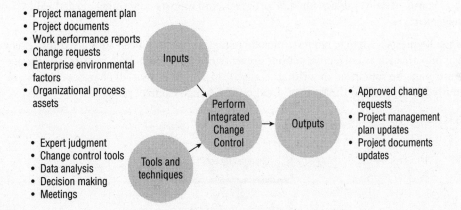

- Project management plan
- Project documents
- Work performance reports
- Change requests
- Enterprise environmental factors
- Organizational process assets

Inputs

- Expert judgment
- Change control tools
- Data analysis
- Decision making
- Meetings

Tools and techniques

Perform Integrated Change Control

Outputs

- Approved change requests
- Project management plan updates
- Project documents updates

For more detailed information on the Perform Integrated Change Control process, see Chapter 10 in *PMP: Project Management Professional Exam Study Guide, Ninth Edition* (Sybex, 2017).

Inputs of Perform Integrated Change Control

There are six inputs of the Perform Integrated Change Control process:

- Project management plan
- Project documents
- Work performance reports
- Change requests
- Enterprise environmental factors
- Organizational process assets

Project Management Plan   The project management plan includes several documents that will be utilized in this process, such as the approved schedule, budget, and scope. These documents will be used when reviewing submitted changes. Other components include the change management plan and the configuration management plan.

Project Documents   The following project documents are typically considered as inputs for this process:

- Basis of estimates
- Requirements traceability matrix
- Risk report

Work Performance Reports   Work performance reports include performance results, such as status of deliverables, schedule progress, and reports containing earned value management.

Change Requests   Change requests include requests that have been submitted for review and approval, such as corrective action, preventive action, and defect repairs. All change requests must be submitted in writing. Figure 8.15 reiterates that all change requests are submitted as inputs into the Perform Integrated Change Control process.

FIGURE 8.15   Change requests

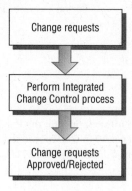

Managing Changes

Modifications to the project are submitted in the form of change requests and managed through the Perform Integrated Change Control process. Here are some examples of factors that might cause change:

- Project constraints
- Stakeholder requests
- Team member recommendations
- Vendor issues

Enterprise Environmental Factors   Enterprise environmental factors used to carry out this process include but are not limited to the following:

- Legal restrictions, including country or local regulations
- Government or industry standards
- Legal and regulatory requirements/constraints
- Organizational governance framework
- Contracting and purchasing constraints

Organizational Process Assets   The following organizational process assets are utilized by this process:

- Change control and authorization procedures
- Process measurement database
- Configuration management knowledge base

Tools and Techniques of Perform Integrated Change Control

The Perform Integrated Change Control process has five tools and techniques that you will need to be familiar with.

Expert Judgment   The following individuals or groups with specialized knowledge or training in the following topics should be consulted:

- Technical knowledge of the industry and focus area of the project
- Legislation and regulations
- Legal and procurement
- Configuration management
- Risk management

Change Control Tools   Change control tools come in the form of manual or automated systems that are used to help facilitate the change management process. Tools should support the following configuration activities:

- Identify configuration item
- Record and report configuration item status
- Perform configuration item verification and audit
- Identify changes
- Document changes
- Decide on changes
- Track changes

 The *PMBOK® Guide* states that the change control board is made up of a group of stakeholders who review and then approve, delay, or reject change requests.

You will also need to know about configuration management systems and change control systems, which are not listed as tools and techniques of the process but directly influence how the process is carried out.

Data Analysis   There are two primary techniques used for this process: alternatives analysis and cost-benefit analysis.

Decision Making   The following decision-making techniques can be used for this process:

- Voting
- Autocratic decision making
- Multicriteria decision analysis

Meetings   Change control meetings are meetings in which the change control board reviews and makes decisions on submitted change requests. Roles and responsibilities for a change control board, when they are needed on the project, are clearly defined and agreed upon by appropriate stakeholders. The change control board is established to review all change requests and is given the authority to approve or deny them. This authority is defined by the organization. The decisions should be documented and reviewed by stakeholders.

Outputs of Perform Integrated Change Control

Know the three outputs of the Perform Integrated Change Control process:

Approved Change Requests   This output reflects the list of submitted changes that have been approved by the change control board.

Project Management Plan Updates   Project management plan updates are made to reflect changes that have been approved or rejected after going through the Perform Integrated Change Control process. This may include changes to the following documents:

- Baselines
- Subsidiary management plans

Project Documents Updates   Project documents updates may include updates to any documents impacted by approved or rejected changes as well as the change request log, which will reflect the status update of the change requests.

Exam Essentials

Describe the purpose of the Perform Integrated Change Control process.   Perform Integrated Change Control is performed throughout the life of the project and involves reviewing all the project change requests, establishing a configuration management and change control process, and approving or denying changes.

Be able to describe the purpose of a change control board.   The change control board has the authority to approve or deny change requests. Its authority is defined and outlined by the organization. A change control board is made up of stakeholders.

Communicating Project Status

Communicating project status occurs throughout activities related to the Executing and Monitoring and Controlling processes, as seen throughout this chapter as well as in Chapter 7 of this book. While project reports help to align the project with the business needs, it is through the Monitor Communications process that the project manager ensures that communication requirements of stakeholders are met.

Monitor Communications

The Monitor Communications process is responsible for monitoring and controlling communications throughout the duration of the project. It is through this process that the project manager ensures that the communications requirements of stakeholders are met, along with their needs and expectations.

Figure 8.16 shows the inputs, tools and techniques, and outputs of the Monitor Communications process.

FIGURE 8.16   Monitor Communications process

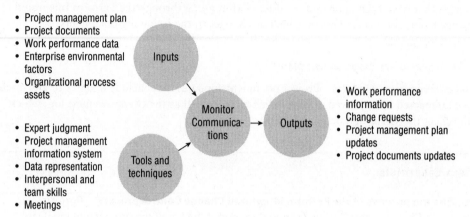

- Project management plan
- Project documents
- Work performance data
- Enterprise environmental factors
- Organizational process assets

- Expert judgment
- Project management information system
- Data representation
- Interpersonal and team skills
- Meetings

Inputs

Monitor Communications

Tools and techniques

Outputs

- Work performance information
- Change requests
- Project management plan updates
- Project documents updates

For more detailed information on the Monitor Communications process, see Chapter 10 in *PMP: Project Management Professional Exam Study Guide, Ninth Edition* (Sybex, 2017).

Inputs of Monitor Communications

The Monitor Communications process includes the following inputs:

- Project management plan

- Project documents

- Work performance data

- Enterprise environmental factors

- Organizational process assets

Project Management Plan   The project management plan components for this process include but are not limited to the following:

- Resources management plan

- Communications management plan

- Stakeholder engagement plan

Project Documents   The following project documents are the primary inputs to this process:

- Issue log

- Lessons learned register

- Project communications

Work Performance Data Work performance data is collected throughout the Monitoring and Controlling processes. Information such as status of deliverables, schedule, and costs is used in the Monitor Communications process.

Enterprise Environmental Factors Enterprise environmental factors used to carry out this process include but are not limited to the following:

- Organizational culture, political climate, and governance framework
- Established communications channels, tools, and systems
- Global, regional, or local trends and practices
- Geographic distribution of facilities or resources

Organizational Process Assets The following organizational process assets are used in the Monitor Communications process:

- Corporate policies and procedures for social media, ethics, and security
- Organization communications requirements
- Standardized guidelines for development, exchange, storage, and retrieval of information
- Historical information and lessons learned repository
- Stakeholder and communications data

Tools and Techniques of Monitor Communications

You should know the following five tools and techniques of the Monitor Communications process:

- Expert judgment
- Project management information system
- Data representation
- Interpersonal and team skills
- Meetings

Expert Judgment Expert judgment is key to assessing project communication and information to understand its impact and then make decisions accordingly. Individuals and groups with specialized knowledge or training in the following topics should be consulted:

- Communications with the public, the community, and the media
- Communications in an international environment between virtual groups
- Communications and project management systems

Project Management Information System The project management information system can be used by the project manager to capture, store, and disseminate information to project stakeholders. These systems may be complex or may be through the use of a simple spreadsheet.

Data Representation   The stakeholder engagement assessment matrix is a primary technique for this process, which can provide information about the effectiveness of communications activities.

Interpersonal and Team Skills   The interpersonal and team skills used in this process are observation and conversation. The most appropriate way to update and communicate project performance is through discussion and dialogue.

Meetings   Meetings are typically used in the Monitor Communications process to facilitate discussion among project team members and other relevant subject matter experts. Examples of discussions that occur as part of this process include analysis and decision making with regard to issue resolution and dissemination of information.

Outputs of Monitor Communications

The Monitor Communications process results in four outputs:

- Work performance information
- Change requests
- Project management plan updates
- Project documents updates

Work Performance Information   Work performance information consists of information that has been analyzed or summarized as a result of carrying out this process. As this information is captured and documented, it can then be distributed to the appropriate stakeholders.

Change Requests   The following changes may be requested as a result of carrying out this process:

- Revision of stakeholder communication requirements, including stakeholders' information distribution, content or format, and distribution method
- New procedures to eliminate bottlenecks

Project Management Plan Updates   Updates to the project management plan typically include the communications management plan and stakeholder engagement plan.

Project Documents Updates   Project documents typically updated as a result of carrying out this process include issue log, lessons learned register, and stakeholder communications register.

Exam Essentials

Describe the purpose of the Monitor Communications process.   Monitor Communications is responsible for monitoring and controlling communications throughout the duration of the project and ensuring that the communication requirements, needs, and expectations of stakeholders are met.

Monitoring Stakeholder Engagement

As the project moves forward, the project manager will need to continuously and carefully monitor the level of stakeholder engagement to ensure that expectations are well met. Stakeholders who are passive and not actively engaged may negatively impact the project at a later point, such as introducing new requirements that could have been addressed earlier in the project life cycle. The project manager may need to adjust the strategy for managing stakeholder expectations and engagement levels as the project progresses.

Monitor Stakeholder Engagement

The Monitor Stakeholder Engagement process belongs to the Project Stakeholder Management Knowledge Area and is responsible for monitoring stakeholder relationships and adjusting the stakeholder management plan as a result of stakeholder engagement. As a result of this process, stakeholder engagement becomes more efficient and effective.

Figure 8.17 shows the inputs, tools and techniques, and outputs of the Monitor Stakeholder Engagement process.

FIGURE 8.17 Monitor Stakeholder Engagement process

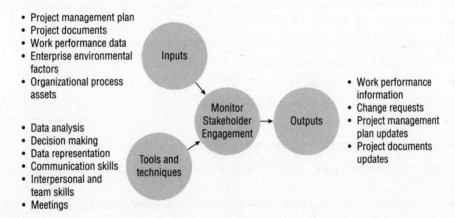

- Project management plan
- Project documents
- Work performance data
- Enterprise environmental factors
- Organizational process assets

- Data analysis
- Decision making
- Data representation
- Communication skills
- Interpersonal and team skills
- Meetings

Inputs

Monitor Stakeholder Engagement

Outputs

Tools and techniques

- Work performance information
- Change requests
- Project management plan updates
- Project documents updates

For more detailed information on the Monitor Stakeholder Engagement process, see Chapter 10 in *PMP: Project Management Professional Exam Study Guide, Ninth Edition* (Sybex, 2017).

Inputs of Monitor Stakeholder Engagement

There are five inputs of the Monitor Stakeholder Engagement process:

- Project management plan
- Project documents
- Work performance data
- Enterprise environmental factors
- Organizational process assets

Project Management Plan   The project management plan contains the stakeholder engagement plan, which guides the project manager in carrying out the process. Additionally, the communications management plan and resource management plan serve as inputs to this process.

Project Documents   Documents typically referred to as part of the Monitor Stakeholder Engagement process include the lessons learned register, stakeholder register, issue logs, risk register, and project communications.

Work Performance Data   Work performance data includes measurements captured throughout the Monitoring and Controlling processes. Examples of data that may be used as part of this process includes what work has been completed, change requests submitted, and technical performance measurements.

Enterprise Environmental Factors   Enterprise environmental factors used to carry out this process include but are not limited to the following:

- Organizational culture, political climate, and governance framework
- Personnel administration policies
- Stakeholder risk thresholds
- Established channels of communication
- Global, regional, or local trends and practices
- Geographic distribution of facilities and resources

Organizational Process Assets   The following organizational process assets are utilized by this process:

- Corporate policies and procedures for social media, ethics, and security
- Corporate policies and procedures for issue, risk, change, and data management
- Organizational communication requirement
- Standardized guidelines for development, exchange, storage, and retrieval of information
- Historical project information

Tools and Techniques of Monitor Stakeholder Engagement

The Monitor Stakeholder Engagement process has six tools and techniques that you will need to be familiar with.

Data Analysis   Three primary data analysis techniques come into play with this process: alternatives analysis, root cause analysis, and stakeholder analysis.

Decision Making   Multicriteria decision analysis and voting are two of the decision-making techniques that can be used for the Monitor Stakeholder Engagement process.

Data Representation   The stakeholder engagement assessment matrix is the primary, but not sole, data representation technique used for this process.

Communication Skills   Feedback and presentations are the two primary techniques used for this process.

Interpersonal and Team Skills   Several interpersonal skills are used for this process:

- Active listening
- Cultural and political awareness
- Leadership
- Networking

Meetings   Meetings are often used to bring experts together to analyze information obtained when carrying out a process and making decisions based on this information.

Day of the Exam

Notice that nearly all processes that fall within the Monitoring and Controlling process group have work performance data as an input and work performance information as an output. The only exception to this rule are the two Monitoring and Controlling processes that fall within the Project Integration Management Knowledge Area.

Identifying trends across the project management processes, such as this one, will help you better understand and break down questions on the day of the exam.

Outputs of Monitor Stakeholder Engagement

Know the four outputs of the Monitor Stakeholder Engagement process:

Work Performance Information   As with other processes that fall in the Monitoring and Controlling process group, performance data that has been captured and analyzed is documented as an output. This information is key in making decisions at the project level.

Change Requests   As the process is carried out, corrective actions or preventive actions may be needed. These are submitted in the form of change requests, which are then funneled into the change control process.

Project Management Plan Updates Various subsidiary plans, such as the stakeholder engagement plan, resource management plan, and communications management plan, may need to be updated as a result of carrying out this process.

Project Documents Updates Project documents typically updated as a result of carrying out this process include the issue log, lessons learned register, risk register, and stakeholder register.

Exam Essentials

Describe the purpose of the Monitor Stakeholder Engagement process. The Monitor Stakeholder Engagement process is responsible for monitoring stakeholder relationships and adjusting the stakeholder management plan as a result of stakeholder engagement.

Bringing the Processes Together

In this chapter, you learned all about the processes that fall in the Monitoring and Controlling process group. If anything is amiss, the processes in this group work together to bring the project back in line with the project management plan.

In addition to correcting any differences between the actual work and the project management plan, the Monitoring and Controlling process group is responsible for preventive actions. During these processes, changes are verified and managed, and the status of identified risks is monitored in order to manage hurdles as soon as they arise. This process group is the project's gatekeeper.

Figure 8.18 summarizes the objectives in the Monitoring and Controlling process group.

FIGURE 8.18 Process group objectives: Monitoring and Controlling

Actions

✓ Observe and manage project performance
✓ Keep the project in line with the project management plan
✓ Take preventive actions
✓ Verify and manage project changes
✓ Monitor risks

In total, the Monitoring and Controlling process group contains 11 processes, covering nearly all of the following Knowledge Areas:

- Project Integration Management
- Project Scope Management

- Project Schedule Management
- Project Cost Management
- Project Quality Management
- Project Communications Management
- Project Risk Management
- Project Procurement Management
- Project Stakeholder Management

We will review the process interactions that occur in each knowledge area during the Monitoring and Controlling process group. This will help you understand how the processes work together.

Project Integration Management Knowledge Area Review

Two key processes in the Monitoring and Controlling process group belong to the Project Integration Management Knowledge Area. Figure 8.19 shows how the project work is tracked and regulated as part of this knowledge area and how all project changes are approved or rejected. Changes are reviewed by the integrated change control system, which determines whether the changes are necessary and in the best interest of the project.

FIGURE 8.19 Process interaction: integration

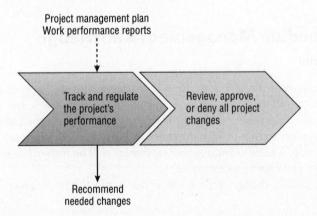

Project Scope Management Knowledge Area Review

As you may recall, scope documents are necessary to keep the project focused by providing it with boundaries and defining exactly what it set out to accomplish (no more, no less). The two processes in the Project Scope Management Knowledge Area fall in the

Monitoring and Controlling process group and ensure that the project is in line with the defined requirements.

Figure 8.20 shows how verified deliverables are formally accepted during this phase and how the project and product scope are monitored and managed. Changes made to the project scope are carefully watched. If something does not align with the project's defined requirements, then recommended changes are made. Performance measurements are also recorded and are used in project quality processes and project communications.

FIGURE 8.20   Process interaction: scope

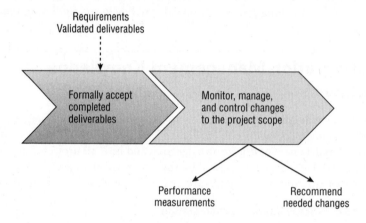

Project Schedule Management Knowledge Area Review

Only one process from the Project Schedule Management Knowledge Area occurs in the Monitoring and Controlling process group. This process is responsible for monitoring and controlling changes to the project schedule. Here, we are also concerned with monitoring the status of the project so that progress updates can be made. Performance measurements emerge from this step. The performance measurements will be important to monitoring and controlling quality and communications.

As Figure 8.21 shows, changes are recommended based on the progress and status of the project schedule.

Project Cost Management Knowledge Area Review

During the monitoring and controlling of project costs, we utilize the budget developed during the execution of the project work. Figure 8.22 shows the single cost-related process in the Monitoring and Controlling process group.

FIGURE 8.21   Process interaction: time

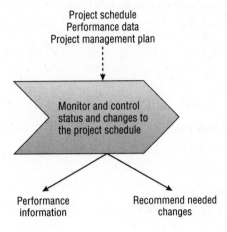

Project schedule
Performance data
Project management plan

Monitor and control
status and changes to
the project schedule

Performance
information

Recommend needed
changes

FIGURE 8.22   Process interaction: cost

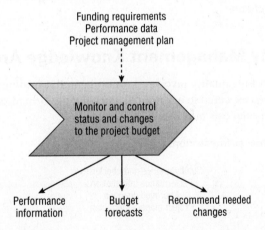

Funding requirements
Performance data
Project management plan

Monitor and control
status and changes
to the project budget

Performance
information

Budget
forecasts

Recommend needed
changes

As you may recall during our review of this process earlier in this chapter, the following items are generated out of this process:

- Budget forecasts

- Performance measurements, which will be used for monitoring and controlling quality and communications (similar to the performance data of the project schedule)

- Recommended changes to bring the budget back in line with the project management plan as needed

Generating the budget forecasts and performance measurements involves the use of earned value management (EVM), which itself includes several formulas. Although we won't go through the formulas and calculations here, you'll need to remember the calculations and various performance measurements in EVM:

- Planned value (PV)
- Earned value (EV)
- Actual cost (AC)
- Schedule variance (SV)
- Cost variance (CV)
- Schedule performance index (SPI)
- Cost performance index (CPI)
- Estimate at completion (EAC)
- Estimate to complete (ETC)
- To-complete performance index (TCPI)

For a review of the cost formulas, see "Control Costs" earlier in this chapter.

Project Quality Management Knowledge Area Review

Monitoring and controlling quality involves monitoring and recording the results of quality activities that have been executed in addition to assessing performance. Figure 8.23 shows how several items carry out this purpose.

FIGURE 8.23   Process interaction: quality

The results of the single quality-related process in the Monitoring and Controlling process group include the following items:

- Quality measurements, which are submitted back into the Manage Quality process (which is part of the Executing process group)
- Verified deliverables and changes, to make sure the results of the project work are correct
- Recommended changes, which are made for changes or deliverables that have been rejected from a quality standpoint

To generate these results, you may recall that several tools and techniques were used. You should be familiar with the tools and techniques of the quality management processes for the exam. Also note that those conducting quality control activities should have a working knowledge of sampling and probability. At the least, project teams should be familiar with the following:

- Prevention
- Attribute sampling
- Tolerances and control limits

Project Communications Management Knowledge Area Review

Monitoring and controlling project communications relies on performance information and budget forecasts; these are collected and distributed as performance reports. The recipients of these reports are outlined in the communications management plan. Figure 8.24 displays the results of the communications process in the Monitoring and Controlling process group.

FIGURE 8.24   Process interaction: communications

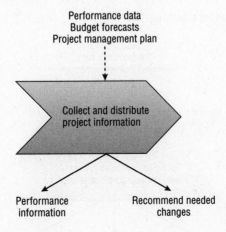

This process generates the following items:

- Measurements of the project's progress, and forecasts
- Any recommended changes made to bring the project back in line with the project management plan, implement preventive actions, or accommodate changes that were made to the product or project as a result of managing stakeholder expectations

Project Risk Management Knowledge Area Review

The Project Risk Management Knowledge Area has only one process that falls in the Monitoring and Controlling process group. As you may recall, this single process accomplishes a lot of things. Within this risk-related process, we will carry out the following actions:

- Implement the risk response plans, which were developed in the Planning process group
- Evaluate the effectiveness of the plans
- Monitor the identified risks
- Identify new risks
- Evaluate the effectiveness of the risk management processes

As shown in Figure 8.25, carrying through these actions results in the following:

- Actual outcomes of the identified risks
- Newly identified risks
- The documenting and recording of the risk outcomes for use by future projects
- The documenting and recording of the risk audits that were conducted to evaluate the effectiveness of the risk response plans and the risk management processes
- Any recommended changes to bring the project back in line with the project management plan as well as corrective actions and preventive actions (typically includes the implementation of contingency plans and workaround plans)

FIGURE 8.25   Process interaction: risk

Project Procurement Management Knowledge Area Review

During monitoring and controlling of the project, vendor relationships and performance are managed and monitored. Figure 8.26 shows what occurs in the single procurement-related process that falls in the Monitoring and Controlling process group.

FIGURE 8.26   Process interaction: procurement

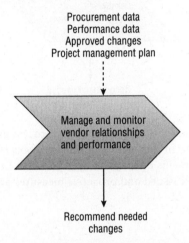

Procurement data
Performance data
Approved changes
Project management plan

Manage and monitor vendor relationships and performance

Recommend needed changes

The following information is used throughout this process:

- Procurement information, such as the procurement contracts and any documents relating to the procurements being administered

- Vendor performance information, including internal performance reports and reports generated by the vendors

- Approved changes, which typically involve changes to the contract terms and conditions

- The project management plan, which contains the procurement management plan

As a result of the Control Procurements process, recommended changes are made to bring vendor performance and progress back in line with the project management plan.

Project Stakeholder Management Knowledge Area Review

As part of managing stakeholder expectations, the project manager must actively monitor the engagement of stakeholders throughout the project's life cycle. This occurs through the single Monitoring and Controlling process that falls within the Project Stakeholder Management Knowledge Area. Figure 8.27 shows how this process interacts with other processes within the Monitoring and Controlling process group.

FIGURE 8.27 Process interaction: stakeholder management

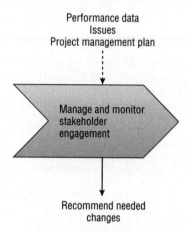

Performance data
Issues
Project management plan

Manage and monitor
stakeholder
engagement

Recommend needed
changes

Keep in mind that the Monitoring and Controlling process group's purpose is given away by its title. The processes in this process group are concerned with making sure the project (performance and status) is moving along as planned. In the event that this is not the case, corrective actions are issued and proactive measures are taken through preventive actions.

Review Questions

1. The Monitor and Control Project Work process results in all of the following *except*:

   A. Change requests

   B. Preventive actions

   C. Defect repairs

   D. Deliverables

2. A project manager of a technical training company is working on a project that will automate the company's course registration process. Due to the expertise involved, the company hired an external vendor to create the backend development of the registration system. While monitoring the project work, the project manager discovered that the vendor was two weeks behind schedule and about to miss an important milestone. What tool and technique did the project manager use to make this determination?

   A. Agreements

   B. Work performance data

   C. Inspection

   D. Work performance information

3. All of the following processes integrate with the Control Procurements process *except*:

   A. Close Procurements

   B. Direct and Manage Project Work

   C. Control Quality

   D. Perform Integrated Change Control

4. Which of the following *best* describes the contract change control system?

   A. Meetings where the change control board reviews and makes decisions on change requests submitted

   B. A subsystem of the PMIS that manages approved changes and project baselines

   C. A system that describes the processes needed to make contract changes

   D. A system that describes how the deliverables of the project and associated project documentation are controlled, changed, and approved

5. While conducting earned value management, the project manager of a software development company receives a request from a stakeholder for the most current cost estimate report. Specifically, the stakeholder needs to know the value of the work completed against actual cost. Which formula will the project manager use to calculate this information?

   A. $EV \div AC$

   B. $EV - AC$

   C. $EV - PV$

   D. $EV \div PV$

6. During a project status meeting, the project manager provided the room of stakeholders with results of a recent quality audit. After the group discussed the results, it was determined that a minor adjustment needed to be made to bring the variance levels under control. The project sponsor, also a meeting participant, agreed and gave her approval to implement the changes immediately. What should the project manager do next?

    A. Inform the quality management team and implement the changes that day.

    B. Obtain the customer's approval for the change, even though the project sponsor has approved it.

    C. Document the change request and submit it for review by the change control board.

    D. Bypass the change control process because the change has already received approval by a high authority.

7. After the implementation of yet another risk response plan, the project manager became concerned about whether the budget was sufficient enough to cover the remaining identified risks. Which of the following tools and techniques can the project manager use to evaluate the status of the budget in terms of risk?

    A. Risk reassessment

    B. Risk audits

    C. Budget analysis

    D. Reserve analysis

8. If budget at completion (BAC) is 1,500 and estimate at completion (EAC) is 1,350, what is the current variance at completion (VAC)?

    A. 150

    B. 75

    C. 0.90

    D. 1.11

9. A project manager is in the process of determining the existing variance between the schedule baseline and actual schedule. To determine the variance, the project manager used schedule variance (SV) and schedule performance index (SPI). The project manager is currently in what process?

    A. Control Costs

    B. Control Schedule

    C. Control Quality

    D. Control Communications

10. What level of accuracy does 3 sigma represent?

    A. 68.27 percent

    B. 95.46 percent

    C. 99.73 percent

    D. 99.99 percent

11. Assuming that the work will proceed as planned, what is the estimate to complete (ETC) if the estimate at completion (EAC) is $250,000 and actual cost (AC) is $50,000?

   A. $300,000

   B. Reestimate

   C. $250,000

   D. $200,000

12. What does the to-complete performance index (TCPI) value tell you?

   A. The measurement of progress to date against the progress planned

   B. The projected performance level the remaining work of the project must achieve to meet the BAC or EAC

   C. The expected total cost of a work component, a schedule activity, or the project at its completion

   D. The amount of effort remaining based on the activities completed to date and what is thought to occur in the future

13. Which process is responsible for ensuring that communication requirements of stakeholders are met?

   A. Monitor Stakeholder Engagement

   B. Monitor Communications

   C. Control Stakeholder Engagement

   D. Control Communications

14. Polly is a project manager tasked with leading a project that will establish business continuity management practices for a major retail coffee chain. The disaster recovery procedures deliverable has just been verified. What process is Polly likely to take the deliverable through next?

   A. Control Scope

   B. Validate Scope

   C. Close Project or Phase

   D. Monitor and Control Project Work

15. Polly is a project manager tasked with leading a project that will establish business continuity management practices for a major retail coffee chain. She has been asked by the project sponsor to provide an update of the expected total cost of the project work. Currently, the project is expected to continue to experience steady performance. What value will Polly report at the next meeting if the BAC = $500,000, EV = $300,000, and AC = $350,000?

   A. Insufficient information provided

   B. −$50,000

   C. $550,000

   D. $583,431

16. If earned value (EV) is 20,000 and planned value (PV) is 35,000, what can you determine about the project?

   A.   Ahead of schedule

   B.   Under budget

   C.   Behind schedule

   D.   Over budget

17. Beans by the Dozen is a company that ships precooked beans to restaurants in the western United States. Recently, the company has decided to expand its operation to the north-ern regions of the country. Ben, the project manager, has just implemented three changes approved by the change control board. What is Ben likely to do next with regard to these changes?

   A.   Approve the changes

   B.   Validate the changes

   C.   Update the change log

   D.   Communicate an update to stakeholders

18. Based on the following information, what can you determine about the project? Earned value (EV) = 160,000, actual cost (AC) = 110,000, planned value = 175,000.

   A.   The project is behind schedule and under budget.

   B.   The project is ahead of schedule and under budget.

   C.   The project is behind schedule and over budget.

   D.   The project is ahead of schedule and over budget.

19. All of the following are outputs of the Monitor Stakeholder Engagement process *except*:

   A.   Project documents updates

   B.   Change requests

   C.   Work performance data

   D.   Work performance information

20. Beans by the Dozen is a company that ships precooked beans to restaurants in the western United States. Recently, the company has decided to expand its operation to the northern regions of the country. The project is currently behind schedule, and the project manager has just been asked to work his magic to get the project back on track. If earned value (EV) is $60,000, actual cost (AC) is $85,000, and planned value (PV) is $75,000, what options are available to the project manager?

   A.   Crash the schedule.

   B.   Fast-track the schedule.

   C.   Crash *or* fast-track the schedule.

   D.   Nothing. He is out of options.

Chapter

9

Closing the Project

THE PMP® EXAM CONTENT FROM THE CLOSING THE PROJECT PERFORMANCE DOMAIN COVERED IN THIS CHAPTER INCLUDES THE FOLLOWING:

✓ **Obtain final acceptance of the project deliverables from relevant stakeholders in order to confirm that project scope and deliverables were achieved.**

✓ **Transfer the ownership of deliverables to the assigned stakeholders in accordance with the project plan in order to facilitate project closure.**

✓ **Obtain financial, legal, and administrative closure using generally accepted practices and policies in order to communicate formal project closure and ensure transfer of liability.**

✓ **Prepare and share the final project report according to the communications management plan in order to document and convey project performance and assist in project evaluation.**

✓ **Collate lessons learned that were documented throughout the project and conduct a comprehensive project review in order to update the organization's knowledge base.**

✓ **Archive project documents and materials using generally accepted practices in order to comply with statutory requirements and for potential use in future projects and internal/external audits.**

✓ **Obtain feedback from relevant stakeholders using appropriate tools and techniques and based on the stakeholder management plan in order to evaluate their satisfaction.**

Closing is the final process group of the five project management process groups and accounts for 7 percent of the questions on the PMP® exam. The primary purpose of Closing is to formally complete the project, phase, or contractual obligations. Finalizing all of the activities across the project management process groups accomplishes this.

By the end of the process that makes up the Closing process group, the completion of the defined processes across all of the process groups will have been verified. Don't forget that the closeout preparations begin early in the project with the clear and well-defined success criteria of the project.

The process names, inputs, tools and techniques, outputs, and descriptions of the project management process groups and related materials and figures in this chapter are based on content from *A Guide to the Project Management Body of Knowledge (PMBOK® Guide), Sixth Edition* (PMI®, 2017).

Obtaining Final Acceptance

All projects must be formally closed out regardless of the reasons for closure (such as successful completion or early termination). According to the *PMBOK® Guide*, the following typically occurs during formal closing of the project or project phase:

- Ensuring that exit criteria are met
- Obtaining formal acceptance by the customer or sponsor
- Closing out procurement contracts
- Conducting phase-end or post-project reviews
- Updating the organizational process assets, which includes documenting lessons learned and archiving project documents in the project management information system (PMIS)
- Recording the impacts of tailoring to any process
- Performing assessments of the project team members
- Transferring the project's product, service, or results to the next phase or to operations
- Measuring stakeholder satisfaction

These activities are carried out through a single process called Close Project or Phase.

Close Project or Phase

The Close Project or Phase process is concerned with finalizing activities necessary to complete a project, phase, or contract; this includes gathering project records and disseminating information to formalize the acceptance of the product, service, or result. The process belongs to the Project Integration Management Knowledge Area. Here are additional notes about the process you should know:

- It involves analyzing the project management processes to determine their effectiveness.

- It documents lessons learned concerning the project processes.

- It closes out procurement activities.

- It archives all project documents for historical reference. You can probably guess that Close Project or Phase belongs to the Project Integration Management Knowledge Area since this process touches so many areas of the project.

- It investigates and documents reasons for a project or phase being terminated prior to its completion.

According to the *PMBOK® Guide*, every project requires closure, and the completion of each project phase requires project closure as well. The Close Project or Phase process is performed at the close of each project phase and at the close of the project.

Figure 9.1 shows the inputs, tools and techniques, and outputs of the Close Project or Phase process.

FIGURE 9.1   Close Project or Phase process

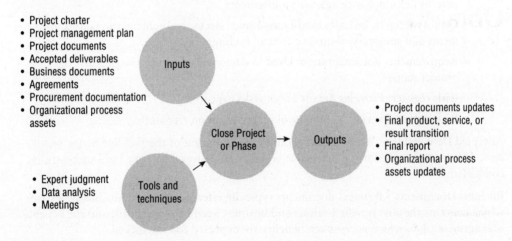

- Project charter
- Project management plan
- Project documents
- Accepted deliverables
- Business documents
- Agreements
- Procurement documentation
- Organizational process assets

Inputs

Close Project or Phase

Outputs

- Project documents updates
- Final product, service, or result transition
- Final report
- Organizational process assets updates

- Expert judgment
- Data analysis
- Meetings

Tools and techniques

For more detailed information on the Close Project or Phase process, see Chapter 12, "Closing the Project and Applying Professional Responsibility," in *PMP®: Project Management Professional Exam Study Guide, Ninth Edition* (Sybex, 2017).

Inputs of Close Project or Phase

For the exam, know the eight inputs of the Close Project or Phase process:

Project Charter   The project charter contains the success criteria and other approval requirements necessary to close out a phase or project.

Project Management Plan   For a project to be considered closed, the project management plan will be reviewed by the project manager to ensure completion of the deliverables and that all objectives of the project have been met.

Project Documents   Several project documents can be referenced to validate that closure requirements have been met. According to the *PMBOK® Guide*, the following are examples of documents that may be referenced:

> **Assumptions log:** Contains assumptions and constraints
>
> **Basis of estimates:** Contains details behind estimates produced
>
> **Change log:** Details status of all change requests
>
> **Issue log:** Contains status of all open issues
>
> **Lessons learned register:** Includes lessons learned from the phase or project to be finalized
>
> **Milestone list:** Contains final dates on which milestones are to be accomplished
>
> **Project communications:** Includes all communications created to date
>
> **Quality control measurements:** Contains results of quality control activities to determine compliance against requirements
>
> **Quality reports:** Includes quality assurance issues, recommendations for improvement, and summary of quality control findings
>
> **Requirements documentation:** Used to demonstrate compliance against the project scope
>
> **Risk register:** Provides details about risks captured
>
> **Risk report:** Provides summary of information on risk status

Accepted Deliverables   Accepted deliverables are an output of the Validate Scope process. This input is necessary to determine whether all deliverables have been successfully completed.

Business Documents   Business documents typically referenced include the business case, which contains the cost benefit analysis and business need being satisfied, and the benefits management plan, which notes when benefits are expected to be achieved.

Agreements   Agreements become a necessary input to the process, since it's through this process that procurement activities are finalized. Agreements contain the terms and conditions related to contract closure.

Procurement Documentation   According to the *PMBOK® Guide*, procurement documentation is collected, indexed, and filed through the Close Project or Phase process. Procurement documentation typically includes the following:

- Contract schedule
- Scope
- Quality
- Cost performance
- Contract change documentation
- Payment records
- Inspection results

Organizational Process Assets   The following organizational process assets are typically used in this process:

- Guidelines for closing out the project or project phase
- Historical information and lessons learned
- Project closure reports
- Configuration management knowledge base

Tools and Techniques of Close Project or Phase

The Close Project or Phase process has three tools and techniques: expert judgment, data analysis, and meetings.

Expert Judgment   Subject matter experts can help ensure that the process is performed according to the organization's standard and to project management standards. Experts typically include other project managers, the project management office, and organizations such as PMI® or other technical organizations that publish standards and resources.

Data Analysis   Analytical techniques may be used to ensure that closure activities are ready to be performed and are performed correctly. Regression analysis and trend analysis are two examples of techniques provided by the *PMBOK® Guide*, as well as document analysis and variance analysis. These data analysis techniques help teams gather lessons learned to improve the performance on projects taken on in the future.

Meetings   Meetings are often used as a means of bringing experts together to validate that deliverables have been accepted. Other uses of meetings at this stage include transferring knowledge, capturing lessons learned, and celebrating successful closure of a phase or project. Meetings may occur in a variety of formats, such as in person or virtual.

Outputs of Close Project or Phase

The four outputs that result from carrying out the Close Project or Phase process are as follows:

Final Product, Service, or Result Transition   *Final product, service, or result transition* refers to the acceptance of the product and the turnover to the customer or into operations. This is where information is distributed that formalizes project completion.

Final Report   The project's final report includes an overall summary of how the project has performed. According to the *PMBOK® Guide*, it may include things such as these:

- Summary description of project or phase
- Objectives and criteria used to evaluate the following metrics:
    - Scope
    - Quality
    - Schedule
    - Cost
- Summary of how the final result achieved the targeted benefits and business needs
- Summary of risks

Project Documents Updates   Any and all project documents may be updated as a result of carrying out this process. One document, in particular, that is important is the lessons learned register.

Organizational Process Assets Updates   The following organizational process assets are typically updated as a result of the Close Project or Phase process:

- Project files, such as the project planning documents, change records and logs, and issue logs
- Project or phase closure documents, which include documentation showing that the project or phase is completed and that the transfer of the product of the project to the organization has occurred
- Project closure reports
- Historical information, which is used to document the successes and failures of the project
- Operational or supporting documents
- Procurement file, which includes all of the procurement records and supporting documents
- Deliverable acceptance, which is a formal written notice from the buyer that the deliverables either are acceptable and satisfactory or have been rejected
- Lessons learned documentation

Exam Essentials

Be able to name the primary activity of the Closing process.   The primary activity of the Closing process is to finalize the project, phase, or contract.

Be able to describe when the Close Project or Phase process is performed.   Close Project or Phase is performed at the close of each project phase and at the close of the project.

Transferring Ownership

The acceptance and turnover of the product to the customer or into operations typically involves a formal sign-off indicating that those signing accept the product of the project. This occurs as a result of carrying out the Close Project or Phase process, which was discussed earlier in this chapter.

Exam Essentials

Be able to name the process responsible for transferring ownership of the project's final product, service, or result. The Close Project or Phase process is responsible for transferring the final product, service, or result of the project to the customer or transitioning it into operation.

Obtaining Financial, Legal, and Administrative Closure

Aside from the Closing process, there are a few additional items to note about the Closing process group and finalizing project closure. To start, project or phase closure is carried out in a formal manner and requires that financial, legal, and administrative closure be obtained. This is important to communicating formal closure and to ensuring that no further liability exists after the project has been completed.

It's important to note that a project can move into the Closing process group for several reasons:

- It's completed successfully.
- It's canceled or killed prior to completion.
- It evolves into ongoing operations and no longer exists as a project.

Formal Project Endings

Aside from these common reasons that result in a project moving into the Closing process, there are four formal types of project endings that you should be familiar with: addition, starvation, integration, and extinction.

Addition A project that evolves into ongoing operations is considered a project that ends because of addition, moving into its own ongoing business unit. Once it experiences this transition, it no longer meets the definition of a project.

Starvation   Starvation occurs when resources are cut off from a project prior to the completion of all the requirements. This results in an unfinished project. Starvation often occurs as a result of shifting priorities, a customer's cancellation of an order or request, the project budget being reduced, or key resources quitting.

Integration   Integration occurs when the resources of a project (such as people, equipment, property, and supplies) are distributed to other areas in the organization or are assigned to other projects. In other words, resources have been reassigned or redeployed, causing an end to the project.

Extinction   Extinction occurs when a project has completed and stakeholders have accepted the end result. This is the best type of ending because the project team has completed what they set out to achieve.

In all cases, if a project ends early, it's important to retain good documentation that describes why the project ended early. Performing a project review in these cases is important to retaining key details and specifics regarding why a project ended before all requirements were completed.

Trends

Another notable piece of information involves stakeholder influence and cost trends that occur during project closure. Stakeholders tend to have the least amount of influence during the Closing process, while project managers have the greatest amount of influence. Costs are significantly lower during the Closing process because the majority of the project work and spending has already occurred.

Administrative Closure

As part of administrative closure, resources will need to be released and the administrative closure procedures carried out.

Release Resources

Although releasing project team members is not an official process, you will release your project team members at the conclusion of the project, and they will go back to their functional managers or be assigned to a new project if you're working in a matrix-type organization. The release of project resources is addressed within the resource management plan, which is created through the Plan Resource Management process.

As you learned in Chapter 5, "Planning Project Resource, Communication, Procurement, Change, and Risk Management," the resource management plan includes a section called "project team resource management," which includes details of how resources will be defined, staffed, managed, and released. The resource management plan is a subsidiary plan of the project management plan. It typically addresses the release of resources (not just at the end of the project, but in general at any point within the project), outlines the method for resource release, and defines when resources are to be released.

Once resources are released, the costs of the resources are no longer charged to the project. The resource management plan helps mitigate human resource risks that may occur during or at the conclusion of the project.

Perform Administrative Closure

Administrative closure procedures involve the following:

- Collecting all the records associated with the project
- Analyzing the project success (or failure)
- Documenting and gathering lessons learned
- Properly archiving project records
- Documenting the project team members' and stakeholders' roles and responsibilities:
  - Approval requirements of the stakeholders for project deliverables and changes to deliverables
  - Confirmation that the project meets the requirements of the stakeholders, customers, and sponsor
  - Documented actions to verify that the deliverables have been accepted and exit criteria have been met

Figure 9.2 shows the elements of the administrative closure procedures.

FIGURE 9.2   Administrative closure procedures

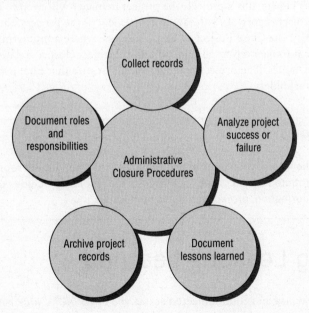

Exam Essentials

Be familiar with key trends projects experience during project closure.   Notable trends during project closure are that stakeholders have the least amount of influence whereas project managers have the greatest amount of influence and that costs are significantly lower.

Be able to name the four formal types of project closure.   The four formal types of project closure are addition, starvation, integration, and extinction.

Know when and how resources are released from the project.   Project resources are primarily released as part of finalizing project closure. The release of project resources is addressed in the resource management plan.

Be familiar with the purpose of the administrative closure procedures.   Administrative closure involves collecting all the records associated with the project, analyzing the project success or failure, documenting and gathering lessons learned, properly archiving project records, and documenting roles and responsibilities.

Distributing the Final Project Report

As part of formally closing out a project, the project manager will need to create and distribute the final project report. As you saw in our review of the process outputs, this generally occurs as part of the Close Project or Phase process, where administrative details are addressed. The final project report should include all project closure–related details, project variances, and any issues. The project manager should ensure that final project status is distributed to the stakeholders.

Exam Essentials

Be familiar with the information distributed as part of the final project report.   The final project report distributed by the project manager to stakeholders includes project closure–related information, project variances, and issues.

Collating Lessons Learned

One of the recurring themes communicated across the *PMBOK® Guide* is the proactive nature of the project manager, expressed by their actions. An example of being proactive is documenting lessons learned as part of the organizational process assets and capturing them within the lessons learned register.

Documenting lessons learned, as mentioned previously, focuses on capturing what went well within the project, what didn't go well, and what can be improved. Although lessons learned are recorded throughout the life of the project, holding a final review with the project team before the team is released at the end of the project is essential. This information can be captured through a comprehensive project review with stakeholders and then can be added to the organization's knowledge base.

Documenting lessons learned occurs as part of the Close Project or Phase process, through the organizational process assets updates output.

Exam Essentials

Be familiar with how lessons learned are captured at the end of the project and what information is recorded. At the end of the project, lessons learned can be documented by holding a comprehensive project review with stakeholders. The focus of lessons learned includes documenting what went well within the project, what didn't go well, and what can be improved.

Archiving Project Documents

As part of the Close Project or Phase process, project documents are archived. This occurs through the organizational process assets updates output, which makes the historical documents available for future reference and use. Archiving project documents provides the following benefits:

- Retaining organizational knowledge
- Ensuring that statutory requirements, if applicable, are adhered to
- Making project data available for use in future projects
- Making project data available for internal/external audits

Exam Essentials

Know the process and output responsible for archiving project documents. Final project documents are archived as part of the organizational process assets updates output through the Close Project or Phase process.

Measuring Customer Satisfaction

According to the *PMBOK® Guide*, project success is measured by the following criteria:

- Product and project quality
- Timeliness
- Budget compliance
- Degree of customer satisfaction

Customer satisfaction is an important goal you're striving for in any project. If your customer is satisfied, it means you've met their expectations and delivered the product or service as defined within the planning processes. Customer satisfaction can be measured through quality management, which in part is concerned with making sure that customer requirements are met. This is done through understanding, evaluating, defining, and managing customer and stakeholder expectations.

As Figure 9.3 illustrates, modern quality management achieves customer satisfaction in part by ensuring that the project accomplishes what it set out to do (conformance to requirements) and that it satisfies real needs (fitness for use).

FIGURE 9.3   Measuring customer satisfaction

Exam Essentials

Understand how to measure customer satisfaction.   Customer satisfaction is measured through quality management, which ensures that the project meets conformance to requirements and fitness for use.

Bringing the Processes Together

The Closing process group consists of a single process that works toward closing out the project or project phase. Before closing out the project, the project manager must first make sure that the project has met its objectives and accomplished what it set out to achieve. The Closing process group is also concerned with the following objectives:

- Obtaining formal acceptance of the project's completion
- Releasing the project resources

- Measuring customer satisfaction
- Archiving the project information for later use

Figure 9.4 reflects the objectives of the Closing process group through several key questions that the project manager should ask before considering the project fully closed.

FIGURE 9.4   Project closure checklist

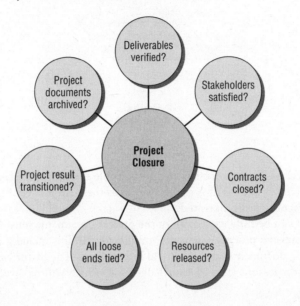

Next, we'll go through the Closing process reviewed in this chapter.

Project Integration Management Knowledge Area Review

A project closeout cannot occur without first finalizing all project or phase activities. The Close Project or Phase process from within the Project Integration Management Knowledge Area is responsible for making this happen. Figure 9.5 shows what occurs within this process. The accepted deliverables are used to verify that the project or the project phase has accomplished what it needed to.

Keep in mind that all procurement contracts must be completed and closed out before the project itself can close. Any loose ends or work on the vendor's end must be finalized as part of closing activities. You may recall that contract closure occurs through the Control Procurements process, part of the Monitoring and Controlling process group, and that all procurement activities are finalized through the Close Project or Phase process.

FIGURE 9.5   Process interaction: integration

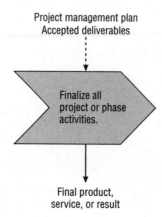

Project management plan
Accepted deliverables

Finalize all
project or phase
activities.

Final product,
service, or result

The Close Project or Phase process is also responsible for administrative closure of the project or project phase. The result is the transition to the customer of the final product, service, or result that the project created.

Before a project can be fully closed, all of the project documents must be archived within the organizational process assets. As you may recall, this includes all of the project files, any closing documents, and historical information. The historical information is archived within the lessons learned knowledge base, which will be a valuable asset to future projects.

Review Questions

1. All of the following are inputs of the Close Project or Phase process *except*:

   A. Procurement documentation

   B. Project management plan

   C. Accepted deliverables

   D. Final product, service, or result transition

2. A project manager of a travel excursion company is currently working on confirming that all project deliverables have been successfully completed to transfer the project to the customer. What process is the project currently in?

   A. Validate Scope

   B. Scope Closure

   C. Close Project or Phase

   D. Close Procurements

3. When closing out a project or project phase, which of the following tools and techniques can be used to ensure that closure has been performed to the appropriate standards?

   A. Records management system

   B. Procurement audits

   C. Expert judgment

   D. Organizational process assets

4. The Close Project or Phase process accomplishes all of the following *except*:

   A. Updating and archiving records for future reference

   B. Closing procurements

   C. Documenting and verifying project outcomes

   D. Transitioning the final product, service, or result to the organization

5. While conducting project closure activities, a relatively new project manager of a whiteboard production company becomes confused as to how the organization verifies that the existing criteria have been met. The project manager has found that some of the procedures followed by the organization are different from the procedures used in previous companies she's worked for. Where can the project manager go to clarify the procedures for verifying that the exit criteria have been met?

   A. Administrative closure procedures

   B. Close Project or Phase

   C. Control Procurements

   D. Expert judgment

6. All of the following are tools and techniques of the Close Project or Phase process *except*:
   A. Claims administration
   B. Data analysis
   C. Meetings
   D. Regression analysis

7. A project manager was in the midst of trying to resolve a dispute with one of the project's largest vendors. The issue revolved around the responsibility of the vendor to comply with changes to the scope. Although this was addressed in the contract, the vendor felt that the scope changes were much larger than the scope of the contract itself. What would be the *best* way to resolve the dispute?
   A. Through the court system
   B. Using an alternative dispute resolution technique
   C. Terminating the contract
   D. Making changes to the contract

8. Project managers have the greatest amount of influence during which stage of the project?
   A. Prior to the start of the project
   B. During the Planning processes
   C. During execution of the project work
   D. During the Closing processes

9. Resource release criteria can *best* be found in which plan?
   A. Project management plan
   B. Staff release plan
   C. Project team resource management
   D. Resource management plan

10. A major deliverable has just been signed off by the sponsor. What is the project manager likely to do next?
    A. Carry out the Close Project or Phase process
    B. Carry out the Validate Scope process
    C. Carry out the Control Quality process
    D. Carry out Integration activities

11. Polly is a project manager tasked with leading a project that will establish business continuity management practices for a major retail coffee chain. The project's sponsor has just informed Polly that due to a major health safety issue discovered, all resources will be pulled from her project for an indefinite amount of time. In this scenario, Polly's project has just been terminated due to what type of project ending?
    A. Addition
    B. Starvation
    C. Integration
    D. Extinction

12. Polly is a project manager tasked with leading a project that will establish business continuity management practices for a major retail coffee chain. The project's sponsor has just informed Polly that due to a major health safety issue discovered, all resources will be pulled from her project for an indefinite amount of time. What is Polly likely to do next?

A. Validate the health safety issue to ensure that resources are being used appropriately

B. Archive all project documentation and release the resources immediately

C. Perform closure activities by carrying out the Close Project or Phase process

D. Refuse to cancel the project, since business continuity is critical to the success of the company

13. The Close Project or Phase process belongs to which project management Knowledge Area?

A. Project Procurement Management

B. Project Integration Management

C. Project Closure Management

D. Project Scope Management

14. Beans by the Dozen is a company that ships precooked beans to restaurants in the western United States. Recently, the company has decided to expand their operation to the northern regions of the country. Ben, the project manager, confirmed that the vendor has recently completed all deliverables outlined within the statement of work and passed a recent audit. He has just closed out the contract and completed the other major deliverables of the project. Which document is Ben likely to use as a guide to ensure that project success criteria have been met?

A. Milestone list

B. Project management plan

C. Project charter

D. Procurement management plan

15. A project manager of a real-estate firm has just been notified that her project has come to an end as a result of resources redirected to work on other projects deemed to be of higher priority. In this scenario, the project has been terminated due to what type of project ending?

A. Addition

B. Starvation

C. Integration

D. Extinction

Appendix A

Answers to Review Questions

Chapter 1: Project Foundation

1. B. Ongoing operations are continuous without a specific end date; projects have definite start and end dates.

2. C. Although all the options appear attractive, a project is not considered successful until it has met the expectations of the project stakeholders.

3. C. Programs include groups of related projects managed in a coordinated fashion. Each project under a program is managed by its own project manager, who reports to a project manager responsible either for that area of the program or for the entire program.

4. A. The functional organization type is considered to be the traditional approach to organizing businesses. Functional organizations are centered on specialties, grouped by function, and displayed as a hierarchy.

5. B. Ensuring efficient use of resources toward a specific business goal is the role of a portfolio manager. Although a PMO may help manage resources across projects, it doesn't manage resources toward a specific goal but rather manages the objectives of a collective set of projects.

6. B. Within a projectized organization, project managers have high to ultimate authority, giving them the capability of assigning resources.

7. A. *Integration* refers to a Knowledge Area within the *PMBOK® Guide*, which will be addressed in a future chapter. Because the word closely resembles *Initiating*, the first process group within the project life cycle, they can easily be confused.

8. B. Costs are highest during the Executing process group, since this is where the most time and resources are used within a project.

9. D. This describes the Plan-Do-Check-Act cycle, which was originally defined by Walter Shewhart and later modified by Edward Deming.

10. B. While having a strong knowledge of finance and accounting principles would be beneficial to a project manager, only a basic level of knowledge is required.

11. C. Within a functional organization, the functional manager has a higher level of authority over the project manager, who has minimal to none.

12. D. Do not confuse the project life cycle that all projects go through with the process groups that are identified in the *PMBOK® Guide*. The project life cycle consists of (1) starting the project, or initiating, (2) planning the work, (3) performing the project work, and (4) closing out the project.

13. A. Business skills listed in this chapter include communication, budgeting, organization, problem solving, negotiation and influencing, leading, and team building skills. Data management skills are a more technical skill set with more of a functional implication than a project management focus.

14. D. According to the *PMBOK® Guide*, the Initiating process group contains the following actions: (1) developing the project charter, which formally authorizes the project, and (2) identifying the project stakeholders.

15. D. According to the *PMBOK® Guide*, the Closing process group contains the following action: finalizing the project work to formally complete the project or project phase.

Chapter 2: Initiating the Project

1. B. Identify Stakeholders, Plan Stakeholder Engagement, and Monitor Stakeholder Engagement are all processes of the Project Stakeholder Management Knowledge Area. Other processes of this Knowledge Area include Manage Stakeholder Engagement. Remember that in several instances, the name of a process can provide key clues in regards to the process group and Knowledge Area it belongs to.

2. D. A feasibility study takes place prior to making a final decision about starting a project and determines the viability of the project or product, the probability of it succeeding, and whether the technology proposed is feasible.

3. C. When projects are evaluated using the scoring model, the project with the highest overall weighted score is the best choice. Therefore, Project C, which has the highest score at 17, is the correct choice.

4. B. Multi-objective programming is a mathematical model technique. Mathematical models are also known as constrained optimization methods, making B the correct choice. As a side note, A and C refer to the same method, and D is a type of benefit measurement method.

5. A. To calculate the present value you would use the following formula:
$$PV = FV \div (1 + i)^n$$
$$PV = \$5,525 \div (1 + 0.10)^4$$
After working out the problem, the result is a planned value of $3,773.65.

6. B. Notice that the question asks for the *best* choice. Both the product scope description and project charter provide information about the characteristics of the product, service, or result of the project, but the product scope description directly defines these characteristics, making B the best choice.

7. D. The Develop Project Charter process contains four inputs: business documents, agreements, organizational process assets, and enterprise environmental factors. The project charter (option D) is an output of this process.

8. D. The project charter isn't complete until sign-off has been received from the project sponsor, senior management, and key stakeholders. The signatures signify the formal authorization of the project. A project charter cannot be published until after sign-off has been obtained.

9. C. There are seven inputs to the Identify Stakeholders process: business documents, project documents, project management plan, project charter, agreements, enterprise environmental factors, and organizational process assets. Option C is reflected within the project charter input (B).

10. A. The stakeholder register is a document that captures all of the details about the identified stakeholders. It typically includes identification information, assessment information, and stakeholder classification. Option A provides the best description from the list of options provided.

11. A. Polly has just performed the Develop Project Charter process. After the creation of the charter, the project manager is likely to begin the process of identifying stakeholders by performing the Identify Stakeholders process. These two processes both belong to the Initiating process group.

12. B. Data representation is a technique used within the Identify Stakeholders process. Data representation is typically used to identify the influences stakeholders have in regard to the project and understand their expectations, needs, and desires.

13. D. The Project Scope Management Knowledge Area includes six processes, which are Plan Scope Management, Collect Requirements, Define Scope, Create WBS, Validate Scope, and Control Scope.

14. C. While a project manager was assigned, the project has not been formally approved. In order to formalize the project and obtain authorization to utilize resources of the organization, a project charter must first be developed and approved.

15. D. According to the *PMBOK® Guide*, project scope identifies the work that needs to be accomplished to deliver a product, service, or result with the specified features and functionality.

16. A. Project scope is measured against the project management plan, which encompasses the various plans and baselines of the project, including the scope baseline.

17. B. Stakeholder analysis is used during the Identify Stakeholders process, and consists of two general steps: (1) identify stakeholders and capture general information about them and (2) assess the reaction or responses of the stakeholder to various situations.

18. D. Life-cycle costing is an economic evaluation technique that determines the total cost of not only the project (temporary costs) but also owning, maintaining, and operating something from an operational standpoint after the project is completed and turned over.

19. A. The Project Integration Management Knowledge Area is responsible for identifying, defining, combining, unifying, and coordinating the various processes and project management activities across the project management process groups.

20. C. Develop Project Charter is the first process of the Project Integration Management Knowledge Area and is responsible for the creation of the project charter. The project charter formally initiates the project within the organization and gives authorization for resources to be committed to a project.

Chapter 3: Planning Project Scope and Schedule Management

1.   C. The project scope statement is an output of the Define Scope process and is not included as part of the project management plan. The following plans and components are included: scope management plan, requirements management plan, schedule management plan, cost management plan, quality management plan, communications management plan, risk management plan, procurement management plan, resource management plan, schedule baseline, cost baseline, and scope baseline.

2.   A. Option A refers to those participating in a focus group, whereas B refers to interviews, C refers to the Delphi technique, and D refers to facilitated workshops.

3.   B. Sam is currently using product analysis, which is a method for converting the product description and project objectives into deliverables and requirements. To do this, Sam may have used any of the following: value analysis, functional analysis, requirements analysis, systems-engineering techniques, systems analysis, product breakdown, and value-engineering techniques.

4.   D. The WBS contains deliverables that are broken down to the work package level. The work packages are not broken down into the activity level until the Define Activities process, which cannot occur until after the WBS has been created.

5.   A. Finish-to-start is the type of logical relationship most frequently used within precedence diagramming methods and therefore the most likely choice. Option B, start-to-finish, is used the least.

6.   C. Option C is another name for the requirements documentation, which is an output of the Collect Requirements process.

7.   B. Option B is the correct answer for the purpose of collecting requirements. The output of the Collect Requirements process is used as an input for the other options, but the overall goal is to ensure that stakeholder expectations have been met.

8.   A. Option A is the best definition of a project constraint. Option B is the definition of a project assumption. Although there may be situations where option C is true, constraining the ability of the project team in terms of time, money, and scope will almost always impact the project outcomes. Option D is not a good answer because constraints can constantly change over the course of a project and need to be reevaluated.

9.   A. The total float of activity B is 4.

   To calculate total float of activity B, you would first need to perform a forward pass and backward pass. Follow the explanation noted in the chapter, then subtract either the early finish from the late finish of each activity or its early start from late start to calculate total float (both calculations produce the same answer).

   The early finish of activity B is 7, and late finish is 11. When subtracting these two numbers, you end up with a total float of 4.

10. **D.** A triangular distribution estimate is calculated by taking the simple average of the optimistic, most likely, and pessimistic estimates provided:

   Triangular distribution = (optimistic + most likely + pessimistic) ÷ 3

   When plugging the numbers into the formula using the values provided, here is the calculation, rounded to the nearest whole number:

   (12 + 23 + 38) ÷ 3 = 24

Chapter 4: Planning Project Cost and Quality Management

1.   **B.** Philip B. Crosby believed that preventing defects from occurring resulted in lower costs and conformance to requirements and that cost of quality transformed to cost of conformance as opposed to the cost of reworking.

2.   **D.** Option D is another name for quality metrics, which is an output of the Plan Quality Management process. Although options A and B are not directly listed as a tool and technique of this process, they are part of data representation and data gathering, respectively, which are both formal tools and techniques of the process.

3.   **D.** Option D is the correct answer for a critical path, which has zero float, meaning that it influences the longest full path on a project.

4.   **B.** Option B is the correct description for the cost baseline, and it is displayed as an S curve.

5.   **C.** Option C is the best answer, and the cost of quality includes all the work necessary to meet the product requirements for quality. The three costs associated with cost of quality are prevention, appraisal, and failure costs (also known as cost of poor quality).

6.   **C.** Option C is not correct for meeting quality requirements as costs are typically lower due to a reduction in rework.

7.   **A.** To calculate the activity duration estimate using a beta distribution, you would use the following formula: (optimistic + (4 × most likely) + pessimistic) ÷ 6. Using the estimates provided by Ron, plug the estimates into the formula to get the following: (15 + (4 × 20) + 50) ÷ 6 = 24.17, or 24 if rounded to the nearest whole number.

8.   **C.** The late start of activity C is 6.

   To calculate the late start of activity C, you must first draw out the diagram using the information provided in the table, then perform a forward pass and backward pass. Remember that to perform a forward pass, you must assume 1 as the early start of the first activity, then add the duration of the activity to the early start and subtract one to calculate early finish. To calculate the early start of a successor activity, add one to the early finish of its predecessor that has the highest number. For a refresher, see Chapter 3.

   To perform a backward pass, you do the reverse, starting with the last activity. The late finish of the last activity will be the same as its early finish. Subtract the duration of the activity and add one to calculate the late start. Subtract one from the late start and carry it over as the late finish of its predecessor activities, and repeat. If an activity has multiple predecessors, use the lowest late start number for your calculation.

The graphic shows the network diagram using the details of the table provided:

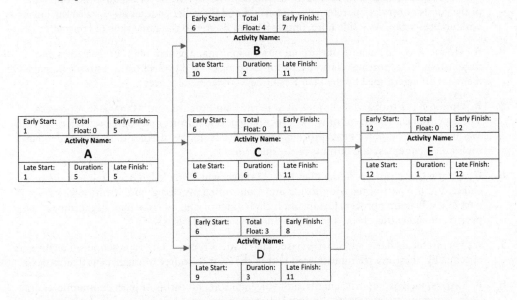

9. B. The early finish of activity D is 8. To calculate the early finish of this activity, follow the explanation provided in this chapter.

10. C. To calculate the critical path, total the duration of each activity for the three network paths possible, and select the highest number:

Path A-B-E has a total duration of 8.

Path A-C-E has a total duration of 12 (this is the longest path in the network diagram).

Path A-D-E has a total duration of 9.

Alternatively, if you've already calculated the total float for each activity, add the duration of the activities with a total float of 0, which all fall on the critical path.

Chapter 5: Planning Project Resource, Communication, Procurement, Change and Risk Management

1. A. The formula for calculating communications channels is *n* multiplied by *n* – 1, all divided by 2, where *n* represents the total number of stakeholders within the project. When you plug in the number of stakeholders in Rodrigo's project, the following formula results:

$$\frac{32 \times (32-1)}{2} = 496$$

2. C. Option A refers to Plan Risk Management, B refers to Identify Risks, and D refers to Perform Quantitative Risk Analysis.

3. C. Cost-reimbursable contracts carry the highest risk for the buyer because the total cost of the goods or services purchased is uncertain and the seller charges all costs to the buyer with no preset cap. As a side note, options A and B refer to the same type of contract.

4. A. Option A is the purpose of the communications management plan. Project roles and responsibilities, reporting relationships for the project, and project team resource management are all determined by the Plan Resource Management process.

5. B. Option B is a tool and technique used in the Plan Procurement Management process. The procurement statement of work, procurement documents, and source selection criteria are some of the outputs of this process. During the exam, be sure not to mix up the inputs, tools and techniques, and outputs in the question.

6. C. Option C is a process in the Plan Risk Management Knowledge Area, but it is the only choice that is a part of the Monitoring and Controlling process group. Identify Risks is a part of the Planning process group and includes identifying all risks that might impact the project, documenting them, and identifying their characteristics.

7. A. Hierarchical charts and matrix-based charts are a type of data representation technique. Specifically, these are techniques used within the Plan Resource Management Plan process.

8. B. Letters, memos, reports, emails, and voicemails are all forms of push communication. Push communication refers to sending information to intended receivers, but it is not concerned with whether it was actually received or understood.

9. A. *Lump-sum contract* is another name for a fixed-price contract. This type of contract carries the least amount of risk for the seller because it tends to set a fixed price for goods or services rendered.

10. C. Interviews is a data-gathering technique used in several of the Planning processes. It encourages anonymity, trust, and unbiased feedback.

Chapter 6: Planning Stakeholder Engagement and Obtaining Project Plan Approval

1. A. The question describes the accept strategy. Option A is a better choice than option D, since the question also notes that no contingency is needed, making option A the more specific choice.

2. A. This describes the stakeholder engagement assessment matrix, which allows for a comparison between current and desired engagement levels of stakeholders.

3.　D. The project manager is likely to point Antwon to the team charter, which documents the team values, agreements, and operating guidelines.

4.　B. Outputs from other processes are a key input, not a tool and technique, of the Develop Project Management Plan process. Options A and C are forms of data gathering, a tool and technique of the process.

5.　C. Simulation is a technique used within the Perform Quantitative Risk Analysis process to determine a probability distribution for the variable chosen, such as cost or schedule duration. Monte Carlo analysis is a popular simulation technique used.

6.　D. Escalate is a risk response strategy used for opportunities or threats that go beyond the authority level of the project manager or are outside of the project, such as within a program, as is the case in this scenario.

7.　A. Source selection analysis is a tool and technique of the Plan Procurement Management process, not an output. Look for clues, such as the word *analysis* in this case, which hints that it is a technique versus a result or outcome of carrying out a process.

8.　B. Kaylee has just carried out the Plan Risk Responses process, which is part of the Planning process group.

9.　D. The project manager has just finished carrying out the Identify Risks process. After performing risk identification, the project is likely to carry out the Perform Qualitative Risk Analysis process next. This process is responsible for determining what effect the identified risks will have on the project objectives and the probability that they will occur. Option A describes the Identify Risks process, Option C describes Plan Risk Responses, and Option D describes the Perform Quantitative Risk Analysis process.

10.　A. Interviews is a technique that is part of data gathering. In addition to interviews, data gathering also includes checklists, focus groups, and brainstorming. Other tools and techniques of the Develop Project Management Plan process include interpersonal and team skills (such as conflict management, facilitation, meeting management) and meetings.

Chapter 7: Executing the Project

1.　B. Jon's upcoming role within the project has been pre-assigned. Be sure to keep your eyes open for clues in the question's scenario. For instance, Jon has been looking forward to this assignment for months, yet the project has not officially begun. This means that Jon would have been included within the project charter as a specific team member assigned to the role of software architect. Although option C, project team member, is also correct, the question asks for the *best* choice.

2.　C. Options A, B, and D are all benefits of virtual teams. A war room requires team members to be colocated, which means that they are based out of the same physical location. Since virtual teams are spread out in various locations, option C is the correct choice.

3. B. Storming, the second of Bruce Tuckman and Mary Ann Jensen's five stages of team development, is when employees tend to be more confrontational with one another as they are vying for position and control.

4. D. The chaotic meeting scenario is a result of a lack of ground rules. Ground rules determine acceptable team behavior and rules that should be applied during meetings. As the scenario exhibits, a lack of ground rules can lead to poor productivity and waste of time.

5. A. The correct choice is social needs, which is the third level from the bottom in Maslow's pyramid. This is the level that describes the need to belong, be loved, and be accepted.

6. C. Collaborating, also called problem solving, is the best strategy for resolving conflict because it brings about a win-win result.

7. C. Communication methods are a tool and technique of the Manage Communications process and include all means that make it possible to communicate project information to the appropriate individuals.

8. B. Quality audits bring about quality improvements and greater efficiency to how processes and activities are carried out, making B the correct choice. Option A describes process analysis. Although quality audits can reveal information on team performance, the purpose is not to conduct performance reviews. Quality audits ensure that applicable laws and standards are being adhered to, but it is not a legal requirement to conduct them.

9. A. Douglas McGregor is responsible for Theory X & Y. Frederick Herzberg defined the Hygiene theory; Abraham Maslow created Maslow's hierarchy of needs theory; and Victor Vroom is responsible for the Expectancy theory.

10. A. The project management plan, specifically the stakeholder engagement plan, is an input to the process as opposed to a tool and technique. Avoid selecting an answer too fast simply because you recognize a connection between a term and a process name.

11. C. The project manager in this scenario is carrying out the Develop Team process. This process is concerned with creating a positive environment for team members; developing the team into an effective, functioning, coordinated group; and increasing the team's competency levels.

12. B. The Executing process group is where the work reflected in the plan is carried out and, as a result, where the majority of the project budget is spent.

13. A. Obtaining and managing resources is a key step to kicking off the execution of the plan, which occurs through processes that fall in the Project Resource Management Knowledge Area and Project Procurement Management Knowledge Area.

14. C. The question describes bidder conferences, which are meetings held with prospective vendors prior to the completion of their response to a seller's proposal. This technique is used as part of the Conduct Procurements process.

15. D. Option D provides the definition of a deliverable as noted within the *PMBOK® Guide*.

16. B. The question describes the work performance data output of the Direct and Manage Project Work process. Work performance data involves gathering, documenting, and recording the status of project work.

17. B. The Direct and Manage Project Work process creates the issue log. Other outputs of this process include deliverables, work performance data, change requests, project management plan updates, project documents updates, and organizational process assets updates.

18. B. Work performance information generates data that has been analyzed and is an output generated from the processes that fall in the Monitoring and Controlling process group. Work performance data, on the other hand, represents raw data produced out of the Direct and Manage Project Work process.

19. C. Change requests are an output of the Manage Quality process, not an input.

20. D. Polly has just carried out the Manage Quality process. Corrective actions are documented through the change requests output of the process.

Chapter 8: Monitoring and Controlling the Project

1. D. Deliverables are an output of the Direct and Manage Project Work process, not of the Monitor and Control Project Work process. Preventive actions and defect repairs (options B and C) are part of change requests.

2. C. Options A and B are inputs of the Control Procurements process, and option D is an output. This leaves C, inspection. Inspection includes a review of the vendor's progress in meeting contract objectives. This question simply tested your ability to distinguish between the inputs, tools and techniques, and outputs of the process.

3. A. According to the *PMBOK® Guide*, you must integrate and coordinate the Direct and Manage Project Work, Control Quality, Perform Integrated Change Control, and Monitor Risks processes during the Control Procurements process. Only Close Procurements, option A, is not included in this list of processes.

4. C. Option A refers to change control meetings, option B refers to the configuration management system, and option D refers to the change control system. Also notice that C, the correct choice, is the only option that specifically mentions contracts.

5. A. In this scenario, the stakeholder is looking for the latest cost performance index, which measures the value of the work completed against actual cost. The correct formula simply takes earned value and divides it by actual cost.

6. C. Change requests should always be documented, even if verbal approval has been provided by a high-authority figure of the project (such as the project sponsor in this scenario). Obtaining the approval of the project sponsor may speed up the approval process, but it may not replace it.

7. **D.** You may have been tempted to choose option C. However, budget analysis is not a tool and technique of the Monitor Risks process, which is the process used in this scenario. The correct choice is reserve analysis. Reserve analysis compares the amount of unused contingency reserve to the remaining amount of risk. This information is then used to determine whether a sufficient amount of reserve remains to deal with the remaining risks.

8. **A.** To calculate variance at completion, simply subtract the estimate at completion (EAC) from the budget at completion (BAC). Plug in the numbers provided in the question and work out the problem as follows:

$$VAC = 1,500 - 1,350$$

9. **B.** The project manager is currently in the Control Schedule process. This can be a tricky question because PV and SPI were mentioned, steering you toward the Control Costs process. In this scenario, the project manager is specifically utilizing the variance analysis technique of the Control Schedule process.

10. **C.** For reference, know the level of quality for 1 sigma (68.27 percent level of accuracy), 2 sigma (95.46 percent level of accuracy), 3 sigma (99.73 percent level of accuracy), and 6 sigma (99.99 percent level of accuracy).

11. **D.** When the work is proceeding according to the plan, calculate ETC using the following formula: $ETC - AC$. When plugging in the values provided by the question, the calculation is as follows:

$$\$250,000 - \$50,000 = \$200,000$$

12. **B.** TCPI is the projected performance level the remaining work of the project must achieve to meet the BAC or EAC. Option A describes SPI; Option C describes EAC; and Option D describes ETC.

13. **B.** The Monitor Communications process is responsible for monitoring and controlling communications throughout the duration of the project. It is through this process that the project manager ensures that the communication requirements of stakeholders are met, along with their needs and expectations.

14. **B.** Deliverables are verified through the Control Quality process. Verified deliverables are then taken through the Validate Scope process, which seeks to obtain formal acceptance of completed deliverables.

15. **D.** Polly has been asked by the sponsor to calculate estimate at completion (EAC). When the project is expected to continue at a steady rate of performance, use the following formula to calculate EAC: $BAC \div CPI$. In order to calculate EAC, you must first calculate CPI with the values provided. To calculate CPI, divide earned value (EV) by actual cost (AC): $\$300,000 \div \$350,000 = 0.857$. Now, plug the values into the EAC formula: $\$500,000 \div 0.857 = \$583,431$ (rounded to the nearest dollar).

16. **C.** Using the EV and PV values provided, calculate the schedule performance index (SPI). The formula for SPI is as follows:

$$SPI = EV \div PV$$

Using the formula provided, plug in the values to get the following: $20,000 \div 35,000 = 0.57$. When the SPI is > 1, it means that the project is ahead of schedule; when it is < 1, it means that the project is behind schedule. Based on the SPI calculated, the project is *very* behind schedule. In order to determine whether the project is over or under budget, we would need the actual cost (AC) value, which was not provided.

17. B. After changes have been implemented, they are validated through the Control Quality process. This process inspects the changes made to ensure that they were implemented correctly and then accepts or rejects them.

18. A. Based on the values provided, calculate CPI and SPI using the following formulas:

$$CPI = EV \div AC$$
$$SPI = EV \div PV$$

Now, plug in the values to get the following:

$$CPI: 160,000 \div 110,000 = 1.45$$
$$SPI: 160,000 \div 175,000 = 0.91$$

Based on the CPI and SPI values calculated, the project is under budget (getting 91 cents of value for every dollar spent) and behind schedule (only 91% on schedule).

19. C. Work performance data is an input of the Monitor Stakeholder Engagement process, not an output. The following are outputs of the process: work performance information, change requests, project management plan updates, and project documents updates.

20. B. Based on the values provided, you can calculate CPI to determine whether there are funds available to crash the schedule. To calculate CPI, use the following formula: $EV \div AC$. Plug in the values to get the following CPI: $\$60,000 \div \$85,000 = 0.71$. Based on the CPI, the project is also currently over budget. Since crashing is typically a costly option, the project manager is likely to fast-track activities on the critical path where possible.

Chapter 9: Closing the Project

1. D. Final product, service, or result transition is an output of the process, not an input. Inputs include project charter, project management plan, project documents, accepted deliverables, business documents, agreements, procurement documentation, and organizational process assets.

2. C. You may have leaned toward selecting option A at first glance because deliverables are validated during the Validate Scope process. However, the project manager is currently confirming that "all deliverables" of the project have been successfully accomplished, not validating the actual deliverables themselves. To make this determination, the Close Project or Phase process uses the project management plan and the list of accepted deliverables.

3. C. This question refers to the Close Project or Phase process, which has the following three tools and techniques: expert judgment, data analysis, and meetings. These are used when performing administrative closure.

4.   B. Closing procurements occurs through the Control Procurements process, while finalizing all remaining procurement activities occurs in the Close Project or Phase process.

5.   A. In this scenario, the project manager would refer to the administrative closure procedures. These procedures address several closure items, such as collecting project records, analyzing the success of the project, and documenting the roles and responsibilities of the project team members and stakeholders. As part of the latter, the administrative closure procedures document the actions to verify that the project deliverables have been accepted and that the exit criteria have been met.

6.   A. Claims administration is a tool and technique of the Control Procurements process, not Close Project or Phase. The Close Project or Phase process uses expert judgment, data analysis (in the form of document analysis, regression analysis, trend analysis, and variance analysis), and meetings.

7.   B. Disputes or outstanding claims are resolved by using alternative dispute resolution techniques, which are considered to be the most favorable ways of resolving disputes. Option A, taking the dispute to court, is the least favorable resolution technique.

8.   D. The project manager has the greatest amount of influence during the Closing processes, whereas stakeholders have the least amount of influence during this stage of the project.

9.   B. This is a tricky question because all the options are technically correct. However, the question asks for the *best* answer. This would be option B, the staff release plan. All of the other options are connected—the project team resource management (which addresses the release of resources) is a component of the resource management plan, which in turn is a component of the project management plan.

10. A. Typically, a phase is marked by the completion of a major deliverable. Sign-off of deliverables occurs through the Validate Scope process, after a quality review has been performed. The next step would be to formally close out the phase through the Close Project or Phase process.

11. B. Polly's project has been terminated due to starvation. Starvation occurs when resources are diverted from or no longer provided to the project.

12. C. Although Polly's project has ended prematurely, she must still perform closure activities by carrying out the Close Project or Phase process.

13. B. The Close Project or Phase process belongs to the Project Integration Management Knowledge Area and is the only process belonging to the Closing process group.

14. C. The project charter, which is an input to the Close Project or Phase process, contains the project success criteria and approval requirements.

15. C. Integration occurs when the resources of a project (such as people, equipment, property, and supplies) are distributed to other areas in the organization or are assigned to other projects, causing an end to the project.

Appendix B

Exam Essentials

Chapter 1: Project Foundation

Be able to describe the difference between projects and operations. A project is temporary in nature with a definite beginning and ending date. Projects produce unique products, services, or results. Operations are ongoing and use repetitive processes that typically produce the same result over and over.

Be able to differentiate between project management, program management, portfolio management, and a project management office. Project management brings together a set of tools and techniques to describe, organize, and monitor the work of project activities; program management refers to the management of groups of related projects; portfolio management refers to the management of a collection of programs and projects that support a specific business goal or objective; and the project management office oversees the management of projects and programs throughout the organization.

Be able to list some of the skills every good project manager should possess. Communication, budgeting, organization, problem solving, negotiation and influencing, leading, and team building are skills a project manager should possess.

Be familiar with the components of the PMI Talent Triangle. The components are technical project management, leadership, and strategic and business management.

Be able to define the role of the project manager. The project manager is the individual assigned to lead the team that is responsible for achieving the project objectives.

Be able to differentiate between the organizational structures and the project manager's authority in each. Organizations are usually structured in some combination of the following: functional, projectized, and matrix (including weak matrix, balanced matrix, and strong matrix). Other types of organizational structures exist, such as multidivisional, virtual, hybrid, and PMO. Project managers have the most authority in a projectized organization and the least authority in a functional organization.

The *PMBOK® Guide* emphasizes that you should not confuse this generic life-cycle structure with the project management process groups because the processes in a process group will consist of activities that may be performed and recur within each phase of a project as well as for the project as a whole.

Be able to name the five project management process groups. The five project management process groups are Initiating, Planning, Executing, Monitoring and Controlling, and Closing.

Chapter 2: Initiating the Project

Be able to name the ten Project Management Knowledge Areas. The ten Project Management Knowledge Areas are Project Integration Management, Project Scope Management, Project Schedule Management, Project Cost Management, Project Quality Management, Project Resource Management, Project Communications Management, Project Risk Management, Project Procurement Management, and Project Stakeholder Management.

Be able to distinguish between the 13 needs or demands that bring about project creation. The 13 needs or demands that bring about project creation are market demand, stakeholder demand, business process improvement, competitive forces, material issues, organizational need, customer requests, technological advances, legal requirements, ecological impacts, political changes, economic changes, and social needs.

Be able to define decision models. Decision models are project selection methods that are used prior to the Develop Project Charter process to determine the viability of the project. Decision models include benefit measurement methods and mathematical models.

Be familiar with payback period. Payback period is the amount of time it will take the company to recoup its initial investment in the product of the project. It's calculated by adding up the expected cash inflows and comparing them to the initial investment to determine how many periods it takes for the cash inflows to equal the initial investment.

Understand the concept of NPV and IRR. Projects with an NPV greater than zero should be accepted, and those with an NPV less than zero should be rejected. Projects with high IRR values should be accepted over projects with lower IRR values. IRR is the discount rate when NPV is equal to zero and IRR assumes reinvestment at the IRR rate.

Be able to identify where the high-level scope is documented and what it is based on. The high-level scope is defined and documented within the project charter and is based on the business and compliance requirements.

Be able to identify where the high-level risks, assumptions, and constraints are documented and what they are based on. The high-level risks, assumptions, and constraints are defined and documented within the project charter and are largely based on the existing environment, historical information, and expert judgment.

Be able to list the Develop Project Charter inputs. The inputs for Develop Project Charter are business documents, agreements, enterprise environmental factors, and organizational process assets.

Be able to describe the purpose of the business case. The purpose of a business case is to understand the business need for the project and determine whether the investment in the project is worthwhile.

Be able to describe the importance of the project charter. The project charter is the document that officially recognizes and acknowledges that a project exists. The charter authorizes the project to begin. It authorizes the project manager to assign resources to the project and documents the business need and justification. The project charter describes the customer's requirements and ties the project to the ongoing work of the organization.

Understand the Identify Stakeholders process. The purpose of this process is to identify the project stakeholders, assess their influence and level of involvement, devise a plan to deal with potential negative impacts, and record stakeholder information in the stakeholder register.

Chapter 3: Planning Project Scope and Schedule Management

Understand the purpose of collecting requirements. Requirements are collected to define and document the project sponsors', customers', and stakeholders' expectations and needs for meeting the project objective.

Know the outputs of the Collect Requirements process. The outputs of the Collect Requirements process include requirements documentation and requirements traceability matrix.

Understand the purpose of the project scope statement. The project scope statement serves as a common understanding of project scope among the stakeholders. The project objectives and deliverables and their quantifiable criteria are documented in the project scope statement and are used by the project manager and the stakeholders to determine whether the project was completed successfully. It also serves as a basis for future project decisions.

Be able to describe the purpose of the scope management plan. The scope management plan has a direct influence on the project's success and describes the process for determining project scope, facilitates creating the WBS, describes how the product or service of the project is verified and accepted, and documents how changes to scope will be handled. The scope management plan is a subsidiary plan of the project management plan.

Be able to define a WBS and its components. The WBS is a deliverable-oriented hierarchy.

It uses the deliverables from the project scope statement or similar documents and decomposes them into logical, manageable units of work. The lowest level of any WBS is called a work package.

Know the difference between the precedence diagramming method (PDM) and the arrow diagramming method (ADM). PDM uses boxes or rectangles to represent the activities (called *nodes*) that are connected with arrows showing the dependencies between the activities. ADM places activities on the arrows (called *activity on arrow*), which are connected to dependent activities with nodes.

Be able to describe the purpose of the Estimate Activity Resources process. The purpose of Estimate Activity Resources is to determine the types and quantities of resources (human, equipment, and materials) needed for each schedule activity within a work package.

Be able to name the tools and techniques of Estimate Activity Durations. The tools and techniques of Estimate Activity Durations are expert judgment, analogous estimating, parametric estimating, three-point estimating, bottom-up estimating, decision making, data analysis, and meetings.

Be able to define the difference between analogous estimating, parametric estimating, and bottom-up estimating. Analogous estimating is a top-down technique that uses expert judgment and historical information. Parametric estimating multiplies the quantity of work by the rate. Bottom-up estimating performs estimates for each work item and rolls them up to a total.

Be able to calculate the critical path. The critical path includes the activities whose durations add up to the longest path of the project schedule network diagram. The critical path is calculated using the forward pass, backward pass, and float calculations.

Be able to define a critical path task. A critical path task is a project activity with zero float.

Be able to describe and calculate beta distribution. This is a weighted average technique that uses three estimates: optimistic, pessimistic, and most likely. The formula is as follows:

$$\frac{Optimistic + (4 \times Most\ Likely) + Pessimistic}{6}$$

Be able to name the schedule compression techniques. The schedule compression techniques are crashing and fast-tracking.

Be able to describe a critical chain. The critical chain is the new critical path in a modified schedule that accounts for limited resources.

Be able to name the outputs of the Develop Schedule process. The outputs are project schedule, schedule baseline, schedule data, change requests, project calendars, project management plan updates, and project documents updates.

Chapter 4: Planning Project Cost and Quality Management

Be able to identify and describe the primary output of the Estimate Costs process. The primary output of Estimate Costs is cost estimates. These estimates are quantitative amounts—usually stated in monetary units—that reflect the cost of the resources needed to complete the project activities.

Be able to identify the tools and techniques of the Estimate Costs process. The tools and techniques of Estimate Costs are expert judgment, analogous estimating, parametric estimating, bottom-up estimating, three-point estimating, data analysis, project management information system, and decision making.

Be able to identify the tools and techniques of the Determine Budget process. The tools and techniques of Determine Budget are expert judgment, cost aggregation, data analysis, historical information review, funding limit reconciliation, and financing.

Be able to describe the cost baseline. The cost baseline is the authorized, time-phased cost of the project when using budget-at-completion calculations. The cost baseline is displayed as an S curve.

Be able to describe project funding requirements. Project funding requirements are an output of the Determine Budget process. They detail the funding requirements needed on the project by time period (monthly, quarterly, or annually).

Be able to identify the benefits of meeting quality requirements. The benefits of meeting quality requirements include increased stakeholder satisfaction, lower costs, higher productivity, and less rework, and they are discovered during the Plan Quality process.

Be able to define the cost of quality (COQ). The COQ is the total cost to produce the product or service of the project according to the quality standards. These costs include all the work necessary to meet the product requirements for quality. The three costs associated with cost of quality are prevention, appraisal, and failure costs (also known as cost of poor quality).

Be able to name four people associated with COQ and some of the techniques they helped establish. They are Crosby, Juran, Deming, and Shewhart. Some of the techniques they helped to establish are TQM, Six Sigma, cost of quality, and continuous improvement. The Kaizen approach concerns continuous improvement and specifies that people should be improved first.

Be able to name the tools and techniques of the Plan Quality Management process. The tools and techniques of the Plan Quality Management process consist of expert judgment, data gathering, data analysis, decision making, data representation, test and inspection planning, and meetings.

Chapter 5: Planning Project Resource, Communication, Procurement, Change, and Risk Management

Be able to define the purpose of the Plan Resource Management process. Plan Resource Management involves defining how to estimate, acquire, manage, and use resources; it is where roles and responsibilities for the project are determined.

Be able to describe the purpose of the communications management plan. The communications management plan determines the communication needs of the stakeholders.

It documents what information will be distributed, how it will be distributed, to whom it will be distributed, and the timing of the distribution.

Be able to define the purpose of the Plan Procurement Management process. The purpose of the Plan Procurement Management process is to identify which project needs should be obtained from outside the organization. Make-or-buy analysis is used as a tool and technique to help determine this.

Be able to identify the contract types and their usage. Contract types are a tool and technique of the Plan Procurement Management process and include fixed-price and cost-reimbursable contracts. Use fixed-price contracts for well-defined projects with a high value to the company, and use cost-reimbursable contracts for projects with uncertainty and large investments early in the project life. The three types of fixed-price contracts are FFP, FPIF, and FP-EPA. The three types of cost-reimbursable contracts are CPFF, CPIF, and CPAF. Time and material contracts are a cross between fixed-price and cost reimbursable contracts.

Be able to name the outputs of the Plan Procurement Management process. The outputs of Plan Procurement Management are a procurement management plan, procurement strategy, bid documents, procurement statement of work, source selection criteria, make-or-buy decisions, independent cost estimates, change requests, project documents updates, and organizational process assets updates.

Be able to define the purpose of the risk management plan. The risk management plan describes how you will define, monitor, and control risks throughout the project. It details how risk management processes (including Identify Risks, Perform Qualitative Risk Analysis, Perform Quantitative Risk Analysis, Plan Risk Responses, Implement Risk Responses, and Monitor Risks) will be implemented, monitored, and controlled throughout the life of the project. It describes how you will manage risks but does not attempt to define responses to individual risks.

Be able to define the purpose of the Identify Risks process. The purpose of the Identify Risks process is to identify all risks that might impact the project, document them, and identify their characteristics.

Be able to define the risk register and some of its primary elements. The risk register is an output of the Identify Risks process, and updates to the risk register occur as an output of every risk process that follows this one. By the end of the Plan Risk Responses process, the risk register contains these primary elements: identified list of risks, risk owners, risk triggers, risk strategies, contingency plans, and contingency reserves.

Be able to define the purpose of the Perform Qualitative Risk Analysis process. Perform Qualitative Risk Analysis determines the impact the identified risks will have on the project and the probability they'll occur, and it puts the risks in priority order according to their effects on the project objectives.

Be able to define the purpose of the Perform Quantitative Risk Analysis process. Perform Quantitative Risk Analysis evaluates the impacts of risks prioritized during the Perform Qualitative Risk Analysis process and quantifies risk exposure for the project by assigning numeric probabilities to each risk and determining their impact on project objectives.

Be able to define the purpose of the Plan Risk Responses process. Plan Risk Responses is the process where risk response plans are developed using strategies such as escalate, avoid, transfer, mitigate, accept, exploit, share, enhance, develop contingent response strategies, and apply expert judgment. The risk response plan describes the actions to take should the identified risks occur. It should include all the identified risks, a description of the risks, how they'll impact the project objectives, and the people assigned to manage the risk responses.

Chapter 6: Planning Stakeholder Engagement and Obtaining Project Plan Approval

Be able to describe the purpose of the stakeholder engagement plan. The stakeholder engagement plan identifies the management strategies necessary to effectively engage stakeholders.

Be able to state the purpose of the Develop Project Management Plan process. The project management plan defines how the project is executed, monitored and controlled, and closed, and it documents the processes used during the project.

Chapter 7: Executing the Project

Be able to describe the purpose of the Acquire Resources process. The Acquire Resources process involves acquiring and assigning physical and human resources, both internal and external, to the project.

Be able to describe the purpose of the Conduct Procurements process. Conduct Procurements involves obtaining bids and proposals from vendors, selecting a vendor, and awarding a contract.

Be able to name the tools and techniques of the Conduct Procurements process. The tools and techniques of the Conduct Procurements process are bidder conferences, advertising, data analysis, expert judgment, and interpersonal and team skills.

Be able to name the contracting life cycle stages. The stages of the contracting life cycle are requirement, requisition, solicitation, and award.

Be able to describe the purpose of the Develop Team process. The Develop Team process is concerned with creating a positive environment for team members; developing the team into an effective, functioning, coordinated group; and increasing the team's competency levels.

Be able to name the five stages of group formation. The five stages of group formation are forming, storming, norming, performing, and adjourning.

Be able to define Maslow's highest level of motivation. Self-actualization occurs when a person performs at their peak and all lower-level needs have been met.

Be able to name the five types of power. The five levels of power are reward, punishment, expert, legitimate, and referent.

Be able to identify the six styles of conflict resolution. The six styles of conflict resolution are forcing, smoothing, compromising, confrontation, collaborating, and withdrawal.

Be able to name the tools and techniques of the Manage Team process. The tools and techniques of Manage Team are interpersonal and team skills and the project management information system.

Be able to identify the distinguishing characteristics of Direct and Manage Project Work. Direct and Manage Project Work is where the work of the project is performed, and the majority of the project budget is spent during this process.

Be able to describe the purpose of the Manage Communications process. The purpose of the Manage Communications process is to collect, retrieve, store, and get information to stakeholders about the project in a timely manner.

Be able to describe the purpose of the Manage Stakeholder Engagement process. Manage Stakeholder Engagement concerns satisfying the needs of the stakeholders and successfully meeting the goals of the project by managing communications with stakeholders.

Be able to describe the various steps that a change request progresses through. Change requests are reviewed by the change control board through the Perform Integrated Change Control process. If approved, the changes are then implemented through the Direct and Manage Project Work process.

Be able to describe the purpose of the Manage Quality process. The Manage Quality process is concerned with making certain the project will meet and satisfy the quality standards of the project.

Be able to describe where risk response plans are documented and when they are executed. Risk response plans, contingency plans, and fallback plans are documented within the risk register and are executed when predefined risk triggers occur.

Be able to describe the purpose of the Implement Risk Responses process. The Implement Risk Responses process is responsible for implementing agreed-upon response plans so that overall risk exposure is managed and to minimize unique project threats and maximize opportunities.

Chapter 8: Monitoring and Controlling the Project

Name the outputs of the Monitor and Control Project Work process. The outputs are work performance reports; change requests, which include corrective actions, preventive actions, and defect repair; project management plan updates; and project documents updates.

Name the processes that integrate with the Control Procurements process. Direct and Manage Project Work, Control Quality, Perform Integrated Change Control, and Monitor Risks.

Name the purpose of the Validate Scope process. The purpose of Validate Scope is to determine whether the work is complete and whether it satisfies the project objectives.

Describe the purpose of the Control Costs process. The Control Costs process is concerned with monitoring project costs to prevent unauthorized or incorrect costs from being included in the cost baseline.

Be able to describe earned value management techniques. Earned value management (EVM) monitors the planned value (PV), earned value (EV), and actual cost (AC) expended to produce the work of the project. Cost variance (CV), schedule variance (SV), cost performance index (CPI), and schedule performance index (SPI) are the formulas used with the EVM technique.

Know the purpose of the Control Scope and Control Schedule processes. The purpose of the Control Scope process is to monitor project and product scope and manage changes to the scope baseline. The purpose of the Control Schedule process is to monitor the status of the project's progress and to manage changes to the schedule baseline.

Be able to name the tools and techniques of the Control Costs process. The tools and techniques of Control Costs are expert judgment, data analysis, to-complete performance index, and project management information systems.

For the exam, be familiar with the tools used to control quality. This includes checklists, check sheets, statistical sampling, and questionnaires and surveys.

Describe the purpose of the Control Quality process. The purpose of the Control Quality process is to monitor work results to see whether they comply with the standards set out in the quality management plan.

Describe the purpose of the Monitor Risks process. Monitor Risks involves identifying and responding to new risks as they occur. Risk monitoring and reassessment should occur throughout the life of the project.

Describe the purpose of the Perform Integrated Change Control process. Perform Integrated Change Control is performed throughout the life of the project and involves reviewing all the project change requests, establishing a configuration management and change control process, and approving or denying changes.

Be able to describe the purpose of a change control board. The change control board has the authority to approve or deny change requests. Its authority is defined and outlined by the organization. A change control board is made up of stakeholders.

Describe the purpose of the Monitor Communications process. Monitor Communications is responsible for monitoring and controlling communications throughout the duration of the project and ensuring that the communication requirements, needs, and expectations of stakeholders are met.

Describe the purpose of the Monitor Stakeholder Engagement process. The Monitor Stakeholder Engagement process is responsible for monitoring stakeholder relationships and adjusting the stakeholder management plan as a result of stakeholder engagement.

Chapter 9: Closing the Project

Be able to name the primary activity of the Closing process. The primary activity of the Closing process is to finalize the project, phase, or contract.

Be able to describe when the Close Project or Phase process is performed. Close Project or Phase is performed at the close of each project phase and at the close of the project.

Be able to name the process responsible for transferring ownership of the project's final product, service, or result. The Close Project or Phase process is responsible for transferring the final product, service, or result of the project to the customer or transitioning it into operation.

Be familiar with key trends projects experience during project closure. Notable trends during project closure are that stakeholders have the least amount of influence whereas project managers have the greatest amount of influence and that costs are significantly lower.

Be able to name the four formal types of project closure. The four formal types of project closure are addition, starvation, integration, and extinction.

Know when and how resources are released from the project. Project resources are primarily released as part of finalizing project closure. The release of project resources is addressed in the resource management plan.

Be familiar with the purpose of the administrative closure procedures. Administrative closure involves collecting all the records associated with the project, analyzing the project success or failure, documenting and gathering lessons learned, properly archiving project records, and documenting roles and responsibilities.

Be familiar with the information distributed as part of the final project report. The final project report distributed by the project manager to stakeholders includes project closure–related information, project variances, and issues.

Be familiar with how lessons learned are captured at the end of the project and what information is recorded. At the end of the project, lessons learned can be documented by holding a comprehensive project review with stakeholders. The focus of lessons learned includes documenting what went well within the project, what didn't go well, and what can be improved.

Know the process and output responsible for archiving project documents. Final project documents are archived as part of the organizational process assets updates output through the Close Project or Phase process.

Understand how to measure customer satisfaction. Customer satisfaction is measured through quality management, which ensures that the project meets conformance to requirements and fitness for use.

Index

E

J

Comprehensive Online Learning Environment

Register to gain one year of FREE access to the online interactive learning environment and test bank to help you study for your PMP certification exam—included with your purchase of this book!

The online test bank includes the following:

- **Chapter Tests** to reinforce what you've learned
- **Practice Exams** to test your knowledge of the material
- **Digital Flashcards** to reinforce your learning and provide last-minute test prep before the exam
- **Searchable Glossary** to define the key terms you'll need to know for the exam

Register and Access the Online Test Bank

To register your book and get access to the online test bank, follow these steps:

1. Go to bit.ly/SybexTest.
2. Select your book from the list.
3. Complete the required registration information including answering the security verification proving book ownership. You will be emailed a pin code.
4. Go to http://www.wiley.com/go/sybextestprep and find your book on that page and click the "Register or Login" link under your book.
5. If you already have an account at testbanks.wiley.com, login and then click the "Redeem Access Code" button to add your new book with the pin code you received. If you don't have an account already, create a new account and use the PIN code you received.